LAUNCHING NEW VENTURES

An Entrepreneurial Approach

Kathleen Allen
University of Southern California

UPSTART PUBLISHING COMPANY, INC.
Chicago, Illinois

Published by Upstart Publishing Company, Inc.
A Division of Dearborn Publishing Group, Inc.
155 N. Wacker Drive
Chicago, Illinois 60606-1719
(800) 448-3181 or (312) 836-4400

Neither the author nor the publisher of this book is engaged in rendering, by the sale of this
book, legal, accounting or other professional services. The reader is encouraged to employ the
services of a competent professional in such matters.

Library of Congress Cataloging-in-Publication
Allen, Kathleen R.
Launching new ventures: an entrepreneurial approach / Kathleen R. Allen.
     p. cm.
Includes index.
ISBN: 0-936894-73-3 (softcover)
1. New business enterprises—Management. 2. Small business—Planning. 3. Business plan-
ning. I. Title.
HD52.5.A46 1995
658.1'141—dc20   94-44966
                       CIP

Interior design by ST Associates, Wakefield, MA.
Cover design by S. Laird Jenkins Design, Arlington, VA.

Printed in the United States of America
10 9 8 7 6 5 4 3 2 1

*This book is dedicated to Jon Weisner, Kelly Stolpe, Sean Entin, and
their classmates in the Entrepreneur Program at the University of Southern California
with thanks for their inspiration throughout the process.
You are the reason I love teaching.*

Contents in Brief

Table of Contents

List of Profiles

Introduction

Entrepreneurship is not about money, and it's not just about starting businesses. At the personal level *it's about passion*—doing what you feel passionate about. Talk to most of the truly successful entrepreneurs in this world, you will probably find that the common denominator is that they are doing something they really love. It has often been written that if you do what you love, money, and success will follow. As trite as that phrase has become, it does appear to be true. The logic makes sense. If you do what you love, you will probably be very good at it; consequently you will establish a name for yourself. What you do will be in demand, and people will pay handsomely for it. Of course, there are no guarantees that passion alone will bring success, but it is passion that drives the entrepreneur to succeed. *Entrepreneurship is about passion, about doing what you love.*

Every semester students attend my classes searching for the rules they need to be successful in business. Everyone wants to learn the "keys to success," but sadly there are no keys—there are no rules. At least if there are, they change from week to week and from situation to situation. You see, entrepreneurs make their own rules. And thank goodness they do, because if they had all followed the same rules when starting their businesses, we would never have seen the stunning breakthroughs of the likes of Apple, Gentech, and Silicon Graphics. It's only what hasn't been done before that excites the world—that leap into the unknown that shakes us up and makes us take notice. It is often said that "imitation is the sincerest form of flattery." That may be true in public relations, but it is the kiss of death for entrepreneurs. What worked last week may not necessarily work this week. One change in any aspect of a business environment can change the dynamics such that a product that was successful one month cannot find customers the next. A technology that was "proven" one year is obsolete the next. That is the excitement and challenge of entrepreneurship today. *Entrepreneurship is about innovation and change.*

For the dynamic entrepreneur the path to success is not usually the path of least resistance, for the path of least resistance does not return the most for the effort. The opportunities that present the greatest challenge also bring the greatest rewards, and so it is with entrepreneurs. They seek opportunities that are innovative and show potential for growth. The challenge of turning such an opportunity into a business is the passion of the entrepreneur. That passion leads the entrepreneur forward with no thought of failure. Failure does not exist in their vocabulary. What others judge as failure—a business that didn't survive, a product that didn't find sufficient demand, the inability to secure growth capital—is but a mere pause on the continual journey to success. For entrepreneurs, success is not measured by how many times they fail but by how many times they get up and try again. Each pause in their progress prepares them for the next step ahead. *Entrepreneurship is about challenge and persistence.*

Often the students who come to my classes from other disciplines—engineering, cinema, English, international relations—feel intimidated by the fact that they are sharing the class with business majors. It stems from the belief that there must be some basic formula for business success, and if there is, business students will certainly have learned it. Well, business students have learned formulas, formulas that work fairly well for middle managers in large corporations. But the mindset that business schools impose on students is actually the antithesis of the mindset needed by someone starting a dynamic new venture. Consequently, many business students come to entrepreneurship with preconceived notions about what the nature of business is. They have in essence lost their innocence, their ability to creatively play with possibilities and do something they weren't taught to do. Business majors are starting from perhaps an even more difficult position than those who are from other fields. They need to regain some of their innocence by learning to look at everyday objects and events from a different perspective so they can begin to recognize the opportunity that is all-round them. *Entrepreneurship is about writing new formulas for how things are done.*

Entrepreneurship in the 1990s has taken on a new dimension. A global economy, the tearing down of trade barriers, and the information superhighway have created a competitive marketplace the likes of which has not been seen before. Today large corporations are looking for ways to act small and flexible so they too can be more competitive in the global marketplace. New ventures will not succeed in this dynamic environment by doing business the way it has always been done. Times have changed; circumstances have changed, and that means the ventures that entrepreneurs create must change as well. Today it is not enough to build a business around an innovative, quality product or service—that's expected. Today to sustain a competitive advantage in a global marketplace means creating a world-class venture.

A world-class venture is one that is customer-driven, is lean and flexible, and pursues excellence in all areas of the business. This book was written to help entrepreneurs and would-be entrepreneurs understand the nature of the new entrepreneurial environment and how to deal with it. It purposely focuses on starting growth-oriented ventures that will potentially impact the economy. But even those who wish to start small, community businesses can learn much from seeing how a world-class venture is created, for small business owners are also facing an increasingly competitive environment and need to strive for excellence in their businesses as well. By the end of this book you will have a good sense of what it takes to build a world-class venture and will understand the competitive advantage that can be gained by doing so. You will realize also that world-class status is not synonymous with big business. On the contrary, one of the key aspects of a world-class venture is that it can remain relatively small and flexible while still exerting a major impact in the marketplace. You will also be in a better position to decide if you have the passion of the entrepreneur. *Entrepreneurship in the 1990s is about creating world-class ventures.*

I believe that the passion of the entrepreneur is like energy. It can change, but it can never be destroyed—it will simply take on another form. When an entrepreneur fails, the passion doesn't die; rather, it sustains him or her in the effort to start again. Fortunately, life grants youth and entrepreneurs a grace period in which to make mistakes, lots of mistakes, and still be able to start over with a clean slate. For me, the joy of working with my students, no matter what their age, is that they are willing to make mistakes in order to learn. Because they are willing to fail, they are learning that failure is a healthy—in fact, necessary—part of success, and they are gaining a real sense of what it's like to be an entrepreneur. I can teach them the tools of entrepreneurship, but the spirit and passion cannot be taught, and no one has a monopoly on passion. Some of the most successful entrepreneurs I know have been teachers, engineers, psychologists, musicians, and film-makers. Many have had no college education at all, but they were all lifelong learners. They built world-class businesses out of a passion for what they believed in, and what they believed in first and foremost was—themselves. Will Rogers once said:

Know what you are doing.
Love what you are doing.
Believe in what you are doing.

He must have been talking about entrepreneurs.

—*Kathleen Allen*

Features of this Book

Launching New Ventures: An Entrepreneurial Approach is written in a practical, how-to style designed to allow any reader or student successfully plan and start a world-class venture. For classroom use, the book includes several elements to aid instructors and students in the start-up process.

Chapter Overviews outline the key topics for each of the 20 chapters.

Key terms are bold-faced when first introduced, and subsequently defined in the text.

An informal *self-test* measures proclivity towards entrepreneurial activity compared to typical entrepreneurs.

Chapters include *Profiles* of real-world entrepreneurs and businesses that clarify the topic at hand and provide starting points for additional discussion and thought.

Throughout the book, numerous elements facilitate the start-up process, including:

- Outline of a feasibility plan
- Outline of a business plan
- Detailed outline of an operational plan
- Outline of a marketing plan
- A 20-point test to verify the status of Independent Contractors
- An incorporation checklist
- A new product checklist to help determine the likelihood of success.

New Venture Checklists at the end of each chapter help organize the start-up process.

Additional Sources of Information are listed at the end of each chapter for more in-depth reading on the topic at-hand, including on-line resources for market research.

Issues to Consider, questions at the end of each chapter, focus the thinking of entrepreneurs and provoke meaningful discussion in the classroom.

Case Studies at the end of each of the seven parts of the book. are designed to illustrate the key components of the section that precedes them, and include discussion questions for classroom use.

An *index* at the end of the book aids location of key topics, people and companies covered in the text.

An *Instructor's Manual*, featuring lecture outlines, overhead transparency masters, discussion points for the case studies and end-of-chapter questions, as well as worksheets and a test bank, is available upon adoption for classroom use. To request a copy, call Upstart Publishing at (800) 235-8866.

Acknowledgments

Thanks first of all to my tireless faculty assistant, Nancy Frost, who has since gone on to establish her career in financial services. Without her research work, this book would have never been completed on time. Thanks to all my students in the Entrepreneur Program at the University of Southern California who used the manuscript in class and made very helpful suggestions. I am grateful to my wonderful husband who kept me on track and edited every chapter of this book. I also appreciate the excellent suggestions of my academic reviewers: Candida Brush, Boston University; Bill Gartner, San Francisco State University; Keith Cox, University of Houston; and Dewey Johnson, California State University, Fresno. Candy and Bill also contributed three of their original case studies to the book. My appreciation to Marianne Szymanski of Toy Tips, Inc., Steve Johnson of Simtek, Inc., Patricia Zinkowski of Flight Time International, and Sandy Gooch of Sandy Gooch Enterprises, Inc. for allowing me to explore their businesses and their entrepreneurial psyches in-depth for the case studies, and to Dan Lauer of Lauer Toys for his help with the Waterbabies doll. Thanks to Jack Savage, my editor, for his sense of humor and patience, and to Spencer, Jean, Karen, Brad, Nancy, and all the great people at Upstart.

PART 1

The Entrepreneur and the Entrepreneurial Venture

Develop a vision, and never lose sight of that vision.

—SANDY GOOCH, FOUNDER,
MRS. GOOCH'S NATURAL FOODS MARKETS

CHAPTER 1

Understanding World-Class Entrepreneurship

Overview

- *The importance of entrepreneurship in a volatile world market*
- *Entrepreneurial characteristics and reasons for wanting to start a business*
- *The new venture creation process*
- *Entrepreneurial ventures versus small businesses*
- *Factors in the entrepreneurial environment that will affect the start-up*
- *Business trends of the 1990s that affect the search for a business idea*

Death, Taxes, and Change—The Only Certainties

The old adage that the only sure things in life are death and taxes needs to be updated for the 1990s to include *change*, for it is clearly evident that change has become a way of life. Today there are no safe companies, no sure customers, no secure jobs, and no such thing as an established market share. The global economy has opened up heretofore unknown opportunities and with it a new network of suppliers, distributors, and outsourcing resources that will compete with and for American goods. Electronic highways like Internet have given virtually anyone instant access to people and information throughout the entire world, giving entrepreneurs the chance to compete with large companies on a more level playing field. The price of money in the global marketplace is changing daily, making it nothing short of a miracle to forecast costs, prices, and interest rates into anything but the very immediate future. Many of the products and services businesses will offer ten years from now cannot even be conceived of today. Technology is constantly changing the business of business, from manufacturing to distribution to customer service.

Tom Peters predicted the dynamic nature of the world today and the consequent need to redefine "excellence" in business in his prophetic 1987 book titled *Thriving on Chaos*. Now more than eight years later, the truth of what he said is being felt. "...Excellent firms of tomorrow will cherish impermanence—and thrive on chaos," or they will not survive. Peters's study focused on America's big companies and demonstrated how failure to adjust to a changing world threatens to destroy them. Change has not been part of the vocabulary of many of America's biggest companies. However, to those who have devoted their lives and energy to entrepreneurship, the concept of change as a constant is not entirely new. Uncertainty is the ubiquitous companion of any new venture. Born into an uncertain environment, start-ups by nature must be flexible, able to change in response to changing needs and requirements. Joseph Schumpeter, a classical economist who often took off that hat when he spoke of entrepreneurs, said the job of the entrepreneur is "creative destruction." Entrepreneurs disrupt the economic equilibrium. Schumpeter's concept of the entrepreneur does not, however, fit easily into the economic models espoused by the followers of Keynes, Friedman, and supply-side economists, whose goals are to optimize existing resources and arrive at economic equilibrium. Consequently, they have a difficult time accepting Schumpeter's model, which contends that economic disequilibrium caused by entrepreneurial innovation is a sign of a healthy economy.

> *Born into an uncertain environment, start-ups by nature must be flexible, able to change in response to changing needs and requirements.*

Nevertheless, the volatile world market cannot be ignored, and no one is better prepared to face the dynamics of the 1990s and beyond than entrepreneurs. Dealing with the new global and technological environment requires a different vision and a different mindset today than it did even a decade ago. Where in the past new businesses started with a narrow geographic focus, purchased equipment and technology to last for the long term, designed products and services before finding customers to purchase them, and built large bureaucratic organizations, today the rules have changed. Today these intrepid risk takers who start their high-growth ventures in this decade have the distinct advantage of starting with flexible, dynamic organizations poised to respond to change and to even create change as well. Certainly it is easier to start a venture with the expectation of change than to attempt to downsize a monolithic giant and re-educate employees to new ways of doing things.

Accordingly, this book refers to these new types of entrepreneurial ventures as **world-class** ventures, created by entrepreneurs who have learned much from witnessing the foibles, failures, and frantic downsizing of big business. World-class ventures will come from a learning curve that says bigger is not more efficient and the largest firms are not always the greatest sources of innovation. While world-class ventures take advantage of current technology for product development and manufacturing, they are not necessarily "high-tech ventures" in the strictest sense of the term. Typically, high-tech companies include such things as computer software and hardware manufacturing and biomedical technology firms. Instead, "world-class" as used in this book is a quality term applied to firms that have certain characteristics. Achievement of world-class status begins at start-up with a vision, strategy, and infrastructure that models these characteristics. Therefore, the successful start-ups of the 1990s and beyond will:

- Be smaller and more responsive
- Look for niche markets at a global level
- Innovate with teams and fast-faced product development
- Be oriented toward quality and customer service
- Have a less hierarchical organizational structure
- Rely on outsourcing, the virtual corporation
- Create value by giving employees a major stake in the organization

This then is the legacy of big corporations of the past—they have effectively carved a new market niche for the dynamic entrepreneur of the future.

What Is an Entrepreneur?

The term **entrepreneur** has existed in our vocabulary for more than 250 years. The United States was founded on the principle of free enterprise, which encouraged entrepreneurs to freely assume the risk of developing businesses that would make the economy strong. However, it wasn't until the 1980s that *entrepreneur* came into popular use in the United States and an almost folkloric aura began to grow around men and women who started rapidly growing businesses. These formerly quiet, low-profile people suddenly became legends in their own time with the appeal and publicity typically accorded movie stars or rock musicians. Extraordinarily creative and enterprising business people like Bill Gates, who created Microsoft, Anita Roddick, who founded The Body Shop, and Steven Jobs and Steven Wozniak, who started Apple Computers, suddenly found that the whole world was interested not only in their businesses but in their personal lives as well.

At the same time, academic researchers sought to define what made these entrepreneurs so successful and to look at the new venture process as something quite different from starting a small business or managing an established company. In the early stages, researchers, with little success, attempted to identify psychological characteristics or traits associated with entrepreneurs to differentiate them from managers. What they discovered was that many of the characteristics normally encountered in entrepreneurs also exist in some managers.

What are the characteristics typically found in entrepreneurs? Research points to the entrepreneur's ability to take calculated risks and to have an achievement orientation, a sense of independence, an internal locus of control and a tolerance for ambiguity.

Risk-Taking

The consensus of the research on risk-taking in entrepreneurs is that they are not big risk-takers.[1] They are, instead, calculated risk-takers who define the risks inherent in any venture and attempt to minimize them while remaining focused on opportunity. In fact, the real risk for the entrepreneur seems to come from the fear of failure and the potential for damage to his or her reputation. Consequently, it is in the best interest of the entrepreneur to analyze a potential opportunity to reduce the risk associated with it.

Need for Achievement

Entrepreneurs tend to have a high desire to be personally responsible for solving problems and setting and reaching goals—in other words—a need for achievement.[2] This need for achievement has often been referred to as "the burning gut." Entrepreneurs are innately driven to start ventures and succeed. They are not daunted by failure, but tend to keep trying until they succeed.

A Sense of Independence

Entrepreneurs also seem to purposely seek independence—to be their own boss in situations that allow them to assume a higher degree of personal responsibility

[1]Brockhaus, R.H. (1980). "Risk-taking Propensity of Entrepreneurs." *Academy of Management Journal*, 23, 509–520; Drucker, P.F. (1985). *Innovation and Entrepreneurship.* New York: Harper and Row.

[2]McClelland, D.C. (1965). "N-achievement and Entrepreneurship: A Longitudinal Study." *Journal of Personality and Social Psychology*, 1, 389–392.

PROFILE 1.1

Turning Failure into Success

No one knows more about how it feels to fail than Wally Amos, founder of Famous Amos Cookies. After building an $80 million business as "the face that launched 1,000 chips," he lost his fortune, his business, and even the right to use his name. He says that failure came because he was irresponsible and didn't take on professional management to grow the company. Instead, he moved to Hawaii, 2,500 miles away from the corporate headquarters, to enjoy the good life.

By the 1980s he was on the verge of losing the company. Out of fear he took on investors who ultimately seized control of the company and left him out in the cold. Taking full responsibility for the loss of his company, Amos set out to start another, Wally Amos Presents: Chip and Cookie in 1991. It was not to be. Within 18 months, the owners of Famous Amos enjoined him against using his own name. On the verge of bankruptcy, Amos, ever persistent, started yet another cookie company in 1993, The Uncle Noname [No-nahm-ay] Cookie Co., which he is promoting nationwide. This time, however, he is donating one percent of net sales to an organization called Cities in Schools, which offers a dropout prevention program. On every bag of cookies is a recipe for lemonade, which reflects Amos's philosophy about life: *If life hands you a lemon, turn it into lemonade.*

for their decisions and achievements. This need for independence, however, often makes it difficult for entrepreneurs to delegate authority to others.

Internal Locus of Control

"Locus of control" refers to the degree to which people believe events in their lives are within their control. Those who believe they have control over aspects of their environment and destiny are said to have an internal locus of control, while those who feel controlled by their environment are said to have an external locus of control. Many studies have determined that entrepreneurs have a strong internal locus of control.[3] In fact, the issue of the entrepreneur's need for control has even been referred to as the "dark side" of the entrepreneur, since the entrepreneur often has difficulty delegating authority or giving up control in any way.

---

[3]Greenberger & Sexton, D.L. (1988). "An Interactive Model of New Venture Initiation." *Journal of Small Business Management*, 1-7.

Tolerance for Ambiguity

The start-up process is by its very nature dynamic, uncertain, complex, and ambiguous. Entrepreneurs, however, seem to work well in this type of environment, possibly because it is challenging, exciting, and offers more opportunity than a more structured environment.

If psychological characteristics are not a good measure of who the entrepreneur is, how then do we describe the entrepreneur? Not by who the entrepreneur is, but by what the entrepreneur *does*. It is the behaviors of entrepreneurs that distinguish them.[4]

Therefore, the act of creating the business—perceiving an opportunity, assessing and risking resources to exploit the opportunity, managing the process of building a venture from an idea, and creating value—is the **entrepreneurial act**. Those who have the passion to build innovative businesses from the idea stage and who continue to act entrepreneurially, making strategic decisions that engage the business in risk-oriented activity, growth, and consequent high performance, are considered *entrepreneurs*.

Why Do Entrepreneurs Start Businesses?

Entrepreneurs start businesses for a variety of reasons. Sometimes they are blocked in their achievement in the company for which they work. Such was the case of Ruth Owades, who founded Gardeners' Eden, sold it, and then started Calyx and Corolla, both successful mail order catalogs. She was working for a large mail order company when she saw a need for a catalog that catered to upscale gardeners, offering interesting and unusual tools and other gardening paraphernalia. Unfortunately, she could not win the support of her company, which was nervous about investing in an idea that strayed from what they were currently doing. She subsequently decided to leave that company and start her own.

Some entrepreneurs have started their businesses as a result of a course in entrepreneurship taken at a community college or university. For Talli Counsel, taking an entrepreneurship course at the University of Southern California in 1985 inspired him to give up medical school and search for a business opportunity. The opportunity came when he started a small business changing tires on fleet vehicles owned and operated by various businesses, and subsequently

---

[4]Gartner, W.B. (1988). "Who is an Entrepreneur is the Wrong Question." *American Journal of Small Business*, 11-31.; Vesper, K.H. (1990). *New Venture Strategies*. Englewood Cliffs, NJ: Prentice Hall.

met someone who gave him a contact with a Fortune 500 company. That contact led to his starting Interfleet, Inc., now a successful business that services the fleet vehicles of the Fortune 500 companies nationwide and consults to the major auto makers.

Figure 1.1: Should You Start a Business?

No quiz can really tell you if you are the kind of person who should start a business. This little quiz and its discussion at the end of the chapter will simply help you learn if you have some of the typical characteristics found in many entrepreneurs. Answer the following questions without spending a lot of time thinking about them. You are looking for a spontaneous reaction. There are no right or wrong answers, but when you have finished, look at the end of the chapter to see what research has found to be the typical responses made by entrepreneurs.

1. Are you
   a. married
   b. single
   c. widowed
   d. divorced

2. Are you
   a. a man
   b. a woman

3. What is your primary reason for wanting to start a business?
   a. to make money
   b. to be independent
   c. to gain power
   d. to give yourself a job
   e. to be famous

4. How comfortable are you with uncertainty and ambiguity?
   a. very comfortable
   b. somewhat comfortable
   c. not at all comfortable

5. To be successful in an entrepreneurial venture, what do you believe you will need?
   a. money
   b. luck
   c. hard work
   d. good idea
   e. all of the above

6. In terms of taking risk are you
   a. a high risk taker (gambler)
   b. a moderate risk taker
   c. small risk taker
   d. not relevant

7. Have you ever been fired?
   a. At least once
   b. Never

8. Did you start any businesses before you were 20?
   a. Many
   b. One or two
   c. None

Others start businesses for very personal reasons. This was the case for Sandy Gooch, who suffered from severe reactions to artificial additives in food. They actually became toxins in her body. Learning that many others also suffered in this way, she decided to become an expert on natural foods, and in 1977 she founded her first Mrs. Gooch's Natural Foods Market in the Los Angeles area. By 1993 the company had seven stores, was doing about $80 million in annual revenues, and had over 800 employees.

Still others simply want to own their own businesses. After World War II, Masaru Ibuka started a company in a rented room of a bombed-out department store in Tokyo with $1,600 of his own savings and seven employees, but no idea as to what the business was. After weeks of brainstorming, they decided to produce a rice cooker, which, unfortunately, didn't work the way it was supposed to. However, Ibuka and his team persisted in spite of failure, and they are known today as Sony Corporation.

Whatever the reason, most entrepreneurs have the intense desire—the passion—to start a business long before they know what that business will be. It is that internal need to be independent and create something, "the burning gut," that drives entrepreneurs.

Entrepreneur Myths

Before leaving the topic of what defines entrepreneurs, some of the myths that have surrounded them over the years need to be dispelled.

Entrepreneurs are born, not made. Entrepreneurs come in all ages and backgrounds. Even though research has demonstrated links to role models of previous generations within a family, the entrepreneurial drive has not been shown to be hereditary. Almost anyone who has a vision for a new venture, tremendous drive, and the willingness to risk failure can acquire the technical skills to be an entrepreneur through education and experience. Entrepreneurial drive, however, is one thing that must exist naturally in a person. It cannot be learned.

Entrepreneurs are gamblers. Entrepreneurs are *not* gamblers! In fact, as stated previously, entrepreneurs attempt to minimize the risk of an undertaking by calculating the consequences of their decisions before they implement them. For this reason, they conduct feasibility studies to determine an idea's potential viability with some degree of accuracy before they expend a lot of time and money on it.

Money is the most important component of the start-up package. Researchers and venture capitalists will tell you that while sufficiently capitalizing the new business is important to its survivability, the most important component is the founding team. An excellent founding team can take an undercapitalized new venture and make it a commercial success. On the other hand, a mediocre team may have a difficult time making even a sufficiently capitalized venture a success. What constitutes an excellent management team is discussed in Chapter 4.

Entrepreneurs are motivated solely by money. As you saw from the stories of Talli Counsel, Ruth Owades, Sandy Gooch, and Masaru Ibuka, entrepreneurs are motivated to start businesses for a variety of reasons, many of which are personal and have nothing whatsoever to do with money. For people like Sandy Gooch, for example, money is a means to an end, providing natural foods that people can eat without worrying about toxic consequences.

The Entrepreneurial Venture

The entrepreneur is only one component in the process of new venture creation. (See Figure 1.2.) The behaviors and experience of the entrepreneur interact with all the other components of the new venture process to create a business.

Figure 1.2: The New Venture Process

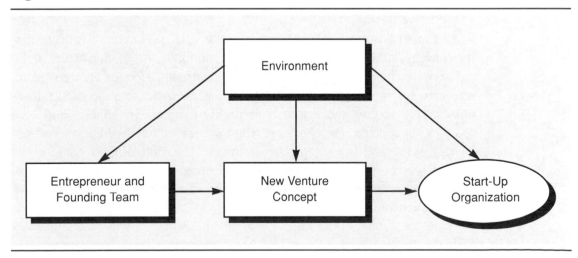

The second component, the environment, is the most comprehensive in the venture creation process. It includes all those factors, apart from the entrepreneur's personal background, that affect the entrepreneur's decision to start a business.

Four categories of environmental variables significantly impact a new venture's ability to start and grow:

1. **Type of Environment**
   - Uncertain
   - Complex
   - Volatile
2. **Resource Availability**
   - Land
   - Skilled labor
   - Capital for start-up
3. **Mechanisms for Realizing Value**
   - Favorable markets for new ventures
   - Access to distribution channels
   - Favorable tax structure
   - Favorable governmental policies
4. **Incentives for New Venture Creation**
   - Enterprise zones
   - Small Business Administration grants
   - Favorable capital gains laws

All these environmental characteristics affect the new venture concept that the entrepreneur develops and will vary depending on the specific nature of the industry in which the new business will operate. For example, entrepreneurs who start high-technology businesses, such as computer and electronics businesses, face an environment at once highly dynamic (changing) and very complex. In contrast, entrepreneurs who start restaurants face a more technologically stable and less complex environment. The more of these components that are present in their favorable form in the environment when the entrepreneur starts the business, the better the chance the new venture will grow and become successful.

While the details of the list of environmental variables will be discussed in their appropriate chapters, in general, the environment for starting new ventures in the 1990s and beyond is characterized by:

1. Global competition
2. Faster product development times
3. Rapidly changing technology
4. Higher expected standards for quality and service
5. The need for strategic alliances
6. A decline in traditional financing sources

Within specific industries and in specific geographic regions, environmental variables and the degree of their impact will differ.

The new venture concept, the third component in the entrepreneurial process, is the development of the initial business idea, taking into consideration the entrepreneur's goals and the environment in which the business will operate. Developing the business concept is the subject of Chapter 3.

Entrepreneurial Ventures vs. Small Businesses

It is important to make a clear distinction between entrepreneurial ventures and small businesses. While many of the venture creation processes discussed in this book are applicable to both types of businesses, in a world-class entrepreneurial venture there is a distinct difference in the vision of the entrepreneur and the goals for the business.

Recall from the earlier description of the process of entrepreneurship that entrepreneurial ventures are essentially

- **innovative**
- **value-creating**
- **growth-oriented**

An entrepreneurial venture brings something new to the marketplace, whether it be a new product or service (the fax machine), a new marketing strategy (Home Shopping Network), or a new way to deliver products and services to consumers (Federal Express). The entrepreneurial venture creates value through innovation and through bringing new jobs to the economy that don't merely draw from other businesses currently existing. Moreover, entrepreneurial ventures are growth-oriented. The entrepreneur has a vision of where he or she wants the business to go and, generally, the vision is on a regional, national, or more often a global level.

By contrast, small businesses are generally started to generate an income and lifestyle for the owner or the family. Often referred to as "Mom and Pop" businesses, they tend to remain relatively small and geographically bound. A specific example will illustrate the difference between entrepreneurial ventures and small businesses.

If you were to start a company that remanufactures machine tools for local manufacturers, you would be starting what is termed a small business, in this case a job shop, because the concept in and of itself is not innovative. Your employees would likely come from other similar businesses. If, however, you were to specialize in re-manufacturing certain types of machinery, using the latest technology or developing proprietary technology, marketing the company on an international level with a plan to go public in seven years, then you would have started an entrepreneurial venture. It would be innovative, and therefore create value by offering something that doesn't currently exist; it would create new jobs; and it would have a growth orientation. Logically many small businesses have the potential to become world-class entrepreneurial ventures. The reason they don't is often a conscious decision of the founder to remain a small, lifestyle business.

> *World-class entrepreneurial ventures focus on people—empowering employees, reshaping the traditional hierarchies, providing training and education, and giving employees responsibility, ownership in the company, and opportunity.*

Additional characteristics are associated with world-class entrepreneurial ventures. They focus on people—empowering employees, reshaping the traditional hierarchies, providing training and education, and giving employees responsibility, ownership in the company, and opportunity. The result is more loyalty on the part of employees, less turnover, and spectacular performance. These world-class ventures are also customer-need driven. More often than not, customers and the marketplace dictate the products and services offered by the entrepreneur and even the direction the new venture will take. They are also in constant pursuit of excellence in all aspects of the business. Finally, they are flexible both in organizational structure and strategy, ready to respond quickly to changes in the environment.

If you understand the differences between world-class entrepreneurial ventures and small businesses, you will realize that knowing what kind of business you are starting is very important since it affects the decisions you make from the outset and your goals for that business. For example, if your intent is to grow the business to a national level, you will make different decisions along the way than if your intent is to own and operate a thriving restaurant in your local community. Generally, a small business requires good management skills, since the owner must perform all tasks associated with the business as it grows. By contrast, entrepreneurs typically do not enjoy the management aspects of the business and would prefer to hire experts to carry out that function, leaving the entrepreneurial team free to innovate, raise capital, and get involved in public relations.

The Role of the Entrepreneur in the Marketplace

From the founding of this country, individuals with an entrepreneurial spirit have started the businesses that are the basis of the free enterprise system. With a careful eye on trends and consumer needs, they have supplied us with new technology and new products and services of every conceivable type while creating jobs. Beyond all this, the most successful entrepreneurs affect our lives, the way we do things, and the choices we make. A legendary example is Steve Jobs and Steve Wozniak, who, in 1976, created the personal computer through their company, Apple, and started a revolution that in less than five years resulted in a whole new industry with hundreds of ancillary businesses and thousands of new jobs that had not existed previously. Entrepreneurs like Jobs and Wozniak shake up the economy. They look for unsatisfied needs and satisfy them. In fact, the most creative entrepreneurs invent needs that consumers and businesses never knew they had.

Today small business—by the Small Business Administration definition, businesses with fewer than 100 employees—accounts for about 90 percent of all new jobs created. How has this happened? Figure 1.3 on p. 16 summarizes the evolution that has taken place since the 1960s.

> *Today small business—by the Small Business Administration definition, businesses with fewer than 100 employees—accounts for about 90 percent of all new jobs created.*

In the mid-1960s, large companies were the norm. In fact, all but two of the biggest companies in the world were American. It is estimated that General Motors in the 1960s earned as much as the ten biggest companies of Great Britain, France, and West Germany combined. The reason American companies enjoyed such unrestricted growth was that at that time they basically had no competition from Europe and Japan.

The 1970s saw the beginning of three significant trends that would forever change the face of business: macroeconomic turmoil, international competition, and the technological revolution. A volatile economic climate pervaded the 1970s, the likes of which had not been seen since World War II. The Vietnam War economy brought with it inflation, the dollar was devalued, food prices skyrocketed due to several agricultural disasters, and the formation of OPEC sent gas prices up 50 percent. Furthermore, by the late 1970s the Federal Reserve had let interest rates rise to a prime of 20 percent. The result was no borrowing, no spending, and a recession that spilled into the 1980s, bringing with it an unemployment rate of ten percent.

To compound the effects of the economy on business, by 1980 one-fifth of all American companies faced foreign competition which had far more favorable cost structures. Imports, particularly in the automobile and machine tools industries, were suddenly taking a significant share of the market from American businesses.

The third event affecting business was the technological revolution brought about by the introduction of the microprocessor by Intel in 1971, the Mits Altair personal computer in 1975, and the Apple II computer in 1977. Microprocessors succeeded in rendering whole categories of products obsolete—such things as mechanical cash registers and adding machines, for example—and effectively antiquated the skills of the people who made them.

Increasing the pressure for business, the government ushered in a new era of business regulation with the Environmental Protection Agency, the Occupational Safety and Health Agency, and the Consumer Product Safety Commission, all of which increased costs to businesses. On the opposite front, deregulation forced planes, trucks, and railroads to compete and, in general, big companies no longer had control of the marketplace.

Figure 1.3: Why is Entrepreneurship So Important Today?

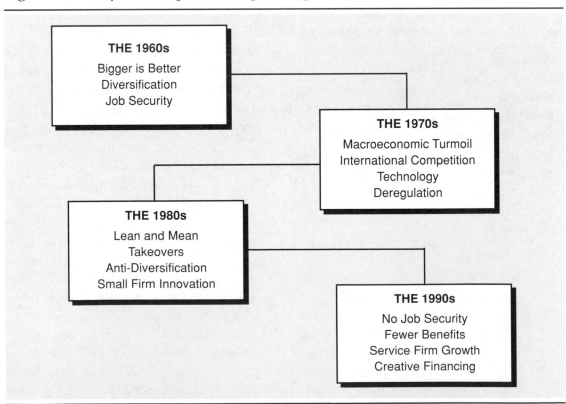

By the early 1980s, business was in terrible shape. The Fortune 500 saw a record 27 percent drop in profits.[5] Large mills and factories were shutting down; manufacturing employment was declining; yet, ironically, productivity remained the same or increased. It was found that new, smaller manufacturers were still generating jobs—and not only manufacturing jobs, but service jobs as well. How was this possible? To become competitive, smaller, more flexible, *entrepreneurial* manufacturers hired subcontractors who could perform tasks such as bookkeeping and payroll more efficiently. These service firms developed to support the needs of the product sector, but they too inspired the creation of other service firms as well—people who work often need day-care service or maid service, so even more jobs were created.

With the creation of all these jobs, it is no wonder that the 1980s have been called the Decade of Entrepreneurship by many, including the dean of management science, Peter Drucker, who was not alone in asserting that the United States was rapidly and by necessity becoming an entrepreneurial economy.[6]

> *All these events have moved this country in the 1990s toward a period that requires the vision, the resources, and the motivation of the entrepreneur.*

Responding to this entrepreneurial drive, big business in the 1980s found it necessary to downsize and reverse the trend of diversification it had promulgated for so long. If big companies were going to compete with the dynamic, innovative, smaller firms and fend off the takeover bids so prevalent in the 1980s, they would have to restructure and reorganize for a new way of doing business. This restructuring and reorganizing actually resulted in improved performance, increased profits, and higher stock prices. It also meant, however, that many jobs would no longer exist, people would receive fewer benefits, and the only "secure" jobs left would be found in civil service.

All these events have moved this country in the 1990s toward a period that requires the vision, the resources, and the motivation of the entrepreneur to seek new opportunities and create new jobs in a vastly different global environment. One measure of the awareness of this entrepreneurial trend is the increasing number of schools worldwide that now offer entrepreneurship courses. Today nearly 400 colleges and universities offer at least one course in entrepreneurship. Community colleges and community-based programs are also seeking to give aspiring entrepreneurs the tools they need to succeed.

---

[5]Case, J. (1992). *From the Ground Up.* New York: Simon & Schuster.
[6]Drucker, P.F. (1985) *Innovation and Entrepreneurship.* New York: Harper & Row.

Trends for the 1990s and Beyond

Today potential entrepreneurs thinking about starting a business need to become aware of the trends that will affect global markets through the 1990s and possibly into the next century. Understanding societal trends is also a good way to prepare yourself to recognize opportunity. What major trends are currently evolving?

The Downsizing of Major Corporations

As discussed in the previous section, the trend is definitely away from monolithic corporations like General Motors to smaller, more flexible companies. The reason is that our economic environment has become more complex and dynamic; businesses need to be able to quickly shift gears to meet changing needs and requirements. The advantages that smaller companies—whose overhead is much less—afford is recognized by major organizations like 3M, which regularly subcontracts with small manufacturers to produce products related to their core product, adhesive tape.

An Emphasis on Social Responsibility

Today an increasing number of businesses are doing more than simply making profits. They are also concerned about giving something back to their community through community-aid programs, by being responsible about the pollutants they create in their production process, and by demonstrating an awareness of their interconnectedness with society as a whole. Anita Roddick's Body Shop, for example, in its commitment to social responsibility, established trade agreements with underdeveloped countries to bring their raw materials to the commercial market in the form of natural skin care products.

A Focus on the Environment

Not only are businesses becoming more responsible about not polluting the environment, many entrepreneurs are starting environmental businesses to help Americans in their efforts to clean up the environment. A good example is Gardeners' Supply, a mail-order company located in Burlington, Vermont, which collects and composts grass clippings, leaves, and food scraps for free. The compost is then passed on to gardeners. The program has been so successful that they are now collecting 3,000 to 4,000 tons a year. Its goal is to recycle 30 percent of the total waste in the community.

A Global Orientation

The old saying that the world is an increasingly smaller place seems to be true. Technology has made access to other countries as easy as contacting the business in the next city. Exporting products and services to other countries has almost become a necessity for a growing business to remain competitive. Today it is just as likely you will purchase some of your supplies overseas as it is that you will purchase them domestically. You may even, like Mattel Toy Company, manufacture in another country.

Fitness and Health

The business of keeping people healthy and physically fit is a huge industry that began taking shape in the 1980s. The ubiquitous baby boom generation, which is fast approaching its 50s, provides the astute entrepreneur with an enormous customer base of people who want to stay "young" as long as possible.

The Aging Population

In less than 20 years, the oldest of the baby boomers will have reached retirement age. We are facing a major population shift; average age is increasing. Consequently, opportunities abound for product and service businesses that meet the needs of this enormous consumer group. Bruce Lunsford is an example of someone who saw this trend and started Vencor, Inc., which specializes in long-term care. Today he runs hospitals in 11 states.

Career Flexibility

Keeping the same job for 30 or more years is a thing of the past. Today adults must be prepared for change, and they must constantly update their skills so when change comes, they can adapt. Roe Hatlen found himself out of a job at age 40. Fortunately, it was just the jump-start he needed to make the decision to start his own company. He managed to build the very successful Old Country Buffet chain of restaurants, offering home-style entrees.

Information is Power

You have no doubt heard the terms *information age* and *information super-highway*. With the advent of the computer revolution, information is more readily available and in greater quantity than ever before. In fact, some would say we are actually suffering from "information overload," too much information and too little time to process it all. Today a company's power—or an individual's power for that matter—comes from staying on top of new information. We are no longer a society that can educate people through age 21 and claim that they are sufficiently educated. "Life-long learning" is the trend, and on just that premise Joline Godfrey founded Odysseum, Inc., an international learning design company serving Fortune 500 companies.

Women in Business

Today women are starting businesses at a rate five times that of men. Moreover, women now employ more people than the Fortune 500 worldwide. Why is this? One reason is that women are no longer comfortable in a big business culture dominated by men, which often prevents them from reaching the highest levels of management. Women also start businesses so they can make the major decisions and create a culture that reflects their different management style. Emyre Robinson, for example, founded Barrios Technologies, an engineering contractor to NASA and major space contractors, to meet a need in the industry but also for the opportunity to create a business culture based on the nuclear family, where people come first. Her door is open to any employee of the company, and all are encouraged to participate in its growth process and its success.

The fact that more women are starting businesses is also important from an economic standpoint; women now require the services they traditionally supplied for their husbands: housecleaning, child care, cooking, and so on. Consequently, some women are starting those very service businesses that help other women move into economic sectors previously dominated by men. While it is true that in general women start small businesses in the retail and service sectors, we are now seeing a significant increase in the number of women who start high-growth ventures in industries previously dominated by men.

Staying Home

Faith Popcorn, a noted market consultant to Fortune 500 companies, has observed a trend she calls "cocooning." Cocooning is simply staying home: entertaining at home or working from home. What this means to entrepreneurs is that people are demanding more delivery services for things such as restaurant food, groceries, dry cleaning, and so forth. They want to entertain themselves at home, so they are purchasing more in-home entertainment systems, renting more videos, and shopping from home via computers.

In the decade of the 1990s and beyond, entrepreneurial skills will be the key not only to economic independence and success, but literally to survival as well. The marketplace places a premium on creativity, initiative, independence, and flexibility, characteristics present in dynamic entrepreneurs. Starting a new venture is a process that begins long before the business ever opens its doors. Consequently, this book takes a process approach to starting a world-class venture. By using the framework of a business plan, it guides the reader through the process, emphasizing the new "rules" for start-ups in the 1990s and giving the reader a clear sense of how to create a world-class venture.

✓ New Venture Checklist

Have you

☐ Concluded that you have what it takes to be an entrepreneur?

☐ Determined why you want to start a business?

☐ Decided if you will start an entrepreneurial venture or a small business?

☐ Determined how the trends for the 1990s will affect your search for a business idea?

Answers to Questionnaire Figure 1.1: *Should You Start A Business?*

1. The average entrepreneur is married, probably because they are older when they initiate their ventures and having a working spouse gives an additional source of income during start-up.
2. Most entrepreneurs today are still men, particularly in high-growth ventures, but women are now beginning to start businesses at a rate much higher than men. And more and more women are starting high-growth ventures.
3. The primary reason most entrepreneurs give for starting a business is to gain independence—the right to do things the way they want.
4. In general, entrepreneurs tend to be very comfortable with ambiguity and uncertainty. An uncertain environment, which is characteristic of start-up ventures, offers a challenge that entrepreneurs enjoy meeting. Moreover, a dynamic, uncertain environment generally offers more opportunity.

5. Entrepreneurs will need all of these factors. But note that entrepreneurs believe they make their own luck.

6. Entrepreneurs are moderate risk takers. They calculate risk and take on risks that have a good probability of producing adequate rewards.

7. Entrepreneurs often report having been fired, probably because they don't easily fit into traditional company molds.

8. Most entrepreneurs have started several ventures before age 20.

Additional Sources of Information

Case, John. (1992). *From the Ground Up*. New York: Simon & Schuster.

Drucker, Peter F. (1986). *Innovation and Entrepreneurship*. New York: Harper & Row.

Godfrey, Joline. (1992). *Our Wildest Dreams*. New York: HarperCollins.

Naisbitt, John and Patricia Aberdene. (1990). *Megatrends 2000: Ten New Directions for the 1990s*. New York: Fawcett Columbine.

Peters, Tom. (1987). *Thriving on Chaos*. New York: Harper & Row.

Issues to Consider

1. Why is it is so difficult to assign "typical" characteristics to entrepreneurs in order to describe them?

2. Do you agree with the notion that entrepreneurs start businesses for more than money? Why or why not?

3. What impact does the environment have on your ability to start a business?

4. What does "creating value" mean to you as a potential entrepreneur?

5. Take a typical "small business" in your community and discuss how you could turn that business into an entrepreneurial venture.

6. What evidence do you find for the statement that we are becoming an "entrepreneurial economy"?

7. Which of the trends for the 1990s do you believe holds the most promise for business opportunity and why?

CHAPTER 2

Recognizing and Testing Opportunity

Overview

- *Creativity exercises to enhance latent creative skills*
- *Techniques for generating new business ideas*
- *The issue of success and what it means to you*
- *A quick test of the business idea to determine if a feasibility study is warranted*
- *Overview of the feasibility study and business plan*

Recognizing Opportunity

Have you ever wondered where people get those great ideas that turn into extraordinarily successful businesses? Is the ability to recognize opportunity something you're born with? Absolutely not! Certainly some people have an easier time generating ideas than others, but that's only because they have better developed creative and awareness skills. This is good news, because even if you have never thought of yourself as a creative person, you have the ability to become one.

What does creativity have to do with entrepreneurship? Very simply, creativity is a key ingredient to entrepreneurial success. Today's entrepreneurs face a very volatile, uncertain environment: a banking industry that is restructuring and moving away from lending to growing businesses; factories that are downsizing or closing; local, state, and federal bureaucracies that have burdensome regulations; and an economic climate that is challenging at best for starting and growing new businesses. Sounds grim.

But even in the worst of environments—in fact, especially in the worst environments—creative men and women find innovative ways of adapting to the environment and making it work for them. It is no wonder then that the worst of times often brings out the best in entrepreneurs. The case of John Wiley and Alan Ackerman is a good example. (See Profile 2.1.) No matter what the environment throws at entrepreneurs, if they put their creative talents to work, they can find a way to succeed.

Enhancing Your Creative Skills

Creative people are curious people who exhibit a strong sense of awareness of their surroundings. They ask questions and aren't afraid to do things differently. They are openly accepting of all ideas, figuring that every idea is worthy of at least initial consideration; and they seem to have a high tolerance for ambiguity.

However, some people resist creativity and ambiguity; they are uncomfortable in uncertain environments and don't know how to use their creative skills to survive. This is not surprising when you consider that many schools do not challenge students to be creative, but instead expect students to follow a structured environment laid out by the teacher, which includes coming up with only the expected correct answers.

PROFILE 2.1

Making Creativity Work

In 1982 John Wiley and Alan Ackerman started a company called Microbits Peripheral Products, Inc. to produce hardware for the Atari personal computer. Within a year and a half, they were doing $3 million in sales and had 55 employees. Then in 1985 the Atari market collapsed, Microbits was unable to keep up its loan payments, and its loan was called by the bank. The company could not be sold, so the bank decided to package the assets and auction them through a sealed bid process. Wiley and Ackerman could have given up at that point, but, instead, they saw a chance to turn a disaster into a creative opportunity by rounding up ten investors who helped them repurchase their assets at auction for 10 cents on the dollar.

With their investors they started Supra, which produces modems and communication devices for a number of different computers. Starting in their garage, Wiley and Ackerman turned a failure into a success within a year.

Entrepreneurship is a creative, not a scientific, process. From the generation of the business idea to the development of the market plan to the management of the growing business, it is creativity in all aspects of the venture that sets the most successful new businesses apart from those that merely survive.

Before considering some specific techniques you can use to generate business ideas, you might want to try a couple of exercises to prepare yourself for thinking creatively.

1. Pick a simple item you have in your home, perhaps a box of granola, and see how many uses you can find for it. There are at least 30! Remember, don't limit your thinking. For example, you could glue the granola to a backing, spray it with shellac, and use it as jewelry! As silly as this sounds, you will find that the more you do this exercise with different products, the easier it gets and the more ideas you are able to generate. Some of them may actually turn out to be sound business ideas.
2. The next time you say to yourself, "I wish there were a way to..." or "I wish I had something that could..." stop yourself and start thinking about how to get from here to there. This is, by the way, how breakthrough products like the fax machine were developed. The question that led to the fax machine was, "How can I get a written document to people as quickly as I can phone them?" For the solution the inventor didn't limit himself by looking only at what was obviously possible. Think of all the inventions and services that are part of life today that wouldn't be here if the inventors had limited themselves to what was "possible."

Sources of New Venture Ideas

It is important to distinguish between an *idea* and an *opportunity*. Everyone has ideas; in fact, you probably have hundreds of them every day. Every time you make a decision to do something, it is based on an idea or thought that came to you prior to making the decision. However, opportunity, in a business sense, is an idea that can be turned into a business or commercialized in some manner. In fact, the very act of moving through the process of creating a business plan turns an idea into an opportunity.

Much of creativity and innovation today occurs within the confines of what is already known: planes to spaceships, drive-in restaurants to drive-in banks. It is only when a few very insightful people break those boundaries and leap into an untried, unknown universe that products like the computer, for which there really was no precedent, are created. Even a simple product like Velcro was inspired by going beyond human boundaries and observing the sticky hook spine of the common burr in nature.

What sets off the creative process is a very personal thing. How many times have you come up with an idea while listening to a dry lecture or a boring sermon? Some people find their best ideas come while they are driving their car, reading a book, or exercising. Do you get ideas through dreams or in the shower? If you can identify where and when you seem to get most of your creative thoughts, you might want, if possible, to do that activity or a similar one more often and actually write down the ideas you get when you get them.

There are several ways you can use your newfound creativity to generate some ideas that may lead to an opportunity and help turn you into an entrepreneur.

PROFILE 2.2

A Creative Way to Generate Ideas

Dr. Yoshiro Naka Mats is truly the essence of a creative, innovative person. He holds more than 2,300 patents, more than double the number that prolific American inventor Thomas Edison held. For example, Naka Mats is responsible for the floppy disk, which he licensed to IBM, the compact disc and player, the digital watch and the water-powered engine. Naka Mats even has a creative way of generating ideas. He starts the creativity process by sitting calmly in a room in his home, which he calls the "static room" because it has only natural things in it, much like the meditation gardens in Kyoto, Japan. It is in this room that he opens his mind to the creative flow of new ideas. He then moves to the "dynamic room," a dark room with the latest audio/video equipment. Here he listens to jazz, easy listening music and Beethoven's Fifth Symphony—one of his favorites. In this room the genesis of new ideas begins to form. Following a period of time in the dynamic room, he heads for the swimming pool where he swims underwater for extraordinarily long periods of time. It is underwater that he finishes the process of "soft thinking" or playing with the idea and is ready to move on to the more practical phase of considering how to implement the idea.

Naka Mats, by the way, also swears by the brain food he eats: dried shrimp, seaweed, cheese, yogurt, eel, eggs, beef and chicken livers!

Keep an Idea File or Notebook

You have often heard about people who keep a notepad by their bed in case they have a good idea during the night. Why not keep a notepad with you all the time? Who knows when the spark of a great idea will come to you? Don't take a chance that you will remember it later. Chances are you won't because other thoughts and activities will invade your consciousness during the day, leaving you struggling later to recall what that great idea was that you had.

Talk to People—Network

Dr. Naka Mats claims (see Profile 2.2) that networking with people wherever he goes is a prime source of inspiration for new product ideas. In talking to people you find out more about their needs, and an unmet need is an opportunity. Talk to consumers, suppliers, your potential competition; there is something to be learned from everyone you meet. When you talk to people, don't just ask one question, ask several, because it is not likely you will get the information you need from the response to your first question. Many businesses like Toyota use this technique with great success to uncover the root cause of problems. After the first question, they ask at least three more. The technique might look something like this:

1. Why is the business failing?
   There is insufficient cash flow to cover expenses.
2. Why is there insufficient cash flow?
   Sales volume is too low.
3. Why is sales volume too low?
   We are not using the best distribution channels.
4. Why have we not used the best distribution channels?
   Our management team has no marketing experience.

Solution:　Hire an experienced marketing person.

If you had stopped after the first question, you would have thought that merely increasing cash flow by any means would correct the problem. By continuing to ask questions, you arrived at the root of the problem, lack of marketing experience, which is something quite different from solving a cash flow problem. Insufficient cash flow was only a symptom of the real problem: management deficiency.

Read Voraciously

Read newspapers, business magazines, and trade journals from the industry that interests you. Keep up with current trends in the marketplace, as well as present and potential governmental policies that may affect your industry. Remember, an idea can come from anywhere. The wealth of new environmental businesses was spawned from the relatively recent awareness of what our business and life practices are doing to the world we live in and also from the regulations that ensued.

Try Thinking in Opposites

Try thinking about what a product or service will *not* do or be. Charles Thompson, who wrote an excellent book on creativity, tells of an unusual technique he developed to collect debts.[1] He did it by thinking in opposites. Most people send formal invoices to their customers reminding them of their debt. He sent a cartoon of himself lying on the floor with a giant knife stuck in his

Figure 2.1: Generating Business Ideas

List some geographical areas that are not being serviced by a particular product/service.

1. _____
2. _____
3. _____

List some market segments (populations) that are underserved.

1. _____
2. _____
3. _____

List some big or troublesome problems for which the solution could turn into a potential business.

1. _____
2. _____
3. _____

[1]Thompson, Charles. (1992) *What a Great Idea!* New York: HarperPerennial.

back and a bubble saying "I trusted you." Most people send bills to the client's office. He sent it to the home. Most people send the bill in a business envelope by regular mail; Thompson sent it in a three-foot package by next day UPS. The technique was extremely successful and even turned into a small business because he thought about a problem from a different perspective; he did the opposite of what everyone else did.

Look for New Uses for Old Things

Johann Gutenberg took two unconnected ideas—the wine press and the coin punch—and came up with the printing press and moveable type. The mechanism for roll-on deodorant was the inspiration for the ballpoint pen. You might try looking a little closer at the products you use everyday and probably take for granted. How many times have you given an item a new use simply because you didn't own the correct tool to do what you wanted to do? Look at everything you use a little more closely to see if there is a way you can improve on it or come up with an entirely new tool. 3M scientist Arthur Fry was working on developing bookshelf arranger tape when he came up with the idea for a sticky-backed book marker, which ultimately became Post-it Notes[R].

Brainstorm Your Way to a New Idea

Brainstorming is a technique whereby you come up with ideas one after the other without stopping to consider if the idea is feasible. The advantage of brainstorming is that it often puts you in a position to come up with ideas as quickly as possible. Brainstorming opens your mind and helps you suspend judgment. Challenging beliefs and assumptions through brainstorming about what may be possible is why computers, fax machines, and space shuttles exist today.

Look to the Government

The federal government or your state government can be a great source of new venture ideas. New laws and regulations often require the use of a product or service that didn't previously exist. For example, the establishment of the Occupation Safety and Health Administration (OSHA) provided an opportunity for people who could provide training to businesses on everything from how to meet the stringent requirements in the workplace to filling out the incredible amount of paperwork associated with those requirements. City ordinances that require that certain products, such as glass and plastic, be recycled have produced many new businesses that provide new uses for these materials.

Where Will the Opportunities Be Next Century?

Organizations that monitor the growth of industry believe that the sectors of the economy that will attract sales and investment in the coming years are in the health industries and computer-related industries, specifically companies working on networking and "the information superhighway." Next are consumer goods and telecommunications. The most successful firms in these industries, generally high-tech and high-growth firms, flourish in an environment of change. This is not to say the business opportunity you find must be in these areas to be successful; it is, however, more likely your firm will grow rapidly and have above average sales if it is. Of course, the way you run your business and the amount of control you exert over its growth will be a function of the type of entrepreneur you are and your goals for yourself and the business.

Success and Failure

Many studies have attempted to determine the factors that contribute to a new business's success, with success usually being defined as monetary—sales or assets. While no one can guarantee a business that has particular attributes will be successful, certain characteristics do seem to be associated with successful ventures.

- They are started by teams
- The entrepreneur or team has experience in the industry
- The entrepreneur has started other businesses
- The business is well financed
- The business has a global market

The free enterprise system is based on the profit motive; consequently, profits are often used by those outside the business—bankers and investors—to measure venture success. But you also need to consider what success means to you. How will you know when your business is a success? For some entrepreneurs it's when they have created a certain number of jobs; for others, like Anita Roddick and The Body Shop, it's when she has established successful trade initiatives with underdeveloped countries. Only you can define success for your business, and that definition reflects both your business goals and your lifestyle goals.

By studying the factors that seem to be associated with success, the factors that contribute to failure also become readily apparent. Research has found that the primary cause of failure is a poor management team. Most books and articles, however, shy away from talking about failure even though failure is an important ingredient in success. It has been said that failure is just a rest stop on the way to success. It was that way for Judy Sims who, with her husband, started a games and educational retail software store that immediately failed. Drawing on her successful experience with cold calling (making unsolicited sales calls), she pulled herself up and began selling business software to local businesses in Dallas. One of her first accounts was Ross Perot's Electronic Data Systems and the rest, as they say, is history. Today her company does over $160 million in sales. The point is that entrepreneurs don't give up no matter how many times an idea they have fails. Instead, they look at failure as a source of opportunity, a wake-up call to listen more carefully to the customer and spend more time observing what is going on in the marketplace.

Testing the Idea Quickly

You know you have a business idea worthy of further consideration when you can't stop thinking about it. When that happens it's time to do a quick test to see if a full-blown feasibility study is warranted. There are several ways to accomplish this.

1. Talk to some trusted friends and get initial feedback on the idea. But don't be discouraged or write off the idea if they tell you it's crazy. People thought Fred Smith was crazy when he said he could deliver a package anywhere in the United States overnight—that is, until he founded Federal Express.
2. Do a quick checklist of the forces working for your idea and the forces working against it. How does the idea stack up? Are there more forces working in favor of the idea than against it?
3. Ask yourself three very important questions.
   Am I really interested in this business opportunity? If you develop this concept, it is going to take all the time and energy you can give it, so it's important that you *like* it.
   Is anyone else interested? You can't have a business without customers and you may need investors, so you'd better be sure that others are interested in what you have to offer.
   Will people actually pay for what I am offering? Often when people hear about a new product or service they express interest, even excitement, over it. But what are they willing to pay for it? If they are not willing to pay what you believe it's worth, that's a clue you may need to rethink the idea.

If your business idea can pass these tests, it is time for the next level of investigation: the feasibility study. A feasibility study gives you an indication of whether there is sufficient demand for your product or service. The estimation of demand is a vital step in deciding if you have a viable business concept, for there is no business without enough satisfied customers. Once you have concluded there is adequate demand for the product or service, other issues such as the operational and financial requirements can be undertaken and a business plan completed. There is no need to spend considerable time and effort on those issues if the feasibility study indicates insufficient interest in your product or service.

Even though the feasibility study is a tool geared primarily toward providing information to the entrepreneur, it's often possible to attract outside interest in your product/service at that point if the results are positive. That interest may result in some funding to help you complete a comprehensive business plan, conclude product development, and start the business. The feasibility study may also assist in attracting quality people to the founding team. As stated in the introduction, this book has a process organization. It follows the new venture creation process from its inception through start-up and growth. The feasibility study and the business plan are part of that process: They, in effect, document the process for the entrepreneur and others who are interested in the business.

The Feasibility Components

This section introduces the feasibility study and the business plan by giving an overview of their components. Each of the components described below has its own chapter detailing how to gather and analyze the information needed to complete that section of the document. Figure 2.2 displays an outline of a feasibility study.

Product/Service Description

The first section of the feasibility study presents a complete description of the product or service being offered, who the target customer is, the unique aspects of the product/service, and the benefits to the customer. It is in this section that the unique features of the product or service will be discussed, as well as possibilities for additional innovation in products, service, or distribution, called spin-offs. If the product needs to be designed and built, this section describes how this will be accomplished. Also note in this section any perceived or actual environmental impact from your business and how to mitigate it.

Figure 2.2: Feasibility Study Outline

EXECUTIVE SUMMARY
I. PRODUCT/SERVICE DESCRIPTION
Purpose of the Business
Description and Uses
Design and Unique Features
The Primary Customer
Spin-Offs
Environmental Impact

II. MANAGEMENT TEAM
Qualifications
Gap Analysis

III. MARKET ANALYSIS
Industry Description
Industry size
Industry status (growing, mature, in decline)
Growth potential
Geographic locations
Trends and entry barriers
Profit potential
Sales patterns and gross margins
Target Market
Primary target markets
Secondary markets
Demographics
Customer needs analysis
Product/Service Differentiation
Unique features
Potential for innovation
Competitors
Direct and Indirect
market share
description
strengths and weaknesses
Emerging
Substitute products
Competitive Advantage
Proprietary protection
Other competitive advantages

IV. PRELIMINARY CONCLUSIONS AS TO FEASIBILITY
Is there a demand for the product/service?
Is there a suitable market opportunity?

Management Team

The management team, the second section, is a critical factor in determining the potential feasibility of the new venture. This section of the study discusses the key members of the founding team and the expertise they bring to the venture. It also includes an analysis of any expertise that may be missing from the team and how the entrepreneur intends to alleviate this weakness.

Market Analysis

The market analysis section of the feasibility study is a crucial section because it presents support for the contention that there is a market and a demand for the product or service. The section begins with a complete understanding of the nature of the industry in which the business will operate. Industry knowledge is enormously important, as it enhances your ability to find a niche market for the product or service. The analysis in this third section of the study includes such things as barriers to entry, stage of growth, competitors, market share, and potential for growth. It also includes information on typical sales patterns and gross margin percentages for the industry. A good understanding of the industry facilitates zeroing in on your target market, the primary customer for the product or service. An in-depth analysis of the customer includes the size, location, buying habits, and needs of the customer base.

Also accomplished in this section is a comprehensive analysis of both direct and indirect competitors. A description of emerging competitors and substitute products demonstrates that the entrepreneur has considered all possible competition. Finally, this section defines those unique competitive advantages the business enjoys.

The Business Plan Components

What is the difference between a feasibility study and a business plan? A feasibility study gives you a preliminary check on the viability of your venture by estimating if you have sufficient demand for your product/service. By contrast, the business plan is a more comprehensive analysis that includes, in addition to the market research, a discussion of the operational and financial management and controls of the new business. The business plan serves three purposes:

• It serves as a reality check
• It is a living guide to your business
• It is a statement of intent for interested third parties

The Reality Check

Usually by the time the business plan is completed you will have an excellent idea if this business concept has a chance of succeeding. You will also know if you are still interested in starting the business. Frequently the period of concept development is much like a "honeymoon" phase. The entrepreneur believes completely this business will be a success and can picture exactly how it will work. Unfortunately, going through the exercise of doing a business plan, researching costs, preparing forecasts, and strategizing about operating procedures sometimes reveals potential problems previously unrecognized. Strong negatives or difficulties can lead to the decision not to proceed. This is not considered a failure for the entrepreneur. It merely indicates the value of doing a business plan in the first place. It is certainly preferable to halt the effort at that point than to go forward and possibly fail farther down the road when significant time and money have been expended.

The Living Guide to the Business

The business plan is a blueprint for the start-up and growth of the new venture. It is called a living document because it is subject to a changing environment. The original business plan for a new business contains estimates of what the entrepreneur expects will happen when the business starts, and it is often prepared with subjective data. Consequently, the entrepreneur typically re-evaluates the plan and updates it periodically the first year, then annually thereafter. This process compares the goals and projections from the original business plan with the actual achievements of the firm during the period under investigation. If significant differences in figures are observed, the entrepreneur attempts to learn what may have caused the difference and adjust projections for the next period to account for any changes. In this way the business plan always reflects what the business is actually doing, thereby improving and refining projections for the future.

Statement of Intent for Third Parties

In addition to the entrepreneur, it may be necessary to induce others to become interested in the new venture. These third parties include:

- Investors
- Bankers
- Potential management
- Strategic partners

Each of these groups looks at the business plan from a different perspective.

Investors.   Investors review closely both the factors that predict growth and the qualifications and track record of the management team. This is because they want to ensure their investment increases in value over the period of time they are involved in the business and that it is in capable and experienced hands. They look at the deal structure, that is, what their investment will buy them in terms of an equity interest and subsequent ownership rights in the company. They also want to know how they will be able to liquidate their investment at some future date.

Bankers/Lenders.   Bankers/lenders are primarily interested in the company's margins and cash flow projections because they are concerned about how their loans or credit lines to the business will be repaid. The margins indicate how much room there is for error between the cost to produce the product or deliver the service and the selling price. If margins are tight and the business finds itself having to lower prices to compete, it may not be able to pay off its loans as consistently and quickly as the bank would like. Similarly, bankers look at cash flow projections to see if the business can pay all its expenses and still have money left over at the end of each month. Bankers also look at the qualifications and track record of the management team and may require personal guarantees of the principals.

Potential Management.   At start-up or some later date, the entrepreneur may want to attract qualified personnel to the key management team to fill the gaps in experience. The business plan provides these people a complete picture of the business and the role they could potentially play in its start-up and growth.

Strategic Partners.   Some entrepreneurs, particularly those who intend to manufacture a product, choose to form a strategic alliance with a larger company so they don't have to incur the tremendous costs of purchasing equipment for a manufacturing plant. They may, for example, license another firm to manufacture and assemble the product and supply it to the entrepreneur to market and distribute. Alternatively, they may enter into an agreement with a supplier to provide necessary raw materials in exchange for an equity interest in the start-up venture.

Strategic partners like these want to review the growth plans of the company and the market strategy, as these plans indicate how much business the strategic partner may get. They are also interested in the new venture's ability to pay them for their work. Knowing in advance what these third parties are looking for will prompt you to address their specific needs in your business plan, facilitating your ability to achieve the goals of the business.

Having considered the value of doing a business plan, it should be noted that some successful businesses were started without one—Crate and Barrel, Pizza Hut, and Reebok, to name just a few. It is certainly possible to start a business without a business plan—people do it every day; however, entrepreneurs today operate in an intensely competitive, complex, and dynamic environment. Unless you are starting a very simple, small business or buying an established firm, you will probably not want to rely solely on your talent or luck. A business plan is one way to compensate for knowledge you don't have and gives you credibility in the eyes of others.

> *A business plan is one way to compensate for knowledge you don't have and gives you credibility in the eyes of others.*

What the business plan is not is a guarantee of success. Businesses have succeeded in spite of poorly done business plans and have failed even when the plan was carefully crafted. *The business plan is a tool entrepreneurs use to enhance their chances of success.* That is why it is important that both the entrepreneur and the founding team be fully involved in the development of the business plan. There are companies that will write your business plan and do research for you, but you know the business better than anyone. And you will understand it that much better if you and your team do the work necessary to put together a business plan.

Figure 2.3, pp. 38-39, presents an outline of the business plan. The first three sections of the business plan are identical to those in the feasibility study.

Operational Analysis

In this section of the business plan, a detailed description of the product/service is presented, including engineering specifications and a description of the prototype. The status of product development is addressed, as well as additional steps that must be taken before having a product that is ready to sell to the public. The time and cost requirements of completing the development tasks are also included. In addition, this section contains a discussion of the distribution channels used to move the product or service from the producer to the end user. A major portion of this section is devoted to a description of how the business will operate, where it will get its raw materials, how they will be manufactured and/or assembled, and what type and quantity of labor is required to operate the

Figure 2.3: Business Plan Outline

EXECUTIVE SUMMARY
I. PRODUCT/SERVICE DESCRIPTION
  Purpose of the business
  Description and uses
  Design and unique features
  The primary customer
  Spin-offs
  Environmental impact

II. MANAGEMENT TEAM
  Qualifications
  Gap analysis

III. MARKET ANALYSIS
  Industry Description
    Industry size
    Industry status (growing, mature, in decline)
    Growth potential
    Geographic locations
    Trends and entry barriers
    Profit potential
    Sales patterns and gross margins
  Target Market
    Primary target markets
    Secondary markets
    Demographics
    Customer needs analysis
  Product/Service Differentiation
    Unique features
    Potential for innovation
  Competitors
    Direct and indirect
      market share
      description
      strengths and weaknesses
    Emerging
    Substitute products
  Competitive Advantage
    Proprietary protection
    Other competitive advantages

IV. OPERATIONAL ANALYSIS
    Technical Description of Product/Service
      Uses, design, prototype
      Issues of obsolescence

Figure 2.3. *(continued)*

Distribution Channels
Status of Development and Related Costs
    Current status of development
    Tasks to be completed, time and cost to complete
    Potential difficulties, resolution
    Government approvals
Manufacturing or Operating Requirements and Associated Costs
    Manufacturing cycle
    Materials requirements
    Inventory requirements (also retail/wholesale business)
    Production requirements (also retail/wholesale or service)
    Labor requirements (all businesses)
    Maintenance and quality control requirements (all businesses)
    Financial requirements (all businesses)

V. MARKETING PLAN
Pricing
    Venture versus competitors
    Value chain
Purpose of Marketing Plan
    Target market
    Unique market niche
    Business identity
Marketing Tools
    Advertising & promotion
Media Plan
    Uses and costs of specific marketing tools
Marketing Budget
    Individual costs and total costs as a percentage of sales

VI. FINANCIAL PLAN
Assumptions
Pro forma Financial Statements
    Cash flow
    Income
    Balance sheet
Capital Expenditures
Break-even Analysis and Payback Period

VII. CONTINGENCY PLAN
Deviations from the Original Plan and Solutions

VIII. DEAL STRUCTURE
Debt and/or Equity Funding Amounts
Projected Return on Investment
Harvest Strategy

business. The outline of the business plan notes where businesses other than manufacturing have the same information requirements as manufacturing.

Financial Plan

The financial plan presents the entrepreneur's forecasts for the future of the business. Generally these forecasts are in the form of financial statements broken out by month in the first year or two, and then annually for the next two to five years. This section demonstrates the financial viability of the venture and the assumptions made by the entrepreneur in doing the forecasts. It is designed to show that all the claims about the product, sales, marketing strategy, and operational strategy can work financially to create a business that can survive and grow over the long term.

The Contingency Plan

The contingency plan is simply a way of recognizing that sometimes the "best laid plans" don't work the way you intended. It presents potential scenarios, usually dealing with situations like unexpected high or low growth or changing economic conditions and then suggests a plan to minimize the impact on the new business.

The Deal Structure

The deal structure section presents the offering to potential investors, including how much capital is required, in what form (equity, debt, or a combination), return on investment, and a plan for harvesting the investment at a later date. This section should be written from the investor's point of view and present the benefits to the investor of putting money into the new venture.

Undertaking a feasibility study and completing a business plan are certainly daunting tasks, but they are an absolutely essential exercise that helps the entrepreneur understand every aspect of the new venture and how all the pieces fit together more clearly. Even successful entrepreneurs who have started businesses without a written plan have had to write business plans when they needed growth capital or a credit line from the bank. Those starting high-growth, global ventures will find they need outside capital and resources fairly quickly. The business plan will be revisited in Chapter 19, where the organization and presentation of the plan are addressed.

☑ New Venture Checklist

Have you

☐ Tried the creativity-enhancing exercises in this chapter?

☐ Started a file to keep track of business ideas?

☐ Started networking and reading in your industry?

☐ Visited the local Chamber of Commerce and Small Business Administration office to see what information and help is available to small business owners?

☐ Defined what success means to you?

☐ Done a quick test on your idea?

☐ Made a list of the information you will need to start collecting to complete the feasibility study and business plan for the new venture?

Additional Sources of Information

Brandt, Steven C. (1982). *Entrepreneurship: The Ten Commandments for Building a Growth Company.* Reading, MA: Addison-Wesley Publishing.

Dacey, John S. (1989). *Fundamentals of Creative Thinking.* New York: Free Pr.

Gumpert, David E. (1990). *How to Really Create a Successful Business Plan.* Boston: The Goldhirsch Group.

Habino, Shozo and Gerald Nadler. (1990). *Breakthrough Thinking.* Rocklin, CA: Prima Publishing.

Longsworth, Elizabeth K. (1990). *Anatomy of a Start-up.* Boston: Inc. Publishing.

Timmons, Jeffry. (1990). *New Venture Creation.* Homewood, IL: Richard D. Irwin, Inc.

van Oech, Roger. (1990). *A Whack on the Side of the Head.* New York: Warner Books.

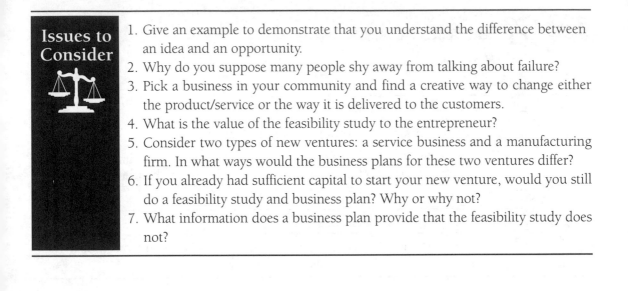

Issues to Consider

1. Give an example to demonstrate that you understand the difference between an idea and an opportunity.
2. Why do you suppose many people shy away from talking about failure?
3. Pick a business in your community and find a creative way to change either the product/service or the way it is delivered to the customers.
4. What is the value of the feasibility study to the entrepreneur?
5. Consider two types of new ventures: a service business and a manufacturing firm. In what ways would the business plans for these two ventures differ?
6. If you already had sufficient capital to start your new venture, would you still do a feasibility study and business plan? Why or why not?
7. What information does a business plan provide that the feasibility study does not?

Developing the Business Concept

Overview

- *Turning an idea into a business*
- *Common methods for protecting an idea*
- *Procedures to follow when obtaining a patent*
- *Advantages and disadvantages of starting a business versus buying a business*
- *The Product/Service Plan section of the feasibility study or business plan*

Protecting the Business Concept

Once an opportunity is identified, the next step in venture creation is to define the business concept—that is, the description of the product or service and what the mission of the business will be. While today more businesses are started within the service sector than in any other, many of the high-growth new business concepts involve manufacturing products. Consequently an understanding of two issues related to the creation of product businesses is important: the relationship between inventors and entrepreneurs, and the issue of proprietary rights. Even if your business is a service, retail, or wholesale business, you may need to protect the use of your name, a logo, or a written document, all of which come under the broad heading of proprietary or intellectual property rights.

Inventors and Entrepreneurs

People often confuse inventors and entrepreneurs, believing that the terms are synonymous. But as with the terms *idea* and *opportunity*, inventors and entrepreneurs are often very different concepts; inventors are normally involved with implementing ideas, while entrepreneurs are involved with implementing opportunity. The reason is that inventors are idea people, representing the essence of creativity. They tend to look at every aspect of life as a problem to be solved or a product to be improved. Sometimes this idea-seeking attitude can serendipitously result in a new product idea. For example, one researcher who was developing an anti-ulcerative drug accidentally licked his fingers and discovered aspartame, which is now sold as Nutrasweet. Whether they are scientists, engineers, mechanics, or just "tinkerers," inventors are continually generating ideas and prototypes for new products, many of which will never see the marketplace. This is because inventors often lack the necessary skills to commercialize their inventions—they are unable to create a business opportunity by which to bring their products to market.

That's where entrepreneurs come in. Entrepreneurs possess the ability to identify a market for the inventor's product, gather sufficient resources to create a business to market the products and create value for both the inventor and the entrepreneur. This is not to say inventors and entrepreneurs cannot be one and the same. Don Beaver and Ben Stapelfeld invented a method for cleaning up industrial waste oil and went on as entrepreneurs to found The New Pig Corporation (see Profile 3.1). Nevertheless, many times it is the serendipitous teaming of an inventor and an entrepreneur that results in a successful new business venture.

Proprietary Issues

If the new venture opportunity involves a product, it is especially important that the inventor and/or entrepreneur investigate the potential for acquiring intellectual property rights—that is, determine if there are legal ways to protect the product idea from competitor duplication until after it goes to market. (See Profile 3.2, p. 46.)

The issue of who owns an idea is a crucial one as it could mean the difference between having a successful business and not having one. The primary legal means to protecting an original idea is through a patent. Other methods of protection include trademarks, copyrights, and contracts to protect trade secrets.

PROFILE 3.1

Making Pigs of Themselves: Inventors Turned Entrepreneurs

For years factories have struggled with the problem of how to clean up greasy spills and leaks on their floors. The method most commonly used was kitty litter, but it tended to be messy and get into the machinery. Don Beaver and Ben Stapelfeld, owners of an industrial cleaning business, began playing around with absorbent materials, putting them in everything from athletic socks to pantyhose, and throwing the concoction away when it became saturated. At one point, facing financial disaster with their business, they decided to push ahead and develop their absorbent sock concept into a real product.

They tried every type of absorbent material and finally hit upon ground-up corn cobs. With an investment of $500,000 from banks and private investors, they began to build the company. Going through the traditional industrial distribution channels was unsuccessful because their product provided relatively small commissions to distributors in comparison with commissions on large hydraulic systems. So they developed a unique market strategy that involved giving the company an unusual name—The New Pig Corporation—using promotional items such as pig coffee mugs and pig hats, and spending 40 percent of revenues on advertising.

The most important thing they did, however, was to define their business not as a one-product business but as a problem-solving business. They encouraged their customers to make suggestions and from these suggestions sprang numerous new products. The company now employs over 140 people.

Patents

The U.S. patent system was designed 200 years ago by Thomas Jefferson to protect the inventions of the independent inventor. Today, although most inventors work in the research departments of large corporations, the basic legal tenets of patent law still remain true to the independent inventor. In fact, the number of patents issued to independent inventors increased 37 percent in the last half of the 1980s. Since the first patent was issued in 1790, more than five million U.S. patents have been granted.

A patent grants an inventor the exclusive right to an invention for a period of years, depending on the type of patent. It also prevents others from

PROFILE 3.2

The Importance of Proprietary Rights

Bob Kearns was tired of windshield wipers that operated either too slowly or too fast. He wondered why they couldn't function like an eyelid and literally blink. Kearns had a damaged eye, the result of being hit with a champagne cork on his wedding night, and had great difficulty seeing while driving one night in a severe rainstorm. That's when the inspiration for intermittent windshield wipers came to him.

For Kearns, generating ideas for products that solved problems was a way of life. His first invention was a comb that distributed hair tonic, then came an amplifier for people who had undergone laryngectomies, followed by an innovative type of weather balloon. Most of the ideas never went beyond the model stage, which is not atypical for inventors. Kearns, who had a masters degree in mechanical engineering, began working on the prototype of the intermittent wiper blade in 1963. When he had a working prototype, which he installed in his car, he arranged to show it to engineers at Ford. They encouraged him to field test it to see if it would achieve three million cycles. When it did, he again contacted Ford which suddenly didn't seem interested any more. He then went to a friend who owned a mid-sized manufacturing firm that supplied parts to the auto industry. Kearns assigned the rights to the patent to his friend in exchange for his friend paying the costs of getting the patents and paying Kearns royalties plus $1,000 a month to continue research and development.

Then, surprisingly, in 1969, Ford came out with an intermittent wiper blade that used the Kearns design. GM followed suit in 1974 and Chrysler in 1977, along with several foreign car companies. Kearns, who by that time had reacquired his patent rights, filed suit against Ford in 1978 for patent infringement and later against Chrysler. It took 12 years of intense work (Kearns represented himself) for the first case to come to trial. In the first suit, Ford agreed to settle for $30 million after the jury found in Kearns' favor, but he turned them down (he was seeking $1.6 billion). In a second trial, Kearns was awarded $5.2 million. Ultimately Ford and Kearns settled for $10.2 million. The Chrysler case, which concluded in June 1992, gave Kearns an additional $11.5 million, but he was still unhappy because the jury didn't find that the automaker had been willful in the infringement. Still, Kearns stands as a role model to other inventors who regularly face patent infringement by large corporations.

manufacturing and selling the invention during the period of the patent. At the end of this time, the patent is placed in public domain. Two types of patents concern most inventors: utility and design patents. Utility patents are the most common type. They protect the functional part of machines or processes, in addition to computer programs associated with hardware. Some examples are toys, film processing, protective coatings, tools, and cleaning implements. A utility patent is valid for 17 years from the date of issuance. Design patents protect new, original ornamental designs for manufactured articles. The design must be nonfunctional and part of the tangible item for which it is designed. Some examples are a gilding, an item of apparel, or jewelry. Design patents are valid for 14 years from date of issuance.

Ever vigilant to changing technology, in 1980 the Patent Office created a new category of protection: life forms. It covers such controversial things as altered human genes and microbes that break down crude oil. Another special category is the plant patent, which protects any new variety of a sexually or asexually reproduced plant.

Computer programs present some special problems requiring several methods of protection. For example, they may be protected by a trade secret contract if the developer/owner merely licenses the program for distribution by someone else to a narrow market. If wide dissemination is the goal, a patent offers more protection and is available if the program contains at least one unique algorithm that is part of the machine or physical process. Copyrights are commonly used for programs that don't qualify for a patent. In addition, the name of the program can be trademarked and the instructions copyrighted.

Is the Invention Patentable?

Before deciding to file for a patent, it is important to first determine the patentability of the invention. There are four basic criteria:

1. It must fit into *one of the five classes* established by Congress:
    * Machine (fax, rocket, electronic circuits)
    * Process (chemical reactions, methods for producing products)
    * Articles of manufacture (furniture, diskettes)
    * Composition (gasoline, food additives)
    * A new use for one of the above

Many inventions can be classified into more than one category. That does not present a problem, however, since the inventor does not have to choose into which category the invention fits.

2. It must have *utility*, in other words, be useful. This is not usually a problem unless you have invented something like an unsafe drug or something purely "whimsical." The Patent Trademark Office (PTO) has been known to issue patents on some fairly strange inventions, such as a male chastity device (#587,994).

3. It must not contain *prior art*. Prior art is knowledge that is publicly available or published prior to the date of the inventions—that is, a date before the filing of the patent application. Accordingly, it is important to document everything that is done in the creation of the invention. Also you must follow the "one-year rule," which says the invention must not become public or available for sale more than one year prior to filing the patent application. This rule is meant to ensure that the invention is still novel at the time of application. Novelty consists of physical differences, new combinations of components, or new uses.

4. It must be *unobvious*. The invention must not be obvious to someone with ordinary skills in the field. This is a tricky definition but has been further explained by the PTO as an invention that contains "new and unexpected results." If your invention is rejected on the first pass as not being "unobvious," it probably means the patent examiner wants you to demonstrate its unobviousness.

The Patent Process

The process for obtaining a patent is well defined; however, it is advisable to use the services of a patent attorney, especially when applying for foreign patents. Attorneys understand the complicated system at the Patent Office in Washington, DC, and can do a better job of expediting the process. The Patent Office is staffed by attorneys and engineers, so a patent attorney may have more success communicating with them than an inventor would.

Understanding the requirements for patents in other countries is a fairly complex specialty given that the laws vary from country to country. An attorney with experience filing foreign patents can ensure that you receive all the rights to which you are entitled. The bottom line is that the patent should be applied for correctly to avoid costly problems later on.

- **Disclosure Document.** The inventor will normally file a disclosure statement that documents the date of conception of the invention. This statement is crucial in the event two inventors are working on the same idea at the same time. The one who files the disclosure document first has the right to file for a patent. The disclosure document is a detailed description of the invention and its uses and may include photos; however, it is *not a* patent application. The inventor has a two-year grace period in which to file a patent application, but must demonstrate diligence in completing the invention and filing the application. If the inventor publicly uses or sells the invention more than a year prior to filing the patent application, he or she will be prohibited from gaining a patent. To file a disclosure statement, send

  - a cover letter requesting that the PTO accept the disclosure statement,
  - a check for the required fee,
  - a copy of the disclosure statement, and
  - a stamped, self-addressed, return envelope.

  Do not use the tactic of mailing a dated description of the invention to yourself by certified mail. It has no value to the Patent Office.

- **Patent Application.** The patent application contains a complete description of the invention, what it does, and how it is uniquely different from anything currently existing (prior art). It also includes detailed drawings, explanations, and engineering specifications. The claims section of the application specifies the parts of the invention on which the inventor wants patents. The description of these claims must be specific enough to demonstrate the invention's uniqueness but broad enough to be difficult for others to circumvent the patent, that is, modifying it slightly and duplicating the product without violating the patent. Be sure you file the patent application no more than one year after offering the product for sale or using it commercially. It is infinitely preferable to file *before* any public disclosures are made.

- **Oath.** The application also contains an oath which the inventor signs testifying to the veracity of what has been said.

The cost, on average, of filing a disclosure statement and patent application is between $1,500 and $2,000. However, the more complex the application, the higher the patent attorney fees. These figures do not include the costs of engineered designs and drawings, which must accompany the application and vary significantly from product to product.

Once the application is received, the Patent Office will conduct a search of its patent records. During this period the invention is said to be "patent applied for," which establishes the inventor's claim and dates relative to prior art. An invention can stay in the patent-applied-for stage for up to two years, the primary advantage of this being that the public does not have access to the patent application and drawings, which might allow someone else the chance to design around the patent.

The Patent Office contacts the inventor and states that they either accept the claims in the application or deny the application and give the inventor a period of time to appeal and/or modify the claims. It is not uncommon for the original claims to be rejected in their entirety by the PTO, usually because of prior art. If and when the Patent Office accepts the modified claims, the invention is in the "patent pending" stage, that is, awaiting the issuance of the patent. The inventor may market and sell the product during this period, but must clearly label it "patent pending." Once the patent is *issued*, however, it becomes public record.

> *The entrepreneur does not have to own a patent to benefit from it.*

If the patent examiner rejects the modified claims, the inventor has the right to appeal to a Board of Patent Appeals within the Patent Office. Failing to find agreement at this point, the inventor may appeal to the U.S. Court of Appeals for the Federal Circuit. This appeals process may take years.

The entrepreneur does not have to own a patent to benefit from it. In some cases it may be possible to license the right to use a patent from the inventor. For example, an inventor may license the entrepreneur to manufacture and distribute the invention and receive a royalty on sales. Alternatively, it may also be possible for the entrepreneur to purchase an assignment of a patent from the inventor, transferring ownership rights to the entrepreneur. Be aware, however, that the patent, once issued, is a powerful document that gives the holder the right to enforce the patent against infringers in a court of law. Under the law, the patent holder is entitled to a reasonable royalty from the infringer and if the infringer refuses to pay, the patent holder can enjoin or close down the operation of the infringer. If the entrepreneur is planning to export products, patent applications should be filed in the countries in which the product will be sold. This can be a costly process if the entrepreneur is dealing with a number of countries. Furthermore, entrepreneurs have often found their patents violated in countries that do not have as stringent patent laws as the United States.

Other Forms of Protection

Trademarks. A trademark is a symbol, word or design that is used to identify a business or a product. For example, Apple Computers uses a picture of an apple with a bite out of it followed by the symbol ®, which means "registered trademark." A trademark has a longer life than a patent, with certain conditions. A business has the exclusive right to a trademark for as long as it is actively using it. However, if the trademark becomes part of the generic language like *aspirin* and *thermos*, it can no longer be trademarked. Furthermore, a trademark cannot be registered until it is actually in use. Before that time the entrepreneur should use ™ (or SM for services) after the name until the trademark is registered.

To register a trademark, an applicant can use one of three methods:

1. If the mark has already been in use, the applicant can file a use application requesting registration and ownership of the mark. You will also have to submit three specimens showing actual use of the mark.
2. If the mark has not yet been in use, you can file an intent-to-use application. After the mark is in use, you must submit the three specimens showing actual use before receiving registration.
3. Depending on international agreements with a specific country, an applicant can file based on having a trademark in another country.

To apply, you need to submit PTO Form 1478 with a drawing of the mark and the appropriate fee. The PTO does not require a search for potentially conflicting marks prior to filing the application. However, it is probably wise to do so since it isn't difficult. You can conduct a search in the PTO public search library or a patent and depository library, or hire a specialist to search for you. The PTO determines whether the mark may be registered and notifies you. If the PTO rejects the application, you have six months to respond.

Marks that cannot be trademarked include:

• anything immoral or deceptive
• anything that uses official symbols of the United States or any state or municipality, like the flag
• anything that uses a person's name or likeness without permission.

Trade Secrets. Trade secrets are those aspects of the business that you wish to protect from disclosure by employees or others involved with the business. The only way to protect trade secrets is through an employment contract that specifically details any trade secrets. Then, should a former employee use a specified trade secret, the company can use legal remedies, such as an injunction or suing for damages.

Aspects of the business that may be considered trade secrets are recipes or ingredients (Mrs. Field's Cookies), source codes for computer chips, customer discounts, manufacturer costs, and so forth.

Copyrights. Copyrights protect original works of authors, composers, screenwriters, and computer programmers. A copyright does not protect the idea itself but only the form in which it appears. For example, a computer programmer can copyright the written program for a particular type of word processing software, but cannot copyright the idea of word processing. This is why several companies can produce word processing software without violating a copyright. They are really protecting the unique programming code of their software. A copyright lasts for the life of the holder plus 50 years, after which it goes into public domain. Copyrighted works cannot be copied without permission of the copyright holder.

To obtain federal copyright protection, the work must be in a fixed and tangible form—that is, you must be able to see or hear it. It should contain copyright notice (although this is no longer required by law) so that a potential violator cannot claim innocence because there was no notice. The notice should use the word "copyright" or the symbol ©, provide the year and the complete name of the person responsible for the work.

Though it is not required, registration of the Copyright Office at the Library of Congress in Washington, DC, is important in order to obtain full protection under the law. Along with the application and fee, you must submit a complete copy of an unpublished work or two complete copies of a published work.

The key point to remember about intellectual property rights is that they can't stop someone from infringing on your rights. What they can do is provide you with offensive rights, that is, the right to sue in a court of law, a long and costly process. Consequently, intellectual property rights should never be the sole competitive advantage a business possesses.

How Will the Business Work?

Developing an idea for a product or service and securing proprietary rights are just the beginning. It is difficult to determine if the product/service idea will have value until the entrepreneur decides what kind of business he or she is creating. Suppose you have developed a new computer program that will revolutionize the way manufacturers control inventory. You have a product; now what is the business? There are actually several options.

1. Start a mail order business to market and sell the program
2. License the program to a major software company to distribute
3. Open a computer software store to sell your program plus other popular business software
4. Give the program to computer software outlets on consignment—that is, the store pays you if they sell the program

The choice of the kind of business to start is a function of your life goals and how much time and money you have to devote to the business. Obviously, opening a computer store is more time consuming, costly, and risky than licensing, for example. It is important to consider all options and their associated risks, costs, advantages, and disadvantages before settling on the type of business you will create.

Starting vs. Buying a Business

Once you know what your product or service is and the kind of business you are creating, you must decide whether to start a new business or buy an existing business and turn it into an entrepreneurial venture that will satisfy your needs. In general, entrepreneurs start businesses when they can't find an existing business compatible with their product/service idea or goals. Starting a business is probably the most common route for entrepreneurs, but it's not the only way. Some entrepreneurs choose instead to buy an existing business.

Buying a Business

Buying a business has several advantages:

- It is less risky than starting from scratch because facilities, employees, and customers are likely to be in place.
- It is an easier route to owning a business if the entrepreneur has limited business experience.
- The chances for success are increased, particularly if the business has a good reputation.
- The business may have established trade credit, which is crucial because relationships with suppliers and others take a long time to develop.

- The owner may be willing to stay on board for a time to help the entrepreneur learn the business.

However, existing businesses rarely come without problems. In the first place, the business may have been put up for sale because it was not successful. It may have developed a negative reputation, its inventory may be outdated, and its location may no longer be appropriate. On top of all this, chances are the owner will price the business at more than it's worth in the marketplace. To further compound the risk, an owner is not likely to confess the real reasons the business is being sold. These reasons may include:

- the company being squeezed out of the market by larger companies
- key employees leaving
- the threat of a major legal action
- competitors' products are better
- the owner has a better opportunity

The owner is more likely to say the business is being sold because the owner wants to retire or is suffering from some illness. With this in mind, there are several questions to ask prior to purchasing a business.

- What is the potential for growth?
- Is the business profitable with a strong cash flow?
- Does it have valuable assets?
- Is it free of legal problems?
- Does it have a good reputation?
- Are you capable of running the business?
- Is the location suitable?
- Is the business compatible with your goals?

Buying a business will take the same kind of research as starting one. In fact, although this book is geared toward starting a business from scratch, many of the same skills apply to buying an existing business and making it grow. You will need to:

- Understand the industry and the market niche in which the business will operate
- Examine the records of the business
- Talk to employees, suppliers, and customers
- Examine equipment and facilities
- Examine all contracts

- Verify the value of the business based on industry statistics (See Chapter 17 for suggestions on valuing the business.)

There are several sources of information on business acquisitions. Probably the best source is talking to bankers, attorneys, and accountants who regularly work with businesses. The business opportunities section of newspapers such as the *Wall Street Journal* and trade publications are another source. It is also possible to investigate business liquidation auctions, but unless you're a turn-around specialist, taking on a business that has experienced severe problems may be more risky than starting from scratch.

Starting a New Business

Creating a business has the principal advantage of allowing the entrepreneur to do everything exactly the way he or she wants, in effect starting with a clean slate. Often, however, starting a new business is a matter of necessity. With limited funds, many entrepreneurs start out of their homes or garages because they do not have the financial ability to purchase an established business. Then, too, entrepreneurs frequently find it difficult to locate an ongoing business sufficiently compatible with what they are trying to do. This was the case for Mo Siegel, who wanted to live in Colorado but couldn't find a business suitable for his new venture idea. So he started his own: Celestial Seasonings, the highly successful herbal tea company.

Starting a business, however, is generally more time-consuming and potentially more costly than buying an existing business. That "clean slate" referred to earlier means the entrepreneur must purchase, rent, or borrow everything it takes to run the business. Furthermore, employees, suppliers, channels of distribution, and customers must all be identified and developed. By the end of this book, you will have a good sense of what starting a business is all about.

Describing the Business

Whether the new venture concept is a product or a service, it will need to be carefully described in as much detail as possible. The description of the business concept is a reflection of the entrepreneur's goals, lifestyle, and philosophy. When placed in the feasibility study and ultimately in the business plan, it will give the reader a clear sense of what this business is intended to do. Consequently, the description of the business concept goes well beyond the mere discussion of the product or service being offered. Recall the example of

The New Pig Corporation in this chapter. Don Beaver and Ben Stapelfeld saw the business in a much broader sense than just a product business. They actually viewed it as a business that provided a service by solving people's clean-up problems. In that way their product offering increased substantially over the initial product, the PIG.

The Product/Service Plan is the first section of both the feasibility study and the business plan. Some of the things you should consider when constructing this section include:

The Product/Service Plan

- The purpose of the business
- Description and uses of the product/service
- The unique features of the product/service
- Proprietary rights
- The primary customer
- Spin-offs
- Environmental impact

The Purpose of the Business

Defining the purpose of the business is a valuable exercise. It forces the entrepreneur to answer the question *Why am I in business?* In other words, what is the reason for the business to exist? One potential entrepreneur with a service business idea wrote:

> Image Designs creates graphics and technical documents to help high-technology companies enhance their image-building and publishing efforts through quality, affordable graphics and technical documentation from freelance professionals.

Description and Uses

It is important that the new venture product or service be described in detail and that pictures be included if necessary for clarity. In the business plan pictures help sell the idea. A color rendering or preferably a color photograph of a prototype will enhance the credibility of the entrepreneur. One potential entrepreneur described her products this way:

> The product mix consists of clothing, ceramics, greeting cards, stuffed animals, and prints using the licensed designs of Will Bullas. These items are considered gifts or collectibles. The combination of the original

characters and the artist's humorous quotes makes the artwork and products attractive and one-of-a-kind.

She also included examples of Will Bullas designs.

Unique Features

Today, even if you are selling a commodity, a standard item like hand soap that people use in their everyday lives, you won't get consumers to purchase your product over the many others in the market if you can't tell them why they should. Consumers want to know the unique features your product or service offers. These features will ultimately form the basis of the marketing strategy. In the case of Image Designs, the entrepreneur was able to identify several unique features, including "one-stop" shopping for all design needs and a management team with a working knowledge of manufacturing, R&D, and high technology company operations.

The Primary Customer

The primary customer is the main purchaser of your product or service. It is crucial to the potential success of the venture that you identify as precisely as possible who is most likely to purchase the product or service. Image Designs targeted high technology firms that need outside graphic or technical documentation support. The New Pig Corporation, with an industrial cleaning product, focused on manufacturers.

Proprietary Rights

It is important to note any ways in which the product/service concept can be legally protected, whether it be through patents, copyrights, trademarks, or trade secrets. Intellectual property rights add value to the product or service; therefore they are an important consideration in new venture creation.

Spin-Offs

Including any related products or services that can derive from the initial one adds more value to the business concept, as it points to directions for future growth. For example, Image Designs could move into mixed-media arts, animation, and 3-D or video production—in other words, expand its services within the same target market. The New Pig Corporation identified many potential spin-offs, such as collectibles with their logo emblazoned on them. As a result of customer suggestions, they even developed a Hazardous Materials PIG with DuPont.

Environmental Impact

Today businesses must be concerned with the impact they may have on the environment either from their products or from the processes that produce those products. Specifying what, if any, impact the new venture will have and how it will mitigate any potential negative impact will go a long way toward establishing a positive image for the company. Potential negative effects are easier to identify in a product-oriented business; however, even a service business can demonstrate a concern for the environment. For example, Image Designs intends to create environmental products using the licensed designs, using recycled materials for all paper and packaging, and supporting local efforts to clean up and protect the environment.

In sum, the detailed description of the business provides the entrepreneur with a focus as he or she begins to study the potential market for the product or service. Understanding the purpose and goals of the business makes the work of determining feasibility more manageable.

✓ New Venture Checklist

Have you:

☐ Decided the kind of business you intend to establish?

☐ Determined if any aspect of your product/service idea can be protected by means of patents, trademarks, or copyrights?

☐ Considered if you will start the new business from the ground up or buy an existing business?

☐ Described your business concept by completing the Product/Service Plan?

Additional Sources of Information

Franchise Opportunities Handbook, U.S. Department of Commerce Publication.

Friedman, Robert. (1993). *The Complete Small Business Legal Guide.* Dover, NH: Upstart Publishing.

Hedglon, Mead. (1992). *How to Get the Best Legal Help for Your Business (At the Lowest Possible Cost).* New York: McGraw.

Henderson, Carter. (1985). *Winners: The Successful Strategies Entrepreneurs Use to Build New Businesses.* New York: Henry Holt & Co.

Knight, Brian. *Buy the Right Business - At the Right Price.* Dover, NH: Upstart Publishing.

Mosely, Jr., Thomas E. (1992). *Marketing Your Invention.* Dover, NH: Upstart Publishing.

Ward, John. (1991). *Creating Effective Boards for Private Enterprise.* San Francisco: Jossey-Bass.

Issues to Consider

1. Compare and contrast buying a business with starting a business in terms of the advantages and disadvantages of each.
2. What is the difference between a disclosure document and a patent application?
3. Suppose you have an idea for a new type of "sunless" tanning lotion. What procedures would you follow to protect your idea?
4. You have succeeded in protecting your new idea for sunless tanning lotion. Name four types of businesses you could start using this idea.
5. What information will you need to have if you decide to consider buying a business?
6. Using the sunless tanning lotion as your product, describe the essential ingredients of the Product/Service Plan.

CHAPTER 4

The Founding Team

Overview

- *The value of a team approach for starting the venture*
- *Criteria for professional advisors to the new venture*
- *The benefits and legalities of using independent contractors for any or all aspects of the business*
- *Outsourcing new venture functions*
- *The initial management team for the new venture and a gap analysis*

The Solo Entrepreneur vs. the Team

By their very nature, entrepreneurs in their quest for independence often attempt a new venture as a soloist. In this way they can retain sole ownership, make all the key decisions, and not have to share the profits. This approach to starting a business is still the most common in small businesses and in the craft or artisan areas. Unfortunately, however, in today's market, it is becoming increasingly difficult to succeed alone, particularly if the goal is to create a world-class company. With more new ventures operating in complex, dynamic environments and requiring more capital, it is highly unlikely any one person will have all the knowledge and resources to start a world-class company as a soloist.

Collaboration is, therefore, an essential ingredient in any world-class start-up. Studies of high technology start-ups in particular have demonstrated that a team effort will provide a better chance for success than a solo effort.[1] There are several other important reasons for using a founding team.

- The intense effort required of a start-up can be shared.
- Should any one team member leave, it is less likely to result in the abandonment of the start-up.
- With a founding team that includes major functional areas—marketing, finance, operations—the new venture can proceed further before it will need to hire additional personnel.
- A quality founding team lends credibility to the new venture in the eyes of lenders, investors, and others.
- The ability to analyze information and make decisions is improved because the lead entrepreneur has the benefit of the varied expertise of his or her team members; in this way ideas may be viewed from several perspectives.

The founders of Compaq Computers, three former senior managers at Texas Instruments, used an integrated, interdisciplinary team approach to start-up that resulted in a phenomenal $111 million in sales in the first year. Their success was attributed to the "smart team," whose philosophy was that every member of the team should contribute to every facet of the venture. The engineer gave input to the market strategist, and the finance expert worked closely with the design engineer. In this way they were able to cut their product development time in half, an important goal in an industry where new products are outdated almost before they are manufactured.

The team approach to starting a business does not stop with the founding members. The founding team, in an effort to ensure a successful start-up, also forms alliances with professionals and industry experts to act as advisors and form what can be called an extended founding team. (See Figure 4.1.)

The Founding Team

When an entrepreneur decides to use a team effort to create the new venture, he or she generally looks for people who have complementary skills. In other words, if the entrepreneur happens to be an engineer, finding a market expert and someone who knows how to raise capital would be advantageous to the new venture. Since the start-up of a new venture is a multifunctional process,

---

[1]Van de Ven, A.H., Hudson, R. & Schroeder, D.M. "Designing New Business Start-Ups." *Journal of Management*, Vol. 10 (1984).

Figure 4.1: The Entrepreneur's Team

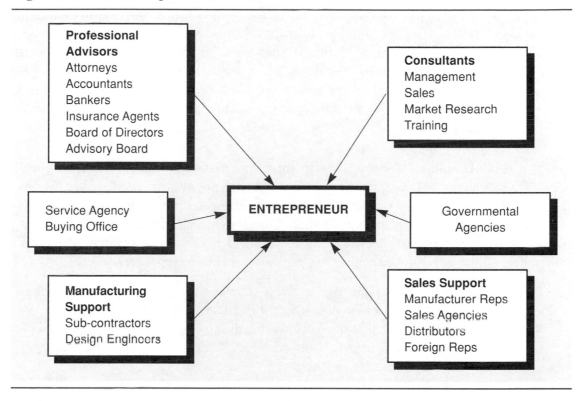

the entrepreneur and the venture will benefit greatly from a team composed of a variety of strengths and disciplines. Another advantage to forming a quality team is that the founding team has a vested interest in the new venture. They invest not only their time but often their money as well. Thus the burden of raising the resources necessary to start the venture is distributed among the team members, giving the lead entrepreneur access to the network of contacts of the other members in addition to his or her own. This vastly increases the information and resources available to the new venture and allows the venture to grow more rapidly.

Of course, it isn't always possible to put together the "perfect" team from the start. You may not have yet found the right person to fill a particular need, or you may have found the right person, but he or she is too expensive to bring on board during start-up. No matter. Talk to that person anyway about joining the team at a later date and keep that person up-to-date on what the company is doing. You would be surprised at how many times an aggressive start-up company can woo an experienced person away from a major corporation.

Professional Advisors

When a new venture is in the infancy stage, it generally doesn't have the resources to hire in-house professional help such as an attorney or accountant. Instead it must rely on building relationships with professionals on an "as-needed" basis. These professionals provide information and services not normally within the scope of expertise of most entrepreneurs, and they can play devil's advocate for the entrepreneur, pointing out potential flaws in the business concept.

Attorneys.   The first thing an entrepreneur should realize when dealing with attorneys is that, for the most part, they are not business people. They are professionals who specialize in one area of the law: tax, real estate, business, patents. Therefore, it is important to select an attorney who specializes in the particular area needed by the entrepreneur. Attorneys can provide a wealth of support for the new venture. Within their particular area of expertise attorneys can:

- Advise the entrepreneur in the selection of the correct legal organizational structure—that is, sole proprietorship, partnership, or corporation.
- Advise and prepare documents for intellectual property rights acquisition.
- Negotiate and prepare contracts for the entrepreneur, who may be buying, selling, contracting, or leasing.
- Advise the entrepreneur on the compliance with regulations related to financing and credit.
- Keep the entrepreneur apprised of the latest tax reform legislation and help minimize the venture's tax burden.
- Assist the entrepreneur in complying with federal, state, or local laws.
- Represent the entrepreneur in any legal actions as an advocate.

Choosing a good attorney is a time consuming but vital task that should occur prior to start-up. Decisions made at inception may affect the venture for years to come, hence, the need for good legal advice. A few tips may facilitate the search.

- Ask accountants, bankers, and other business people for recommendations.
- Retain an experienced attorney who is competent to do what you want.
- Look for an attorney who is willing to listen, has time for you, and will be flexible about fees while the business is in the start-up phase.
- Check out the firm by phone first. You can learn a lot about the law firm by noting who answers the phone and with what tone of voice.
- Confirm that the attorney carries malpractice insurance.

Accountants. Your lawyer is your advocate, but your accountant is bound by rules and ethics that do not permit advocacy. Therefore, where an attorney is bound to represent you no matter what you do, the accountant, who is bound by the Generally Accepted Accounting Principles (GAAP), cannot defend you should you choose to do something that violates the GAAP.

Accounting is a fairly complex form of communication that the entrepreneur needs to understand. In the beginning of the business, the accountant may set up the company's books and maintain them on a periodic basis. Or, as is often the case, the entrepreneur may hire a bookkeeper to do the day-to-day recording of transactions and go to the accountant only at tax time. The accountant will also set up control systems for operations as well as payroll. A growing business has to:

- Verify and post bills
- Write checks
- Issue invoices
- Make collections
- Get suppliers to cooperate
- Balance the checkbook
- Prepare financial statements

- Establish inventory controls
- File yearly tax returns
- Prepare budgets
- Prepare stockholder reports
- Make payroll tax deposits
- Secure insurance benefits
- Keep employee records

The accountant can assist in all these areas. Once the new venture is beyond the start-up phase and growing consistently, an annual audit is needed to determine if the accounting and control procedures are adequate. Additionally, the auditors may also require a physical inventory. If everything is in order, they will issue a certified statement, which is important should the entrepreneur ever decide to take the company public on one of the stock exchanges. Accountants are also a rich networking source in the entrepreneur's search for additional members of the new venture team. Much like attorneys, accountants tend to specialize, so finding one who is used to working with young, growing businesses will be an advantage. It is highly likely that the accountant who takes your business through start-up and early growth may not be the same person to take care of the company's needs when it reaches the next level of growth. As the financial and recordkeeping needs of the business increase and become more complex, the entrepreneur may need to consider a larger firm with expertise in several areas.

Bankers. There is a saying that all banks are alike until you need a loan. Today that phrase is even more true. Having a qualified banker on the advisory team of the new venture is an issue not only when you need a line of credit for operating capital or to purchase equipment but from the moment you open the business account. An entrepreneur should think of a banker as a business partner who can:

- Be a source of information and networking
- Help the entrepreneur make decisions regarding capital needs
- Assist the entrepreneur in preparing proforma operations and cash flow analyses and evaluate projections the entrepreneur has made
- Assist the entrepreneur in all facets of procuring financing

Selecting a bank should be as careful a process as that for an attorney or accountant. The entrepreneur needs to develop a list of criteria that defines the needs of the new venture with respect to the banking relationship to narrow the search for a banker. The entrepreneur should also talk to other entrepreneurs in the same industry to identify a bank that works well with the type of venture planned. Talking to an accountant or attorney for suggestions of the best bank for the new venture is another way to find a good banker.

When choosing a banker, seek out an officer with a rank of assistant vice president or higher as these officers are trained to work with new and growing businesses and have a sufficient level of authority to quickly make decisions that affect the new venture.

Insurance Agents. Many entrepreneurs overlook the value of a relationship with a competent insurance agent, but a growing venture will require several types of insurance.

- Property and casualty
- Medical
- Errors and omissions
- Life on key management
- Workers' compensation
- Unemployment
- Auto on firm's vehicles
- Liability (product and personal)
- Bonding

Major insurance firms can often handle all types of insurance vehicles, but many times the entrepreneur will need to seek specialists for certain kinds of protection like bonding (which is common in the construction industry to protect against a contractor not completing a project), product liability insurance, and errors and omissions (which protects the business against liability from unintentional mistakes in advertising). The new venture's insurance needs will change over its life, and a good insurance agent will help the entrepreneur determine the needed coverages at the appropriate times.

Board of Directors. The decision to have a board of directors is influenced by the legal form of the business. If the new venture is a corporation, a board of directors is required. If the business requires venture capital, a board will be necessary and the venture capitalist will probably demand a seat on it. Boards of directors serve a valuable purpose: If chosen correctly they provide expertise that will benefit the new venture. In that capacity they act as advisors. They also assist in establishing corporate strategy and philosophy, as well as goals and objectives.

It is important to distinguish between boards of privately owned corporations and those of publicly owned corporations. In a privately owned corporation, the entrepreneurial team owns all or the majority of the stock, so directors serve at the pleasure of the entrepreneur, who has effective control of the company. On the other hand, directors of publicly traded companies have legitimate power to control the activities of the company.

> It is important to distinguish between boards of privately owned corporations and those of publicly owned corporations.

Boards can be comprised of inside or outside members or a combination of the two. An inside board member is one who is either a founder, employee, family member, or retired management of the firm, while an outside member is someone with no direct connection to the business. Which type of board member is best is a matter of opinion and circumstance as research has not provided any clear results on this issue. In general, however, outside directors are beneficial for succession planning and capital raising. They can often bring a fresh point of view to the strategic planning process and expertise that may not be held by the founders.

Insiders have the advantage of complete knowledge about the business; they are generally more available and have demonstrated their effectiveness. They will usually have the necessary technical expertise as well. On the other hand, there are political ramifications when the board members report to the CEO. For that reason they may not always be objective and independent in their thought process. Insiders may also not have the broad expertise necessary to effectively guide the growth of the business.

Consider carefully whether the new venture requires a working board. Most working boards are used for their expertise, for strategic planning, for auditing the actions of the firm, and for arbitrating differences. These activities are not as crucial in the start-up phase when the entrepreneurial team is gathering resources and raising capital. However, a board of directors can assist the entrepreneurial team in those functions and can network with key people who can help the new venture. At this juncture in the new venture some potential directors will ask to be included on the board so they can monitor their investment in the company. This is common with large private investors, bankers, and even accountants. To ensure that you get only the best people on the board, standards should be set in advance and strictly adhered to.

> *The board members can offer the struggling team an objective point of view and the benefit of their considerable experience.*

During the growth period of the new venture, the entrepreneurial team is normally buried with operational details, the need to generate sales, and the problem of maintaining a positive cash flow. Dealing with a board of directors is not something they will want to do. But the board members can offer the struggling team an objective point of view and the benefit of their considerable experience.

When choosing people to serve on the board of directors, you should consider those who have:

- The necessary technical skill related to the business
- Significant, successful experience in the industry
- Important contacts in the industry
- Expertise in finance, capital acquisition, and possibly Initial Public Offerings (IPOs)
- A personality compatible with the rest of the board
- Good problem-solving skills
- Honesty and integrity

If the entrepreneurial team is not careful, they may learn too late that a director they have appointed to the board considers the position an appointment for life, much like being appointed to the Supreme Court. To avoid a situation—you'll want new directors at times in order to bring new life to the board—ask directors to serve on a rotating basis for a specified period of time.

The board is headed by the Chairman, who, in a new venture, is typically the lead entrepreneur. The entrepreneur will also, most probably, be the President and Chief Executive Officer (CEO). The additional positions of secretary and treasurer may be held by a single person, often another member of the founding team.

Boards normally meet an average of five times a year, depending on the type of business. How often the board meets will largely be a function of how active it is at any point in time. Directors typically spend about nine to 10 days a year on duties related to the business and are usually paid a retainer plus a per-meeting fee with their expenses also reimbursed. The compensation can take the form of cash, stock, or other perquisites.

Today it is more difficult to get people to serve as directors because in some cases they can be held personally liable for the actions of the firm, and the frequency with which boards are being sued is increasing. For this reason, potential directors may require that the business carry directors and officers' (D & O) liability insurance on them; however, the expense of this insurance is often prohibitive for a growing company. Additional expenses related to the development of a board of directors include meeting rooms, travel, and food.

Advisory Board. The advisory board is an informal panel of experts and people who are interested in seeing the new venture succeed. They are generally unpaid and may meet once or twice a year to advise the entrepreneur. Advisory boards are often used when a board of directors is not required or in the start-up phase when the board of directors consists of the founders only. It can provide the new venture with the needed expertise without the significant costs and loss of control associated with a board of directors. In a wholly owned corporation there really is no distinction between the functions of a board of directors and a board of advisors, as control remains in the hands of the entrepreneurial team.

Mistakes to Avoid

Putting together the extended founding team is a serious undertaking that, if unsuccessful, could have severe ramifications for the future of the business. Several common mistakes in forming the team should be avoided.

- Forming the team casually or by chance—that is, without careful consideration of the experience and qualifications each one brings to the team.
- Putting together a team whose members have different goals, which could impede the growth of the company.
- Using only insiders for the board of directors—that is, friends and family instead of the most qualified people to advise the business.

- Using family members or friends as attorney and accountant for the business. As these professional advisors must remain objective at all times to best represent and assist the entrepreneur, choosing relatives can cause unnecessary problems.
- Giving the founding team all stock in lieu of salary. The lead entrepreneur does not want significant shares of stock in the hands of people who may later leave the company. Furthermore, loose stock can land in the hands of the firm's competitors. In a later chapter, the issue of a buy-sell agreement to prevent this problem will be discussed.

Outsourcing Savvy – Independent Contractors

New ventures typically do not have the resources to hire all the management staff they might need to run the business. In fact, most entrepreneurs "bootstrap" in the early stages of growing a business. **Bootstrapping** in this context means "begging, borrowing, or renting everything" to get the business off the ground. Bootstrapping represents collectively all the creative techniques employed by entrepreneurs in the start-up phase. The general rules of thumb for bootstrapping include:

- Hiring as few employees as possible (employees are usually the single largest expense of a business).
- Leasing rather than buying so as not to tie up limited funds in equipment and facilities. With a lease, there is often no down payment and the cost is spread over time.
- Arranging longer terms with suppliers.
- Where possible, getting customers to pay in advance.

The first rule of thumb above is relevant to this chapter. How does a new venture survive with as few employees as possible and still grow? One solution is to hire employees from a temporary service; another is to use independent contractors, a process known as **outsourcing.** Independent contractors own their own businesses and are hired by the entrepreneur to do a specific job. They are under the control of the entrepreneur *only* for the result of the work they do and *not* in the means by which that result is accomplished. There are several advantages to the entrepreneur in using independent contractors.

- Independent contractors are usually specialists in their field.

- Hiring an independent contractor often costs less than hiring an employee because the entrepreneur does not supply the contractor's medical and retirement benefits, unemployment insurance, Social Security tax, or withhold income tax. These benefits can amount to as much as 32 percent of the base salary.

If, however, the entrepreneur does not follow the rules regulating classification of workers as independent contractors, the entrepreneur can be held liable for all back taxes plus penalties and interest, which can result in a substantial sum. Entrepreneurs using independent contractors should:

- Consult an attorney.
- Draw up a contract with each independent contractor that specifies that the contractor will not be treated as an employee for state and federal tax purposes.
- Be careful not to indicate the time or manner in which the work will be performed.
- Verify that the independent contractor carries worker's compensation insurance.
- Verify that the independent contractor possesses the necessary licenses.

More specifically, the IRS uses a 20-point test for classifying workers. (See Figure 4.2 on p. 72.) Even if you follow all the IRS rules, however, there is no guarantee the IRS won't challenge your position. Therefore it is important to document the relationship with an independent contractor through a legal agreement that explicitly demonstrates that the independent contractor owns his or her own business. The IRS can decide that a worker is an employee if even one of the 20 points is true.

If all the IRS rules are followed, independent contractors can make the very small start-up venture look like an established corporation to anyone on the outside. A large corporation will generally have vice presidents for departments of operations, sales, marketing, and finance. It is possible for the entrepreneur to replicate the corporate bureaucracy using independent contractors thereby lowering costs and remaining more flexible. Figure 4.3 on p. 72 shows how a growing entrepreneurial venture can imitate the strength, stability, and expertise of a much larger, more established company through the use of independent contractors. The concept is called the "virtual corporation" and will be discussed at length in Chapter 10.

Figure 4.2: The 20-Point Test for Independent Contractors

The worker is an *employee* if he or she:

1. Must follow the employer's instructions about the work
2. Receives training from the employer
3. Provides services that are integrated into the business
4. Provides services that must be rendered personally
5. Cannot hire, supervise, and pay his or her own assistants
6. Has a continuing relationship with the employer
7. Must follow set hours of work
8. Works full time for an employer
9. Does the work on the employer's premises
10. Must do the work in a sequence set by the employer
11. Must submit regular reports to the employer
12. Is paid regularly for time worked
13. Receives reimbursements for expenses
14. Relies on the tools and materials of the employer
15. Has no major investment in facilities to perform the service
16. Cannot make a profit or suffer a loss
17. Works for one employer at a time
18. Does not offer his or her services to the general public
19. Can be fired at will by the employer
20. May quit work at any time without incurring liability

Figure 4.3: The Virtual Entrepreneurial Company

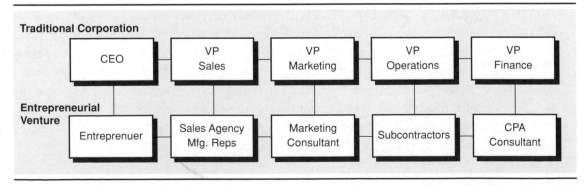

The Shadow Team

Many types of independent contractors operate behind the scenes of the new venture but make a valuable contribution nonetheless.

Consultants. The consulting industry is one of the fastest growing industries in the U.S., and they can provide a variety of services for the new venture.

- Train the sales staff and/or management
- Conduct market research
- Prepare policy manuals
- Solve problems
- Act as temporary key management
- Recommend market strategy
- Design and engineer product
- Design a plant layout and equipment
- Conduct research and development
- Recommend operational and financial controls

Since they tend to be fairly expensive, consultants are best used for critical one-time advice or problem solving. However, this is a matter of perspective, as a quality consultant can accomplish a mission or job more efficiently and effectively than an employee because their greatest strengths are usually problem solving and working quickly within a strict budget.

Manufacturing Support. Even those new ventures that involve manufacturing a product can avail themselves of the benefits of independent contractors. Because the cost of building and equipping a new manufacturing plant is immense by any standards, many entrepreneurs choose to subcontract the work to an established manufacturer. In fact, it is possible for the entrepreneur with a new product idea to subcontract the design of the product to an engineering firm, the production of components to various manufacturing firms, the assembly of the product to another firm, and the distribution to yet another firm.

Sales Support. Hiring a sales staff can be an expensive proposition for any new venture, not only from the standpoint of benefits but because they must be trained as well. As new, high growth ventures seek a geographically broad market, even global, it is vital to consider manufacturer's representatives (reps) and foreign reps who know those markets and can act as the entrepreneur's representative. Using distributors allows the entrepreneur to reach the target market without having to deal with the complex retail market. In addition, sales agencies can provide fully trained sales persons to the new venture in much the same manner as temporary services supply clerical help. Some can also provide advertising and public relations.

Service Agencies. With many established firms downsizing and contracting out for services, some entrepreneurs have seen an opportunity to provide those services and have built highly successful, high growth businesses. As a result, it is now possible for a new venture to subcontract for payroll services, computer services, and temporary help, to name a few. The service firm employs the individual and provides the benefits while the entrepreneur pays a fee for the services.

Buying Offices. When the entrepreneur is ready to consider a global market, he or she may opt to use either an import/export agency or broker or the international department of a major bank. These people understand the laws, customs, and currency exchange rules in the countries with which the entrepreneur will deal.

Governmental Agencies. There are many agencies at the federal, state, and local levels that offer various services to new ventures. Notable among them are the Small Business Administration, which provides education, loans, and grants to small business; the Department of Commerce, which can assist the entrepreneur on issues of trade; and state and local economic development corporations.

By taking advantage of the many services available, the entrepreneur can literally start a business from home to reduce start-up capital requirements, yet still operate like a major corporation. This was the route Talli Counsel of Interfleet took (see Chapter 1). He now handles over $14 million worth of fleet

Outsourcing Your Staff

Leasing your staff, *outsourcing* as it is called, is a way for a new business to enjoy the advantages of major corporations without incurring the expense. The way it works is that a leasing company assumes the payroll and human resource functions for the business for a fee that generally ranges from three to five percent of gross payroll. Each pay period the new venture pays the leasing company a lump sum to cover payroll plus the fee. The National Staff Leasing Association reports that there are about one million leased employees in the U.S. and the industry is growing at an annual rate of 30 percent.

vehicles, and he and his wife are still the only employees of the company. This is not to suggest that a company can always avoid hiring employees and still grow. That will depend on the type of business started. However, it does suggest that in the start-up, bootstrapping phase of a new venture the use of independent contractors can help ensure that the business survives long enough and generates enough revenues to hire employees.

The Management Team Section of the Feasibility Study or Business Plan

There is an advantage to the entrepreneur going it alone initially, that is, doing a feasibility study, formulating the preliminary business plan, incorporating, and in general doing as much as possible until the rest of the team is actually needed. By going beyond the mere conceptual stage, you establish ownership of the business concept and will be in a better position to negotiate with potential team members while remaining the lead entrepreneur. However, if you intend to eventually persuade others—lenders, investors, potential management—that the new venture is a good idea, you will need to convince them that not only is your plan viable, but that you have key personnel with a diversity of expertise and experience in place to implement the plan. That is the purpose of the management section of the feasibility study or business plan.

The key questions that need to be answered in this section of both the feasibility study and the business plan are:

1. Who is on the management team?
2. What are their qualifications and what expertise do they bring to the new venture?
3. What gaps in expertise need to be filled and how will that be accomplished?

The discussion of the management team should focus on persuading the reader that a competent team has been formed and the entrepreneur has identified areas in which expertise is still needed. In general, be sure you have covered the three major functional areas of the business in describing the team—marketing, finance, and operations—and can show you have someone on the team who has demonstrated expertise in the industry or business you are starting. Descriptions of the team should incorporate only *relevant* education and experience. Formal resumes can be placed in the appendices. The key point to remember is that many investors and lenders read this section first, so you need to impress them that the new venture is in good hands.

☑ New Venture Checklist

Have you:

- ☐ Identified the members of the founding team or at least the expertise needed to start the venture?

- ☐ Begun asking questions about potential professional advisors such as an attorney or accountant?

- ☐ Determined if you will need a board of directors, advisory board, or both?

- ☐ Identified at least one type of independent contractor the new venture could use?

- ☐ Determined what expertise is missing from the management team and how you will take care of it?

Additional Sources of Information

Baty, G.B. (1990). *Entrepreneurship for the Nineties.* Englewood Cliffs, NJ: Prentice Hall. Chapter 5.

Covey, S.R. (1989). *The 7 Habits of Highly Effective People.* New York: Simon and Schuster Trade.

Ford, R.H. (1992). *Boards of Directors and the Privately Owned Firm.* New York: Quorum Books.

Timmons, J.A. (1990). *New Venture Creation.* Homewood, IL: Richard D. Irwin, Inc., Chapter 7.

Ward, J. (1991). *Creating Effective Boards for Private Enterprise.* San Francisco: Jossey-Bass.

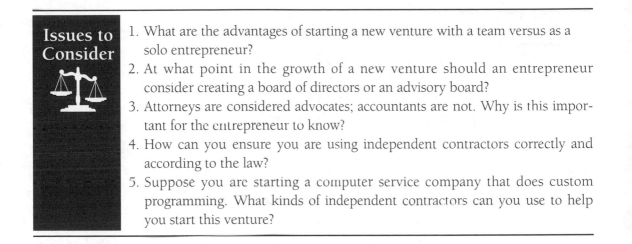

Issues to Consider

1. What are the advantages of starting a new venture with a team versus as a solo entrepreneur?
2. At what point in the growth of a new venture should an entrepreneur consider creating a board of directors or an advisory board?
3. Attorneys are considered advocates; accountants are not. Why is this important for the entrepreneur to know?
4. How can you ensure you are using independent contractors correctly and according to the law?
5. Suppose you are starting a computer service company that does custom programming. What kinds of independent contractors can you use to help you start this venture?

Mrs. Gooch's Natural Foods Markets

Entrepreneurs start businesses for many reasons, but not many do it because they want to save their lives. Sandy Gooch was one such entrepreneur. In 1974 she was a wife, mother, ex-teacher, and full-time homemaker who, like millions of other Americans, often relied on convenience foods even though she knew they contained potentially harmful chemicals. One day she woke up with persistent sniffles for which the doctor prescribed tetracycline. A few days later, however, she thought she suffered a heart attack and was rushed to the hospital. The doctors could not find the cause for her symptoms. Two weeks later she developed an ear infection and was again given tetracycline. This time her "attack" lasted three days, and she nearly died. Her father, a biologist/chemist, began what was to be a year of research into food manufacturing practices. He found that Sandy was allergic to chemicals and additives commonly found in food. They affected her body in such a way that it was unable to fight off disease.

From the information her father had gathered, Sandy decided a natural diet was her best weapon and she proceeded to get rid of everything that was not natural in her kitchen. Within a period of about three months she was feeling better, and within nine months she was healthier than she had been for years. As she began to study nutrition and whole foods, Sandy found others who shared her problem. But, like Sandy, these people had to travel from health food store to health food store, along with shopping at grocery stores, to find the natural foods they needed.

Sandy felt frustrated. Coming from a family that had always helped people in the community, it was natural that she began to explore ways to make life easier for people who wanted to eat healthy foods. There were lots of things she could do—start a newsletter, form a coop, give seminars—but the only idea that allowed her to make a real impact on people's lives was the idea of a natural foods store that would carry only things that were good for you. Excited by the possibilities, Sandy began to consult with herbologists, chemists, biologists, cosmetologists, and physicians to gather all the information she could about diet, wholesome foods, and food allergies.

Armed with a wealth of nutritional knowledge, Sandy realized that all the knowledge in the world about food could not compensate for a lack of experience in business. She would need to take on a partner. Fortunately, she had a friend who was managing a health food store in the San Fernando Valley, and she succeeded in convincing him to help.

They had to find a store location that was accessible and in a good area of town. After much driving around and consulting newspapers, they found a market on the west side of Los Angeles that had gone out of business. It was obvious that the owners had run it into the ground, but to Sandy it couldn't be more perfect. Using her teacher retirement money and all of her savings, she opened her first natural foods market on this site in 1977. The store was an overnight success in spite of the fact that she had done no location studies or psychographic studies. She was not simply lucky, however. She had correctly determined that there were a lot of people who shared her problems with unnatural foods. In other words, she had innocently and intuitively found a niche in the market. Customers lined up and kept her at the register for six hours straight without a break.

One of the problems they faced early on was a shortage of cash.

High demand for what you have to offer has its obvious pluses and its not-so-obvious minuses. One of the problems they faced early on was a shortage of cash. Often cash flow problems are the result of poor management, but in Sandy's case, it was caused by the need to stock sufficient inventory to meet demand. And that required a lot of capital, which they didn't have. By keeping overhead costs down and scrimping anywhere that it didn't affect the customer, they were able to keep up with demand pretty well.

Sandy's passion for her business and her need to help people, coupled with the tremendous demand for what she had to offer, led to the opening of a second store within a year. To finance this store, Sandy offered limited partnerships to raise $125,000. From then on, using internal cash flows, five more stores followed over a period of 15 years, with each store reflecting Sandy Gooch's philosophy and mission for the business:

Mrs. Gooch's is committed to offering the highest quality natural foods, related products, service and information which optimize and enrich the health and well-being of the individual as well as the planet. (From the Company Mission of Mrs. Gooch's)

The mission statement guided all of the decisions she made about the stores. Accordingly, Sandy required that her suppliers guarantee the quality of their products and be able to furnish laboratory analyses or signed affidavits if requested. The products she carried could not contain chemicals, white flour, sugar, preservatives, artificial colors or flavors, caffeine, chocolate, hydrogenated vegetable oil, or irradiated food. The mission statement also gave her a way to expand the product line to include, in addition to food, nutritional supplements and body care products. To increase efficiency as the company grew, she opened a produce/grocery distribution center, a food commissary for the preparation of deli and bakery foods, a design studio to create store decor and a construction shop to build the displays.

> She knew that an informed consumer would be an advocate for the type of nutritional lifestyle she was proposing.

A former teacher, Sandy Gooch's love of education found its way into her business. To help achieve her mission, her 800 employees were carefully trained to be knowledgeable about the products she carried. Sandy believed strongly that their product was really knowledge and information. That belief formed the basis of her marketing strategy. She knew that an informed consumer would be an advocate for the type of nutritional lifestyle she was proposing. As advocates they would return again and again to purchase those products and gain more knowledge. She promoted health awareness by offering seminars, producing a newsletter, and giving her customers free brochures on nutrition. A mini-bookstore in each store contained all the latest research on foods and their relationship to the body. Even the ads that appeared in newspapers were educational in nature.

Sandy incorporated the business early in its development and set up a Board of Directors, which included herself, her partner, the general manager, and their attorney. As this privately held company began to grow, Sandy wondered if she had made the correct decision putting all "insiders" on the board. Would they continue to share her mission for the business?

1. Why is Mrs. Gooch's considered an entrepreneurial venture?
2. How does the mission statement of Mrs. Gooch affect the decisions she made as the business grew?
3. What intellectual property rights could she acquire?
4. What other kinds of businesses could Sandy Gooch have started given her philosophy?
5. What potential effect could there be from using insiders on the Board of Directors? What can she do to remedy the situation?
6. What are some spin-off products or services Mrs. Gooch's could offer?

PART 2

Finding, Analyzing, and Testing Opportunity

The man with a new idea is a crank–
until the idea succeeds.

—MARK TWAIN

CHAPTER 5

Understanding the Industry: Prelude to Success

Overview

- *Identifying the industry in which the new venture will operate*
- *Industry carrying capacity, dynamism, and complexity*
- *Sources of secondary industry information*
- *Sources of field data on the industry*
- *Effective field interviews*
- *Presenting the industry profile in the feasibility study or business plan*

Defining the Industry

One of the environmental variables that affects both the creation and strategy of the new venture is the industry in which it will operate. A strategic position in a growing, dynamic, and healthy industry can go a long way toward ensuring a successful venture. On the other hand, a weak position in a mature industry may sound a death knell for the business before it even opens its doors. A young, growing industry with many new entrants will present at once a highly competitive environment for the new venture and a chance to gain significant market share if entry is early. This was the case in the software industry in the 1980s. A more mature industry, by contrast, may have already passed through the period of "survival of the fittest" and will now be comprised of a few firms with large market shares, as in the automobile, semiconductor, and airline industries, to name a few.[1]

Research has identified three dimensions of the industry environment that help the entrepreneur evaluate the new venture's potential in the industry: carrying capacity, dynamism, and complexity.[2]

Carrying Capacity

Capacity is the extent to which the industry can support growth. Entrepreneurs will typically seek out an industry that can support expansion, thus allowing the new venture to grow and obtain the resources it needs. Difficulty in entering a specific industry suggests that the industry may be approaching its carrying capacity—that is, the production capability of the existing firms equals or exceeds the demand for industry products. The only way to enter such an industry then is through the introduction of new technology or by discovering a niche where a need has not been met. The was the strategy of Gentech Corporation in introducing new technology in a niche market of the large and very mature generator and compressor industries.

Dynamism

Dynamism is the degree of certainty or uncertainty in the industry, as well as stability or instability; in other words, a dynamic environment is one that is difficult to predict because it is in constant flux. Industries that operate in volatile environments, like the computer industry, contain higher degrees of uncertainty or risk. Consequently, the rewards are usually higher as well.

Complexity

Complexity is the number and diversity of inputs and outputs facing an organization. Firms that operate in complex industries usually have to deal with more suppliers, customers, and competitors than other industries, and they usually produce a greater number of dissimilar products for global markets. Industries with a high degree of complexity by their very nature make it difficult for new

---

[1]N.C. Churchill, J.A. Hornaday, B.A. Kirchhoff, O.J. Krasner & K.H. Vesper. "Venture Survivability." *Frontiers of Entrepreneurship Research*, Wellesley, MA: Babson Center for Entrepreneurial Studies. (1987).

[2]Starbuck. W.H. "Organizations and Their Environments." (1976). In M.D. Dunnette (Ed.) *Handbook of Industrial and Organization Psychology*. Chicago: Rand McNally. Pfeffer, J. & Salancik, G.R. (1978). *The External Control of Organizations*. New York: Random House.

businesses to enter. They are also extremely competitive; therefore, new ventures often find a great deal of hostility rather than collaboration.

Industry Structure

In studying the industry in which the new venture will operate, develop a broad picture of how the industry works, how friendly it is to new entrants, and where it is going in the future. Michael Porter asserts that there are five forces in any industry that affect the ultimate profit potential of a venture in terms of long run return on investment. They are:

1. Threat of new entrants into the industry
2. The bargaining power of suppliers
3. Threat of substitute products
4. The bargaining power of buyers
5. Rivalry among competitors in the industry[3]

These are the forces that drive competition and affect the long run profitability of the new venture as well as other firms in the industry. Short run profitability, by contrast, is affected by such things as economic forces, changes in demand, material shortages, and so forth.

Threat of New Entrants

In some industries barriers to entry are high and will discourage new entrants. These barriers may include:

- *Economies of scale.* Many industries have achieved economies of scale in marketing, production, and distribution. This means that their costs to produce have declined relative to the price of their goods and services. A new venture cannot easily achieve these same economies, so it is forced into a "Catch-22" situation. It can enter the industry on a large scale and risk retaliation from those established firms in the industry, or enter on a small scale and not be able to compete because of high costs relative to everyone else. Another version of this dilemma is an industry where the major players are vertically integrated; that is, they own their suppliers and/or distribution channels. What most new ventures attempt to do when faced with

---

[3]Porter, Michael E. (1980). *Competitive Strategy: Techniques for Analyzing Industries and Competitors.* New York: The Free Press. p. 3.

economies of scale is to form alliances with other small firms to share resources and compete on a more level playing field.

- **Brand loyalty.** New entrants to an industry face products and services that have loyal customers, so an extensive marketing campaign focused on re-educating the customer about the benefits of the new venture's products will be required. The cost of undertaking this strategy is a significant barrier to entry.

- **Enormous capital requirements.** The cost of entering many industries is prohibitive for a new venture. These costs may include up front advertising, R&D, and expenditures for plant and equipment to compete on par with established firms in the industry.

- **Switching costs for the buyer.** Buyers in most industries don't readily switch from one supplier to another unless there is a demonstrated reason to do so. This is because it costs the buyer money and time to retrain staff and potentially learn a new technology. For example, users of the Microsoft Windows graphical interface will not easily switch to a different system because they have spent a lot of time learning the Windows environment and are used to it.

- **Access to distribution channels.** The new venture must convince established distribution channel members to accept the new product or service and prove that it will be beneficial to distributors to do so. This persuasion process can be costly for the new venture.

- **Proprietary factors.** Barriers to entry also include proprietary technology, products, and processes. Where established firms hold patents on products and processes that the new venture requires, they have the ability to either keep the new venture out of the industry or make it very expensive to enter. Most favorable location is another form of proprietary barrier. Often entrepreneurs will discover that existing firms in the industry own the most advantageous business sites, forcing the new venture to locate in a less competitive site. Established firms, being further along on the learning/experience curve, are probably more cost efficient in their operations—something that will take time for the new venture to achieve. These proprietary factors are all substantial barriers to entry for a new venture.

- **Government regulations.** The government can prevent a new venture from entering an industry through strict licensing requirements and by limiting access to raw materials through laws or high taxes and certain locations via zoning restrictions.

- **Industry hostility.** Some industries are extremely retaliatory toward new businesses that attempt to compete in the industry. This typically occurs where there are many well established firms that have sufficient resources to spend the time and money going after a new entrant. It is also common in mature industries where growth has slowed, so rivalry for market share intensifies as profits decline. Weaker firms ultimately exit the industry.

Threat from Substitute Products

A new venture must not only compete with products and services in its own industry but with those that are logical substitutes in other industries as well. Generally, these substitute products and services accomplish the same basic function in a different way or at a different price. For example, restaurants regularly compete with other forms of entertainment for the consumer's disposable dollars. The threat from substitute products is more likely to occur where firms in other industries are earning high profits at better prices than can be achieved in the new venture's industry.

Threat from Buyers' Bargaining Power

Buyers of products and services can force down prices in the industry through volume purchases. This is particularly true where the industry products comprise a significant portion of the buyers' requirements. Under this scenario, the buyer is more likely to seek the lowest possible price. The largest buyers also pose a threat of backward integration, where they actually purchase their suppliers, thus better controlling costs and affecting price throughout the industry. The more buyers understand the nature of the industry and the more the products are standardized, the greater the likelihood that these buyers will have significant bargaining power. In industries where buyers have bargaining power, it is more difficult for a new entrant to gain a foothold and grow.

Threat from Suppliers' Bargaining Power

In some industries suppliers exert enormous power through the threat of raising prices or changing the quality of the products that they supply to manufacturers and distributors. If the number of these suppliers is few relative to the size of the industry, or the industry is not the primary customer of the suppliers, that power is magnified. Moreover, if these suppliers are the primary source of materials and components for the new venture, the ability to compete on cost may be negatively affected. A further threat from suppliers is that they will **forward integrate**—that is, they will purchase the outlets for their goods and services, thus controlling the prices at which they are ultimately sold.

It is interesting to consider that labor is really a source of supply. In certain industries where highly technical skills are required or where unions are strong, labor as a supplier has enormous bargaining power and can significantly impact costs for the new venture.

Rivalry among Existing Industry Firms

In general, it can be said that a highly competitive industry will drive down profits and ultimately the rate of return on investment. To position themselves in a competitive market, firms will resort to price wars, advertising skirmishes, and enhanced service. Once one firm decides to make such a strategic move in the industry, others will follow. The clearest example is the airline industry; when one airline discounts its prices significantly, most of the others immediately follow. The problem with this tactic is that it ultimately hurts everyone in the industry and may even result in forcing some firms out because competitive prices drop below cost. Most new ventures can't compete on price and can't afford costly advertising battles to build an image. To compete in an industry that is highly competitive, they must find a market niche that has not been served by the major industry rivals and enter the industry without causing movement on the part of the major players.

The Special Case of Emerging Industries

Emerging industries are those that are just coming into being. Some examples are interactive television and telecommunications. In these types of industries there are no rules initially. Instead, technical uncertainty exists until the major technology developers enter the industry and it becomes apparent which technology is the best. Consequently, there is no standardization of products and processes in the industry for some time, and as a result costs to produce are high. Securing sufficient raw materials may also be difficult.

Buyers in an emerging industry are, for the most part, considered first-time buyers. They will pay a premium for the product at its introduction but will usually see that price decline significantly as competition increases and standardization of technology occurs.

For entrepreneurs, an emerging industry is at once exciting, challenging, and extremely risky. Certainly the strongest position is to own the technology being introduced and be able to enter the market with sufficient resources to establish a firm market share and brand identity. If, however, others are also entering the market at the same time with similar proprietary technology, resources will have to be directed toward promoting the benefits and superiority of the entrepreneur's technology. This was the case for Microsoft's Windows, which ultimately overcame the threat of IBM's OS/2 technology. If major companies from other compatible industries are entering the new industry, the task is that much harder. That is the situation for new ventures hoping to garner a piece of the action in the telecommunications industry, where they are competing for market share against the likes of QVC and Microsoft.

Competitive Strategies

The new venture's entry strategy will largely be a function of the structure of the industry into which it seeks entry. In general, three broad strategies are available to the new venture: cost superiority, product/process/service differentiation, and niche.

Cost Superiority

Essentially, **cost superiority** entails entering the industry with an organizational structure that is "lean and mean," with tight controls on costs. To accomplish this usually requires designing the production process and distribution mechanisms to operate under strict controls, meeting stringent quantity targets. This strategy is very difficult for a new venture to achieve in that it most often results from being further along on the experience curve and from producing in high volumes. It is rare that a new venture will have the infrastructure and resources in place, and sufficient product/service demand from the beginning to allow it to use cost superiority as an entry strategy.

Differentiation

Differentiation is a strategy that involves distinguishing the new venture from others in the industry through product/process innovation, or a unique marketing or distribution strategy. Differentiation often creates brand loyalty among customers, thereby making the product or service less sensitive to price. Consequently, margins are usually increased, which better insulates the company against supplier and buyer bargaining power, and moves the focus away from the cost to produce. Additionally, substitute products are less likely to be a threat where differentiation is the strategy.

Niche Strategy

The third strategy is often referred to as a **niche** strategy, which simply means that the new venture focuses on a particular customer group or specific geographic region not currently served by the industry effectively. Many a new venture has entered an established industry via a niche. This strategy may include either a cost leader or differentiation strategy as well, with the key distinction being that the niche strategy tackles only a segment of the industry rather than the industry as a whole. Where competition is weak and exposure to substitute products is a minor issue, the niche strategy offers a safer route to establishing a foothold in the industry. Gentech, whose *PowerSource* industrial machine competes in the generator/compressor industries, is focusing on a niche market in equipment rental outlets as a strategy to enter a large industry with established firms.

Competing on a Global Level

Porter (1980) contends that while there are many differences when competing in an industry on an international basis, structural factors and general market forces are essentially the same. Entrepreneurs can go global through licensing products and services to international firms, exporting, or investing in plant and equipment in another country.

   While the advantages of competing on a global level include increased potential for growth, there are a number of difficulties that often impede the process. Transportation and storage of product in other countries is often difficult. Many times products made in the United States must be modified to meet the specifications and demands of customers in other countries. For example, sizes of clothing vary from country to country, and electrical current, which is 110v in the United States is 240v in many other countries. Distribution channels inside the borders of other countries usually operate differently. Sometimes the problem is a matter of political clout or government regulation. Finally, the legal protections, such as patent laws, that are enjoyed by entrepreneurs in the United States are not always respected in the same manner in other countries.

   The complexity of investigating an industry on a global level is exacerbated by the fact that not only must you grasp how the industry works in that country, but you must also have a good understanding of the culture and political process. These issues related to marketing on a global level are treated more fully in Chapter 16.

Competitive Analysis

Within any industry, it is important to hypothesize about the competitive strategy of the competition—in other words, to know the competition as well as you know your own business. Studying the history and management style of your major competitors will give insight into what motivates them and how they may potentially react to your strategy. You need to identify their current strategy to learn how they have positioned themselves in the industry. In the same way that you would analyze your strategy's strengths, weaknesses, opportunities and threats, you should also study theirs.

Not all of your competitors will exhibit the same strategy, so it is useful to categorize them to get a handle on what the new venture is facing. Once the competitors have been categorized, you will more readily see into what strategic grouping the new venture lies, that is, who your key competitors are. From there the new venture's position in that group will be determined as well as the strategic group's position in the industry as a whole. To have the best chance for success, the new venture should be positioned in the strategic group that offers the best profit potential, yet a reasonable cost of entry.

Industry Evolution

Industries do not remain static or stable over time. In fact, they are in an almost constant state of evolution. Like a business, an industry moves through a life cycle that includes birth, growth, maturity, and ultimately decline. Of course, for every industry the life cycle stages occur at different rates and last for varying lengths of time. Some industries like the auto industry avoid decline by constantly innovating to meet market demand and satisfy governmental regulations.

As an industry grows, it sees demographic shifts, changes in costs of materials and labor, product and process innovations, and changes in its customer markets. Industry products tend to become commodities over time, so the competitive tendency to differentiate products is enhanced. With time, uncertainty is reduced and proprietary rights become less exclusive, which may result in larger, risk-averse firms entering the industry. These larger firms have the resources to integrate vertically, gaining control of suppliers and distribution channels, and instituting product and process innovations that can result in larger volumes of goods being produced and sold. These actions can cause a change in the cost structure of the industry and the exit of firms unable to compete in the new industry structure. A few firms will finally dominate the industry.

Industry Analysis

The importance of understanding the industry in which the new venture will operate cannot be overstated because the industry environment has a direct impact on how the new venture does business and on its potential for success. The nature of the industry certainly must be taken into consideration when establishing the competitive strategy for accomplishing the goals of the venture.

An industry analysis requires a plan of attack to avoid wasting time hunting for inadequate information and not knowing what to do with it once it is collected. The analysis will include:

- Identifying the industry
- Examining secondary resources
- Talking to people in the industry
- Analyzing the data and drawing conclusions

Standard Industrial Classifications

It is possible to determine the specific industry in which the new venture will operate by identifying the Standard Industrial Classification (SIC) for the product or service. Knowing the four-digit SIC code for the business allows the entrepreneur access to a wealth of information typically categorized by SIC code. Standard Industrial Classification Codes were developed by the U.S. Bureau of the Budget in 1972. The major classifications include such industries as agriculture, mining, construction, manufacturing, and wholesale. For example, under the major classification of manufacturing, the types of businesses and their respective codes can be found listed in Figure 5.1.

Sources of Industry Information

An industry analysis usually begins with a search of secondary data sources— journals, trade magazines, reference books, government publications, and annual reports of public corporations—sources that are all normally found in a university or community library. Historical data, such as annual reports over

Figure 5.1: Manufacturing Industrial Classifications

2400	Food & Kindered Products
2600	Paper & Allied Products
2700	Printing, Publishing & Allied Industries
2800	Chemicals & Allied Products
3000	Rubber & Miscellaneous Plastic Products
3200	Stone, Clay, Glass & Concrete Products
3300	Primary Metal Industries
3400	Fabricated Metal Products, except machinery & transportation equipment
3500	Machinery, except electrical
3900	Miscellaneous Manufacturing Industries

Figure 5.2: Categories of Data for Industry Analysis

- Growth
- Complementary/substitute products
- Competitors
- Market strategies
- Economic environment
- Regulatory environment
- Socio-political environment

- Technology of production
- Distribution channels
- Innovation
- Suppliers
- Product lines
- Buyer behavior

a 10 to 15 year period, can often help the entrepreneur spot trends, cycles, and seasonal variations in the industry. Trade magazines provide a good sense of who the key firms are and the directions the industry may be taking. Figure 5.2 provides a listing of some of the essential raw data on the industry that should be collected. Some of this information will also be useful later for the market analysis.

After the secondary data are collected, they must be organized and analyzed. In general, the key questions about the industry that should be answered are:

- Is the industry growing?
- Where are the opportunities?
- What is the status of any new technology?
- How much does the industry spend on research and development?
- Who are the major competitors?
- Are there young, successful firms in the industry?
- What does the future look like?
- Are there any threats to the industry?
- What are the typical margins in the industry?

The Importance of Primary Data

Secondary research paints the broad brush of the industry; however, given the lead time from data gathering to print, it is rarely the most current information available. Therefore, to access the most timely information, it is extremely important to gather primary field data on the industry. (See Figure 5.3 on p. 94.) In other words, you need to talk to people in the industry—"pound the pavement" so to speak. Some of the sources to tap are:

- *Industry observers,* those who study particular industries and regularly report on them in newspapers, newsletters, or through the media.

- *Suppliers and distributors*, who are in an excellent position to comment on the health of the industry in terms of demand for products and services, as well as the financial strength and market practices of major firms.
- *Customers*, who can be a clue to satisfaction with the industry and the product or service supplied.
- *Employees of key firms* in the industry, who are a good source of information about potential competitors.
- *Professionals from service organizations* such as lawyers and accountants who regularly work with a particular industry.
- *Trade shows*, which give a good indication of who the biggest competitors are and who has the strongest market strategy.

Tactics for Talking to Key Industry People

Field research is usually accomplished via interviews or casual discussions with people in the industry. Getting people to open up and talk to you will be easier if you follow a few simple rules.

- Where possible, secure an introduction from someone who knows the interviewee. You will find that once you talk to the first person, that person will recommend someone else, and you'll be on your way to gathering more information than you could ever use.

Figure 5.3: Sources of Field Data for Industry Analysis

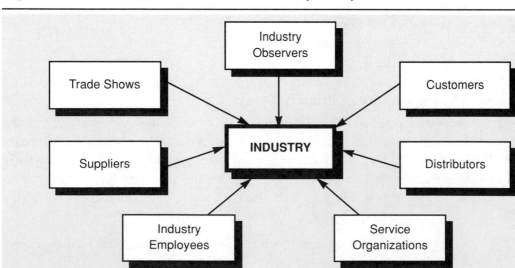

- Seek out individuals who regularly deal with the media since they are easier to approach; however, be aware that they are also used to being very careful about what they say.
- Allow sufficient lead time for the meeting since you are probably dealing with very busy people on tight schedules.
- Offer something that might be of value to them such as a summary of the results of the industry analysis or to take them to lunch.
- Be honest about your affiliation, either with a university or business. Interviewees want to know you understand the value of their time.
- To give yourself credibility, demonstrate your knowledge of the interviewee's business. Of course, to do this you will have had to research the business before the meeting.
- If possible, take a colleague or business partner along to ensure that you obtain all the needed information and catch all the visual cues. This is particularly true when talking to potential competitors.
- Carefully observe the surroundings. Physical clues and non-verbal communication are often excellent indicators of the nature of the industry.
- Be sure your opening questions are easy and non-threatening and show a genuine interest in the interviewee's business.

The Ideal Industry

While no industry is perfect, an industry comprised of the following features offers more opportunity for a new venture.

- An industry with over $50 billion in sales will probably have niche markets of sufficient size to allow for the attainment of an adequate market share.
- An industry that is generally growing at a rate greater than the GNP offers more potential for growth of the new venture.
- An industry that allows for after-tax profits of greater than five percent of sales within three to five years will enhance the new venture's chances for success.
- An industry that is socially and environmentally responsible will be one that is compatible with current societal and political trends and, consequently, may be eligible for special grants and other types of funding.

New ventures entering an emerging industry will not have the luxury of a history and information that can indicate potential for growth and profits. They can, however, look to the experiences of other recently formed industries that are similar to theirs to predict patterns and potential market demand.

These characteristics are merely benchmarks. With so many variables involved, no one can guarantee a new venture will survive or become a success even if the industry possesses all these characteristics. However, as with anything, the more information the entrepreneur has, the better chance there is of not making costly mistakes.

Presenting the Industry Data in the Feasibility Study or Business Plan

Industry Profile
- *Current Size*
- *Growth Potential*
- *Geographic Locations*
- *Industry Trends*
- *Seasonality*
- *Profit Potential*
- *Sales Patterns*
- *Gross Margins on Products*
- *Technology*
- *Government Regulation*

The industry analysis provides the entrepreneur and others with the information necessary to determine if the industry in which the business will be started appears conducive to new ventures. The data collected should be presented in the feasibility study or business plan in a way that highlights the key points and answers the major questions addressed in this chapter. Often this can be accomplished best through the use of tables and graphs. These can display data efficiently and should be used where appropriate; however, the entrepreneur must never assume readers will pick out the most salient points from tables, graphics, or the narrative for that matter. It is important to point out key trends and patterns in the data as the entrepreneur sees them.

A comprehensive industry analysis will include:

- The *current size* of the industry as measured by total sales volume, total number of firms, and total number of employees.
- The *growth potential*, based on historical trends in size. Is the industry growing, shrinking, or remaining stable?
- *Geographic location*, where the industry seems to cluster (i.e. semiconductors in Silicon Valley, California; Route 128 in Massachusetts, and so forth).
- *Industry trends* in terms of products, services, innovation, and technology.
- *Seasonality* of demand for products and services, based on days of week, months, or seasons of the year.
- *Profit potential*, based on performance of existing firms in the industry.
- *Sales patterns* as measured by frequency and quantity of purchase.
- *Gross margins on products* as an indicator of how easy or difficult it will be to cover overhead.
- *Technology*, both process and product as an indicator of barriers to entry and potential for innovation.
- *Government regulation* of aspects of the industry that may affect the new ventures growth potential.

Both the entrepreneur and other interested parties will want to know that the industry is healthy, growing, and provides an excellent window of opportunity for the new venture.

✓ New Venture Checklist

Have you:

☐ Identified the SIC code for the industry in which your new venture will operate?

☐ Collected secondary data on the industry?

☐ Conducted field research by interviewing suppliers, distributors, customers, and others?

☐ Developed an industry profile that will tell you and others if the industry is growing, who the major competitors are, and what the profit potential is?

Additional Sources of Information

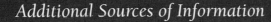

Darnay. A.J. (Ed.). *Manufacturing USA: Industry Analyses, Statistics, and Leading Companies.* Detroit: Gale Research Inc.

R. J. Elster (Ed.). *Small Business Sourcebook.* Detroit: Gale Research Inc.

Gumpert, D.E. & Timmons, J.A. (1982). *The Insider's Guide to Small Business Resources.* Garden City, NY: Doubleday & Co.

Schwartz, C.A. *Small Business Sourcebook.* Detroit: Gale Research Inc.

Thomas Register

U.S. Census Data: State and County Business Patterns

Issues to Consider

1. How does your industry measure up in terms of dynamism and complexity?
2. Which primary and secondary information will tell you if the industry is growing and favorable to new entrants?
3. What kinds of information can suppliers and distributors give you?
4. What information about the industry can trade shows provide?
5. How should tables and graphs be used in the industry profile?

CHAPTER 6

Evaluating the Target Market

Overview

- *Defining and describing the target market*
- *Direct, indirect, and emerging competitors*
- *Competitive advantage*
- *Secondary sources of data on the target market*
- *Techniques for estimating demand for the product or service*
- *Presenting the market analysis in the feasibility study or business plan*
- *Determining initial feasibility*

Defining the Target Market

One of the most important tasks the entrepreneur must undertake is the identification of the primary customer for the product or service being offered by the new venture. The **target market** is that segment of the marketplace that will most likely purchase the product or service. It is referred to as the **primary market.** The **secondary market,** by contrast, consists of those customers outside the target market for whom a different market strategy will be required.

The ability to identify the target market is based on an analysis of customer need, which usually begins at the earliest stages of business concept development. In fact, often the idea for an innovative product or service springs from a need observed by the entrepreneur (e.g., Bob Kearns and the intermittent wiper blade). The preliminary needs analysis is then refined through target market research and eventually becomes the focal point for many of the decisions and

99

strategies of the new venture. Unfortunately, most entrepreneurs don't place enough emphasis on in-depth market analysis. Instead they assume levels of need and demand without any evidence to support them. As a result, they tend to overestimate their market forecasts for demand by as much as 60 percent.[1]

The Market Niche

The term **niche** refers to that very specific segment of the market toward which the new venture is targeting its efforts. It is usually a relatively small, well-defined segment that is often not currently being served by the products and services available in the industry. Sandy Gooch's natural food markets is one example of a niche product/service. The PIG industrial cleaning device is another. The advantage of defining a market niche is that it permits entry by the new venture into virtually any industry without having to compete at the level of General Motors. The start-up venture in a niche market can more quickly become the "big fish in the little pond," establishing a secure customer base before it expands into larger, more competitive markets. Starting with a niche also facilitates a better understanding of customers' needs and purchasing patterns on a smaller, more manageable scale.

Describing the Target Customer

No matter what the size of the target market, it is crucial that the entrepreneur know as much as possible about the customer. Gooch determined early in the development of her concept for a natural foods market that her primary customer is a well-educated, working woman over 30 years old who is concerned about what she puts into her body. Over the years of growing her business, Gooch has refined that description and can now describe her target customer in even greater detail. The important point is that knowing as much as possible about the customer will guide you in making decisions about how to reach that customer. For example, since Mrs. Gooch's customer is thirsty for nutritional knowledge, Mrs. Gooch's Natural Foods Markets distributes a newsletter containing the latest nutritional information. Her stores are full of educational pamphlets in addition to trained clerks who answer any questions her customers might have. As long as she can meet the specific needs of her customers, Gooch's business will thrive. Therefore, defining the target market

---

[1]Hills, G.E. "Market Analysis and Marketing in New Ventures: Venture Capitalist Perceptions" in *Frontiers of Entrepreneurship Research*. Babson Center for Entrepreneurial Studies, (1984), p.43.

really means describing the primary customer for your product or service—that customer who will help your business grow and succeed.

In the beginning stages of market analysis, you will probably have a fairly loose description of the target market. This description will be refined and may even change as you talk to the target customers during the field research. The key questions you will be attempting to answer are:

- Who is my customer?
- What do they typically buy and how do they hear about it?
- How often do they buy?
- How can my new venture meet the customers' needs?

Some techniques for gathering this information will be discussed later in this chapter.

Identifying the Competition

There are three types of competitors for your product or service: direct, indirect, and emerging. Identifying specifically who these companies are—their strengths, weaknesses, and market share—will put the new venture in a better position to be a contender in the industry and particularly in the target market.

Direct Competitors

Those businesses that supply products or services that are the same or similar to yours, or are a reasonably good substitute for yours, are **direct competitors** to the new venture. However, be careful: the term **competition** is not quite that simple. Suppose you are going to open an entertainment center that incorporates virtual reality computer games in a shopping mall. One possible direct competitor that comes to mind is a video arcade. But if you consider your venture to be in the entertainment business, you will see that other direct competitors for the consumer dollars you are seeking are movie theaters, miniature golf courses, bowling alleys, and video rental stores. That certainly complicates the picture, and it's not the only source of competition for the new venture.

Indirect Competitors

Indirect competitors may not even be in the same industry as the new venture but who compete alongside it for consumer dollars. Using the example above, consumers may choose to spend their limited dollars at restaurants rather than on entertainment, or, perhaps, on a weekend vacation. Indirect competitors, therefore, are often substitutes outside the entrepreneur's industry or target market.

Emerging Competitors

When entering a market as a new business, it is vital not only to assess the existing competition but also the potential for new competition—emerging competitors—at some time in the future. In many industries today, technology and information are changing at such a rapid pace that the window of opportunity to successfully start a new venture has been closing. Consequently the entrepreneur must be ever-vigilant to new trends and new technology in both the industry in general and in the specific target market.

Competitive Advantage

Understanding who your competitors are is one step in learning what the new venture's competitive advantages are. If your product or service has intellectual property rights—patent, trademark, copyright—*that* is a significant competitive advantage. Other advantages may be found in the market strategy, the distribution strategy, and the operations strategy. The bottom line in competitive advantage is innovation in all aspects of the business. What this suggests is that knowing your competitors as well as you know your new venture allows you to seek more ways in which the new venture can innovate, can distinguish itself from its competitors, and can attain an important level of competitive advantage in the marketplace.

PROFILE 6.1

The Importance of Satisfying Customer Needs

Robert Shaw is chairman of International Jensen, a manufacturer of audio speakers whose primary target market is the automotive industry. He supplies speakers to companies like Ford, Chrysler, and Honda. Shaw believes that the success of his company, even during slow years for the auto industry, is due in large part to his company's concern for what the customer wants, *not* what his company wants. He empowers his workers at the local level to stay in touch with customers' demands. If the trend is for more sophisticated, lightweight speakers, Shaw is prepared to give the customers what they want. Sales are increasing at a rate of about 10 percent per year, suggesting that he is doing just that.

Researching the Target Market

The research conducted on the target market will provide some of the most important data needed by the entrepreneur to decide if the new venture is feasible. To ensure that useful and correct conclusions can be drawn the research methods must be sound. A four-step process will ensure the information needed to make this crucial decision is gathered and used correctly. (See Figure 6.1.)

Figure 6.1: Steps to Market Research

- Assess your information needs
- Research secondary sources first
- Measure the target market
- Forecast demand for the product or service

Assessing Information Needs

Before you can begin to collect market data, you must determine how that data will be used in the market analysis section of the feasibility study and the business plan. Will it demonstrate a demand for the product or service? Will it describe the target customer? You may be wondering how you can decide how data will be used and analyzed when it hasn't yet been collected. Precisely the point. A good researcher will decide *first* what he or she is attempting to accomplish with the research so the correct type of data needed for the analysis will be gathered. Nothing is more discouraging to a researcher than finding out after all the data are collected that a crucial piece of information is missing.

Also, once you know what it is you want to determine with the data, it will be easier to choose a particular type of analysis that will lead to the desired result. For example, if one of your research goals is to refine the description of the target market, you may decide to seek the most common characteristics or demographics (the statistical mode) of the customer—in another words, indicate the most common age, education level, income, and so on. To do this, you will need to gather numerical data. Granted this is a rather simple and obvious example; however, others are not so apparent.

Suppose, for example, you wish to calculate demand for the product or service by using a statistical forecasting technique. The type of technique you choose will dictate the kind of data you must collect. For example, if the technique requires continuous numerical data (i.e. all values for an answer are

Figure 6.2: Sample Demographics of the Target Market

Average age of customer	32
Average income level	$35,000
Average number of years of education	14
Marital status	Married

possible), you would not gather data or design a questionnaire that would give you "yes-no" answers. Fortunately, the market research most entrepreneurs do involves simple, descriptive statistics as seen in Figure 6.2 above.

Recall that the entrepreneur collects both primary and secondary market data. It is important, however, to gather the secondary data first so you have a better understanding of the market prior to designing a sampling plan and doing the field research.

Researching Secondary Sources

Secondary data on the target market give the entrepreneur an understanding of the market before going into the field to talk directly with customers, suppliers, distributors, and others. The library is an excellent starting point. The government publications section will contain Federal Census Bureau data which allows you to define your market by region of the country, major metropolitan area, city, or even neighborhood. The *1990 Census Basics* provides demographic information such as age, education, income, and workers per household. It permits you to determine if the geographic area you have defined is growing or declining, aging or getting younger, if the available work force is mostly skilled or unskilled, along with other trends.

Some groups of demographics (age, income, race, occupation, and education) help identify the likelihood that a person will choose to buy a product.[2] This is true even for industrial products. Demographic data also allow you to segment the target market into subgroups that are estimably different from one another. For example, if your target market is retired people over the age of 60, you may find that buying habits (requirements and quantity of purchase) vary by geographic region or by income level.

Finally, census data can be used to arrive at an estimate of how many target customers are within the geographic boundaries of the target market. Then,

2 Hall, J.A. (1991) *Bringing New Products to Market*. New York: AMACOM.

within any geographic area, those who meet the particular demographic requirements of the product/service can be segmented out.

Most communities have economic development departments or Chambers of Commerce that keep statistics on local population trends and other economic issues. Some communities have Small Business Development Centers (SBDCs), branches of the Small Business Administration that contain a wealth of useful information, as well as services, for small and growing businesses. Other sources available in the library are reference books and trade journals on all types of industries. Apart from the library, useful information can be found from trade associations like the National Association of Manufacturers, commercial research firms, and financial institutions. These resources will assist you in determining the size and characteristics of the target market.

Measuring the Market with Primary Data

There are many ways to collect primary data in the target market. Among them are mail surveys, phone surveys, interviews, focus groups, and product clinics. Each has advantages and disadvantages over the other, and a decision to use one or more of them is usually based on time and money.

Mail Surveys. Doing a mail survey entails designing a survey instrument, usually a questionnaire, that provides the entrepreneur with the desired information. Questionnaire design is not a simple matter of putting some questions on a piece of paper. There are, in fact, proven methods of constructing questionnaires to help ensure unbiased responses. It is not within the scope of this text to present all the techniques for questionnaire construction; however, a few key points should be remembered.

- Keep the questionnaire short with lots of white space so the respondent is not intimidated at the outset.
- Be careful not to ask leading, biased questions.
- Ask easy questions first, leading up to the more complex ones.
- Ask demographic questions (age, sex, income) last when the respondent's attention span has waned. These questions can be answered very quickly.
- For questions people generally hesitate to answer (age, income), group possible responses in ranges (25-35 for age, $35,000-$45,000 for income) so the respondent doesn't feel he or she is giving away very private information.
- Keep in mind that people generally increase their income classification one class and decrease their age one class.

Mail surveys are a relatively easy way to reach a lot of people in the target market and take less time than many other methods. However, mail surveys do have a few weaknesses.

- The response rate is generally very low, usually around 15 percent, which means that about 85 of every 100 persons sampled do not respond. Consequently, the potential for non-response bias makes it difficult for the entrepreneur to feel very comfortable about the reliability of the results.
- The entrepreneur does not have the benefit of non-verbal communication as would be the case with an interview. This is significant when you consider at least 85 percent of all communication is non-verbal.
- The entrepreneur has no way of questioning or clarifying a response.
- There is no control over the accuracy of the information given.
- Normally, a second, follow-up mailing is necessary to achieve the desired response rate.

Phone Surveys. Like mail surveys, phone surveys also use questionnaires so consistency in the questions asked can be achieved. Phone surveys have two particular advantages over mail surveys. They allow for explanation and clarification of questions and responses, and the response rate is higher. However phone surveys take more time to accomplish and are more prone to surveyor bias; that is, there is more opportunity for the person conducting the survey to bias the results by the tone in his or her voice or by unscripted comments. In addition, phone surveys lack the benefits of observing non-verbal communication.

Interviews. Although more costly and time consuming than mail or phone surveys, interviews have many advantages.

- They provide more opportunity for clarification and discussion.
- They enjoy the advantages of non-verbal communication. The entrepreneur will be better able to discern the veracity of what the interviewee is saying.
- The response rate is high.
- Interviews permit open-ended questions that can lead to more in-depth information.
- They provide an opportunity to network and develop valuable contacts in the industry.

Where time and money permit, interviews are probably the best source of valuable information from customers, suppliers, distributors, and anyone else who can help the new venture. It is also possible, however, to use a combination of techniques. For example, the entrepreneur may start with phone surveys to obtain basic information and follow up with interviews with the most useful sources.

Choosing the Sample. All three techniques described above require the selection of a sample from the target market. This step in measuring the market should be done with great care for it will determine the validity of the results achieved. In general, you want to attempt to choose a **random** sample, that is, one in which you have as little control as possible over who will be selected to participate in the sample. Most entrepreneurs, because of cost and time, choose to use what is called a **convenience sample.** This means that not everyone in the defined target market has a chance of being chosen to participate. Instead, the entrepreneur may, for example, choose to select the sample from people who happen to be at a particular shopping mall on a particular day. Clearly, the entrepreneur will not be reaching all possible customers at that mall, but if the target customer typically shops at malls, there's a good chance of achieving at least a representative sample from which results can be derived fairly confidently.

> The credibility of your market research results will be measured by the quality of the sample you select.

Even if a convenience sample is used, there are ways to ensure the randomness of selection of the participants. Using the mall example, the entrepreneur can decide in advance to survey every fifth person who walks by. In this way, the person is not chosen based on their attractiveness or lack of it, or any other reason for that matter. A random number generator on a computer can select names from a telephone book. Whatever system is employed, the key point is to make an effort not to bias the selection.

Often you will hear potential entrepreneurs say they took a sample of friends and relatives who loved the new product idea. Friends and relatives may be able to give you some initial feedback, but they are *not* the best source of unbiased information. Remember, one of the reasons you are doing a feasibility study and, ultimately, a business plan is to convince others about the viability of the new venture concept. The credibility of your market research results will be measured by the quality of the sample you select.

Focus Groups. One more efficient way to gain valuable information before investing substantial capital in production and marketing is to conduct a focus group. The entrepreneur brings together a representative sample of potential customers for a presentation and discussion session. Assuming the new venture involves a consumer product, the entrepreneur may choose to introduce the new product in concert with other products to test the unsolicited response to the product when presented with its competition. For example, suppose your product is a new type of non-alcoholic beverage. You might serve the new beverage along with several competitors' beverages in glasses labeled with numbers, and then solicit feedback on taste, aftertaste, and so on.

Some products and services do not easily lend themselves to blind studies like the one just described. In those instances, the product can simply be presented to the focus group and their opinions and feedback can be solicited. It is important that the person leading the focus group have some knowledge of group dynamics and be able to keep the group on track. Many times these focus group sessions are videotaped so the entrepreneur can spend more time analyzing the nuances of what occurred. Thus, in many ways, focus groups can often prevent the entrepreneur from making the costly error of offering a product or service for which there is little or no interest.

Clinical Studies. Clinical studies are one of the more expensive routes to gathering market data, and, in general, are used by large corporations introducing new products. A clinical study takes place in a controlled setting and is most often used for consumer products. Consumers are asked to visit a test center, which may be set up as a small store. They are given a certain amount of money and asked to choose among a variety of new products available in the test store, which helps the company learn which products are most attractive to customers. In another type of study, consumers may be asked to do blind testing of products such as shampoos or food products to compare tastes and preferences.

Forecasting New Product/Service Demand

One of the most difficult tasks facing the entrepreneur is forecasting the demand for the new product or service, particularly if that product/service has never existed previously in the marketplace. Adding to this difficulty is the fact that most entrepreneurs do their own research because they generally don't have sufficient resources prior to start-up to hire professional market research firms. However, doing your own market research does have the advantage of giving you a clearer sense of your target market and its needs. A number of different techniques can assist you in arriving at a realistic forecast of demand.

Using Historical Analogy or Substitute Products

If the new product is an extension of a previously existing product, it may be possible to extrapolate from that product's demand to yours. For example, the demand for compact discs was derived from the historical demand for cassette tapes and records. In other cases it may be possible to substitute another product in the same industry to give an indication of demand potential, assuming the same target market.

Interview Prospective End-Users and Intermediaries

No one knows the market better than the men and women who work in it every day. They are typically very astute at predicting trends and patterns of buyer behavior. Spending time in the field talking to customers, intermediaries (distributors or wholesalers, sometimes referred to as "middlemen"), retailers, and the like can provide a fairly good estimate of demand.

Go into Limited Production

Sometimes the only way to test the reaction of potential customers is to produce a small number of products and put them in the hands of people to test. This is also an appropriate next step if the first two techniques have produced positive results. Not only will limited testing of the product gauge customer satisfaction, but it may suggest possible modifications to improve the product. These samples of the product are called **prototypes.** Prototypes are generally associated with product companies but, in fact, service businesses must also develop a prototype of the operation or procedures involved in delivering the service. Prototyping permits the testing of a product or service in the actual environment in which it will be used. It is difficult to conduct meaningful market research without a working prototype as most potential customers need to see and use the actual product before they can become enthusiastic about it. Construction of a prototype will also facilitate estimating costs to actually produce the product later on.

Do a Formal Test Market

Where the product is fairly complex and expensive to produce, doing a formal test market in a selected geographic area can provide valuable information on demand and acceptance of the product prior to spending substantial capital for a major product roll-out. The movie industry regularly introduces new movies with a "limited release" in a few strategic theaters. In this way, they can gauge

The WaterBabies Prototype

Daniel Lauer became an entrepreneur by entering one of the most difficult industries of all, the toy industry. At the annual International Toy Fair in New York, about 5,000-6,000 toys are introduced, but fewer than 100 actually survive in this cutthroat market. Daniel Lauer was one of the lucky ones. His first toy, the WaterBabies® doll, sold 2 million copies in 1991. The prototype for the water-filled baby doll consisted of two water-filled balloons for the head and body, and 4 water-filled condoms for the arms and legs. No one was interested at that stage of development. It was not until Lauer had raised the money to make the finished doll, the production quality prototype, run television commercials, and sold the doll in 85 stores that he was able to interest major toy companies. Playmates outbid two other companies for the doll. The WaterBabies® doll is now in her fifth year with over five product extensions and sales of over 4.5 million total units.

the audience's reactions and make changes based on them before releasing the film on a national basis. Major product companies like Procter and Gamble will put a new product into certain geographical test markets like Denver, Colorado to get feedback from customers. Many a new product has met an untimely death as a result of these test market studies.

The Cost/Benefit of Market Research

Market research is undoubtedly one of the more expensive aspects of starting a business, and it is time consuming as well. For these reasons, and because many entrepreneurs don't know how to conduct market research or they believe their product or service is so good that customers will automatically desire it, the market analysis section is probably the least-well-researched and written section of the business plan. Yet good market research answers the question, "Is there a demand for my product or service?" Surely that is the most crucial question an entrepreneur can answer.

Despite the importance of market research, the entrepreneur needs to weigh the cost of doing certain types of market research against the benefits of getting the product/service into the market quickly. In today's dynamic business environment, this is a real concern. Spending too much time on market research can result in losing a window of opportunity for entering the market. Some basic market research techniques can provide excellent information at very little cost and relatively quickly.

- Use focus groups to gauge potential customer reaction.
- Observe buyer behavior at random times in outlets where the product may be offered.
- Use small, representative segments of the target market to test the product/service.
- Examine case studies of similar companies.
- Study census data for demographic information.

Presenting the Market Analysis in the Feasibility Study or Business Plan

As with the industry profile, the data collected during target market research needs to be presented so the reader gets a clear picture of who the targeted customer is and how much the new product/service is desired by that customer. Following the outline in Figure 6.3 will help you organize this section of the feasibility study or business plan.

Figure 6.3: Market Analysis

Target Market
Primary target markets
Secondary markets
Demographics
Customer needs analysis
Product/Service Differentiation
Unique features
Potential for innovation
Competitors
Direct and Indirect
Market share
Strengths and weaknesses
Emerging
Substitute products
Competitive Advantage
Proprietary protection
Other competitive advantages

Preliminary Conclusions as to Feasibility

Once the market study is completed, the entrepreneur is in a good position to answer the question:

Is there sufficient demand for the product or service
the new venture will offer?

If the entrepreneur has personally conducted the research and done all the work to this point, he or she will not only have important information to help make the decision but will also have an intuitive or "gut feeling" as to whether the new venture concept is viable or not. If market indicators are positive, it is time to consider other aspects of feasibility and proceed to test the business concept further.

On the other hand, many entrepreneurs will find it difficult to abandon an idea with which they have "fallen in love," even in the face of market data indicating demand for the new product/service is weak. When this happens, it is important to remember that without customers there is no business. It is far better to abandon a business concept at this point than to venture ahead to the more costly aspects of a business start-up and ultimately fail.

☑ New Venture Checklist

Have you:

☐ Defined the target market for your product or service?

☐ Identified direct, indirect, and emerging competitors?

☐ Described your product or service's competitive advantage?

☐ Listed the information you need to gather to do the market analysis?

☐ Researched secondary data sources such as census data on demographics?

☐ Determined the most effective method for gathering primary data on your target market?

☐ Estimated demand for the product or service?

☐ Organized, analyzed, and presented the data to answer the key question: Is there sufficient demand for the product or service?

Additional Sources of Information

Andreason, A.R. (1988). *Cheap But Good Marketing Research.* Burr Ridge, IL: Irwin.

Breen G. & Blankenship A.B. (1989). *Do-It-Yourself Marketing Research.* New York: McGraw-Hill, Inc.

Crispell, Diane. (1990). *The Insider's Guide to Demographic Know-How.* Chicago: Probus.

Findex: The Directory of Market Research Reports, Studies and Surveys. (1990). Gaithersburg, MD: Cambridge Information Group Directories.

Levinson J.C. (1984). *Guerrilla Marketing.* Boston: Houghton Mifflin.

Issues to Consider

1. What is the value of defining a market niche?
2. Why is it important to do secondary market research before primary market research?
3. What advantages do interviews have over other data collection methods?
4. Suppose you want to determine the demand for your new product, a new type of fast food dessert. What methods would you use to forecast demand?
5. Market research can be an expensive, time-consuming process. What can you do to minimize the costs while still achieving your goals?

CHAPTER 7

Distribution Channels: Getting the Product or Service to the Customer

Overview

- *Consumer versus industrial distribution channels*
- *The role of the distributor in the marketing of a product*
- *The role of manufacturers' reps*
- *Adding value through distribution channels*
- *Distribution channel information in the feasibility study and business plan*

Choosing a Distribution Channel

With a target market well defined and sufficient demand estimated to exist, the entrepreneur faces the important task of deciding how to get the product or service to the customer. A **distribution channel** is, quite simply, the route a product takes from the manufacturer to the customer or end-user. Depending on the type of new venture, there are many choices available. Each choice will have distinct advantages, disadvantages, and consequences, and will to some extent dictate the kind of organization the new venture becomes.

Recall the business concept of the computer program that will revolutionize the way manufacturers control inventory in Chapter 3. Each of the different methods of getting the product to the customer involves the development of a different type of business: retail, mail order, licensing, and so forth. Furthermore, the channel of distribution determines to some extent your product's cost, the potential for loss or damage through transit, and how quickly the product reaches the customer. Finding the most efficient and effective channel can provide a new venture with a distinct competitive advantage.

There are two types of distribution channels: direct and indirect. In a direct channel of distribution, the product or service moves from the manufacturer or producer directly to the customer. Service businesses generally operate in this fashion. For example, when you call a plumber to fix a pipe or call your accountant to do your taxes, the work is handled directly by the company you called with no one else involved. Selling through mail order is another way of using a direct channel. When manufacturers sell to the customer through one of their manufacturer's outlets, they are also using a direct channel.

An indirect channel of distribution involves one or more intermediaries, people who move products from the manufacturer or producer to the end user. They include wholesalers, retailers, distributors, and agents. For example, suppose you are producing paper products such as cups and plates, etc. When the product leaves the production facility, it may go to a wholesaler who will then secure retailers. The retailer's job is to advertise and find customers who will buy the product. Depending on the kind of business the entrepreneur plans to start, he or she will be dealing either with consumer channels or industrial channels of distribution.

Consumer Channels of Distribution

Consumer market channels are used by businesses that sell to people who purchase consumer goods at the wholesale or retail level. There are several routes by which manufacturers can reach their target customers. (See Figure 7.1.)

Figure 7.1: Channels of Distribution

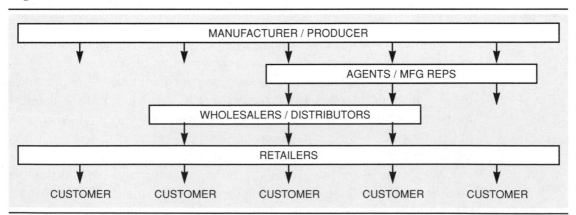

Direct Selling

The most direct channel in the consumer market is to sell to the customer using no intermediaries. As discussed earlier, service businesses usually fall into this category. However, in the past few years a number of manufacturers have also begun bypassing intermediaries and selling directly to their customers. Clothing, household, and furniture manufacturers, to name a few, have opened "outlets" in special factory outlet malls located away from major metropolitan areas. Generally manufacturers sell direct after they have an established following through their normal channels so name recognition is present and little marketing effort is necessary. The outlets are a good way to get rid of excess inventory and slightly defective merchandise that can't be sold in their normal retail outlets. The substantial discounts attract customers from considerable distances.

Retailers

The most common way for manufacturers to get their products to customers is through retail stores, which are responsible for sales and advertising of the product. Using this channel, the manufacturer does not have to incur the expense of maintaining a sales staff or stores. However, without a distributor, the manufacturer needs manufacturer's reps or in-house sales people to locate potential retail customers and arrange for distribution of the product.

Wholesalers/Distributors

Wholesalers or distributors (the terms are interchangeable in common usage) buy products in bulk from manufacturers and then seek retail outlets to reach the consumer. The wholesaler removes from the manufacturer the responsibility of finding suitable retail outlets for the products. A distributor can mean the difference between success and failure for a business. When you realize you are entrusting your most valuable assets—your customers—to the distributor, it becomes clear that selecting a distributor is a crucial part of the start-up process. Not only will good distributors contribute to increased sales, but they will help with product planning for the future. The specifics of what a distributor may do depend on the distributor. Some of the tasks performed by them are:

- Warehousing products
- Advertising and promotion

- Packaging and displays
- Training retail sales personnel
- Assisting with transportation to retailers
- Providing service back-up
- Restocking retailers' shelves

The key to finding a good distributor is knowing whom to ask. Some of the sources of information on distributors are:

- Customers
- Suppliers
- Lawyers
- Business consultants
- Bankers (they have knowledge of a distributor's payment record)

Look for a distributor who provides good service, prices competitively to retail outlets, and is trustworthy. When that distributor is chosen, execute a written contract with the distributor and monitor performance on a regular basis by sampling retail customers to determine if they are satisfied with the product and the service they are receiving from the distributor.

Logistics Firms

It takes a long time before a new venture can justify having its own distribution center. Consequently many growing companies are outsourcing their packaging, warehousing, inventory control, and trucking requirements to third-party logistics firms. In distribution terminology, logistics is the timely movement of goods from the producer to the consumer. In addition to other services, logistics firms can negotiate the best deals and the most efficient carriers, potentially saving the growing venture thousands of dollars.

Agents/Manufacturers' Reps

Often manufacturers/producers retain agents, brokers, or manufacturers' reps to find suitable outlets for their products. These agents arrange agreements with wholesalers and retailers for the manufacturer. Agents usually do not buy or hold an inventory of goods from the manufacturer; instead, they bring together manufacturers and distributors or retailers to establish the most efficient distriution channel. The manufacturer or producer shares the cost with other manufacturers represented by the agent and pays a commission only on what the agent sells.

Manufacturers' representatives are essentially independent salespeople who handle the manufacturer's business in specific territories and are paid on commission. Unlike agents who bring buyers and sellers together for individual transactions, manufacturers' reps work with a specific manufacturer on a continuing basis, receiving a commission per product sold. Reps may also provide warehousing in a territory and handle shipping the product to the retailer.

Industrial Channels of Distribution

Industrial markets consist of customers who purchase goods for use in their businesses. In these markets the manufacturer is targeting another business, perhaps even another manufacturer, for the sale of its products. The options for industrial markets are similar to those in the consumer market. The manufacturer can choose to sell directly to the industrial user using no intermediaries or can use distributors or manufacturers' reps, who market to end-users. Another alternative is to work with agents, who act as a sales force for the manufacturer and either go through a distributor or directly to the industrial user. (See Figure 7.2.)

Figure 7.2: Industrial Channels of Distribution

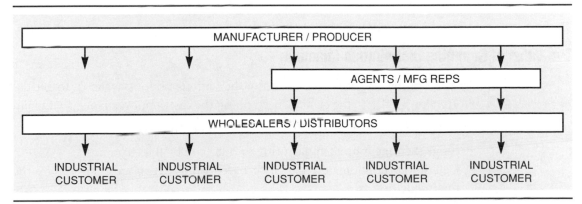

PROFILE 7.1

CALYX & COROLLA
Innovation in Distribution

Jumping from a catalog called "Gardener's Eden," which sold specialty gardening tools, to a fresh flower catalog does not seem like a tremendous feat, but for Ruth Owades it was a true leap of faith. Her goal in starting Calyx & Corolla was to give customers the ability to see the fresh flowers they were buying in the catalog one day and receive them the next. How was this idea different from sending flowers through FTD?

Most flowers are cut (often in South America), shipped to a wholesaler (equivalent to a manufacturer/producer), then to a distributor and finally to a retailer. Before they reach the customer, the flowers are six to ten days old. Owades wanted to streamline this complicated distribution system to get the flowers to the customer more quickly.

To accomplish her dream, Owades had to convince growers to be in the gift business and send smaller quantities than usual. She also had to find an overnight shipper who was used to dealing with perishable items, and a way of shipping the flowers undamaged. Federal Express agreed to work with her on the project.

Ruth Owades ultimately succeeded by making the people in her distribution channel part of her start-up team, having them give input during each phase of the start-up process. The alliances were formed to be mutually beneficial to all parties, and as a result, Calyx & Corolla completed the start-up phase of the business more quickly than most new companies.

The Value of Graphing Distribution Channels

Apart from the obvious value of seeing the various options available to get the product or service to the customer, graphing the distribution channels will help the entrepreneur do the following:

- Judge the time from manufacturing to purchase by the customer
- Determine the ultimate retail price based on the required markups by the intermediaries
- Figure the total costs of marketing the product

All these factors are a function of the distribution channel chosen. Suppose you are manufacturing a consumer product in the sporting goods industry. Here is how you might compare the distribution options available to you. The most common route to the consumer is:

Manufacturer → *Wholesaler* → *Retailer* → *Consumer*

At each stage the channel member adds value to the product by performing a service that increases the chances the product will reach its intended customer (see Figure 7.3). The wholesaler seeks appropriate retail outlets, and the retailer advertises and promotes the product to its customers. This value created allows each channel member to increase the price of the product to the next channel member. For example, the manufacturer charges the wholesaler a price that covers the costs of producing the product plus an amount for overhead and profit. The wholesaler, in turn, adds an amount to cover the cost of the goods

Figure 7.3: The Value Chain

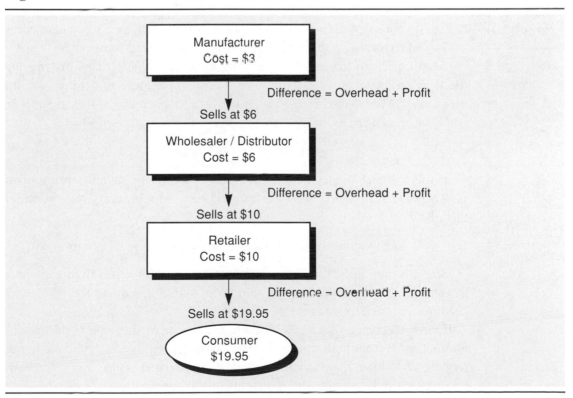

purchased and his or her overhead and profit. The retailer does the same and charges the final price to the customer. That price can typically be 4-5 times what it cost to manufacture the product (labor and materials).

Suppose you decide to bypass the wholesaler and sell directly to retailers:

Manufacturer → Retailer

It appears on the surface that the final retail price could be substantially lower, perhaps even priced at the rate the wholesaler sold to the retailer in the first example. However, there is a flaw in this reasoning. The wholesaler performed a valuable service. He or she made it possible for the manufacturer to focus on producing the product and not incur the cost of maintaining a larger marketing department, a sales force, additional warehouses, and a more complex shipping department. All these activities now become a cost to the manufacturer of doing business with retailers and must be factored into the decision to choose this distribution channel. This is not to say it never makes sense for manufacturers to sell direct to retailers. However, it is important for the entrepreneur to consider all the costs, advantages, disadvantages, and consequences of choosing a particular market channel to reach the customer.

> *It is important for the entrepreneur to consider all the costs, advantages, disadvantages, and consequences of choosing a particular market channel to reach the customer.*

Other aspects of starting the new venture can also be examined by studying the distribution channel options. For example, location and transportation decisions will be affected by the method chosen to reach the customer. Suppose you have chosen the following channel:

Manufacturer → Retailer

In this instance it may be advantageous to locate the manufacturing plant near major transportation networks to hold down shipping costs. Now consider the following channel:

Manufacturer → Wholesaler → Retailer → Consumer

Here it is not important for the manufacturer to be located conveniently near the retailer. Having a location that minimizes shipping costs to the wholesaler becomes a more relevant issue.

If the entrepreneur is a retailer (or wholesaler), he or she looks at the distribution channel from both directions. The customer will be reached directly but looking back down the distribution channel, the retailer is also concerned with finding a good distributor who represents quality manufacturers.

Presenting the Distribution Channel Information in the Feasibility Study or Business Plan

Upon completing the market analysis, you can make a preliminary determination of the feasibility of the business concept, at least to the extent of whether there is sufficient demand for the new product or service. If sufficient demand appears to exist, you can proceed to gather and analyze the information needed to complete a full business plan, which will show whether the business concept makes sense from a financial and operations perspective. Describing the distribution channels for the new product/service is the first step in gathering that information. (See Figure 7.4.)

As the business plan outline indicates (Figure 2.3, p. 38), the distribution channel section is a relatively small, albeit critical, section of the plan. It is eminently important the entrepreneur seek out the most efficient and effective means to reach the customer. For service businesses such as consulting or financial services, the issue of the distribution channel is quite simple. The entrepreneur normally sells those services directly to the customer. Where the entrepreneur is a manufacturer/producer who sells to a distributor, he or she needs to be concerned about how the product will reach the customer and at what price, because, ultimately, the end-user determines the entrepreneur's success as a manufacturer.

The information on the distribution channel is normally placed in the operations section of the business plan where the details of logistics and distribution partnerships can be addressed. However, a general statement of the channel of distribution to be used by the business should also be placed in the Product/Service Plan as part of the description of the business. The issue of distribution channels is revisited in Chapter 12, which discusses the marketing plan.

Figure 7.4: Channels of Distribution

Define the Channel of Distribution
  Channel Members
  Comparison to Industry Norms
  Justification for the Channel
Future Distribution Channels

✓ **New Venture Checklist**

Have you:

☐ Decided if your new venture will operate in a consumer or industrial distribution channel?

☐ Determined the most effective channel of distribution to get your product or service to the customer?

☐ Planned how you will get information on the members of your distribution channel so you can choose the best people to serve your business?

☐ Figured the costs associated with the distribution channel you have chosen?

☐ Determined the length of time it will take to get your product to the customer?

☐ Organized the distribution channel section of the business plan?

Additional Sources of Information

American Logistics Management Association, 2000 Santa Cruz St., Anaheim, CA 92805. 714-937-8970; FAX 714-937-0402.

Davidson, J.P. (1989). *Marketing Sourcebook for Small Business.* New York: John Wylie Publishing.

Davidson, J.P. (1991). *Selling to the Giants.* Blue Ridge Summit, PA: Liberty Hall.

Inbound Logistics Magazine. 5 Penn Plaza, Eighth Floor, NY 10001.

Levinson, J.C. (1989). *Guerilla Marketing Attack: New Strategies, Tactics and Weapons for Winning Big Profits for Your Small Business.* Boston: Houghton-Mifflin.

Lele, M. M. (1988). *The Customer is Key.* New York: John Wiley and Sons.

North American Logistics Association, 1300 W. Higgins Road, Suite 111, Park Ridge, IL 60068. 708-292-1891; Fax 708-292-1896.

Transportation and Distribution Magazine. 100 Superior Ave., Cleveland, OH 44114. 216-696-7000; Fax 216-696-4135.

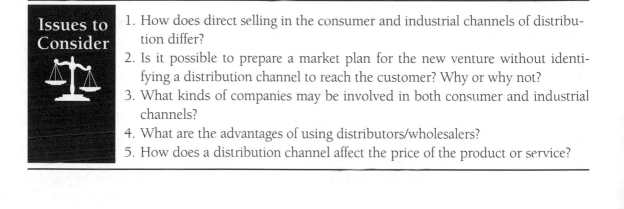

Issues to Consider

1. How does direct selling in the consumer and industrial channels of distribution differ?
2. Is it possible to prepare a market plan for the new venture without identifying a distribution channel to reach the customer? Why or why not?
3. What kinds of companies may be involved in both consumer and industrial channels?
4. What are the advantages of using distributors/wholesalers?
5. How does a distribution channel affect the price of the product or service?

2 GENTECH CORPORATION

In 1988, John Allen was doing commercial real estate development in the San Joaquin Valley in California. Allen had a group of subcontractors whom he regularly hired to do various construction tasks. One of these subcontractors was a man named Bill Nelson, a finish carpenter with a penchant for tinkering and inventing things. Through prior conversation, Nelson had learned that Allen had advanced degrees in engineering and had been previously employed as an engineer by an aerospace firm. Nelson had invented a portable machine to provide a single source of power for electric and pneumatic tools. On the job, Nelson had seen the need for such a product but felt that he didn't have the skills to commercialize the product. Consequently, Nelson approached Allen with his invention to explore the possibility of retaining Allen for technical and financial advice and support. He believed that Allen's unique knowledge of engineering, finance, and construction would result in a good match for his invention.

The original invention was a generator and compressor sitting on twin four-gallon air tanks, and coupled to a small gasoline-drive engine. The concept was quite simple: when the user started a power tool, a signal was sent to the compressor head to open a valve and vent the compressor to the atmosphere, thus reducing the demand on the drive motor and allowing full power to go to the generator. This feature allowed the unit to be powered by a smaller, less costly, lighter-drive motor. Prior attempts by other manufacturers to make a combined unit resulted in heavy, bulky, and expensive products. Nelson felt he had discovered the answer to this with his invention and had applied for a patent to protect his idea.

Allen was intrigued by the concept but lukewarm on getting involved. As a favor to Nelson, Allen made several inquiries to engineering and business associates but received very little encouragement for Nelson's invention. The topic was dropped.

In 1989, Nelson came back to Allen and claimed that he had invented an improvement to his original machine that would make it much more marketable, unique, and innovative than his first attempt; however, he couldn't divulge his new invention until he had completed the prototype and had a non-disclosure statement signed by Allen. He then asked Allen for financial assistance in patenting and developing this new invention without disclosing what the invention was. Allen was naturally hesitant; however, he agreed to consider getting involved after a demonstration of the working prototype.

Several months later, Nelson called Allen to ask if he could come over to demonstrate his new invention. Nelson showed up in a dilapidated old Toyota pick-up with the machine in the back, along with several other tools, electrical cords, air hoses, and general clutter. The invention matched the general appearance of the vehicle and its cargo. It looked like it was put together in a blacksmith's shop from spare parts. Nelson removed the unit from his truck and plugged an electrical cord into one of the household receptacles attached to a piece of wood, which was attached to his machine. The other end was plugged into a power tool. He proceeded to walk away from the unit with the power tool in his hand. At approximately 100 feet from the unit he pulled the trigger of the power tool and the drive motor of the unit started up, and then the power tool started working instantaneously. When he lay the tool down, the motor stopped. He repeated this process several times. Needless to say, Allen was impressed. Nelson had a modified air starter (small air drill) coupled to the drive motor that would start the motor with a signal sent from the power tool. He was using compressed air in the tanks (storage from the compressor) as a "battery" for the air starter. It was ingenious. Allen agreed to get involved and assist in the financial needs to file the patent and construct an engineered, functional prototype. About this time, Allen formed *Gentech Corporation* to manufacture, sell, and distribute the product. Through five years of engineering and prototype building, the invention was improved to incorporate a solid state, programmable controller which, with its additional features, has made the functions of the machine more efficient and intelligent.

> It looked like it was put together in a blacksmith's shop from spare parts.

The Corporation

Gentech Corporation, a privately held California corporation, was established to manufacture and distribute portable power equipment incorporating patented, state-of-the-art technology and satisfying a need for efficient, energy-saving, and environmentally friendly power equipment. *PowerSource,* the first product to be offered by *Gentech Corporation,* is a combination air compressor and generator unit mounted on a typical twin-tank, wheelbarrow-style frame. Driven by a single gasoline engine, the dual purpose *PowerSource* provides both AC electric power and air power from one portable, lightweight unit. When operating as a generator, it supplies electrical power to 110-volt outlets. When an electrical tool is in use, an electronic switching unit automatically sends a signal to open a valve to vent the compressor piston to the atmosphere, thus significantly reducing the demand on the engine. As long as there is air stored in the tanks, air tools and power tools can be used simultaneously. A powerful AC generator and a high output air compressor, the *PowerSource* eliminates the need to transport both a generator and compressor to the work site.

The benefits to the user are that *PowerSource:*

- Substantially reduces operating costs, using the power of one engine to provide the output of two in a single, portable unit
- Significantly reduces fuel consumption, pollution, and costly maintenance repairs with its on demand start/stop system
- Reduces the normal nuisance level of noise associated with gasoline engine-powered generators and compressors that must run continuously

Improvements were accomplished through the use of programmable solid-state electronics with a central control system containing the unique features and functions of the invention on a 3 x 7 printed circuit board. The control board is lightweight, relatively inexpensive, durable, and reliable. It is also easily adapted and incorporated into other machinery benefiting from its functions. Patents for the switching unit (utility patent) and the configuration of the combined unit (a design patent) were issued, while patents for a demand/sensor, start/stop feature, timer delay mechanism, and idle down feature are patent pending.

Allen negotiated with the inventor for a world-wide exclusive license to manufacture, distribute, and sell the patented control system as a free-standing "black box" for use on existing machines. A worldwide non-exclusive license was granted to manufacture, distribute, and sell the combination unit incorporating the patented control system. A royalty based on wholesale selling price will be paid to Nelson.

The company intends to develop several different configurations and sizes of the *PowerSource* so that it can be used in a variety of industries.

The Management Team

John Allen has a broad spectrum of education and experience in engineering and business. With bachelors degrees in aerospace and industrial engineering and master degrees in operations research and business administration, Allen was an engineer for McDonnell-Douglas Astronautics. In the late 1970s, he left engineering to start a successful company specializing in real estate development and investments. To date, he has managed matters pertaining to the engineering, development, patenting, and licensing of *PowerSource* for *Gentech Corporation*.

Kathleen R. Allen, Ph.D. is an assistant professor in the Entrepreneur Program of the University of Southern California and published author in the field of entrepreneurship. She brings to *Gentech Corporation* ten years of business experience including the cofounding of two businesses. She also consults to growing businesses on project feasibility, business planning, and market strategy. She is responsible for the development of the business plan, marketing strategy, and creating the infrastructure for the organization of *Gentech Corporation*.

Michael D. Ream brings 20 years of experience in mechanical engineering, marketing, sales management, and manufacturing to Gentech. He has successfully developed and launched new products into U.S. and international construction rental markets. He has extensive experience with JIT manufacturing and Quality Function Deployment as well as P & L responsibility. He is presently a vice president and officer of a leading international manufacturer of serial work platforms.

Industry Profile

Gentech Corporation and its product *PowerSource* will operate in the motors and generators (SIC 3621) and air and gas compressors (SIC 3563) industries, which are mature industries with many companies. The industries and leading 75 companies in each industry in the United States are summarized as follows:

	Motors & Generators	Air & Gas Compressors
Number of establishments in total industry	467	241
Total sales in leading 75 companies ($ million)	80,554	4,370
Total employment	72,600	24,500
Proportion of total industry in GENTECH's target market	5.2%	8%

The motors and generators industry in the United States is dominated by General Electric (GE), which does over $59 billion in annual sales as compared to its closest competitor, Emerson Electric Co, which does over $7.5 billion. By comparison, more than half of the leading 75 companies do under $100 million in annual sales. It should be noted that most of GE's motors go into their own products, such as household appliances.

The air compressor industry is comprised of much smaller companies. The largest producer is Thomas Industries Inc., with annual sales of $462 million. Three-quarters of the 75 leading American companies have sales under $100 million.

Several manufacturers of either gas or electric air compressors and gas generators produce individual generator and compressor units for the market under consideration by *Gentech Corporation.* Thomas, Emglo, Ingersol-Rand, Rol-Air, and Campbell-Hausfeld are strong in air compressors, while Honda, General Electric, Generac, Kohler, and Winco are their counterparts in generators. Rol-Air and Emglo were the only companies found to produce a combined unit; however, their units weigh in excess of 600 pounds and cost over $2,400. Also, the air compressor and generator functions cannot be used simultaneously, but must be manually switched at the machine. Therefore, as far as could be determined through a preliminary search, there is no comparable product on the market today providing all the functions and features of this unit. Utilizing the patent rights protection and an aggressive market strategy, this situation has a high probability of continuing into the foreseeable future.

Gentech Corporation is targeting a niche market and incorporating new technology with proprietary rights.

The number of new motor and generator companies increased at an annual rate of about three percent per year for the past two years. Employment declined by six percent between 1989 and 1990; similarly the value of shipments declined by six percent during the same period.

The number of air compressor companies has been declining at about three percent per year; however employment was up three percent between 1989 and 1990, and the value of shipments increased nine percent during the same period.

Both industries are mature, fairly stable, with little room for substantial growth using the current technology. For this reason *Gentech Corporation* is targeting a niche market and incorporating new technology with proprietary rights that can also be used on existing motors, generators, and compressors. The industry in general has experienced little or no significant technological or innovative advancements for several years. The use of a patented, solid state, programmable control system to enhance the efficiency and function of the power plant is unique and will result in a competitive advantage during the market entry and roll-out program.

Target Market

Initially the target market is the niche market of the small building contractor or subcontractor. During the first year of operation, the marketing effort will be limited territorially to California and the western states, with the initial entry through construction equipment rental outlets. There are over 12,000 equipment rental outlets nationally and over 2,000 in California alone. Equipment rental outlets typically replace their equipment annually, selling the used equipment. This practice allows *Gentech Corporation* the ability to generate clients who will have a need to purchase *PowerSource* on a regular basis. Using a preproduction quality prototype, demonstrations to potential distributors, end-users, and investors were conducted. The response indicated that there is a need for this product, and the special features make it competitive with existing single purpose units. The consensus has been that this niche market product could have a significant customer base; those participating in the demonstrations were extremely enthusiastic about the product potential. Based on these findings *Gentech Corporation* is conservatively estimating demand at 1,800 units in the first year, 3,600 in the second year in the western United States.

As the market and product mix are expanded, additional users will be identified and targeted. Other classes of users may include farmer, mechanics, commercial fishermen, domestic do-it-yourselfers, the military, utility companies, and federal, state, and local government services and agencies.

Assembly and Distribution

During the early stages in the development of the business *Gentech Corporation* does not intend to manufacture any parts but will subcontract to specialty manufacturers for parts that cannot be purchased "off the shelf" from suppliers. Initially, the product will be assembled in California, but discussions are under way with a compressor manufacturer/distributor on the east coast with the potential for either subcontracting with the east coast company or merging the two companies and producing the product on the east coast. One advantage to this strategy is that the bulk of *Gentech Corporation's* suppliers are located east of the Mississippi River, which would cut transportation costs and delivery time significantly.

The initial distribution strategy will be direct shipment to equipment rental outlets and the use of manufacturer's reps to contact wholesale distributors. After the start-up phase is successfully completed, other distribution channels will be examined.

- Direct shipment to customers from the plant
- Contracting with existing wholesale distributors
- Setting up factory-owned regional wholesale distribution outlets with some direct sales to customers
- Exporting the product

At this time, the founding team is not certain what the post start-up strategy should be.

1. What is the competitive advantage that *Gentech Corporation* has?
2. What are *Gentech Corporation's* options for types of businesses to start?
3. How would you evaluate the management team for start-up?
4. Given the information in the case, should *Gentech Corporation* move to the next level of evaluation? Why or why not?

PART 3

The New Venture and the Law

If laws could speak for themselves, they would first complain of the lawyers who wrote them.

—LORD HALIFAX

CHAPTER 8

The Legal Structure
of the Business

Overview

- *The legal structure options for new ventures*
- *The pros and cons of incorporating*
- *The requirements, advantages, and disadvantages of a sub-chapter S election*
- *Forming a 501(c)(3) non-profit corporation*

The Legal Structure of the New Venture

All businesses operate under one of several legal structures—sole proprietorship, partnership, or corporation—with variations on each. The legal structure of a new venture has both legal and tax ramifications for the entrepreneur and any investors; consequently the entrepreneur must carefully consider the advantages and disadvantages of each form. It is also quite possible a business might change its legal form sometime during its lifetime, usually for financial, tax, or liability reasons. These situations will be discussed as each legal form is considered.

Before examining the various legal forms, consider the following questions, as they affect your ability to select certain legal structures:

1. Do you have all the skills needed to run this venture?
2. Do you have the capital required to start the business alone or can you raise it through cash or credit?
3. Will you be able to run the business and cover your living expenses for the first year?

135

4. Are you willing and able to assume personal liability for any claims against your business?
5. Do you wish to have complete control over the operation of the business?

If you answer "yes" to all these questions, you may be able to use the sole proprietor form of organization for the new venture.

Typically, issues arise when setting up your company. Figure 8.1 compares the various legal forms of ownership.

Figure 8.1: Comparative Legal Structures

Issues	Sole Proprietorship	Partnership	C-Corporation
Number of Owners	One	No limit	No limit on shareholders
Start-Up Costs	Filing fees for DBA and business license	Filing fees for DBA. Attorney fees for partnership agreement	Attorney fees for incorporation documents, filing fees
Liability	Owner liable for all claims against business	General partners liable for all claims. Limited only to amount of investment	Shareholders liable to amount invested. Officers may be personally liable
Life of Business	Dissolution on the death of the owner	Dissolution on the death or separation of a partner unless otherwise specified in the agreement. Not so in the case of limiteds	No effect
Transfer of Interest	Owner free to sell	General partner requires consent of other generals to sell interest. Limiteds' ability subject to agreement	Shareholders free to sell unless restricted by agreement
Distribution of Profits	Profits go to owner	Profits shared based on partnership agreement	Paid to shareholders as dividends according to agreement and shareholder status
Management Control	Owner has full control	Shared by general partners according to partnership agreement	Rests with the board of directors who are appointed by the shareholders

Sole Proprietorship

Nearly 76 percent of all businesses in the United States are sole proprietorships, most probably because it is the easiest form to create. In a **sole proprietorship,** the owner is the only person responsible for the activities of the business. Likewise, the owner is the only one to enjoy the profits and suffer the losses.

To operate as a sole proprietor requires nothing more than a DBA if the entrepreneur does not use his or her name as the name for the business. A DBA is a "Certificate of Doing Business Under An Assumed Name" and can be obtained by filing an application with the appropriate local government agency. The certificate, sometimes referred to as a "fictitious business name statement," ensures that yours is the only business in the area (usually a county) using the name you have chosen and provides a public record of business ownership for liability purposes. For example, *Anthony Jackson and Associates* does not require a DBA if the entrepreneur's name is Anthony Jackson, but *Corporate Consultants* does.

Sole proprietorships have several advantages.

- They are easy and inexpensive to create.
- They give the owner complete authority.
- The income from the business is taxed only once at the owner's personal income tax rate.

There are, however, some disadvantages that deserve serious consideration.

- The sole proprietor has unlimited liability for all claims against the business; that is, any debts incurred must be paid from the owner's assets. Therefore, the sole proprietor puts at risk his or her home, bank accounts, and any other assets. In the current litigious environment, exposure to lawsuits is substantial. To help mitigate this liability, a sole proprietor should obtain business liability insurance, including errors and omissions coverage.
- It is more difficult to raise debt capital because the owner's financial statement alone often may not qualify for the amount needed.
- The sole proprietor usually relies on his or her skills alone to manage the business. Of course, employees with specific skills can be hired to complement the skills of the owner.
- The business's ability to survive is dependent on the owner and, therefore, the death or incapacitation of the owner can be catastrophic for the business.

Often small businesses such as shoe repair shops and boutiques are run as sole proprietorships. This is not to say that a high-growth venture cannot be started as a sole proprietorship; it just will in all likelihood not remain a sole proprietorship for long as the entrepreneur will typically want the protections and prestige a corporation afford.

Partnership

When two or more people share the assets, liabilities, and profits of a business, the legal structure is termed a **partnership.** The partnership form is an improvement over the sole proprietorship from the standpoint that the business can draw on the skills, knowledge, and financial resources of more than one person. Like the sole proprietorship, however, the partnership requires a DBA when the last names of the partners are not used in naming the business. Professionals like lawyers, doctors, and accountants frequently employ this legal structure.

A partnership is essentially a sole proprietorship involving more than one person in terms of its advantages and its treatment of income, expenses, and taxes. However, where liability is concerned, there is a significant difference. In a partnership, each partner is liable for the obligations another partner incurs in the course of doing business. For example, if one partner signs a contract with a supplier in the name of the partnership, the other partners are also bound by the terms of the contract. However, creditors of an individual partner can only attach the assets of that individual partner, including their interest in the partnership.

Partners also have specific property rights. For example, each partner owns and has use of the property acquired by the partnership unless otherwise stated in the Partnership Agreement. Each partner has a right to share in the profits and losses, and each may participate in the management of the partnership. Furthermore, all elections such as depreciation and accounting methods are made at the partnership level and apply to all partners.

Though the law does not require it, it is wise for a partnership to draw up a written partnership agreement, based on the Uniform Partnership Act, that spells out business responsibilities, profit sharing, and transfer of interest. This is because partnerships are inherently fraught with problems that arise from the different personalities and goals of the people involved. A written document executed at the beginning of the partnership will reduce the eventual disagreements and provide for an orderly dissolution should irreconcilable differences arise. Partnerships are burdened by the same disadvantages as sole proprietorships with the additional encumbrance of personal conflicts, usually over power and authority, that can result in the dissolution of the partnership. Many partnerships have solved much of this problem by assigning specific responsibilities to each of the partners.

There are two types of partnerships: general and limited. In a general partnership, all the partners assume unlimited personal liability and responsibility for the management of the business. In a limited partnership, by contrast, the general partners seek investors whose liability is limited to their monetary investment; that is, if a limited partner invests $25,000 in the business, the most he or she can lose if the business fails is $25,000. It is important to note, however, that limited partners have no say in the management of the business. In fact, they are restricted by law from imposing their will on the business. The penalty for participating in the management of the business is the loss of their limited liability status.

Corporation

A **corporation** is different from the preceding two forms in that it is a legal entity in and of itself. The U.S. Supreme Court has defined the corporation as "an artificial being, invisible, intangible, and existing only in contemplation of the law." It is chartered or registered by a state and can survive the death or separation of the owner(s) from the business. The owners of the corporation are its stockholders who invest capital in the corporation in exchange for shares of ownership. Like limited partners, stockholders are not liable for the debts of the corporation and can only lose the money they have invested.

Most businesses form what is known as a **closely held corporation;** that is, the corporate stock is owned privately by a few individuals and is not traded publicly on a securities exchange such as the New York Stock Exchange. This chapter will focus on private corporations. The issue of "going public" typically arises after the business is established and desires to raise substantial capital for growth by issuing stock through an initial public offering (IPO). The IPO and public corporations in general are the subject of Chapter 17.

A corporation is created by filing a Certificate of Incorporation with the state in which the company will do business and issue stock. It also requires the establishment of a board of directors, which meets periodically to make strategic policy decisions for the business. The regular documentation of these meetings is crucial to maintaining the corporation's limited liability status. The board also hires the officers who will run the business on a day-to-day basis.

The C-corporate form (a variation of this most common form, the S-corp., will be discussed later) has several important advantages.

- It enjoys limited liability in that its owners are liable for its debts and obligations only to the limit of their investment. The only exception to this protection is payroll taxes that may have been withheld from employees' paychecks but not paid to the Internal Revenue Service.

- Capital can be raised through the sale of stock up to the amount authorized in the corporate charter; however, the sale of stock is heavily regulated by federal and state governments. A corporation can create different classes of stock to meet the various needs of its investors. For example, it may issue non-voting preferred stock to conservative investors who, in the event the corporation must liquidate its assets, will be first in line to recoup their investment. Common stock is more risky because holders of it are paid only after the preferred stockholders. Common stockholders are entitled to vote at stockholders' meetings and divide the profits remaining after the preferred holders are paid their dividends, assuming these profits are not retained by the corporation to fund growth.

> *A corporation can create different classes of stock to meet the various needs of its investors.*

- Ownership is easily transferred. This is at once an advantage and a disadvantage as the entrepreneur will want to be careful, particularly in the start-up phase, that stock does not land in the hands of undesirable parties such as competitors. This problem is normally handled through a buy-sell clause in the stockholders' agreement that states that stock must first be offered to the corporation at a specified price before being offered to someone outside the corporation.

- The corporation can enter into contracts, sue, and be sued without the signature of the owners. In a start-up or young company, bankers, creditors, and such will likely require that majority stockholders or officers personally guarantee loans. This is because often a new corporation will be wholly owned by the entrepreneur; that is, the entrepreneur or the founding team holds all the issued stock. As the company does not have a track record and is in a high-risk phase of development, creditors protect themselves against the potential failure of the corporation by requiring the signatures, thus giving them the ability to pursue the assets of the owners.

- Corporations often enjoy more status and deference than do other legal forms, principally because they are a legal entity that cannot be destroyed by the death of one or all of the principal shareholders. Moreover, to enter the public equity markets, a business must be incorporated. Also, the perception is that corporations probably keep better records than other forms of ownership because they tend to be under greater scrutiny from governmental agencies. The reason for this scrutiny is the fact that the assets of the corporation are separate from the assets of the individual owner/shareholders.

- Corporations can take advantage of the benefits of retirements funds, Keogh and defined-contribution plans, profit-sharing, and stock option plans. These fringe benefits are deductible to the corporation as an expense and not taxable to the employee.
- The entrepreneur can hold certain assets such as real estate in his or her own name and lease the use of the assets to the corporation.

Corporations do, however, have disadvantages that must be carefully considered. They are certainly more complex, subject to more governmental regulation, and cost more to create. While it is possible to incorporate without the aid of an attorney, it is not recommended. Too many cases can be cited of businesses that ultimately failed or endured significant financial hardship because they did not incorporate properly at the start of the business.

A more cumbersome disadvantage derives from the fact that the corporation is literally a person for tax purposes. Consequently, if it makes a profit, it must pay a tax whether or not those profits were distributed as dividends to the stockholders. And unlike the partnership or sole proprietorship, stockholders of C-corporations do not receive the benefit of losses (in the next section a corporation form that does enjoy these benefits will be discussed). In a C-corporation those losses, if they can't be applied in the year they were incurred, must be saved to be applied against future profits. Accordingly, C-corporations pay taxes on the profits they earn and their owners (stockholders) pay taxes on the dividends they receive, hence, the drawback of "double taxation." It is principally for this reason that many entrepreneurs who operate alone or with a partner do not employ this form. However, if the entrepreneur draws a salary from the corporation, that salary is expensed by the corporation, effectively reducing its net income subject to taxes, and is taxed instead only at the entrepreneur's personal income tax rate.

> *C-corporations pay taxes on the profits they earn and their owners (stock-holders) pay taxes on the dividends they receive, hence, the drawback of "double taxation."*

By creating a corporation and issuing stock, the entrepreneur is giving up a measure of control to the board of directors. Many an entrepreneur has found himself or herself "out of a job" because he or she did not retain sufficient stock to prevent this type of occurrence. It is not always necessary, however, that the entrepreneur retain 51 percent of the stock to maintain control. As long as the entrepreneur's skills and vision are vital to the success of the venture, and as long as most of the shareholders share that vision, the entrepreneur will have effective control of the organization no matter how much stock has been given up. Nevertheless with a corporate form, unlike the sole proprietorship or partnership, the entrepreneur is accountable principally to the stockholders and secondarily to anyone else.

A corporation must endeavor in all ways to act as an entity separate from its owners. It must keep personal finances completely separate from corporate finances, hold directors meetings, maintain minutes, and not take on any financial liability without sufficient resources to back it up. Failing to do any of the above can result in what is known as "piercing the corporate veil," which leaves the officers and owners open to personal liability.

Apart from legal considerations, where to incorporate is also an important issue. It is normally advantageous to incorporate in the state in which the entrepreneur intends to locate the business so that it is not under the regulatory powers of two states (the state in which it is incorporated and the state in which it must file an application to do business as an out-of-state corporation.)

Normally, however, a corporation will not have to qualify as a "foreign" corporation doing business in another state if it is simply holding directors/shareholders meetings in the state, or holding bank accounts, using independent contractors, or marketing to potential customers whose transactions will be completed in the corporation's home state. It has often been said that you should incorporate in Delaware because it has laws favorable toward corporations. If you don't intend to do a substantial amount of business in Delaware, however,

Incorporation Checklist

1. Determine in which state to incorporate.
2. Select the name of the corporation.
3. Find a registered agent who will receive legal service for the business in another state, if necessary.
4. Fill out a certificate of incorporation and file with the Secretary of State with filing fees.
5. Hold a meeting to elect directors and transact necessary business.
6. During the first organizational meeting of the Board of Directors, select the corporate seal, stock certificates, issue shares, elect corporate officers (Chief Executive Officer, President, etc. as necessary).
7. Open bank accounts and apply for an Employer Identification Number.
8. Chose the corporation's fiscal year.
9. If necessary, file a DBA certificate.
10. Fill out applications to do business in other states if necessary.
11. Apply for required state and local licenses or permits.
12. If appropriate, elect an S-corporation status.

the cost and hassle of qualifying in another state may overcome the benefit of a Delaware incorporation. The entrepreneur should also consider the favorableness of the laws governing corporations in the state chosen. Some states, like California, have a required, minimum annual corporate income tax whether or not the business has a taxable income.

The S-Corporation

An S-corporation, unlike the C-corporation, is not a tax-paying entity. It is merely a financial vehicle that passes the profits and losses of the corporation to the stockholders. It is treated much like the sole proprietorship and the partnership in the sense that if the business earns a profit, that profit becomes the income of the owners/stockholders, and it is the owners who pay the tax on that profit at their individual tax rates.

The rules for election of the S-corporation option are very specific.

- The business must first be incorporated.
- It can have no more than 35 stockholders.
- Shareholders must be U.S. citizens or residents (partnerships and corporations cannot be shareholders). It is important that the shareholder agreement protect shareholders against termination of the S-corporation election through transference of shares to an unqualified person or entity.
- It can have only one class of stock issued and outstanding, that is, either preferred or common.
- The S-corporation cannot be a financial institution, a foreign corporation, or a subsidiary of a parent corporation.

It is always wise to check with an attorney to make certain the election of S-corporation status is valid. If a C-corporation elects to become an S-corporation and then reverts back to C-corporation status, it cannot re-elect S-corporation status again for five years.

The S-corporation is different from the C-corporation in several ways.

- The entrepreneur is taxed on corporate earnings whether they are distributed as dividends or retained in the corporation.
- Any losses incurred by the S-corporation can be used as a deduction on the entrepreneur's personal income tax up to the amount invested in the corporation. If there is more than one shareholder, the loss is shared according to the percentage of ownership.

- If the entrepreneur sells the assets of the business, the shareholder pays a tax on the amount of appreciation. With a C-corporation, the gain is taxable to the corporation and the balance paid to the stockholder is also taxed.

The businesses that benefit most from an S-corporation structure are those that don't have a need to retain earnings. In an S-corporation, if the entrepreneur decides to retain, say, $100,000 of profit to invest in new equipment, the stockholders must still pay taxes on that profit as if it had been distributed. Furthermore, while most deductions and expenses are allowed, S-corporations cannot take advantage of deductions based on medical reimbursements or health insurance plans. Another consideration is that unless the business has regular positive cash flow, it could face a situation where the business makes a profit which is passed through to the owners to be taxed at their personal rate, but generates insufficient cash to pay those taxes.

> The businesses that benefit most from an S-corporation structure are those that don't have a need to retain earnings.

The S-corporation was a valuable financial tool under the 1986 Tax Reform Act because personal tax rates were significantly lower than corporate rates. However, there is some question about the tax advantages under the 1993 Tax Code, as top personal rates have increased and surcharges have been imposed so that a C-corporation might be preferable at higher profit levels. For some small businesses, however, the S-Corporation may still be less costly in the long run because it avoids double taxation of income. A good tax attorney or CPA should advise the entrepreneur on the best course of action.

Ventures that typically benefit from election of the S-corporation status include service businesses with low capital asset requirements, real estate investment firms during times when property values are increasing, and start-ups that are projecting a loss in the early years. Entrepreneurs should probably not elect the S-corporation option if they want to retain earnings for expansion or diversification or if there are significant passive losses from investments such as real estate.

Limited Liability Corporation

A new corporate form has recently emerged and is now available in a number of states. It is known as a Limited Liability Corporation (LLC) and, like the S-corporation, enjoys the pass-through tax benefits of partnerships in addition to the limited liability of a C-corporation. It is, however, far more flexible in its treatment of certain ownership issues, income tax, and in its implementation.

Only privately held companies can become LLCs and they must be formed following very strict guidelines.

- The owners of an LLC are called "members" and their interests are known as "interests."
- An LLC will have two or more members and is formed via filing articles of organization, which resembles a limited partnership agreement.
- The management of the company can be undertaken by the members or by people they have elected to do so.
- The members create an "operating agreement," which is very similar to a partnership agreement that spells out rights and obligations of the members.
- Managers, officers, and members are not personally liable for the company's debts or liabilities except as they have personally guaranteed these debts or liabilities.
- Most LLCs will be organized for tax purposes like partnerships so that income tax benefits and liabilities will pass through to the members. In New York and California, however, the LLCs will be subject to state franchise taxes or fees. To avoid being taxed like a corporation, the LLC must not have at least two of the four corporate characteristics: limited liability, continuity of life, centralization of management, and free transferability of interests. The two that are least likely to be eliminated to meet the test are continuity of life and free transferability of interests. In fact, several states have "bulletproof" statutes that insure that LLCs will always be classified as partnerships for federal income tax purposes.
- Transfer of ownership is with the consent of members who in the aggregate own at least a majority of the company.
- Unless the members owning the majority interest in the aggregate deem otherwise, the LLC will dissolve upon the death, resignation, expulsion or bankruptcy of a member.
- Interests in LLCs where members participate in the management and control of the company are considered securities for federal and most state securities laws, very much like limited partnership interests. This means that the offering or sale of interests must be registered, which then exposes the organizing members to potential liability for material omissions and misrepresentations of fact under securities laws.

The LLC is most often compared to the limited partnership and the S-corporation. There are, however, differences. In a limited partnership, one or more people (the general partners) agrees to assume personal liability for the actions of the partnership; this is not the case with an LLC. Unlike a limited partnership, in an LLC a member does not have to forfeit the right to participate in the management of the organization to retain his or her limited liability status.

In an LLC, unlike in an S-corporation, there are no limitations on the number of members or their status, such as corporation, pension plans, or non-resident aliens. Also, while S-corporations can't own 80 percent or more of the stock of another corporation, an LLC may actually have wholly owned subsidiary corporations. LLCs are not limited to one class of stock and in some ways they receive more favorable tax treatment. For example, unlike an S-corporation shareholder, the LLC member can deduct losses in amounts that reflect the member's allocable share of the debt of the company.

If at a later date, the entrepreneur decides to go public, the LLC can become a C-corporation by transferring the LLC assets to the new corporation. It is, however, a bit more difficult to go the other way, as you must pay capital gains tax on the appreciation.

LLCs are also becoming a popular vehicle for companies that may have global investors, as the S-corporation does not permit foreign ownership. As this is still a fairly new legal structure, an attorney should be consulted to find out if this form is available in the entrepreneur's state and to help the entrepreneur understand and abide by the requirements associated with it.

The Nonprofit Corporation

It is not outside the realm of possibility for a nonprofit corporation to be a high-growth, world-class company; however, they are not generally started with that goal in mind. A nonprofit corporation is a corporation established for charitable, public (i.e. scientific, literary, and educational), religious, or mutual benefit (i.e. trade associations, tennis clubs) purposes as recognized by federal and state laws. Like the C-corporation, the nonprofit corporation is a legal entity and offers its shareholders and officers the benefit of limited liability. There is a common misconception that nonprofit corporations are not allowed to make a profit. As long as the business is not set up to benefit a single person and is organized for a nonprofit purpose, it can make a profit on which it is not taxed if it has also met the IRS test for a tax-exempt status. However, income derived from for-profit activities is subject to income tax.

There are two distinct hurdles that nonprofit corporations must pass if they want to operate as a nonprofit corporation and have tax-exempt status:

1. meeting the state requirements for being designated a non-profit corporation that can operate as such in a given state, and
2. meeting the federal and state requirements for exemption from paying taxes (IRS 501(c)(3)) by forming a corporation that falls within the IRS's narrowly defined catgories.

In forming the nonprofit corporation, the entrepreneur gives up proprietary interest in the corporation and dedicates all the assets and resources of the corporation to tax-exempt activities. If a nonprofit corporation is ever dissolved, its assets must be distributed to another tax-exempt organization.

Some Final Thoughts

Choosing the legal structure of the new venture is one of the most important decisions an entrepreneur can make, for it affects the tax strategy of the company for years to come. The correct selection depends on the type of venture the entrepreneur is starting, the profits the venture generates, the personal tax bracket of the entrepreneur, the assets used by the business, its potential for growth, and state incorporation laws. Again, particularly in the case of incorporation, it is important that an attorney review the documents to ensure that you have followed the rules and will receive all of the benefits to which the business is entitled.

 New Venture Checklist

Have you

☐ Answered the questions that will determine if you can operate as a sole proprietor?

☐ Considered the advantages and disadvantages of the partnership structure for the new venture?

☐ Examined the advantages and disadvantages of the corporate structure for the new venture?

☐ Talked with an accountant or attorney to determine if the S-corporation election with be advantageous to the new venture?

Additional Sources of Information

Bangs, D.H. (1994). *The Start-Up Guide, 2nd edition.* Dover, NH: Upstart Publishing Co.

Barlett, J.W. (1988). *Venture Capital—Law, Business Strategies and Investment Planning.* New York: John Wiley & Sons.

Friedman, R. (1993). *The Complete Small Business Legal Guide.* Chicago: Dearborn Enterprise.

Mancuso, J.R. (1988). *Mancuso's Small Business Resource Guide.* New York: Center for Entrepreneurial Management.

Nicholas, T. (1993). *The Complete Guide to "S" Corporations.* Chicago: Dearborn Publishing Group, Inc.

Whitmyer, C., S. Rasberry & M. Phillips. (1988). *Running a One-Person Business.* Berkeley, CA: Ten Speed Press.

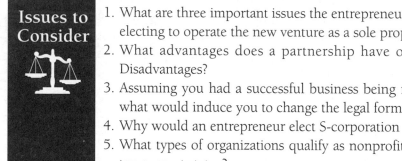

Issues to Consider

1. What are three important issues the entrepreneur should consider prior to electing to operate the new venture as a sole proprietorship?
2. What advantages does a partnership have over a sole proprietorship? Disadvantages?
3. Assuming you had a successful business being run as a sole proprietorship, what would induce you to change the legal form to a corporation?
4. Why would an entrepreneur elect S-corporation status over C-corporation?
5. What types of organizations qualify as nonprofit corporations and 501(c)(3) tax-exempt status?

CHAPTER 9

Regulations Affecting New Businesses

Overview

- *The importance of laws and regulations on all aspects of a new venture*
- *The requirements for a valid contract*
- *Laws and rules that will affect the choice of a site for the business*
- *Laws related to the hiring and firing of employees*
- *Laws that regulate dealings with consumers*
- *Taxes for which the business is responsible*

Regulation as a Way of Life

No matter what size your business is or becomes, it will be affected on a daily basis in a myriad of ways by the laws, regulations, requirements, and restrictions of federal, state, and local government authorities. A number of governmental agencies write and enforce the various regulations by which businesses are bound. Probably no one would dispute the need for government regulation where it protects businesses, employees, and the general public from actions and products that would cause harm or deny people their rights. Many, however, believe that the red tape and paperwork have become so overwhelming that it now costs businesses over two billion hours per year just to fill out government forms. They are concerned that this burden and its accompanying costs appear to exceed any benefit that might be accrued from regulation. The United States is considered by many international business owners, such as

Figure 9.1: Regulations that Affect Business

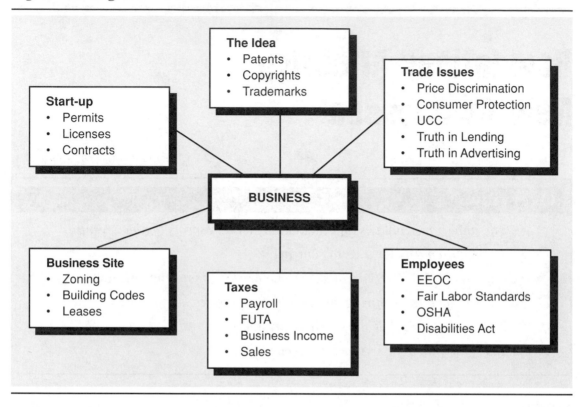

Gordon Roddick of The Body Shop, to be the most regulated country in the world. Roddick believes that compliance with regulations adds at least five percent to the cost of doing business, reducing the number of businesses that are able to start[1] because a new venture must often spend its scarce resources on attorneys and accountants to ensure compliance with the law.

This chapter looks at the process of starting a business from a regulatory point of view, considering which regulations affect which aspects of the new venture. As can already be observed from Figure 9.1, a young business—any business for that matter—is affected in every arena of its existence by laws and regulations.

---

[1]"Regulation Time: 60 Seconds with...Gordon Roddick." *Inc.* magazine, June, 1993, p. 16.

From Idea to Start-Up

One of the first areas where the entrepreneur is affected by laws and regulations occurs at the idea stage before the new venture even begins. Laws determine whether or not an invention or design can be protected by intellectual property rights, and whether a symbol or logo that represents the business can be trademarked so no one else can use it. These legal protections can give the business a significant competitive advantage.

In all likelihood, you will enter into several contracts before the business is up and running. These may include agreements with suppliers, a lease for the business site, a partnership agreement, independent contractor agreements, employment contracts, and so forth. If you have established a relationship with a business attorney, he or she will probably be able to create standard contract forms reflecting the specific needs of your business that can be used over and over again in similar situations. On the other hand, when presented with a contract created by a third party (your supplier's attorney, for example), you should ask your attorney to review the document to make sure you are protected and are not agreeing to something that could ultimately harm the business. In general, contracts should be drawn in such a way as to be legally binding so you will have legal remedies should the other party not comply with the terms of the contract.

To be a legally binding contract, there must be an **agreement,** which is an offer or promise to do something or refrain from doing something. For example, a vendor may offer to sell you a copy machine, which constitutes an offer to do something. For the agreement to be valid, however, there must also be **consideration,** which is your promise to supply or give up something in return—a check or purchase order, for example. Furthermore, to be legally binding, the parties to the contract must have **capacity;** that is, they must be legally able to enter into a contract. Contracts cannot be entered into legally by intoxicated persons, persons who are not of sound mind and body, or minors. If these people do enter into an agreement, the contract may be contested and ruled to be void, as never having existed

A lawyer's time is normally very expensive, but lawsuits can be devastating to a growing business, not to mention time-consuming. It may, however, be possible to save money by taking advantage of some of the new self-help legal software and books now available. While they should not be used as a substitute for sound legal advice on complex issues, they are excellent for basic legal issues such as simple agreements. Both software and books usually provide standard

PROFILE 9.1

Sub Pop Learns the Hard Way

Breaking into the multi-billion dollar recording industry as an independent label is no easy trick. But that didn't stop transplanted mid-westerners Bruce Pavitt and Jonathan Poneman from starting an independent recording company in Seattle known as Sub Pop, which featured local rock groups. Their first production was an album by a group called Soundgarden, which was marginally successful. A year later Soundgarden left Sub Pop to sign with A & M Records and produce *Badmotorfinger*, a record that sold over 900,000 copies. Unfortunately, Sub Pop didn't receive a dime because they had never had a contract with Soundgarden.

Sub Pop quickly learned they needed to have tough contracts that made it difficult for a group to leave them without paying something. Fortunately, they learned that lesson early because another of their groups, Nirvana, went on to sign with David Geffen's DGC label. Because of the contract with Sub Pop, DGC had to pay a royalty of over two percent to Sub Pop on Nirvana's future record sales. Nirvana's *Nevermind* album alone brought over $1 million in royalties to Sub Pop. They also own the rights to songs that Nirvana recorded before leaving Sub Pop. Having a valid contract in the beginning was a valuable lesson!

forms with blanks to fill in. Some interactive programs even guide the entrepreneur through a series of questions that lead to a customized document. When using these programs, be aware that the deletion or addition of even one word can change the meaning of a sentence with potentially disastrous consequences.

Choosing a Business Site

When considering a place to locate the new business, you can't just go anywhere that seems appropriate to you. Cities and counties have laws restricting businesses from locating in areas designated for residential dwellings, agricultural development, and open land. Within areas designated for businesses, there are even more regulations, called zoning laws, that dictate what type of business can locate at a certain location. In general, business zoning laws fall into four categories: commercial, office/professional, light industrial, and heavy industrial. Commercial zoning includes retail stores, restaurants, and supermarkets. Office zoning permits general office uses plus some banking/financial, but no manufacturing. Light industrial zoning allows for distribution and warehousing, while heavy industrial includes major manufacturing and assembling of products. In general, as you move from commercial zoning to heavy industrial, the cost per square foot of the land declines. Consequently, manufacturing facilities that normally require considerably more square footage of buildable space enjoy less expensive land and rent costs. This is because as you move from commercial to industrial zoning, the importance of the specific location for business success decreases. Therefore, you are more likely to find commercial zoning in the vicinity of residential zoning than you are to find industrial. This subject is treated more fully in Chapter 10. You can learn more about city and county zoning ordinances from the planning department or building and safety department of the city in which the business will be located. Unincorporated areas normally have their own county planning department.

Most municipalities require that a business have a license to operate within the limits of the city or town.

Not only will the business have to abide by zoning ordinances, but also by building codes. Whether you build the facility or buy an existing facility, you have to ensure that the building meets local and state building standards. Such things as structural codes for earthquake safety, fire codes, and electrical codes are all mandated by these standards. If you are building, you should hire an experienced, licensed general contractor who will see that all requirements and inspections are met. If you are buying an existing building, you can hire a professional contractor or inspector to verify that the building meets all codes. If you are renting, make sure the landlord can provide proof that the building meets all code requirements so you don't face having to move when a building inspector condemns the building after your business is already there.

Most municipalities require that a business have a license to operate within the limits of the city or town. If the business is located within the unincorporated areas of a county, it may also be required to obtain a license. License requirements vary from city to city, but you can find out your city's requirements by going to the business license division, usually located in the city hall or planning department. Depending on the nature of the business, you may also be required to hold a permit, which can be obtained in the same location as the license. Some typical permits that may be required are building, health, electrical, fire, and sign permits.

More recent environmental regulations affect the choice of site. Most states now have environmental quality regulations that protect against businesses emitting pollutants into the ground, air, or water. They also define who can handle toxic wastes and how they must be disposed of. Check with local government agencies to determine if any permits are required for your business (this is normally for manufacturing or extraction businesses). Also contact federal and state agencies like the Environmental Protection Agency, the Office of Health and Emergency Planning, and the Occupational Safety and Health Administration (OSHA) for information. Some states like California have Environmental Business Resources Assistance Centers that provide access to the latest environmental regulatory compliance resources for small and medium-sized businesses by phone, fax, or electronic bulletin board as well as through a personal visit to the center.

Hiring Employees

Several laws exist related to hiring, firing, and compensating employees, so the entrepreneur must be aware of his or her obligations under the law *before* hiring anyone to avoid any future problems. An employer's obligation begins with the language used in advertising for positions in the company and extends to the interviews conducted with potential hires. The Equal Employment Opportunity Commission (EEOC) is charged with protecting the rights of employees. It mandates that you cannot refuse to hire someone based on age, race, national origin, religion, gender, or physical challenge. The only time sex or race can be a valid consideration for a job is when it is a bona fide occupational qualification, for example, an acting job calling for an Asian male over the age of 40. This also means written job descriptions must be accurate and defensible and contain clear language that differentiates essential tasks of the job from non-essential ones. It is only on the basis of the essential tasks that you can seek someone who is of a certain gender, who has no physical disability, or who can speak a certain foreign language.

If you have written a good ad, you will probably receive several résumés. With jobs being generally more difficult to find, applicants are likely to embellish their résumés somewhat to be more competitive in the marketplace. You, however, must protect yourself against hiring someone whom you may later have to fire, because firing someone is no longer as easy as it used to be. The laws protecting the employee, combined with a litigious society in general, make for a very delicate situation for any employer attempting to fire an employee. It is, therefore, probably dangerous to take any résumé on face value. A few phone calls to references can give you a sense of the veracity of the résumé.

Tips for Looking at Résumés and Selecting a Qualified Candidate

1. Don't feel that just because the person has experience in only one arena, he or she is not qualified to do what you want them to do. Look for core skills like writing, speaking, organizing, leading, and so forth. These basic abilities can be put to use in a variety of scenarios.

2. Consider promoting from within—training current employees so that they can move up when the time comes.

3. Look for people with successful experience in the general field in which you are interested.

4. Look for people who have successfully worked in teams.

5. Look for demonstrable success, not just statements like, "I was a successful salesperson for ABC," but rather statements like, "Over the past five years I have increased my sales volume by 20 percent per year."

6. Look for people who have stayed with a company for a reasonable length of time.

At the interview stage, certain questions are not permitted by the EEOC. These include questions about

- Health
- Disabilities (You may ask, "Do you have any conditions that would preclude your doing this job?")
- Age (To protect those under 21 and over 40)
- Medical history
- Living arrangements
- Religious preference
- Type of military discharge
- Pregnancy plans
- Arrest record (You may ask: "Have you ever been convicted of a felony crime?")
- Ancestry

In general, the rule is to keep all questions related to the job requirements, including skills, experience, and attitudes. One last point on this issue: It is illegal to request a photo with a job application or résumé unless the job is specifically known to be predicated on appearance, such as a modeling job.

Wage and Hour Laws

Consider the following situation. You hire an employee on salary. The employee asks if she can stay an hour late each day so she can catch a ride home with a co-worker. A year later you fire her, and she files a federal wage-and-hour claim for back pay for the extra hour each day she spent during the year. It is likely she will win her claim. Why? Because even salaried employees are entitled to protection under the Department of Labor's Fair Labor Standards Act, which establishes minimum wage. There are a disparately large number of claims against small businesses as opposed to large organizations. This is because small businesses rarely have personnel departments with people whose responsibility is to make sure the hiring and firing of employees is handled correctly so as to avoid claims.

In general, four types of job categories are exempt from minimum wage and hour laws: executive, administrative, professional, and outside sales. This is only true, however, if strict guidelines are followed. The Department of Labor's basic criteria for establishing an employee as exempt are:

• Does the employee receive a salary?
• Does the employee make more than $250 a week?
• Does the employee perform managerial duties over a unit at least 50 percent of the time?

As there are so many regulations designed to protect employees, every new business owner should become aware of federal and state laws regarding employees' hiring, firing, and working conditions. If you do not comply, you could find yourself being sued by the Department of Labor for back pay and liquidated damages, as well as attorneys' fees and costs of litigation. Some of the key laws are discussed in this chapter.

Occupation Health and Safety

Nothing strikes fear in the heart of a business owner like workers' compensation. Workers' compensation insurance is a no-fault system under which workers receive guaranteed compensation for injury at work and employers are protected from unlimited liability by covering the cost of the premiums. Nevertheless, the cost of worker accidents and false claims has threatened the life of many a businesses. On average a business spent $564 per employee on workers' compensation insurance in 1992, double the amount spent seven years ago, according to the Small Business Administration. The dollar amount of claims has also risen to an average of $23,000 per claim, double that in 1985. To further exacerbate the situation, premium rates, which are based on the type of business you are in and your accident history, vary from state to state, resulting in some states having a competitive advantage over others in certain industries. Among the fastest growing and most vexing claims are those for repetitive motion injury (such as carpal tunnel syndrome) and stress-related disabilities.

The high cost of workers' compensation premiums has led many small businesses to join consortiums to self insure. While this is a complex process, there are many consultants who are able to help businesses through it. In some instances, trade associations have formed a consortium for self-insuring businesses in the same industry and facing the same potential injury claims. Fortunately, the bright spot in all this is that a business can control its costs through active accident prevention and education programs. The issue of safe and healthy work environments is the purview of the Occupational Safety and Health Act of 1970 (OSHA) and its administrative unit. OSHA requires that employers eliminate hazardous areas in the workplace and maintain health and safety records on all employees. OSHA inspectors regularly target businesses that have certain hazards inherent in the nature of the business, such as asbestos, and conduct rigorous inspections, liberally dispensing fines and penalties where violations have occurred (the basic fine is $7,000).

Before the new business is faced with an OSHA audit, call OSHA and ask to receive some of their helpful pamphlets (See *Additional Sources of Information* on p. 165) or ask an OSHA consultant to conduct a free, confidential, on-site test of your business and give you compliance advice. Also local colleges usually offer seminars in safety management.

PROFILE 9.2

Taking Care of Workers' Comp

Mid-Atlantic Packaging, Inc., a corrugated box producer, faced severe workers' compensation premiums in 1991 that threatened the financial health of the business. In one year Mid-Atlantic's 80 employees experienced 17 injuries totaling more than $400,000 in workers' compensation claims. The result: premiums for insurance rose sharply, foreshadowing the downfall of the company.

They decided to take a pro-active approach with regard to accident prevention. Corporate gave the general manager "carte blanche" to pursue a safety program. He started by setting up an accident prevention committee comprised of representatives from every department. They set up financial incentives and a method for reporting unsafe actions. Finally they brought in instructors to train workers in how to lift and bend properly to avoid injury. In the year after the new program was implemented, Mid-Atlantic posted no injuries and no claims.

Several tips will help you avoid high premiums and the stress of OSHA audits.

- Develop a safety program.
- Get employees back to work as soon as possible after an injury.
- Increase job satisfaction. Happy employees translate into fewer claims.
- Pay premiums only on straight time (not overtime or vacation time).
- Check the rate categories for all employees carefully.
- Pay the smaller claims yourself.
- If your company has a higher safety record than average, ask for a discount in premium.
- Check your insurance records carefully, especially for claims from people who don't currently work for you or haven't for a long period of time.
- Shop around for the best rates and don't be afraid to change agents midstream.
- Take care of injuries quickly.
- Help employees understand that high premiums mean lower profits, so less money in their pockets.

Americans with Disabilities Act

In July of 1992 the Americans with Disabilities Act (ADA) became law and represented the most sweeping employment reform in over 30 years. Essentially, the ADA prohibits discrimination against anyone with a physical or mental impairment or disability that substantially limits one or more life activities like walking, seeing, or hearing. Other disabilities specifically mentioned in the law are diabetes, cancer, AIDS, arthritis, epilepsy, and emotional illness. The law also protects those who have had drug and alcohol dependencies in the past but have undergone treatment. It does not, however, protect those who are dependent at the time they apply for a job. The candidate, in any case of disability, must qualify for the job in terms of skills and experience in the first place. Of the estimated 45 million Americans with disabilities, approximately 15 million are of working age.

The law applies to businesses with fifteen or more employees. For those businesses that deal with the public, the public-access provisions provide that restaurants, theaters, stores, and the like must modify their facilities to provide access to people with disabilities as long as the modification doesn't create an undue hardship on the business. These modifications might include entry ramps, Braille control panels on elevators, or wider aisles to accommodate wheelchairs. The public access rules fall under the purview of the Department of Justice, while the employment rules are regulated by the EEOC. As the law is stated in broad terms such as "undue burden" and "reasonable accommodations," many business owners are concerned that this ambiguity translates into more litigation for them. The laws related to disability will evolve over time, so it is important that the entrepreneur maintain an awareness of the status of ADA.

Sexual Harassment

The rulings regarding unwanted attention and harassment on the job began to get very tough in the 1980s. The courts have expanded the definition of sexual harassment, and businesses are now developing policies in an effort to ward off embarrassing and expensive lawsuits. The EEOC reports that sexual harassment complaints grew from 4,400 in 1986 to 5,600 in 1990. In its first ruling on the subject, the Supreme Court held that sexual harassment violates Title VII of the 1964 Civil Rights Act when the act is unwelcome and represents an abuse of power in the workplace. Generally, harassment can be divided into two categories: *quid pro quo* where advancement on the job or a raise is conditional on certain sexual favors, and hostile working environment cases where the employee is subjected to a sexually offensive environment against his or her will. Harassment includes but is not limited to verbal and non-verbal assaults of a sexual nature, and physical harassment. As a result, business owners should establish policies that educate and make clear to employees what conduct is not acceptable in the workplace. In doing so, entrepreneurs can solicit guidance from the EEOC.

Trade Issues

In the United States great value is placed on the free marketplace, and generally any attempts by government to interfere in the free market process are shunned. Nevertheless, since the 1800s the government has imposed certain laws specifically designed to preserve competition and the free market. The Sherman Antitrust Act of 1890, one of the first, prohibited any restraint of free trade. Other regulations followed, and they are discussed in several categories.

Price Discrimination

The Clayton Act of 1914 and the even stricter Robinson-Patman Act of 1936, enforced by the Federal Trade Commission, assert that businesses cannot sell the same product to different customers at different prices without justification. In other words, they must demonstrate that the lower price was based on a quantity-sold discount, quality of the product (seconds or slightly damaged), or a cost savings on the part of the seller (the manufacturer discounted the product to the retailer beyond the normal purchase price). Therefore, the entrepreneur must be careful to be fair to all customers when setting prices.

Consumer Protection

The greatest number of laws affecting trade come under the heading of consumer protection. They include:

- Unscrupulous sellers
- Unreasonable credit terms
- Unsafe products
- Mislabeling of products

One of the largest federal agencies monitoring product safety is the Food and Drug Administration (FDA), which is responsible for research, new product testing, and inspection of the operations of food and drug manufacturers. If your new product is a cosmetic, a drug, a food item, or anything applied to the skin, like suntan lotion, you will need FDA approval before marketing the product.

The Consumer Product Safety Commission was established in 1972 as the watchdog for consumers over products considered hazardous. Additionally, it is charged with setting standards for such things as toys for children under the age of five. If your product falls into one of these categories, you will need to be aware of the standards and requirements for marketing and producing that product.

The Fair Packaging and Labeling Act was designed to provide consumers with information so they could shop more wisely. The act mandates that manufacturers truthfully list all raw materials used in the production of the product on a clearly marked label. This is in addition to the size and weight of the packaging. If your product is a food product, the percentages of nutrients, vitamins, carbohydrates, calories, and fat contained in one normal size serving of the product must be displayed. By becoming aware of the regulations affecting products manufactured for public consumption, you can avoid both the possible recall of your product and potential lawsuits.

The Uniform Commercial Code

The Uniform Commercial Code (UCC) is really a group of laws that affects everything from bank deposits and investment securities to sales. It is this latter category that impacts the entrepreneur. Any time you enter into an agreement to sell a product, you create a contract governed by the laws of contract. However, if you are a merchant, you must also abide by the laws of the UCC, which can be different. To use a simple example, suppose you have ordered some supplies from a manufacturer under a contract that contains the terms of place, delivery date, and quantity, but you have failed to ask the price. The supplies arrive and the price is higher than expected. Under the regulations of the UCC, a price that is reasonable at the time of delivery is assigned, based on the fact that both you and the manufacturer are professionals who understand how the business operates. You can't claim lack of knowledge the way a lay person can; you are presumed to know the rules of the game since you are in business.

The UCC also deals with product liability issues. Historically, the philosophy of the marketplace in the United States has been *caveat emptor* or "let the buyer beware." In contemporary times, the burden of that philosophy has shifted to "let the seller beware" as consumer groups and advocates like Ralph Nader have forced businesses to take responsibility for the quality and safety of what they produce. Whenever you sell goods, you also sell a warrant of merchantability, which is an implied warranty that the product is of at least average quality and suitable for the purpose for which it was intended. Consequently, the shift in the burden of responsibility has resulted in numerous lawsuits by consumers and higher premiums for product liability insurance. For example, it is estimated that about 25 percent of the cost of a football helmet pays for product liability insurance. Any entrepreneur who intends to manufacture and sell a consumer product should be careful to include clear instructions on its use and warnings about the consequences of misuse.

Consumer Credit

Like consumer protection laws, the laws regulating consumer lending are pervasive in an effort to protect consumer rights. The Equal Credit Opportunity Act (ECOA) provides for fair and equitable treatment of all borrowers without regard for marital status, source of income, race, color, or national origin. It also requires prompt disclosure of the reasons for any denial of credit. It applies to all banks, credit unions, retailers, and business creditors. Before any credit granting can be completed, the Truth-in-Lending Act (Regulation Z) mandates detailed disclosures concerning the cost of credit. It also requires disclosures on the method of billing on open-ended contracts, personal property leases, and credit card accounts as well as the number and amount of payments required, and the type of collateral given to secure the loan. It applies to anyone who regularly extends credit, imposes a finance charge, or permits an obligation to be repaid over more than four installments.

The Fair Credit Billing Act (FCBA) provides procedures for dispute resolution, and the Fair Credit Reporting Act (FCRA) mandates standards for reporting information on credit recipients to credit reporting agencies. If you intend to grant credit to your customers, you must make yourself aware of all of the applicable regulations. The bottom line is: merchant lender beware!

Truth in Advertising

The Federal Trade Commission is charged with protecting the rights of consumers against false or misleading advertising. It has come down hard on many businesses for misleading customers about what a product can do, offering a reduced (sale) price on an item that was never advertised at a higher price, using list price as a comparison if the business has never sold the item at list, and using bait-and-switch techniques to lure customers into the store only to switch them to a higher-priced item.

Taxes

As a business owner, you are also legally responsible for paying certain taxes in a timely fashion. Since no one wants to pay more taxes than required, business owners must understand which transactions qualify as tax-free and what the tax consequences are of any transaction. For example, a $2,000 transaction is worth $2,000 to the business if it is tax-free; however, if it is taxable it may only be worth $1,400—a sizable difference. In general, the following are tax-free receipts:

- Compensation from accident and health plans for injuries or illness and life insurance benefits
- Contributions by the employer to a qualified accident and health plan
- Workers' compensation benefits
- Meals and lodging provided for the convenience of the employer, as in business trips
- Interest on municipal bonds.
- Income from the discharge of indebtedness if the taxpayer is insolvent or bankrupt

Beyond these items, most business transactions are taxable.

Payroll Taxes

One of the payroll taxes you will deduct from an employee's paycheck is FICA (social security tax). The deduction is based on a percentage of the employee's income and as of 1994 was 7.65% on wages up to $60,600 (this includes

1.45% for Medicare). Beyond the $60,600, 1.45% for Medicare must still be deducted as there is now no limit on wages for this deduction. In addition, the employer contributes an amount equal to the FICA deduction from the employee's pay, hence the fact that it costs more to employ a person than the mere face value of the paycheck. State and federal income taxes must be withheld according to the current tax law and the employee's W-4 form. This amount is a percentage of taxable gross pay after allowable deductions.

You as the employer are also required to make contributions under the Federal Unemployment Tax Act (FUTA), which provides compensation to workers who are temporarily unemployed. This tax amounts to 6.2% of the first $7,000 of gross pay. If you pay your state unemployment tax in a timely fashion, it is credited against the federal unemployment taxes paid. For example, in California the unemployment tax rate is 5.4%. Subtracting that from the federal rate of 6.2% leaves a net federal tax rate of .8%. Some states like Pennsylvania, Alabama, Alaska, and New Jersey also collect FUTA from employees.

In some states you may be required to pay state disability insurance. In California, for example, this amounts to 1.30% on wages not to exceed $31,767.00 and paid by the employer

If your business accumulates $100,000 or more of FICA and federal income tax withholdings during any pay period, you are required to deposit that amount in an approved depository by the close of the next business day or face a penalty of 2 to 15 percent of the amount. Consequently it is very important to monitor payroll taxes carefully, particularly if you have a labor-intensive business. Don't assume all banks have the same rules for date-of-deposit. You should either deposit withholding tax on the same day you pay employees or by the end of the bank's next business day, and deposit in a commercial bank rather than a Federal Reserve bank, which always credits deposits to the next day. A one-day error can cost your business a lot of money.

Sales and Use Taxes

Regardless of the legal form of the business, anyone who sells tangible products or services is required to collect sales tax. A use tax is collected from the purchaser if a sales tax has not been paid and is equivalent in amount to the sales tax. Local jurisdictions may tax occupancy, personal property, real estate property, stock transfer, real estate transfer, and alcoholic beverages, to name a few. As local governments look for additional sources of revenues, they often find them in the business community. State laws regarding sales and use taxes vary considerably, however, so the entrepreneur should discuss the business's obligations with the appropriate state authority.

Business Income Tax

The business itself must pay federal, state, or local taxes on income it earns as well, depending on the legal form of the business. A sole proprietor or a partner in a partnership pays these taxes one time as personal income from the business. If you are a self-employed business owner, you also pay a FICA tax of 15.3 percent, double that of an employee because you are both the employer and the employee. A corporation, on the other hand, pays a corporate income tax. If you receive a salary from your corporation, you also pay a personal income tax on it.

The number of regulations, taxes, and laws affecting a new business can be daunting, hence the need to consult a good attorney and accountant. In most cases, particularly in those involving the IRS, the penalties for failure to pay or follow the rules are severe. Many a new business owner has discovered this too late. You must prepare in advance for the start of the business by understanding your obligations and planning to meet them.

☑ New Venture Checklist

Have you

☐ Identified the types of laws and regulations that will impact your particular type of business?

☐ Protected aspects of your business concept that fall into the intellectual property rights categories?

☐ Found an attorney who can review any contracts you enter into?

☐ Written clear and legally defensible job descriptions?

☐ Identified all the taxes for which you are responsible and set up a plan for meeting payment deadlines?

Additional Sources of Information

All About OSHA and OSHA Inspections. Call OSHA at 202-219-4667.

The OSHA Handbook for Small Businesses. Call 202-783-3238.

What Businesses Must Know About the Americans With Disabilities Act. U.S. Chamber of Commerce, call 1-800-638-6582. Ask for publication No. 0320.

U.S. Equal Employment Opportunity Commission, 1801 L Street, NW, Washington, DC 20507. ADA Helpline: 1-800-669-EEOC.

Job Accommodation Network, P.O. Box 6123, 809 Allen Hall, WVU, Morgantown WV 26506-6123. Call 1-800-232-9675.

Issues to Consider

1. How will you know when you have a legally binding agreement?
2. What is the purpose of zoning laws?
3. What does the Truth-in-Lending law require of businesses, and which businesses are affected by it?
4. Which laws is the Equal Opportunity Commission charged to regulate?
5. You have an interview with a candidate for a position as bookkeeper for your business. What are some questions you can ask, and what cannot be asked of this candidate?

3

Toy Tips®, Inc.

In September of 1991, 23 years old and only two years out of college, Marianne Szymanski left her job and started Toy Tips®, Inc., a toy research and consulting firm. For most people this would have been a very frightening thing to do, but Marianne had no doubts her new business would succeed. Having graduated from Marquette University with a bachelor of arts degree in psychology and marketing, she had been working for a toy manufacturer selling toys to retailers and sometimes stocking shelves. Naturally customers would come up to her and ask questions. Often they were grandparents who didn't recognize any of the new toys and consequently had no idea what to purchase.

As a result, Marianne decided to find out if there was any information out there on the best toys to buy for kids of various ages. Consulting the major magazines related to children, she found they all seemed to have their own version of the "Top Ten" list of toys. Upon closer inspection, however, she discovered that invariably the toys on the lists were made by the manufacturers who had purchased advertising space in the magazine. Moreover, she found that the self-proclaimed "experts" in the field were actually paid by the manufacturers to review their products. This was certainly not a very unbiased way to judge these toys. Marianne, who hadn't yet decided what she wanted to do with her life, immediately saw an opportunity to provide a much needed service and create a career opportunity for herself.

The Start-Up

Marianne puzzled about the best way to start this business so that she could reach the most people. At the time, 900 telephone numbers were becoming a popular business venture that could be started quickly and with relatively little capital. Marianne decided to try this avenue. So Toy Tips began as the National Toy Information Hotline, a 900 number, that people could call to receive the latest information on toy safety, product recalls, and tips on age-appropriate toys. To start the business, Marianne drained her savings account and then took her business plan to nearly every banker in Milwaukee. She was turned down time and time again with "This is great; this is wonderful—good luck." But no money.

Fortuitously, two days before actually starting the business, she was asked by a local talk show to appear. That free publicity was worth more than any bank loan. From that point on, the media picked up on what she was doing, and her business grew much more quickly than she expected. By the end of the first year, little town gazettes all over Wisconsin had picked up on the hotline; but when the AP and *USA Today* got hold of it the business exploded. She started receiving phone calls from all over the United States.

> That free publicity was worth more than any bank loan.

At the same time she had also sent some information about her hotline to the Toy Manufacturers of America in New York, which is the voice of the toy industry, and they published her information in their monthly PR release to toy manufacturers. All of a sudden she was inundated with information and hundreds of samples from toy companies. Still working out of her home testing toys on the living room floor with neighborhood children, she decided she needed to look for another site for the business because the toys were taking over her home. She went to a pediatrician she knew and worked out a barter arrangement that allowed her to fill up four rooms of his office with toys for his patients to "test." That worked for a while, but soon she had overgrown the space and needed to move again. By now her ability to convince people of her credibility was well honed, so she went to the President of Marquette University, Father DiUilo, who helped to come up with the idea of working out of the child care center at Marquette. The arrangement was that the children would test the toys, she would observe them, and the toys would be donated to the university. And so it was that Toy Tips, Inc. moved into the child care center, a series of rooms bursting with primary colors, bustling with activity, and alive with the sounds of children.

By the end of 1991, she was working with 50 manufacturers. By the end of 1992, that number had swelled to 140, and her revenues had doubled. She had also created a magazine to carry her message and publish the notices of toy recalls. The magazine also contains Marianne's "Top Ten" lists: "The Top Ten Travel Toys," "The Top Ten Educational Toys," and even "The Top Ten Environmental Toys."

Bootstrapping Genius

Even though the company was growing, Marianne did not have enough money to hire the employees she needed to help her handle the ever increasing load of work. But Marianne, who is the essence of the bootstrapping entrepreneur, knew that there must be a way to get help by bartering, the way she had done for her office space. Once again she went to the university and suggested that they offer an internship program with Marquette students who would work for university credit in her research center. The university agreed and "Toy Tips 101" was born. Engineering students tested the toys and even designed a "toy crusher" for her. Working with one of the engineering professors, she was able to develop new tests for toys, such as tests for flammability and toxicity. Journalism students helped her do fact checking and gather information for articles, while a public relations student helped her with her media tour. Psychology and education majors were involved in the focus groups and testing. She also used marketing students to develop questionnaires and research on the needs of parents. Until just recently, Marianne had no "employees" in the traditional sense. She has now hired two assistants to help her carry the load.

With all the media attention she was receiving, Marianne had to travel, but she didn't have an appropriate wardrobe, and since all her money was going into the business, she didn't have the money to go out and buy one. So Marianne again demonstrated her bootstrapping creativity when she went to JH Collectibles clothing company and bartered for a new wardrobe for her media tour. In exchange for the wardrobe, JH Collectables was given a page of advertising in her magazine, which was handed out during the tour.

Marianne used a similar technique to "buy" time with an attorney. She happened to attend a seminar on "Global Marketing in Europe" given by the Wisconsin trade center. Being the only woman at the seminar became an advantage, because when she later called the attorney who led the seminar, he remembered her. She arranged for an appointment ostensibly to talk to him about trademarks, but actually this was just an excuse to approach him about becoming the attorney for her small, but growing, business. She asked if he would consider working with her at a reduced rate with the understanding that when she got bigger and had the money, she would pay his regular rate. He laughed appreciatively at her assertiveness and agreed to work with her. He continues to do so, always charging for his time but being flexible in billing depending on her business's financial situation.

Growing the Business

As the business grew, it became obvious that the 900 hotline was becoming a problem. Young children, who had seen her on TV and knew that she worked with toys were finding her 900 number and calling asking for "the toy tester." She imagined their parents weren't too happy about the phone bills, so she discontinued the line. The 900 number had by then served its purpose. It gave her the resources to get her business off the ground and also gave her extraordinary media attention. She now has over 850 media contacts and appears as a regular "toy guest" on "Good Morning America."

Marianne incorporated the business to protect herself and her assets from liability, but also to give the business a perception of permanence and credibility. This became increasingly important as she began to do more than toy testing. She started consulting to private companies (never toy manufacturers), including McDonalds, Rayovac, HDI Engineering, and Candy & Kids Shoes. One battery manufacturer, for example, asked her to test their batteries in her toys to see exactly how long they last. A French company wanted to learn how American children play, which gave her a chance to go to Europe and study how European children interact and play.

> Growing a business means looking beyond current markets to new ones.

Toy Tips was hired by Toys "R" Us to conduct research on toys for "differently abled" kids. The contract allowed her to set up 18 testing centers at hospitals and clinics and use kids with special needs to test the toys. The result was a special guide for parents of "differently abled" kids that helps them choose toys that children with special needs can enjoy and learn from.

Growing a business means looking beyond current markets to new ones. Marianne understood that children aren't the only people who like toys, so she organized The Annual Toy Tips "Executive Toy Test." Each year she invites 50 executives from all industries to play with toys to discover which are the best stress relievers. This event is held in a different city every year, which gives her a chance to observe differences in toy play from region to region. Marianne also now has six summer camps where kids test computer software.

Toy Tips has a five-year plan and is currently ahead of schedule in terms of growth. Marianne's goal is to make Toy Tips the only unbiased source of information on toys in the nation. The philosophy of Toy Tips has remained constant as a guide for the growth of the business: "Top Tips does not endorse or warrant any toy that it reviews." It considers itself an independent source for informed decision-making on the purchase of toys. With this mission in mind Marianne must decide where she should take the business from here. She has considered forming a non-profit corporation for research purposes as this would give her access to foundation grants. But establishing a non-profit corporation is more complicated and has more rules and regulations than a C-corporation. At this point, she is not sure what the advantages and disadvantages would be.

1. What regulations will specifically impact Toy Tips?
2. Into which other markets can Marianne take her business?
3. Are there any problems this business is likely to face?
4. Is there another corporate form that might work for this business?

PART 4

The Operating Structure of a New Venture

Until someone has a small business, they have no comprehension of how hard it is. People who start businesses from scratch, if they survive, are the toughest people on the face of the earth.

—SUE SZYMCZAK, SAFEWAY SLING

CHAPTER 10

The Big Picture

Overview

- *The nature of a virtual enterprise*
- *The steps in seeking a site for the new venture*
- *Characteristics of retail, service, and manufacturing sites*
- *The advantages and disadvantages of building, buying, or leasing a building*

What Does the Business Look Like?

If the entrepreneur has concluded there is a need or market for the new business concept, the first test of feasibility has been passed. The second test involves determining if the business is operationally feasible; that is, is there a viable way to produce the product or deliver the service to the customer profitably? What must be considered is:

- Where the business will be located
- How it will operate
- What the market strategy will be
- What the organizational infrastructure will look like

Defining and establishing the operational strategies will assist in answering these questions and the ultimate question,

Is the new venture operationally feasible?

Doing this section of the business plan will also force the entrepreneur to seriously consider how the business will work. It's one thing to come up with a great idea that people love. It's quite another to turn that idea into an operating business.

The Virtual Enterprise

When entrepreneurs contemplate starting businesses, perhaps they picture a traditional office, manufacturing plant, or retail outlet with employees. But that vision is changing. Out of necessity, the 1990s have ushered in a new type of business—the "virtual enterprise." The term **virtual enterprise** comes from the computer industry's latest offering in entertainment—virtual reality—which essentially allows the user to be an integral part of a video game's environment without leaving the safety of the real world.

In business, a "virtual enterprise" has much the same purpose. It allows the owner to actively build a company in an industry without incurring the risk of employees, costly equipment, and enormous overhead. The virtual enterprise's goal is to deliver to the customer the highest quality product at the lowest possible cost in a timely manner. To do this requires the participation and management of the entire distribution channel from producer to customer through a series of strategic alliances. Traditionally this was accomplished by building the business to the point where it could afford to buy out its suppliers and/or distributors, giving the company more control over quality and delivery. This strategy is known as **vertical integration.**

Today, however, it is much more difficult for a new venture to accomplish total in-house control of its value chain. The global marketplace is more complex, time to market has decreased, and it is difficult for any one company to have the expertise needed to master all the functional levels of the distribution channel. Today a growing company is more likely to increase its flexibility by choosing one function to concentrate on and sub-contracting other functions it does not want to handle. The general rule is, if the resources to manufacture, assemble, and distribute the product effectively already exist in the market in which you wish to do business, don't duplicate the effort. Form alliances. Besides streamlining the operation, these alliances have the added benefit of establishing peer-to-peer relationships rather than hierarchical ones as is seen in a vertically integrated channel. It becomes more of a team effort, with everyone having the ultimate goal of producing a successful product.

For example, a new equipment manufacturer, Gentech Corporation (See Case Study 2, p. 126), decided the only way to get off the ground and succeed in a very competitive market was to purchase existing components from established manufacturers so it wouldn't have to incur the heavy costs of tooling up a manufacturing plant. Gentech chose to establish an assembly operation and distribute its product initially through an established channel of equipment rental outlets. Gentech also formed alliances with its suppliers so the parts it received were made to their specifications, saving time and money.

Often a business whose competitive advantage lies in proprietary rights on its product will choose to maintain control of strategic functions and outsource such things as warehousing, transportation, and some aspects of marketing.

> *Becoming a virtual company allows the new venture to be more innovative, closer to the customer, and quicker to market.*

Becoming a virtual company allows the new venture to be more innovative, closer to the customer, and quicker to market. Of course, the ultimate in virtual enterprises is one where the entrepreneur literally outsources all business functions and acts as the ringmaster in a three ring circus. Profile 10.1 on p. 176 is an excellent example.

Yet another way that businesses are becoming more flexible and responsive is by forming alliances or teams of businesses to share resources and reduce costs. These alliances accomplish more than simple outsourcing. They may purchase major equipment jointly, or share the costs of research and development, and training. Particularly in the area of R&D, it is very difficult for any one small company to manage the expense alone. For example, the Massachusetts Metalforming Network put together $25,000 of its own money, which gave it the ability to secure $40,000 in grants. That $65,000 allowed the network to collaborate on research to find a good solvent to clean metal parts. This example demonstrates that even competing companies can enjoy the benefits of networking.

Small manufacturers like Erie Bolt Company were instrumental in starting a network of 16 suppliers in their industry. The network operates like a "virtual enterprise" that sub-contracts jobs to the network members who can do them most efficiently. The fact that they also share resources and facilities has given them an economy of scale that has produced a savings of 30 percent to the customers and more than doubled their business.

Networking and business alliances allow smaller businesses to bid successfully against large companies. They offer the convenience and savings of one source for everything, shared quality standards, and coordination of vendors. The key to success with a small business alliance is being willing to share internal information such as manufacturing processes, quality control practices, and product information for the good of all.

PROFILE 10.1

Taking the Virtual Concept to the Limit

Walden Paddlers is a one-person, start-up business located in Acton, Massachusetts. Its purpose is to design, produce, and market a technically advanced kayak made from recycled plastic that outperforms and under-prices the competition. Walden Paddlers' founder, Paul Farrow, comes out of the corporate world, having lost his job to restructuring. Not wanting to build his way back up in the corporate world, he sought to start a business that would allow him to work in the environment he enjoyed most—outdoors—and provide him with plenty of exercise. It took a vacation with his sons, kayaking on a lake, to come up with the perfect idea. Paul quickly realized that the kayak they were using, which was fairly basic, probably cost all of $17.50 to make (it was plastic); yet it retailed for $400. An opportunity was presenting itself.

Upon returning home, he dove into the world of kayaks, talking to anyone who knew anything about them and learning everything he could about design, products, manufacturing, and distribution. As a result of his research, he believed he could carve out a niche in the entry-level kayak market—which was not being well served by the three major manufacturers of kayaks—with a boat that was cheaper than others yet performed better. He identified his target market as a middle-aged person just learning to kayak and who would probably use it in fairly calm waters.

Paul knew he didn't have the resources to do it all himself and he wanted to get into the market very quickly, so he set out to form a series of alliances with established companies. The first alliance was with Hardigg Industries, a Massachusetts rotomolder of plastics. Paul convinced them to put to use some of their unused capacity molding kayaks. This was a fortuitous relationship as Hardigg believed in what Paul was trying to do and knew they held the key to his business getting off the ground. They also saw this as an opportunity to develop a new customer and another profit center for the business.

Paul also needed a designer. Through a series of contacts with various people, he finally found who he was looking for in Jeff Allott. They agreed to spread the payments for his work over the stages of development of the prototype.

The third alliance was with boat dealers. Paul decided to provide prospective dealers with demo boats they could use for 30 days. His only stipulation was that at the end of 30 days they either paid him or returned the boat. The plan worked and soon he had sold his first 100 boats. Farrow's operational strategy is to outsource as long as he can and ultimately create a deal with a major national distributor to reach a mass audience.

Building a virtual corporation and dealing with strategic alliances is not without its problems. For the entrepreneurial team that wants to maintain control of every aspect of the growing venture, it is frustrating to have to give up some of that control to other companies. It can also be a long and difficult process getting virtual partners to meet entrepreneurs' demands for quality, timeliness, and efficiency. Consequently, it is important that the entrepreneur and the virtual partner come to written agreement on their duties and responsibilities and that the relationship be beneficial to both parties. Many entrepreneurs have found that the benefits of virtual partners far outweigh the problems and that the virtual corporation is the most efficient and effective way to get the venture off the ground.

Looking Like a Major Corporation from the Start

The virtual enterprise is a concept whose time has come, but to take advantage of it the entrepreneur must understand what kind of business he or she will have and where it lies in the value chain. In Chapter 3 you learned about how to turn an idea for a product or service into a business. In Chapter 7 you saw how many different ways you can deliver a product or service to a customer. By this time you probably have a good idea whether you will have a retail business, a service business, a distributorship, or a manufacturing plant. This is an important first step because the operational decisions you make will depend in large part on the kind of business you have. Even if you have decided after reading about the virtual enterprise that this is what you want to accomplish, you will still need to visualize the big picture of how the business will work.

It is possible through the use of independent contractors and alliances to create what appears to be a large, complex organization. A major corporation has several key functional areas that are usually headed by upper level management—vice presidents. It may look something like this:

CEO			
VP Sales	**VP Marketing**	**VP Operations**	**Chief Financial Officer**

An entrepreneur generally does not have the financial resources to take on the high salaries and benefits of this type of management team. However, through the judicious use of independent contractors, an operational team that accomplishes these functions can be achieved through subcontractors without high-cost overhead.

Entrepreneur			
Sales Agents	Marketing Consultant	Subcontract	CPA
Sales Reps		Manufacturing	Bookkeeper

To the business world the entrepreneur is accomplishing the same functions as the major corporation; he or she is just not doing it with employees.

Technology has also contributed to helping start-up ventures perform like major corporations for relatively little money. Desktop computers and the latest software, such as computer-aided design, allow new ventures to do things that previously required experts. Electronic networks make it easier to communicate with strategic alliance partners and to access commercial information databases around the world. Computerizing control systems on machine tools permits growing entrepreneurial manufacturers to compete with major companies.

The Fantasy Tour of the Business

To make the job of defining the operations and requirements of the business easier, take an imaginary tour of the business. In this way you can begin to list all the functions, people, equipment, supplies, and space required to run the business. As you enter the imaginary door of the business, ask yourself three questions:

1. Who does the work in this business?
2. Where do they work?
3. What do they need to do the work?

Then begin making lists of tasks, equipment, and people needed to run the business. This information will also be useful when you need to figure expenses for financial projections later on.

The Site for the Business

You may already be familiar with the three key factors for determining value in real estate: "location, location, location." The location of the business has a serious impact on its success. Location determines who sees the business, how easily they can access it, and whether or not they will want to access it. And since many business owners consider their business site as permanent, selecting the best site becomes one of the most crucial decisions to make, one that will need to be justified to the readers of the business plan.

Site decisions begin at a macro level with the state or region of the country and work their way down to the parcel on which the facility is located. That is the process followed in the discussion of the site.

Choosing the Region or State

Locating a site for a high-growth venture normally begins by identifying the area of the country that seems best suited to the type of business being started. "Best suited" may mean that firms in that industry tend to congregate in a particular region, such as the high-tech firms that gravitate to Rte. 128 in Massachusetts. For some businesses "best suited" may mean that a state is offering special financial and other incentives for businesses to locate there. In yet another case, "best suited" means a manufacturer choosing to locate near major suppliers. Unfortunately, often the entrepreneur starts the business in a particular region because that's where he or she happens to live. This may be fine during the incubation period, but the area must be considered carefully for what it contributes to the potential success of the business.

Of course, there is another important factor that must be included in the decision mix, and that is the entrepreneur's desire for a certain lifestyle. Sometimes the desire to maintain a particular lifestyle in a particular location far outweighs the potential negative effects of locating the business in a less than optimal location. Mo Siegal, Founder of Celestial Seasonings, was one such entrepreneur. He was adamant about remaining in his beloved Colorado when he started his now enormously successful venture. Doing business there may have cost more and not have been as convenient for shipping purposes, but the ability to run his business from his home town was more important. In fact, as it turns out, the image of Colorado with its Rockies, cool streams, and beautiful blue skies actually enhanced the image of his herbal teas.

Choosing a Community

The community in which you currently reside may not necessarily be the best place in which to start the business. Certainly it is always easier to deal with something you know well, particularly when starting something as risky as a new business, but don't assume the location factor applies only to decisions within your own neighborhood. Many potentially successful new ventures have failed because they were not located in a region or community that supported that type of business.

To start, it is important to examine the major competitors in the industry to see where they tend to locate. Is it in particular areas of the city, in specific regions of the country, or near major transportation routes? Doing this will give the first clue to a potentially successful location with the required infrastructure and a skilled work force. You also want to define your business's specific needs in terms of labor (skilled/unskilled), land (amount and type), and transportation (highways, ports, international airports). Three important factors about any area under consideration should be examined: economic base, financial incentives, and demographics.

Economic Base. The economic base of a region or community is simply the major source of income for the area. Communities are viewed as primarily industrial, agricultural, or service-oriented. In general, industrial communities export more goods out of the community than they import into it. For example, suppose the community's principal income is derived from farming and the associated products it ships to other communities. This activity brings money into the community. Now suppose the citizens of the community must travel to another community to do major shopping. This activity takes money out of the community. The important thing to learn about the community is whether the money brought in from farming exceeds the money leaving for shopping. If that is so, the community appears to have a growing economic base, which is a favorable factor for new businesses.

You can learn more about the economic base of any community in which you are interested by contacting the state or regional economic development agency in the area. These organizations exist to bring new business into the region, so they have to stay on top of what is going on. They can give you all the statistics you will need on the economic condition of the region as well as estimate the cost of doing business there.

Financial Incentives. Most community governments are faced with cash needs that go well beyond the tax tolerance level of its citizens; consequently, they work diligently with economic development agencies to attract new businesses and the accompanying tax revenues into the community. One of the ways they attract business is to offer incentives such as lower taxes, cheaper land, and employee training programs. Some communities have enterprise zones, which give the businesses that locate in them favorable tax treatment from the state based on the number of jobs created, as well as lower land costs and rental rates. They also expedite permit processes and help in any way they can to make the move easier.

Look carefully, however, at communities that offer up-front cash in compensation for the community's lack of up-to-date infrastructure. They may be hiding a high corporate tax rate or some other disincentive that could hurt your business's chances of success. In general, the larger the incentives, the more careful you should be in doing your homework.

Demographics. In addition to studying the economic base and the community's attitude toward new business, look carefully at the population base. Is it growing or shrinking? Is it aging or getting younger? Is it culturally diverse? The level of and quantity of disposable income in the community will indicate whether there is enough money to purchase whatever you are offering. Demographic information is usually based on the U.S. Census, which tracks changes in population size and characteristics. The U.S. is divided into *Standard Metropolitan Statistical Areas (SMSAs)*, which are geographic areas that include a major metropolitan area like Los Angeles or Houston. These are further divided into *census tracts*, which contain approximately 4,000-5,000 people, and neighborhood blocks. With this information you can readily determine, for example, if the city in which you want to locate a new software development firm has enough people with sufficient technical and educational skills to support it. Population data also indicate the number of people available to work. Demographic data is easily obtained from the economic development agency, the public library, or the post office, which tracks populations by zip code.

Incubators. Some entrepreneurs find it helpful to start their new venture's life in a business incubator, which has the same purpose as an incubator for an infant—to create a controlled environment that will enhance the chances of the business surviving the start-up phase. Private and state-sponsored incubators can be found in nearly every region of the country for almost any type of business. They offer space at a lower than market rate to several businesses who may then share common support functions like receptionist, copy machine, and conference room. The incubator may even offer business courses and training to help new entrepreneurs with the myriad details involved in running the business. After about three to five years, depending on the incubator, the young business is required and helped to move into its own site elsewhere in the community.

Some incubators cater only to high-tech firms or to service firms. Others like the Entrepreneur Partnership Program at the Mall of America in Bloomington, Minnesota, help entrepreneurs determine if their retail or service businesses are suited to the demands of a major mall. This particular program helps the entrepreneur formulate a business plan and open a store. It also provides incentives such as waiving the costs of improving the store space and consulting in marketing and operations.

Choosing a Retail Site. With a retail business, the entrepreneur is dealing directly with the consumer, so, naturally, one of the first considerations is being near the customers. Since a retail business lives or dies based on the number of consumers who have access to the business, it is important to locate where there are suitable concentrations of consumers.

The Trade Area

The trade area is the region from which the entrepreneur expects to draw customers. The type of business will determine to a large extent the size of the trade area. For example, if the business sells general merchandise that can be found almost anywhere, the trade area is much smaller as consumers will not travel great distances to purchase common goods. On the other hand a specialty outlet, for example a boutique clothing store with unusual apparel, may draw people from other communities as well.

Once the location within the community is identified, the trade area can be calculated. With a map of the community, designate the site for the business; then, using a compass, place the epicenter on the proposed site and draw a circle that represents the distance (the radius) you expect people to drive to reach the site. Within the circle is the trade area, which can now be studied in more detail. Using the demographics and a census tract map, identify census tracts within the trade area and look at the census data to determine how many people reside within the boundaries of the trade area. The demographic information will also describe these people in terms of education level, income level, average number of children, and so forth.

Competition

Within the trade area you can also identify the competition. To do this, drive through the area (assuming it is not too large) and spot competing businesses. Note their size and number, and also gauge how busy they are at various times of the day by observing their parking lots or actually entering the business. If competitors are located in shopping malls or strip centers, look for clusters of stores similar to yours and low vacancy rates. This would indicate a strong attraction for the site. Look at the stores near your proposed site to check for compatibility. Often locating near a competitor is a wise choice because it encourages comparison shopping. Observe the character of the area. Does it appear to be successful and well maintained?

Accessibility

It is important to identify the routes your customers might take to reach the proposed site: highways, streets, and public transportation routes. If the site is difficult to locate and hard to reach, you can be certain potential customers will not exert the effort to find you. Also check the parking situation. Most communities require a sufficient amount of parking space for new construction, either through lots or garages; however, in some older areas, street parking is the only available option. If parking is a problem to find or too expensive, you will lose customers.

Do a foot and car traffic count for your proposed site to determine how busy the area is. Remember, retail businesses rely heavily on traffic for customers. Whether you need a high volume of foot traffic is a function of the type of business. Obviously, a coffee house benefits immensely from a high volume of foot traffic, whereas for a warehouse hardware store it may not be as vital. A traffic count is easily accomplished by positioning yourself near the targeted site and tallying the customers going by and into the business. City planning departments and transportation departments maintain auto traffic counts for major arterials in the city.

Choosing the Service/Wholesale Site

If a service or wholesale business has customers who come to the place of business, the needs for a site will parallel those of the retailer in some respects. Accessibility, attractiveness, and a trade area of sufficient size are all important factors in the selection of a site. The entrepreneur does not, however, need to choose from the more expensive commercial sites as the expectations of the customers may not be as great for a wholesale outlet that sells to the public, for example. Customers going to these types of businesses usually want to save money, so they don't expect the "Cadillac" version of a business site. Some service businesses, on the other hand, require attractive office space that is easily accessible. These are usually professional businesses—lawyers, accountants, consultants and so forth. The image they present through the location and appearance of their office is crucial to the success of the business.

Many service and wholesale businesses do not have customers coming to their places of business. Some examples are distributors, contractors, and certain types of consultants. In these cases, it is more prudent for the business to be located in less expensive, less high-profile areas of town where they are still near the customers they serve but can take advantage of a savings in rent or land costs.

Choosing the Manufacturing Site

For the manufacturer, the location choices narrow significantly. Communities have zoning laws that limit manufacturing companies to certain designated areas away from residential, retail, and office commercial sites to reduce the chance of noise, odor, and pollutants affecting the citizens. Often these areas are known as **industrial parks,** and they usually are equipped with electrical power and sewage plants appropriate to manufacturing. By locating in one of these parks, the new business may also benefit from the synergy of other manufacturing nearby. Opportunities for networking and sharing resources and costs are enhanced.

Another common location for manufacturing is **enterprise zones,** which are public-private partnerships designed to bring jobs to inner cities, downtown areas, and rural areas suffering from the shift of jobs and population to the suburbs. There are 35 states (plus the District of Columbia) with authorized enterprise zones. The draw for businesses is tax incentives, regulatory relief, and employee training programs. However, the enterprise zone program is not without its critics. The principal criticism is that there is no net economic gain for the community. Since businesses often move from one area of town to the enterprise zone simply to take advantage of tax breaks, no new jobs are created. Yet another criticism comes from established businesses in the area who complain that the zones are nothing but incubators for competitors. In spite of these criticisms, enterprise zones are likely to continue as one method for creating jobs and rebuilding decaying inner cities.

Wherever an entrepreneur looks for a manufacturing site, he or she is concerned with four key factors: access to suppliers, cost of labor, access to transportation, and cost of utilities. These factors may not be equally weighted.

Depending on the type of manufacturer, one or more factors may have greater importance in evaluating a site.

Access to Suppliers

Manufacturers and processors usually try to locate within a reasonable distance from their major suppliers to cut shipping time and save transportation costs. Certainly a food processor attempts to set up business near the growing fields so the food is as fresh as possible when it arrives at the processing plant. Similarly, a manufacturer that uses steel as one of its main raw materials might want to locate in the same region of the country as the steel mills to save the high costs of trucking heavy steel great distances.

Cost of Labor

Today many manufacturers choose a location based on the cost of labor rather than proximity to suppliers, since labor is generally the single highest cost in the production of goods. Wages and laws relating to workers, such as workers' compensation, vary from state to state, and sometimes from city to city. For example, California laws and cost of living tend to make it a more expensive place to hire employees than those same employees might cost in Missouri. Some labor-intensive businesses have found that the only way they can compete is by having plants in Mexico or China, where labor costs are a fraction of those in the U.S., and where laborers are not protected by as many laws. Mattel Toy Company, for example, has a plant in China to produce the hundreds of different toys it markets every year. The bottom line is that the entrepreneur must weigh the costs in terms of access to labor carefully when considering a particular location for a manufacturing plant.

Access to Transportation

Most manufacturers prefer to locate near major transportation networks: railways, major highways, airports, and ports of call. The reasoning is obvious: The greater the distance between the plant and a major transportation network, the higher the cost to the company and ultimately the customer. Also, the more transportation people who handle the product, the greater the cost. Thus, in terms of simple economics, to remain competitive manufacturers must consider the cost-benefit of locating away from a major transportation network. The higher transportation costs will result in a smaller profit margin for the company or higher costs for the customers. Either way you lose.

Cost of Utilities

Utility rates vary from state to state, and usually from city to city within a given state. If the new venture is heavily dependent on electricity, gas, or coal, this factor could be a significant variable in the cost of producing a product and therefore should be examined carefully.

The Building: The Lease-Buy-Build Decision

To this point, only the site itself has been considered. Naturally there is a building or facility involved as well, which makes the site decision that much more complex. If the site contains an existing building, the question becomes whether to lease or buy. If the site is bare land, building a facility is the only choice. As a significant portion of a new venture's start-up costs is contained in a facility, each of these scenarios is looked at in more detail.

The Existing Building

Any existing building on a potential site must be examined carefully with consideration to the following questions:

- Is the building of sufficient size to meet current and reasonable future needs?
- Do the building and site allow for future expansion?
- Is there sufficient parking?
- Is there space for customers, storage, inventory, office space, and rest rooms?

Allowing for future growth is essential. The initial higher cost of a larger building is often offset by avoiding the extraordinarily high costs of moving and the potential for lost sales and time away from the fundamental work of the business while the business is in transition.

When examining an existing building, begin with the exterior and ask the following questions:

1. Does the building have curbside appeal, assuming customers will come to the site?
2. Is the building compatible with its surroundings?
3. Does it have enough windows of sufficient size?
4. Is the entrance inviting?
5. Is the signage attractive and does it satisfy the local regulations?
6. Is the parking adequate to meet customer and employee demand and satisfy local building codes?

7. Does the interior of the building meet your needs in terms of walls, floors, and ceilings?
8. Are there sufficient lighting fixtures, outlets, and enough power to run equipment?

These are just a few of the questions to ask before finalizing a decision on a building. Most entrepreneurs can answer the above questions to their satisfaction, but to be certain the building is not hiding anything that could come back to haunt the entrepreneur and be costly for the business, it is wise to hire a licensed contractor or inspector to examine the building for structural soundness.

Leasing a Building

The speed of change, innovation, and technological advancement has and will continue to shorten product and service life cycles, and this has an impact on the facilities in which businesses operate. Buildings, on the other hand, have long physical lives and typically are very expensive to refurbish and remodel. Consequently in many communities factories and retail outlets can be seen lying vacant for long periods of time, even years. Ultimately they sell for or are leased at an amount far below what it cost to build the building in the first place.

It has been suggested that one solution to the problem is for businesses to hold short leases of five years or less. In this way the company does not tie up precious capital that it may not be able to recover, and it has the ability to move on when a product or service is deemed technologically antiquated and no longer in demand. There are, however, some serious disadvantages to short-term leasing.

Rents are escalated more frequently due to short-term renewal. Many a business has found itself in this awkward position. Demand for the product or service has been successful beyond initial predictions, so the business needs to remain in its current location beyond the term of the lease. When the entrepreneur goes to renegotiate the lease terms, he or she inevitably finds the landlord intends to raise the rents for a new lease. This is usually justified by increasing market rents; however, at the same time, the landlord is aware that it would be costly for the tenant to relocate. The business would have little time to do so and still maintain its current production rate. Furthermore, the potential for having to replace employees and create new logistics for suppliers and buyers is daunting. All these factors put the entrepreneur in a very weak position to negotiate a new lease.

To strengthen your position, when the lease is first negotiated, include a clause that permits the option to renew at a specified rate, and an escape clause in case the business must be closed. These two clauses may cost a bit more initially, but can yield long-term savings.

It will be more difficult to remodel mid-term. If you have a short-term lease, the landlord will be less likely to approve any substantial tenant improvements if they do not increase the value of the building to future tenants.

When the lease is first negotiated, come prepared with a five-year plan for the facility and be able to demonstrate the benefits to the landlord of allowing the remodeling of the building.

You will not be able to show a substantial asset on the balance sheet. Therefore, it will not be a good vehicle for raising capital.

If you own the building, you can later sell it to raise needed capital and lease it back, thereby avoiding moving costs and providing the new landlord with an instant tenant, a factor that increases the value of the building to the new owner.

The cost of leasing a building is a function of the demand in the marketplace for rentals as well as a number of other factors.

- Buildings that are newer, suitable for a variety of uses, and well-located generally enjoy higher lease rates, as do buildings in short supply.
- Since rent is normally paid based on square footage of space, the larger the space, the more costly the lease.
- Retail and service business sites are generally more expensive than industrial sites.
- A retail site in a regional mall will likely be the most expensive.

Be aware, though, that while manufacturing sites enjoy low rental rates, they usually pay higher amounts for water, power, and sewage. That is why it is important to consider all the costs related to leasing a facility. Not including the cost of expensive utilities or a common use area fee could spell disaster to the business's cash flow.

Businesses face three basic types of leases.

- **Gross lease.** This lease allows the entrepreneur to pay a fixed rate per month, with the landlord covering the cost (and getting the benefit) of insurance, taxes, and building operating expenses such as outdoor lighting, security, and so forth.
- **Net lease (Also known as triple net).** This lease has the entrepreneur paying a fixed monthly rate plus taxes, operating expenses, essentially every-

thing but the mortgage and the building insurance, which the landlord pays. What the entrepreneur actually rents is a shell with stipulated improvements.

- **Percentage lease.** This is the most complicated of all the lease types because it has several variations. It can be written as a percentage of the net income of the tenant or as a flat rate plus a percentage of the gross revenues. The latter is very common in retail operations.

Fortunately for businesses seeking lease facilities, it's a renters' market and will probably remain so for the foreseeable future as demand lags the over-supply created in the 1980s. Moreover, savvy customers in the 1990s expect businesses to reflect the trend toward "less is more" by controlling costs and simplifying operations. In a renters' market, businesses can expect to negotiate leases that provide a certain period of free rent, free parking, allowances for tenant improvements, and greater flexibility to extend or shorten the lease. For example, one Chicago-based company renegotiated its high-rent lease, reducing its obligation from $36 per square foot to $22. In addition, the landlord agreed to cover the $1 million tenant improvements, which would be recovered over the term of the new ten-year lease.

Even more savings in a lease can be achieved by reading it carefully.

- Make sure there is a provision for examining the books of the landlord to view the costs related to the building. In this way you may discover "pass-throughs," or costs in the form of capital improvements that should not be passed on to the tenants, such as the cost of a new security system. You may also find charges to the tenants for expenses that are rightfully the owner's, such as personal services to the owner who is also a tenant of the building.
- Check carefully for clerical mistakes, particularly the easily overlooked simple items like addresses, suite numbers, square footage, and rental amounts.
- Talk to other tenants of a building to find out common needs that may be achieved through a unified effort.
- Ask for a breakdown of taxes and operating expenses for the previous three years and projections for the next five years.
- Ask for a work letter that explains all improvements the landlord will make for the tenant as well as work the tenant must complete and all costs associated with the completion of these improvements.
- Make certain the building meets requirements and safety levels prescribed by the Environmental Protection Agency.

Remember first and foremost, leases are written from the landlord's point of view and are, therefore, negotiable. Just because something appears in printed form does not mean it is true or that you have to agree to it. A lease represents a significant portion of a business's overhead, and you will most likely have to live with it for a long time, so make sure it's what you really want. Leases are a great way for start-up businesses to get into the marketplace, but don't let your enthusiasm for starting the business blind you to the potentially disastrous terms of a poorly written lease. The best advice is to seek the assistance of an attorney who can represent your interests.

Buying a Building

If the entrepreneur has the resources, buying a building has some advantages. A valuable asset is immediately created on the balance sheet, which can be leveraged later on when growth capital is needed. For example, the building could be sold and leased back (called a sale-leaseback), withdrawing equity for other uses and negotiating favorable long-term lease terms. Sale-leasebacks are attractive options for investors and so these buildings generally sell quickly. Of course, when you sell the building, you effectively lose control of it, so be certain to negotiate terms that allow you to remodel and extend the lease should you wish to do so.

One advantage of owning a building is that it can be traded in a tax-deferred exchange for other property you need. For example, suppose you owned an office building but needed a distribution warehouse to support a new direction your business was taking. You might take advantage of a tax-deferred exchange by trading the office building for the warehouse. The exchange would defer capital gains tax on the sale of the office, and you would have the warehouse you need.

One other option to consider is a joint venture between you, the entrepreneur, and a real estate developer on a building in which you will be one of the tenants. If you are able to occupy a substantial portion of the building, it is easier for the developer to acquire a mortgage and additional tenants. Of course, this type of arrangement has the inherent problems of any partnership and should be considered carefully with the advice of an attorney before any agreement is executed.

Buying a building requires a contract, much like a lease agreement. It spells out the terms of the purchase and the items included and excluded from the purchase agreement. As always, read it carefully to make sure that what you agreed to verbally has been translated correctly on paper. It would be wise to hire a due diligence team (inspector, contractor, CPA, attorney) to inspect the building and the agreement so your interests are protected.

Building the Facility

When you can't find the type of building in the location you want, building the facility from the ground up becomes the only option. This will entail an architect, permits, possibly zoning variances, a construction bidding process, off-site improvements (curbs, gutters, water and power lines, roads), and a lengthy building and inspection process. This option should not be undertaken without the aid of a licensed general contractor. Be sure to check the reputation of any contractor you are considering. This is important should the contractor have a dispute with any of the subcontractors hired for the various aspects of the job. The subcontractors have a right to lien the property, which is owned by you. You will then have to sue the contractor to resolve the issue and remove the lien (you cannot receive a Certificate of Occupancy if any liens are present), and this is a time-consuming and costly process.

Constructing a building is no doubt the most complex option; however, you will end up with a building that completely meets your needs.

Also, as you are most probably responsible to the lender for the construction loan, you can ensure that any subcontractors are paid by 1) using a voucher system, which is a cumbersome method whereby the subcontractor receives a voucher for work completed and must take it to the lending bank for payment and release of liens, or 2) by paying the subcontractors directly and receiving lien releases. The latter is known as "jointing a check." It prevents the general contractor from using the funds for other purposes and potentially not having the money to pay the subcontractor.

Constructing a building is no doubt the most complex option; however, you will end up with a building that completely meets your needs. This option is most suitable when the needs for the building and/or the location are unique, when you have the time to wait, and when you intend to remain in the facility long term.

Starting the Business from Home

Almost 20 percent of the 92 million households in America have home offices that produce an income for the owner. It is estimated that more than 1,200 new home businesses begin every day. Add to that the increasing number of people employed in traditional offices who work at least part of the week from home as telecommuters and you have approximately 38 million people who work from home!

Some of the largest, most successful companies in the world today started from home, including Apple Computers, to name just one. The biggest reason so many new ventures start from home is cost, as one of the biggest line items in the budget of a start-up is rent or the cost of buying a building. Consequently, many new companies choose to start with minimal overhead until their product or service gets off the ground to better ensure that the company survives the risky start-up phase. Once orders or clients start coming in regularly, the business can move to a more permanent location.

For some entrepreneurs, however, the goal is to never leave home, but to subcontract all activities that cannot be accomplished from home. This new type of business is a phenomenon of the 1990s and is likely to continue in popularity as people seek more control over their lives, to reduce stress, and to avoid interruptions and traffic jams. With a phone, fax, copier, and computer, technology has made possible the era of the telecommuter and the virtual enterprise.

Anyone considering working from home, even for the short term, should consult with local government agencies to see what the zoning ordinances are. In general, most communities frown on home-based businesses in residential areas, especially if the business receives a lot of auto traffic. For example, Los Angeles prohibits home-based businesses, even those of typical home-office users like consultants, free-lance writers, and artists. However, in spite of the ban, it is estimated that more than 2.2 million households in the Los Angeles area contain a full- or part-time home business. To avoid potential penalties, check the laws and restrictions regarding home-based businesses in your local community.

Final Thoughts

The information collected on where to locate the business and whether to lease, buy, or build the facility will be used in various parts of the business plan. For example, the information on the trade area for the product/service will be useful in the marketing plan section where you elaborate on how to reach the target market. One of the "Four P's" of that marketing plan is *place*—where the business will be located. Information on rental rates and building costs will certainly play a role in the financial plan section of the business plan.

✓ New Venture Checklist

Have you

☐ Determined how your business will operate?

☐ Found ways to operate like a virtual enterprise?

☐ Located a site for the business?

☐ Examined the economic base, incentives, demographics, and trade area?

☐ Decided whether to lease, buy, or build the facility?

Additional Sources of Information

"The Survey of Buying Power," *Sales and Marketing Management* (Annual).
Choosing a Retail Location, SBA Pub. No. MP10.
Locating or Relocating Your Business, SBA Pub. No. MP2.
Practical Business Use of Government Statistics, SBA Small Business
    Management Series, Stock No 045-000-00131-8.
Using Census Data to Select a Store Site, SBA Pub. No. MA2.023.

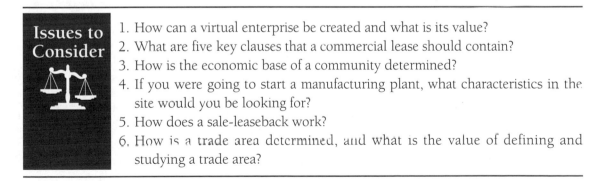

Issues to Consider

1. How can a virtual enterprise be created and what is its value?
2. What are five key clauses that a commercial lease should contain?
3. How is the economic base of a community determined?
4. If you were going to start a manufacturing plant, what characteristics in the site would you be looking for?
5. How does a sale-leaseback work?
6. How is a trade area determined, and what is the value of defining and studying a trade area?

The Operational Plan

Designing an Operational Plan

Many high-growth ventures involve new, innovative products. For these product manufacturing or assembly ventures, the operational plan for the business consists of a fairly complex analysis that includes product development, prototyping, production processes, and inventory control mechanisms. The depth of analysis is a function of the type of product or service being offered, the technological newness of the product, and the number of different ways the product can be produced. Generally speaking, product companies must undergo more in-depth, thorough technical analysis than service companies, although a lack of thoroughness in either case can spell disaster for a new venture.

While this chapter focuses on product development and manufacturing, it does so only because generally speaking, that type of business is the most complex. Those readers who have an interest in service, retail, wholesale, or other types of businesses can pick and choose from the chapter the information appropriate to their type of operation. The fundamental issues of designing a prototype, testing it, and planning for how the business will produce the product are the same for all types of businesses.

New Product Development

The processes, techniques, and time lines—in fact the whole area of product development in the United States, has undergone profound change. Those who study this area are convinced this change has been brought about by three factors:

- International competition
- Sophisticated customers in fragmented markets
- Widely diversified and changing technologies[1]

International Competition

Since the 1980s the number of companies competing in the global marketplace has increased enormously. Couple that with the fact that similarity in product concepts has expanded and you have the makings of an intensely competitive arena for product development. An American company finds it is no longer competing simply with other American companies, but with companies from diverse regions of the world who bring their own trademark to the process and the products.

Sophisticated Customers from Fragmented Markets

The ability of today's customer to differentiate products on a very subtle level and the demands of customers for products that reflect their lifestyles and value systems make it incumbent upon product developers to create products that differentiate themselves on many levels in the marketplace. Where once product performance and price were the main competitive measures, today these two factors are givens. They must be present for a company to even begin to be competitive. This means that a manufacturing company can never

---

[1]Clark, K & T. Fujimoto. (1991). *Product Development Performance*. Boston: Harvard Business School Press.

stop improving its design and manufacturing processes if it wishes to remain competitive.

Widely Diversified and Changing Technologies

Certainly it is recognized that technology is important and essential to product development, and today the marginal cost of added technological capability is small. But a growing business cannot build its competitive advantage around technology alone. Customers are primarily interested in a product that will meet a need or desire, and not necessarily interested in the technology or technological processes that produced it. Often a customer is not willing to pay for or is not interested in having added technology just because it's easily available.

A company operating in a technology-based industry like electronics must keep up with changing consumer demand as well as the technological innovations of its competitors. Competitive advantage can be built around a line of market-differentiated products, but is enhanced by proprietary processes. In the case of a new product, it must not only create value for the customer, but must also be difficult for someone else to produce at the same quality level and for the same cost.

Product Development the Entrepreneur's Way

Most large corporations have separate departments responsible for research and development, engineering, and testing. In many cases, the budgets for these particular departments are astronomical, since new product development, as well as the continual improvement of existing products and processes, is considered one of the most important and challenging tasks of high-performing, world-class businesses.

In the case of start-up ventures, the task is equally challenging; however, most new ventures, unlike large corporations, have very limited or nonexistent budgets. Funding research and development, engineering, and testing for a new company is considered the highest risk stage by most investors; consequently, this type of funding is difficult, if not impossible, for entrepreneurs to secure. They are left with a dilemma: how to perform the R & D that will result in a factory-quality, engineered prototype as quickly as possible yet as inexpensively as possible. It is not surprising then that many good product ideas fail to achieve market introduction.

Other difficulties faced by entrepreneurs at this pre-start-up stage include finding the right consultants to do the engineering, material and parts sourcing, and model building. This effort can be expensive and time consuming, so choosing the wrong consulting firms can be devastating. As engineers tend to specialize (mechanical, electrical, civil), it is possible that one product may require the services of more than one type of engineer. Some of the areas of product development that require engineering analysis, design, and expertise include:

- Component design
- Materials specifications
- Machinery to process
- Ergonomic design
- Packaging design
- Assembly drawings and specifications
- Parts and material sourcing (suppliers)
- Operator's and owner's manuals

Entrepreneurs who develop products usually go through a process much like that shown in Figure 11.1.

Figure 11.1: The Product Development Cycle

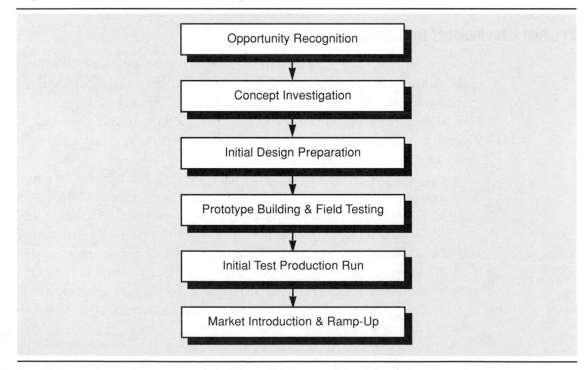

Opportunity Recognition

Recall from Chapter 2 that the first stage in the development of a business concept is opportunity recognition: identifying a niche that has not been served, detecting an improvement in an existing product, or seeing an opportunity for a breakthrough product. Once the opportunity has been identified, it is critical to move forward with the next stage, concept investigation, to shorten the product development cycle as much as possible.

Concept Investigation

Concept investigation is simply doing some investigation to determine if the idea currently exists, if there is a potential market, how much it will cost to produce the product, and how much time will it take. This last piece of information is crucial since an enforced shorter development cycle allows the company to have a first-mover advantage, better meet its customers' needs, lower the costs of production, and cut off the tendency by the entrepreneur or inventor to keep "improving the product," instead of getting it out into the market.

Initial Design Preparation

The first stages of design preparation go hand in hand with concept investigation because the entrepreneur normally needs some preliminary working drawings of the product to estimate costs and manufacturing processes. These preliminary drawings are also used to apply for a patent if the product is patentable. However, once it has been determined the product has real potential, it is time to bring in the design engineers and the other members of the functional team—marketing, operations, and finance—to put together accurate drawings of the product and initial specifications.

Prototype Building and Field Testing

From the initial engineered drawings will come the prototype or model of the product. Often the first prototype does not closely resemble the final product in appearance, but usually does in function. In fact, today it is important to reach the physical stage of prototyping as quickly as possible because involving key functional team members is much less expensive at this early stage. The importance of involving key functional players in the development of the prototype cannot be overstated. It is far less costly to discover at this stage from the marketing expert that the customer will not like the ergonomics of the product, or from the operations and finance experts that the equipment to produce the product is beyond the current budget. With little money invested, team members are free to simulate the use of the product and make mistakes while finding the best version of the prototype.

Technology has even entered the prototyping stage of product development in the form of "rapid prototyping." Today you can purchase a device that, working from information in your computer, will cut and shape metal or other raw materials into three-dimensional parts. In this way, you can actually design a part on the computer screen and then cut it into a real prototype virtually instantly in your office. The obvious advantage of this is avoiding the shipping of two-dimensional drawings to a parts manufacturer and then waiting for the part to be made.

With a prototype it is also easier to acquire more accurate target market demand information, more accurate cost estimates, and a clearer sense of whether the product will work as proposed in the design phase. The added benefit is that eliminating features that do not create value in the mind of the customer can reduce manufacturing costs 25-40 percent. Moreover, through field testing the prototype, adjustments and modifications can be made, leading to a production-quality prototype: in essence, the final product.

> *Businesses that do not manufacture products—service, retail, wholesale, and so forth—still need to design a prototype.*

Various engineers can be employed to take the crude prototype and determine the best assembly design, the types of materials to use, the most effective components, the required suppliers, and which other subcontractors might be needed to make the product ready for production. From the engineered assembly drawings, parts lists, and specifications, the production-quality prototype can be assembled. Small engineering firms or solo engineers who support entrepreneurs and inventors, small job shops, machine shops and/or model builders may be used to complete the prototype. These sources are normally quicker and less expensive than the larger, better-known firms. When seeking an engineer or model builder, the entrepreneur must use caution. Careful analysis of qualifications, experience, and references relative to the task are essential. A good source of referrals is a major university engineering department and/or other engineers.

Businesses that do not manufacture products—service, retail, wholesale, and so forth—still need to design a prototype, but the prototype in this case will not be physical. Instead it will be a design for how the business will provide a service or product to its customer, maintain and control inventories, hire employees, and guarantee quality and satisfaction. Entrepreneurs who intend to start nonmanufacturing businesses should read this chapter substituting the design for their service as the product where appropriate.

One of the time-consuming aspects of this stage of product development is sourcing the components and raw materials for the product. Deciding which switch to use, who should mold the plastic, or which vendors provide the best materials at the lowest prices requires a lot of leg work. Of course, the entrepreneur could leave these decisions to the design engineers, but at $150 an hour, it doesn't make sense to have the engineer searching for and comparing all the parts and materials. The engineer may, however, offer suggestions based on experience, but the actual leg work is usually done by the entrepreneur and the founding team. What the engineer does is ensure the product meets OSHA standards (assuming it needs to) and suggest warning labels that may be required on the product.

Initial Test Production Run

The number of prototypes used in the field testing stage is limited. The entrepreneur has usually not yet met the supplier's volume level for discounts, so the cost to produce at this stage is very high. After conducting a small initial test production run in a limited market, the product is honed to completion and market-ready status. It is also the first opportunity for the entrepreneur to test the manufacturing and assembly processes and determine accurate costs of production at varying levels of volume.

Product Market Introduction and Ramp-Up

At this stage the product is ready for introduction into the market, and the manufacturing processes are in place to meet projected demand.

Today it is simply not enough to produce a high-quality product at a fair price. To become and remain competitive, the new business must strive for a product development cycle that achieves low cost and high quality as quickly as possible.

Quality Function Deployment

The team-based approach to product development referred to previously is known as Quality Function Deployment (QFD). QFD was developed in 1972 at Mitsubishi's Kobe shipyards and was later adopted by Toyota because it was thought to reduce design costs by 60 percent and design time by 40 percent. QFD was introduced in the United States in 1986 at Ford and Xerox.

PROFILE 11.1

Shortening Development Time Through Teams: The 3M Experience

While 3M manufactures a variety of consumer and industrial products, it is probably best known for its adhesives, namely Scotch Tape® and Post-it Notes®. Because it focuses on unpatentable products whose origins lie in customer needs, it is crucial that 3M be able to identify and solve problems quickly to get new products to market. Using the traditional engineering development cycle would put 3M at a disadvantage, as it would be fairly easy for a competitor to replicate the production process and come out with a competing product shortly after 3M's introduction of its product.

To solve this problem, 3M built a research and design center in Austin, Texas, and housed both its engineers and its marketing staff there. Working together, the Austin group found they could work from physical prototypes almost immediately without the need for detailed drawings. In fact, it made more sense to customize and modify the design using a physical prototype, resulting in the right version being reached much more quickly. This was true, for example, with their mechanical splicing device for optical cables; they were able to go into full production without detailed blueprints, and the product worked. Interestingly enough, when they ultimately did create the blueprints according to the original design, the product didn't work!

The purpose of QFD is to insert customer input throughout the design, manufacturing, and service delivery phases of product development. The market research done for QFD addresses strategic decisions such as performance versus comfort, and functional or ergonomic decisions such as where to place a handle. It does this through customer input known as "Voice of the Customer," which is a prioritized, hierarchical set of "customer needs."

QFD is depicted through the use of four houses:

Customer Needs. Customer needs is a description in the customer's own words of what their needs are with regard to the product. For example, in the case of a new portable computer, the customer may say, "It must be easily carried in a briefcase." A list of several hundred needs may be developed, but they generally fall into three categories: basic needs or assumptions about the product (e.g. that it must be small); desired functions (e.g. what they want it to do); and unusual or unexpected desires (e.g. needs that may surprise or excite the customer).

Figure 11.2: The House of Quality

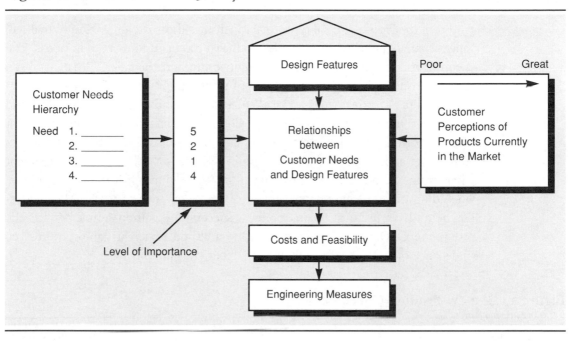

Hierarchy of Needs. Customer needs are structured into three categories: primary, secondary, and tertiary. Primary needs are strategic and consist of the top five to ten customer needs. These direct the engineers as to whether, using the laptop computer as an example, the size, weight, or functions of the computer should be the focus of their efforts. Each primary need then is expanded into three to ten secondary or tactical needs—in other words, what the product development team must do to satisfy that primary need. For example, how is the desired size achieved, or what is the optimal shape? Tertiary or operational needs provide the engineers and R&D personnel with details needed to develop the solutions to the tactical requirements. For example, how you know when the desired size is achieved.

Importances. Importances are the priorities customers place on certain features like size, weight, and so forth. These priorities are then weighed against the cost and feasibility of satisfying a particular need.

Customer Perceptions of Performance. Customer perception is a measure of how customers perceive other products in the market that are currently satisfying the need. Where no such product exists, it measures the way that customers attempt to satisfy the need.

From the House of Quality, the team identifies those design attributes that will affect customers' perceptions of the product if modified to meet their needs. The team also considers the realities of engineering and the costs. What has been presented here is merely an overview of the QFD process. What has not been covered are the possibilities for mathematical operations to develop indices and scales for enhancing decision making. Check *Additional Sources of Information* at the end of the chapter for more information on this subject. The key point to remember about QFD is that it represents a philosophy of product development that brings all members of the team in at the beginning of the design phase, including the most important member of the team—the customer. Many entre-preneurs have used this team approach successfully without implementing the complete QFD process, a fairly complex method which usually requires the assistance of an outside consultant with experience in QFD.

Figure 11.3: New Product Checklist

	Yes	No	Perhaps
The Market			
Is there an existing need for this product in the marketplace?	___	___	___
Will I be first in the marketplace with this product?	___	___	___
Can I protect the product legally?	___	___	___
Can I erect entry barriers?	___	___	___
SWOT Analysis			
Do the strengths of this product exceed any weaknesses?	___	___	___
Are there various opportunities for commercializing this product?	___	___	___
Do any significant threats exist to the development of this product?	___	___	___
Design/Development/Manufacturing			
Is the product innovative?	___	___	___
Can it be developed quickly to market-ready state?	___	___	___
Can it be easily manufactured?	___	___	___
Do I have the resources to manufacture the product?	___	___	___
Is it more practical to subcontract the manufacturing?	___	___	___
Is there a possibility for spin-off products?	___	___	___
Financial			
Is the return on this investment sufficient to justify the effort?	___	___	___
Are the development costs within reason?	___	___	___
Can the manufacturing investment be minimized while still maintaining quality and control?	___	___	___
Is the money needed to produce the product available?	___	___	___

The Product Manufacturing Cycle

A typical manufacturing plant has five functional areas:

The Product Manufacturing Cycle

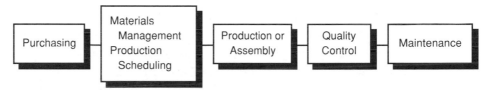

The *purchasing* function is responsible for the purchase of raw materials or components. Its effectiveness is judged by the quality of the raw materials, the cost, and the timeliness of their delivery. The *materials management/production scheduling* section is responsible for moving the raw materials through the production process and storing them. Its effectiveness is judged by the cost of inventory and its ability to meet demand for raw materials. *Production* converts raw materials into finished goods. Its effectiveness is judged by the quality of the goods produced, their cost, and the timeliness of production. These effectiveness factors also apply to assembly plants. The *quality* function is responsible for the quality of the finished product and is judged by its ability to detect defective goods before they leave the factory and to develop methods to reduce the number of defects during production. The *maintenance* function maintains and upgrades the manufacturing equipment. Its effectiveness is judged on the basis of cost as well as the percentage of unscheduled downtime that the equipment experiences.

Manufacturing firms are typically organized as **product-focused** or **process-focused** organizations. A product-focused organization generally is highly decentralized so it can respond better to market demands. Therefore, each product group acts essentially like a separate company, a profit center. This type of organization is well suited to products that don't require huge economies of scale or capital-intensive manufacturing technologies. Process-focused organizations, on the other hand, are common among manufacturers with capital-intensive processes such as those seen in the semiconductor industry. These organizations are highly centralized in order to control all the functions of the organization. Whether the company is product or process-focused, it must be able to extend its control beyond the five functional areas so it is not at the mercy of its suppliers at one end and its distributors at the other. This control is usually accomplished through strategic alliances.

As discussed in Chapter 10, the virtual enterprise, consisting of strategic alliances between every link in the value chain, is one way to achieve control of the entire process from raw materials to distribution, while still remaining small and flexible enough to meet changing needs and demands. This model is similar to that of the Japanese *keiretsu*, which links banks, suppliers, electronics, and auto firms together through a series of cross-ownerships.

The United States' model, however, leaves ownership in the hands of the individual owners but links the organizations into a virtual entity that acts as a team with a common goal. Wal-Mart is probably the best example of this type of partnership and integration. It has established point-of-sale linkups with its suppliers and given its manufacturers the responsibility for handling inventory. The ultimate goal is to construct one organization with a common purpose that encompasses the entire supply chain from raw materials supplier to retailer, with each link along the chain performing the task that it does best.

Materials Requirements

Any business that purchases raw materials or parts for production of goods for resale must carefully consider the quality, quantity, and timing of those purchases. Quality goods are those that meet specific needs. The quantity purchased is a function of demand, manufacturing capability, and storage capability. Planning purchases so that capital and warehouse space are not tied up any longer than necessary is the result of good timing. As materials account for approximately 50 percent of total manufacturing cost, it is important to balance these three factors carefully.

Locating vendors to sell you raw materials or goods for resale is not difficult, but finding the best vendors for your purposes is another matter entirely. The first decision is whether to buy from one vendor or more than one vendor. Obviously, if a single vendor cannot supply all your needs, that decision is made. There are several advantages to using a single vendor where possible:

- You will probably get more individual attention and better service.
- Your orders will be consolidated so you may be able to get a discount based on quantity purchased.

However, the principal disadvantage of one vendor is that if that vendor should suffer a catastrophe (its facility burns to the ground like the Japanese company that was the prime supplier of RAM chips), it may be difficult or impossible to find an alternate source in a short period of time. To ensure against this contingency, you may want to follow the general rule of using one supplier for about 70 to 80 percent of your needs, and one or more additional suppliers to supply the rest.

When considering a specific vendor as your source, ask yourself several questions:

1. Can the vendor deliver enough of what you need when you need it?
2. What is the cost of transportation using the vendor you are considering? If the vendor is located far away, costs will be higher and it may be more difficult to get the service you require.
3. What services is the vendor offering you? For example, how often will sales representatives call on you?
4. Is the vendor knowledgeable about the product line?
5. What are their maintenance and return policies?

It is also important to shop vendors to compare prices, just as you would if you were purchasing equipment. Check for trade discounts and quantity discounts that may make a particular vendor's deal more enticing.

The computer technology revolution has made materials planning more of a science than ever before. Information systems can now provide purchasing managers with detailed feedback on supplier performance, delivery reliability, and quality control results. Comparing results across suppliers gives the purchasing person more leverage when it's time to renegotiate the annual contracts with suppliers.

Inventory Requirements

Today businesses that hold inventories of raw materials or goods for resale have found they must reduce these inventories significantly to remain competitive. Instead of purchasing large quantities and receiving them on a monthly basis, businesses are purchasing daily or weekly in an effort to avoid costly inventories. Of course, some inventory of finished goods must be maintained to meet delivery deadlines; therefore, a delicate balance must be achieved between goods coming into the business, work in progress, and goods leaving the business to be sold.

Inventory Costs

There are many costs associated with inventories that can add as much as 25 percent to the base cost of the inventory. They include:

- **Financing Costs.** The interest paid on the money you borrow to purchase the inventory.
- **Opportunity Cost.** The loss of use of the money tied up in inventory.
- **Storage Costs.** The amount spent on warehouse space to store the inventory.
- **Insurance Costs.** The cost of insuring the inventory.
- **Shrinkage Costs.** The money lost from inventory that is broken, stolen, or damaged.
- **Obsolescence.** The cost associated with inventory that has become obsolete.

Inventory Turnover

It is important to understand how often inventory turns over in your industry to help determine how much inventory, and specifically what goods, to maintain in greater quantities. Inventory turnover is the average number of times an inventory is sold out during the year for a particular product line. If you know the turnover rate for an industry (men's clothing is 3; restaurants, 22; and some chemical manufacturers, 100), you will be able to estimate how much inventory to keep on hand. For example, suppose an industry has an inventory turnover rate of 5.

$$\frac{12}{5} = 2.4 \text{ month's supply}$$

A 2.4 month's supply of inventory needs to be on hand. Once this quantity is known, you can calculate the cost. Do this by dividing the company's forecasted sales for the upcoming year by the cost of goods sold (COGS). For example, if you are forecasting $200,000 in sales and the COGS is 50 percent of sales, then

$$\frac{\$200,000 \times .50}{5} = \$20,000$$

It will cost $20,000 to maintain a 2.4 month's supply in inventory. Naturally, if you deal in several product lines or use a variety of raw materials, calculations for each need to be done as they may have varying turnover rates.

Tracking Inventory

In a start-up venture, keeping track of inventory may simply be a matter of visually inspecting and counting, since the business is growing in a fairly controlled manner in the beginning. However, once the business is really off the ground, these simple techniques will no longer suffice, and it is best to be prepared for this eventuality early on.

Perpetual Inventory Systems. Perpetual systems keep a running count of items in inventory. As items are sold, they are subtracted; as they are purchased, they are added. An electronic point-of-sale system (such as those now used in most grocery and retail stores) allows a business to have instant access to the status of its inventory.

Physical Count System. Most businesses do physical counts even if they have an electronic system to detect errors in the system and account for items that may have been stolen or lost and wouldn't show up as a sale. To make the counting process more efficient, it's important to get the inventories down as low as possible before the count takes place.

Combined Inventory Systems. Some businesses use both perpetual and physical count systems simultaneously, perpetual for the items that make up the bulk of their sales, and physical counts for less commonly sold items.

Just-in-Time System

In the past, inventories were built up based on the state of the economy or in reaction to problems in their inventory control system. If times were good, producers increased stocks of inventory to meet expected demand. Then when the economy slowed, they were usually left with shelves of leftover stock. Reductions in inventory succeeded in exposing typical problems: equipment imbalances, paperwork backlog, excessively long setups, vendor problems, and problems with purchase lead time.

Newer systems, like Just-in-Time (JIT), help manufacturers maintain better control of their inventories by eliminating production and inventory problems and then reducing inventory to only that which is needed. The Just-in-Time system of materials and inventory management deserves its own heading as it is fundamentally different from other inventory systems. Coming originally from Japan, JIT is beginning to take hold in the United States. The philosophy behind JIT is "to produce the minimum number of units in the smallest possible quantities at the latest possible time."[2] A well-devised and implemented JIT system can:

• Increase direct and indirect labor productivity
• Increase equipment capacity
• Reduce manufacturing lead time

---

[2]Hay, E.J. (1988). *The Just-in-Time Breakthrough.* New York: John Wiley & Sons.

- Reduce the cost of failure
- Reduce the cost of purchased materials
- Reduce inventories
- Reduce space requirements

In essence, the goal is to eliminate waste in the manufacturing process. Consequently, to implement JIT it is necessary to look beyond mere inventory to all other aspects of the manufacturing process as well. Starting with the last operation, which is usually the customer requirement, work backwards through the manufacturing process. Customer demand determines how many products are produced. The number of products to be produced determines the production capability requirements, which in turn determine the amount of raw materials needed. In general, a firm maintains an inventory no larger than needed to support one day of production. To do this, it has to have the cooperation of its suppliers and its distributors with severe penalties for not being on time, either too early or late. This, of necessity, reduces the number of suppliers a JIT firm typically deals with. JIT also requires strict quality control because with minimal inventories, there is no excess inventory to cover rejects.

A traditional factory is laid out by functional department, usually based on a particular process or technology. The result is that products are produced in batches. This is the antithesis of JIT, which specifies that the plant be laid out by product. With JIT the equipment is positioned in the order in which it is used to produce a particular product or family of related products. It is also important to plan production so you only produce enough to meet demand. For example, suppose you expect to sell a total of 100 units of your product next month. Then:

$$100/20 \text{ work days} = 5 \text{ units a day}$$
$$5/8 \text{ work hours} = .63 \text{ unit per hour}$$
$$\text{or } 1 \text{ unit every hour and a half}$$

This calculation must be reworked every month as demand changes.

One way suppliers are meeting the needs of a company using JIT is to involve independent contractors specializing in "time-sensitive" deliveries. For example, one company has installed two-way satellite communication on its trucks so shipments can be tracked in real time. Other businesses like American Distribution Systems, Inc. help businesses that need to ship to retailers. They stock merchandise in their warehouses, process orders, make deliveries, and handle billing. In that way retailers don't incur the costs associated with a backup supply of items. Avoid carrying too much inventory seems to be the trend in the 1990s. It requires, however, careful coordination and cooperation of all members of the supply chain to work effectively.

Production Requirements

The production function of a manufacturing business is its life blood. Decisions made in this area directly impact output level, product quality, and costs. Planning for production, therefore, is key to manufacturing efficiency and effectiveness. Most manufacturers begin by *scheduling,* that is, identifying and describing each activity that must be completed to produce the product and the amount of time it takes to complete each activity. Two methods traditionally used to aid the scheduling process are Gannt Charts and Pert Diagrams.

Gannt Charts. Gannt Charts are a way to depict the tasks to be performed and the time required for each. Consider Figure 11.4, The task to be completed is outlined on the vertical axis, with the time to completion on the horizontal. Notice that the solid line represents your plan for completion, while the dashed line depicts where you are in the process toward completion. Gannt Charts are best for simple projects that are independent of each other.

PERT Diagrams. PERT is an acronym for Program Evaluation and Review Technique. This method is helpful when the production being scheduled is more complex and subject to the interdependence of several activities going on either simultaneously or in sequence. In other words, some tasks cannot be started until others have been completed. To begin, you must identify the major activities involved in producing the product and arrange them in the order in which

Figure 11.4: Gannt Chart

Order	Order	September				October				November			
Number	Quantity	6-9	12-16	19-23	26-30	3-7	10-14	17-21	24-28	1-5	7-11	14-18	21-25
5348	1,000												
5349	1,500												
5350	500												

Scheduled Time ▬▬▬▬
Actual Progress -------------

Figure 11.5: PERT Diagram

Activity	Description	Immediately Preceding Event
a	Initial working laboratory prototype	———
b	Patent application	a
c	Hire design engineer	a
d	Engineered prototype with assembly plans and specs	c
e	Field testing/market testing	b, d
f	Sourcing final material and parts suppliers	d, b
g	Production quality prototype	e, f

they occur. Be sure to identify any activities that must occur in sequence; that is, one activity cannot occur until another is finished. Construct a pictorial network that describes the process. Then estimate the time to complete each activity and note it on the chart. This is usually calculated as most optimistic, most likely, and most pessimistic. The statistics involved in analyzing the network are beyond the scope of this book, but essentially consist of 1) identifying the critical path, which is the longest path and is important because a delay in any of the activities along the critical path can delay the entire project; 2) computing slack time on all events and activities (difference between latest and earliest times); and 3) calculating the probability of completion within the time allotted.

The numbered nodes on the diagram (Figure 11.5) refer to the start and completion points for each event. The dummy line was placed in the diagram to account for the completion of Event e being preceded by Events b and d. Both must be completed before Event g can start.

There are several popular software products on the market, such as Micro Planner X-Pert and Microsoft Project, that can help entrepreneurs schedule their production capacity. Tracking production from the outset of the business allows entrepreneurs to make more realistic strategic decisions about growth and expansion.

PROFILE 11.2

The Virtual Distribution Channel:
The Case of Lee Apparel Co.

Based in Merriam, Kansas, the Lee Apparel Company learned that creating strategic alliances up and down its distribution channel would allow it to fine-tune its production and better meet the demands of its retailers. Using Point-of-Sale (POS) data transmitted electronically from the retailer to Lee on a daily or weekly basis, the retailer is able to replenish high-demand products within a matter of days instead of weeks. In some cases Lee has agreements with retailers to ship automatically when POS data indicate stock has reached a critical level based on demand.

To accomplish this, Lee sends every item from its factory with a Universal Product Code (UPC) bar code attached. When the bar code is scanned, the retailer's computer records the item number, color, and size. This information then helps Lee adjust its manufacturing process to meet demand. The success of this program is ultimately dependent on businesses' willingness to share information. In the end, everyone benefits.

Identifying all the tasks in the production process makes it easier to determine what equipment and supplies are needed to complete the tasks. If it is determined the equipment necessary to produce the product is beyond the start-up resources of the entrepreneur, it may be time to consider outsourcing part or all of production to a manufacturer who has excess capacity with the needed equipment.

After the production tasks are identified, a preliminary layout of the plant to estimate floor space requirements for production, offices, and services can be made. It may be beneficial to consult with an expert in plant layout to ensure you make the most efficient use of the limited space you have.

Quality Control

Quality control is the process of reconciling product output with the standards set for that product. It has been said that one thing manufacturers have learned from history is that "the primary objective of the company is to put the quality of the product ahead of every other consideration. A profit or loss notwithstanding, the emphasis will always be on quality."[3] Today thousands of manufacturers have embraced the philosophy of quality first, but have focused principally on equipment and processes rather than on the human element. Both must be done as *total* quality control must permeate every aspect of the organization.

The Inspection Process

One way manufacturers control quality is to implement a regular inspection process that takes place during several stages of the manufacturing operation. Often, primarily due to cost, a random sample of products is chosen for the inspection. This method catches potential defects early in the process before the products become finished goods. Whether each item produced is checked or a random sample is conducted is a function of what is being produced, the cost, and whether the item will be destroyed by the inspection process. For example, if you are producing an expensive piece of machinery, it may be prudent to subject each item to the inspection process, as the cost of inspection is more than made up for in the price of the item. If, on the other hand, you are producing a food product, once it is inspected it cannot be sold, so you can't afford to do more than a representative random sample of each batch.

Quality Circles

Quality circles are groups of employees who regularly work together on some aspect of the production process. They meet several times a month with the help of an outside facilitator to discuss problems and ideas related to their work environment. They often come up with new solutions to problems that are then put into effect, thus improving the efficiency and effectiveness of the manufacturing process and the product as well. Using quality circles gives employees a vested interest in what they are producing; consequently, they are more likely to pay close attention to improving the way their task is completed.

Using the Human Resource for Quality Control

In reality, the real success or failure of the quality control effort is dependent on the human element in the process: customers, employees, and management. Quality begins with satisfying the needs of the customers, and that cannot be accomplished unless those needs and requirements are communicated to

---

[3]Hopper, Kenneth. (1982). "Creating Japan's New Industrial Management: The Americans as Teachers." *Human Resource Management*, p. 13-34.

management and employees. An entrepreneur with a new venture has a unique opportunity to create a philosophy of quality from the very birth of the business, in the way the business is run and in the employees hired. The entrepreneur also has the advantage of creating new habits and patterns of behavior instead of having to change old ones.

Using Customers for Quality Control. Recall the discussion of Quality Function Deployment. At its core is the philosophy that a company produces what the customer needs, when he or she needs it. How does this translate into quality control? Customers, by their demands for reliability and performance in a highly competitive market, establish the standards that must be met when the product is designed and produced. If customers perceive that the product does not meet their needs or does not meet them as well as another product could, lost sales result.

Using Employees for Quality Control. If you want the employees to buy into the notion of quality control at every level, they must be given the responsibility and authority to make changes that will improve the process and product at every level. If you are going to install new technology to improve the process, the employees need to be trained not only in how to use it but how to look for potential problems that would affect quality. The continual use of awareness and training programs will help employees understand their importance in the whole manufacturing process.

Using Management for Quality Control. For total quality management to work, key management must be "on the floor," learning every aspect of production and supporting the efforts of employees. It is their job to bring the requirements of customers to the people who will satisfy those requirements. It is also management's job to establish company-wide, measurable quality goals. Too often management focuses more on productivity goals than quality goals. Ultimately it is quality, not productivity, that will sell product.

In an increasingly global market, it is not surprising that the need for international quality standards would arise. ISO 9000, developed by the International Organization for Standardization in Geneva, is a series of international quality standards and certification that makes it easier for a product to enter the export market. Approved by 95 countries, the standards apply to both manufacturing and service businesses and certify quality control procedures.

PROFILE 11.3

The Baldrige Award Criteria

The Malcolm Baldrige National Quality Award is the United States' highest quality honor. Competition is tough and the selection process daunting, but the award creates a standard to which small companies can compare themselves. The following is a list of the Baldrige criteria:

1. **Leadership.** Demonstrate evidence that senior management promotes quality values, and that those values influence day-to-day management.
2. **Information and analysis.** How effectively is the company using competitive comparisons and does it support quality objectives through data analysis?
3. **Strategic quality planning.** Does the business plan incorporate quality requirements?
4. **Human resources development and management.** What are the systems and practices that involve employees in education, training, assessment and recognition?
5. **Management of process quality.** Check for quality in product and service design, process control, quality assessment and documentation, and assurance of the quality of supplies.
6. **Quality and operational results.** Examine trends and levels in improvement of products and services, business services, and suppliers' quality.
7. **Customer focus and satisfaction.** Evaluate customer service standards, customer satisfaction ratings, and the use of customer complaints and suggestions.[4]

For a small, growing firm, however, it is a fairly costly process that includes, among other things, writing a quality control manual. The cost of achieving the standards is not as great as the cost of obtaining certification, which is subject to audit semiannually and must be renewed annually. But these costs must be weighed against the advantages. With certification, the companies with which the entrepreneur does business don't have to inspect to know the company's standards for quality, and it makes it much easier to enter the export market. Two ways to reduce the costs involved include:

• Compare fees charged by ISO consultants to find the best rate.

---

[4]Adapted from Warren H. Schmidt and Jerome P. Finnigan. (Feb. 1993). "The Race Without a Finish Line." in *Small Business Reports*, Vol 18 No. 2.

- Check with major customers to see if they will help subsidize the cost of certification.
- Determine if you really need certification. Perhaps just meeting the standards is sufficient in your business.

Product/Process Maintenance Requirements and Warranties

Maintenance in the manufacturing process refers both to the maintenance of plant and equipment used to produce the product and the maintenance or servicing of the product after it is sold.

Process Maintenance

At some point any machine will break down, which can mean lost sales and costly repairs. To prevent unexpected breakdowns from disrupting the production process, one of three things can be done. The process can be organized so when one machine is down, the work can be shifted to another. Another way is to build up inventories at each stage of the production process so that machines can keep working as long as the inventory lasts. (This method, however, will probably not work in a company that has chosen a JIT system of inventory management.) The third, and perhaps the best, approach is to regularly undertake preventative maintenance by checking and fixing the machines *before* they break down. The advantage of this approach is that *you* control when the down time occurs.

Product Maintenance

The entrepreneur who subscribes to total quality management will likely wish to provide warranties with products to protect against potential liability and to demonstrate that the company stands behind the product. Today product warranties have also become a marketing tool to sell the product.

Some of the decisions to be made regarding warranties include:

- *Length of warranty*. This depends on industry standards.
- *Covered components*. Some components may come from other manufacturers who have their own warranties. In this case, it is important to have your use of that component on the product certified by the OEM (Original Equipment Manufacturer) so you don't invalidate the warranty. Then if a warranted component from that manufacturer becomes defective, it can be sent back. However, it is probably good business practice to have customers return the

product to you or your distributors for service, repair, or exchange under your warranty, which covers the whole product.

- *Product scope*. Will the warranty cover one or all products in a line or will there be separate warranties?
- *Market scope*. Will the same warranty apply in all markets? This will be a function of state and foreign laws.
- *Conditions of the warranty that the customer must fulfill*. Is there anything the customer must do to keep the warranty in force, such as servicing or replacing disposable parts? These conditions should not include registering the product via a postcard. Today a product is covered by warranty from the moment it is purchased whether or not the purchaser returns a postcard stating when and where it was purchased and answering a short, informational questionnaire. What many companies do to get the postcard information is to offer update notification and potential discounts on future products.
- Who executes the warranty? The entrepreneur must decide who will handle warranty claims (manufacturer, dealers, distributors), recognizing that customers do not like to mail products back to the manufacturer.
- How the public will be educated about the warranty.
- Policies for refunds and returns, and shipping and handling costs. This is a function of the entrepreneur's philosophy about doing business. A customer-oriented company would probably offer a generous return policy and pay for the cost of returns.

Providing a warranty involves a cost to the manufacturer; however, that cost must be weighed against the potential loss of business if no warranty is provided. In the case of a new business with a new product, it is difficult to anticipate the number of problems that might occur as the product gets into the marketplace. Careful and adequate field testing of the product prior to market entry will go a long way toward eliminating many potential problems and the possibility of a recall, which is very costly for any firm, let alone a growing new business.

Financial Requirements

Once the raw materials and parts list has been developed, and the manufacturing or assembly process defined, including labor requirements, it is possible to calculate the total investment required to start the business and the per unit cost of manufacturing the product. To be sure, the initial units produced will cost significantly more to manufacture and assemble because the volume will usually not be sufficient to achieve industry discounts on raw materials and parts, and the plant and equipment will not be used to full capacity. Consequently, gross margins may be extremely small in the early stages until a sufficient increase in volume allows an economy of scale that reduces the per unit cost.

The calculation of the up-front investment in plant and equipment, coupled with the high per unit cost of production, has resulted in many entrepreneurs deciding to outsource manufacturing to an established manufacturing firm. Some products that consist of off-the-shelf components from OEMs can give the entrepreneur the option to set up an assembly operation, which is far less costly than a manufacturing plant. In any case, the process of outlining all the costs of setting up a product company is invaluable in making the final decisions about how the business will operate.

Including the Operational Plan in the Business Plan

Doing the work involved in presenting the technical and operational information in the business plan helps the entrepreneur decide the best alternative for producing the product and gives the reader a good background on how the production function of the new business will operate. The information gathered helps the entrepreneur derive estimates of working capital requirements, start-up costs, and manufacturing costs, all of which will be needed when developing the financial plan for the business.

The operational plan requires the collection of a significant amount of information about the business from a variety of sources. Some of these sources include existing manufacturers (especially competitors), trade publications, trade associations, and equipment suppliers. Once this information is collected, it can be organized and placed in the business plan using the outline of the operational plan section as shown in Figure 11.6 on p 221. You should feel free to modify this outline in any way to reflect the unique requirements of your business.

The business plan is not the place to provide pages and pages of technical specifications and description in an effort to describe how the product or process works. Remember that the reader, whether he or she is an investor, lender, or potential management hire, is interested in how the business will work, the benefits of the product/service, and who the entrepreneur is. The exact specifications related to the new product or process are of less importance. The question to keep in mind when organizing the operational section of the business plan is:

> *Does the reader of the business plan need to know this piece of information to understand the business?*

The technical analysis may warrant the creation of two versions of the business plan. The highly technical version can be reserved for the founding team and the technical staff and the less technical version for all other readers.

The Product

Several aspects of the product should be presented in the operational section of the business plan.

The Purpose of the Product/Service. Let the reader know whether the product solves a problem, recognizes an opportunity, satisfies a need, or is purely for entertainment purposes.

The Unique Features of the Product/Service. The unique features can result in a competitive advantage in the marketplace. They may include not only special features or benefits of the product/service but also any proprietary rights you own such as patents, trademarks, and copyrights. In the case of patents, be sure to state where the product is in patent process. If licensing the product is an option under consideration, the licensee will probably be looking to see that the patent has been "issued," or at the very least is "patent pending." (Recall that when the product is "patent pending" it has, for all practical purposes, been conditionally approved by the PTO.) If your business involves licensing and/or paying royalties to someone else, like an inventor, include that information as well. Only the major points should be presented in this section with a copy of any agreement or details in the appendix.

Include discussion of features such as the design, quality, capabilities, and cost of the product. It is also important to incorporate any photographs or drawings of the product. Again remember that the reader is primarily interested in *what the product functions are,* not *how it functions from an engineering point of view.*

Figure 11.6: Technical/Operational Plan

Product Specifications

Design and performance specifications

Level of quality

Service requirements

Status of development

Materials Requirements

Raw materials and parts required

Availability of raw materials and parts

Source of supply for raw materials and parts

Delivery lead time for suppliers

Inventory Requirements

Description of inventory system

Raw materials and purchased parts in inventory

Work in process inventory

Finished goods inventory

Production Requirements

Explanation of production process

Equipment needed, costs and alternatives

Output capacity from production

Materials handling equipment

Labor Requirements

Skills required

Availability of labor and cost

Support staff required

Maintenance Requirements

Plant equipment maintenance and repair

After sale service and warranties on product

Financial Requirements

Start-up investment in equipment and inventory

Manufacturing costs—raw materials, labor, equipment usage

☑ New Venture Checklist

Have you

- ☐ Developed a prototype of your product?
- ☐ Field-tested the prototype?
- ☐ Sourced the components of the prototype?
- ☐ Outlined the production process?
- ☐ Found suppliers for your material requirements?
- ☐ Determined how inventory will be handled?
- ☐ Developed quality control measures?
- ☐ Determined the product/process maintenance requirements?

Additional Sources of Information

Clark, K & T. Fujimoto. (1991). *Product Development Performance.* Boston: Harvard Business School Press.

Griffin, A. and Hauser, J.R. (1993). "The Voice of the Customer." *Marketing Science,* Vol. 12, No. 1. p. 1.

Hay, E.J. (1988). *The Just-in-Time Breakthrough.* New York: John Wiley.

Hayes, R.H., Wheelwright, S.C. & Clark, K.B. (1988). *Dynamic Manufacturing.* New York: The Free Press.

Hopper, K. (1982). "Creating Japan's New Industrial Management: The Americans as Teachers." *Human Resource Management,* pp. 13-34.

Issues to Consider

1. What is the purpose of a technical analysis of the business concept?
2. How can the product development process be shortened without affecting quality?
3. What value does the philosophy that forms the foundation of the QFD, team-based approach to product development have for entrepreneurs developing new products?
4. What is the difference between product-focused and process-focused companies?
5. What are three factors that should be taken into consideration when choosing vendors to meet materials requirements?
6. How can PERT diagrams aid the entrepreneur in production scheduling?
7. In what ways can the human resources of the business help control quality in all areas of the organization?

CHAPTER 12

The Marketing Plan

- *The focus of entrepreneurial marketing in the 1990s*
- *Preparing a marketing plan*
- *Product, place, promotion, price in the marketing strategy*
- *Using the marketing plan as part of the business plan*

Marketing in the 1990s

Marketing includes all the strategies, tactics, and techniques used to raise customer awareness and to promote a product, service, or business. Traditionally marketing has consisted of a **push strategy,** where a customer who has not necessarily expressed a need for or interest in the product or service is convinced to purchase it through selling techniques. In other words, the focus was on the product, not the customer. In contrast, with world-class marketing in the 1990s, the primary focus is on the customer. If the product or service is designed with the customer's needs in mind, much of the "selling" that would otherwise have to be done has been taken care of by giving the customers what they want. What is left then is to make them aware of its availability and how and where they can purchase it.

In Chapter 6, the importance of researching the target market to determine if there is a big enough market to warrant producing the product or service was stressed. The demographics gathered during this research, as well as information about customers' buying habits, will all be useful in putting together a marketing plan for the new business. Market research is definitely a necessity for operating in the 1990s and beyond. Knowing who your customer is and how, why, and when they buy is the minimum required information any business must have.

Entrepreneurial Marketing

If you studied marketing in college or gained experience in marketing by working for a large company, it is possible that you have seen only one side of marketing. The kind of marketing done by Coca Cola, Burger King, K-Mart, and the like is an entirely different game, calling for different strategies than those entrepreneurs use for start-up ventures. Unfortunately, entrepreneurial marketing is not often taught in business curricula because it isn't as exciting or competitive as brand name marketing in big companies. As a result, unsuspecting entrepreneurs often attempt to employ the same techniques as more established companies; however, since they usually don't have the required resources to market at the same level as the large corporations, the desired results are rarely achieved.

Entrepreneurs must approach marketing from a distinctly different point of view. While *they* may employ some of the same techniques as a large corporate marketer, they will also take advantage of many other marketing opportunities that the corporate marketer may ignore. In fact, some entrepreneurial strategies, such as personalized customer service, are so successful that many large, established companies are now adopting similar programs. Levinson has called the entrepreneurial marketing approach "Guerrilla Marketing," which is an alternative to traditional, expensive marketing tactics.[1] Given that entrepreneurs don't have the time or money for elaborate, high-profile marketing strategies, they essentially mimic what the "big boys" do, but do it for much less money and for a shorter period of time.

This chapter presents some suggestions for creating an entrepreneurial marketing plan that provides the best results for the least amount of money possible. It begins by looking at the marketing plan in general and then considering the traditional "4 P's" of marketing—product, price, place, promotion—in more detail and from an entrepreneurial point of view.

---

[1]Levinson, J.C. (1993). *Guerrilla Marketing*. Boston: Houghton Mifflin.

The Marketing Plan

Many people find the marketing plan section of the business plan the easiest to work on and write. After all, how difficult can it be to conclude that TV, radio, and the newspaper will be needed to advertise the product or service? Unfortunately, it's not that simple. Advertising is just one small component of a total marketing strategy. Moreover, a poorly constructed marketing plan cannot only give weak results in terms of sales, but can ruin a business financially.

A few steps taken before the actual writing of the marketing plan ensures that the plan is on target and is one you can live with for a long time to come. Saying you must live with the plan for a long time probably sounds inconsistent with the need of the entrepreneur to remain flexible and adapt to change in the marketplace. It is not. One of the biggest problems with most marketing plans is that they are not followed long enough to achieve the desired results.

Typically, the business owner does not see immediate results from the marketing effort and decides it must not be working. So he or she changes it and starts the cycle all over again. Changing the plan precipitously is precisely the wrong thing to do. It takes time to make customers aware of the product or service. It takes time for a particular marketing strategy to take hold and build confidence in the customer. From the first time a customer sees an ad, for example, to the point at which the customer actually buys the product may be weeks or even months. On average, the customer will see the ad 15 or 20 times before the product is actually purchased. Therefore, just like a good stock market investor, you must think of the marketing plan as an investment in the future of the business, and any investment takes time to mature. Reaping the benefits of a well-structured marketing plan requires persistence and unwavering dedication until the plan has an opportunity to perform.

There are several steps to take prior to writing a marketing plan.

1. **Make a list of the options**. To even begin to know which marketing options should be considered, you need to talk to other business owners, customers, and suppliers. Read some books and articles on marketing strategies for entrepreneurs, like those suggested at the end of this chapter. This process will produce a list of possibilities that may range from sponsoring a business conference to advertising in a national trade publication. Determining which strategies are the most effective, or even feasible, can be left for later.

2. **Think like a customer.** Imagine the business from the customer's point of view. What would entice you to enter that store, buy that product, take advantage of that service?

3. **Study the competition**. Take a look at the businesses that will be competing with yours and determine what makes them successful or unsuccessful. What marketing strategies do they seem to employ, and are they effective? How could you improve on what they are doing?
4. **Analyze the options and rank them.** Eliminate first those that either don't meet the needs of the target market or are simply not feasible at this time (usually for budgetary reasons). Then rank the top ten choices. You are now ready to begin writing the marketing plan.

The Marketing Plan in One Paragraph

Many experienced marketers suggest that the first step in creating the marketing plan is to condense all the ideas about marketing strategy into a single paragraph that says it all. Impossible? Not at all. A single, well-written paragraph will force you to focus carefully on the central point of the overall marketing strategy. The paragraph should include:

- The purpose of the marketing plan.
  What will the marketing plan accomplish?
- The benefits of the product/service.
  How will the product/service help the customer or satisfy a need?
- The target market.
  Who is the primary buyer?
- The market niche.
  Where do you fit in the industry or market? How do you differentiate yourself?
- The marketing tactics to be used.
  What specific marketing tools will be employed?
- The company's convictions, its identity.
  How will the customers define the company?
- The percentage of sales the marketing budget will represent.
  How much money will you be allocating to the marketing plan?

Here is an example of an effective one-paragraph statement of the marketing plan for a product business.

The purpose of *Gentech Corporation* is to sell innovative, portable power source equipment at the highest quality and the lowest possible cost. *Gentech* will accomplish this by positioning itself as the leader in providing reliable, dual power source products that reduce the number of pieces of equipment a user must own. The target market is the construc-

PROFILE 12.1

What's in a Name?

Even the name of your business should be part of the overall marketing plan because it's the first point of identity you establish with the customer. It should be easily remembered and should relate to what you are selling. A name like "Useful Products," the name of one California company, would not win any prizes for originality and style, but "Higher Ground," an Oregon coffee company, might.

tion industry, and more specifically, those who use power tools in areas where no power is available. The niche *Gentech* will enter is that of construction companies that own or lease power equipment. Initial marketing tactics will include direct sales to equipment rental outlets, advertisements in trade publications, and trade shows. *Gentech's* customers will see the company as service-oriented with a quick response to customer needs both in service and product design. Twelve percent of sales will be applied to the marketing strategy.

With your paragraph in hand and the focus established, a more detailed marketing plan can now be created. Every marketing plan incorporates the four Ps of marketing: product, price, place, and promotion. Once these aspects of the plan have been dealt with, the creative aspects such as the advertising goals can be addressed. You will also develop a media plan that details what media will be used, when they will be used, and how much it will cost.

The Product

There are a number of considerations relative to the product or products that must be addressed in the marketing plan. They include product features—identity, branding, packaging and labeling—product positioning, and product mix.

Product Features

For marketing purposes, think of the product as a bundle of benefits to the customer. These benefits include a wide variety of things: attractiveness, distinctive characteristics, quality, options, warranties, service contracts, delivery, and so forth. But more important to the customer, the product offers intangible benefits like convenience, savings in time and money, or improved

PROFILE 12.2

Effective Niche Marketing:
The Bombay Company

Entrepreneur Robert Nourse began his career as a stereotypical college professor with a doctorate from Harvard Business School. After teaching for nine years, he joined a venture capital firm where he learned about what it takes to grow a business. By 1979, when he was 40 years old, he decided it was time to run his own business. The only problem was he didn't know what that business should be.

As luck would have it, he met an old college friend who had invested in The Bombay Co., a mail order company that sold replicas of 18th and 19th Century English furniture. Shipped in boxes, they needed to be assembled by the customer. The company was called The Bombay Co. after the jewel of the British Empire. Nourse managed to meet the owner of the company, (Harper's mail order, which at that time was losing money) and saw an opportunity. Spelling out the deal on the back of a napkin during lunch, Nourse bought the Canadian rights to Bombay for $1 and a 4% royalty.

The first thing Nourse decided was that mail order was not the best marketing channel for the company. He saw shopping malls as the best outlet because of the high foot traffic. He understood his target market to be the impulse buyer who saw something and didn't want to wait six or eight weeks for delivery. With savings and a loan from the bank, he opened his first store in 1980 with 2,000 square feet in the Eaton Centre in Toronto, Canada's premier shopping center. It was an immediate success.

In 1981, Harper's mail order business was acquired by Tandy Brands, Inc., a holding company in Fort Worth, Texas, which then bought Nourse's Canadian store, giving him the rights to control it. By 1983, with the financial backing of Tandy, Nourse was able to grow the business in Canada to 13 stores. The Bombay stores in the United States, however, were losing money. Tandy decided it wanted to merge the United States and Canadian operations and make Nourse the CEO of all of it. It was an offer he couldn't refuse. Within a year of taking over his new position at the helm of Bombay, Nourse turned the company around. Bombay grew from 75 stores in 1986 to 272 in 1990, and eventually Tandy Brands sold off its other holdings, changing its name to Bombay Co. Inc. In 1991, Nourse became president and CEO. Today Bombay Co. has more than 385 stores and sales in excess of $235 million.

Their marketing niche is the scaled-down piece of furniture appropriate for a small mall store. Their pricing strategy is to offer exclusive furniture and accessories at 30 to 60 percent below other furniture retailers. Keeping costs down has been achieved by controlling the distribution channel from producer to retailer. Their furniture is mass produced according to their trademarked specifications in Asia. The "ready-to-assemble" technology, packaged in flat boxes, saves on shipping and handling. Products can be shipped in standard 40-foot containers. The stores, therefore, maintain only enough stock to meet demand, and excess stock is stored in regional warehouses. They have, however, tested the concept of a superstore with larger, functional pieces of furniture like sofas with great success and are now in the process of converting many of their stores to superstores. Nourse is also introducing a new concept, Alex & Ivy, a store that will feature American and French casual furniture.

health. This bundle of benefits is the information the customer must know about the product/service in order to feel comfortable about buying it.

Merely offering these benefits is not enough, however. They must be offered consistently. In other words, the benefits the customer derives from using the product/service must be received time and time again. Often, for example, a company will focus on a high level of quality without concerning itself with minor fluctuations in that quality. The only way to build confidence in customers and, hence, increase the chance of return customers, is to provide consistency in all the product benefits.

Product Branding, Packaging, and Labeling

Product hype via mass marketing seems to be the strategy of the 1990s. It is seen in everything from Coca-Cola versus Pepsi ads to the auto manufacturers who tell us "It just feels right!" Creating an image through branding, packaging, labeling, and advertising is pervasive because it works. While an ad featuring a young, athletically slim, young woman drinking a "lite" beer seems to be an oxymoron, subliminally it hits the mark. Drinking lite beer is sexy, healthy, youthful, and low in calories. Whether it is true or not is irrelevant; the image remains.

For companies that participate in the war of the images, the battle is everything. They will do anything to win. What is important is the brand name, keeping it in the public eye. Most times we don't even know what company is promoting the brand. Often the name appears only briefly at the end of the ad. This is the strategy of Calvin Klein and Nike. Image and reality are frequently separated by an enormous gap. The belief is that if you repeat a slogan—for example, "We're number one"—often enough, people (including the company) will believe it, even if it's not true. Eventually, however, the lie catches up and customers begin to lose faith in the product (not necessarily in the company, however, because its name was never used).

A counter movement, however, has begun to occur among world-class entrepreneurial ventures. A number of very successful businesses like the Body Shop, Ben and Jerry's, Smith and Hawkens, Apple Computer, and Starbucks Coffee are resisting image positioning as the way to communicate their message. Instead of promoting brand names, they choose to communicate the philosophy of their business, which is at the core of all their products, and

> *A number of very successful businesses are resisting image positioning as the way to communicate their message.*

which by its very nature differentiates these companies from others in the market. They do not go head to head with their competitors in a war of images; they create their own niche in marketing strategy by seeking ways to increase pride and loyalty not only in their customers but in their employees as well. They break with tradition to make themselves stand out.

For example, Starbucks Coffee places great importance on its employees. In an industry that regularly experiences high employee turnover and low wages, Starbucks sees the employees as its competitive advantage. The comprehensive compensation package, health care, and stock options it offers all employees gives them a vested interest in the company and a desire to see it succeed. This philosophy is communicated to customers in a more personal manner than through mass marketing. It is communicated in the way Starbucks' employees treat their customers.

Anita Roddick, who with her husband Gordon founded the Body Shop, opposed the traditional messages of the image-laden cosmetic industry by offering her customers not just a "quick fix" but a "sense of well being." Instead of coming out in a massive ad campaign to say this, however, she chose to demonstrate the philosophy of her business by using inexpensive, recyclable containers (packaging), and products whose origins lie in nature.

The differences in products that these new marketing strategists promote are real and can be measured. These real differences not only distinguish them from the false reality of their competitors' images, but expose those images for what they are. Of course, developing a sound company philosophy or culture is not an overnight achievement. It takes time, and while you are working at building that philosophy, the image builders will probably receive the bulk of the attention. Nevertheless, persistence will pay off when you are able to deliver precisely what you said you would.

Packaging. The way a product is packaged reflects the philosophy of the business. If you are producing a consumer product, attractive packaging will grab the consumer's attention as it sits among many competing products on the shelf. In global marketing packaging can often be as important as the product itself. In Japan, for example, consumers value products that come in artistically beautiful boxes and will pay more for such packaging.

In general, packaging should depict

- What the product is
- Its key product benefits
- The company philosophy
- The level of quality

When Jan Davidson of Davidson, Inc., a leading educational software manufacturer, first studied the packaging of software back in 1979, she noted that most of it was in plastic bags hanging on hooks in the stores. Since she was an educator herself, she wanted her software to be more associated with books and education, so to differentiate her product at the retail level, she packaged it in binders that looked like colorful books on the shelf.

Labeling. Today many companies are promoting products they call environmentally friendly, but they often stretch the limits of that term. In an effort to protect consumers, the Federal Trade Commission has issued guidelines for the use of environmental terms in advertising and product labeling. For example, a product can only be labeled *recyclable* if the entire product can be collected or separated from solid waste and used in the manufacture of other products. A product may be labeled *recycled content* if the recycled materials in the product came from solid waste stream. You also have to distinguish between materials recycled from manufacturing and those from consumer waste by weight. To use the terms *degradable, biodegradable, and photodegradable,* there must be evidence that the product will completely break down and return to nature in a relatively short period of time. Otherwise you have to qualify just how degradable it really is.

Product Positioning

Product positioning is the way customers view the product in relation to competitors' products. Is the product more luxurious, of higher quality, less expensive, more attractive and so forth? In other words, product positioning really defines the product by its benefits to the target customer. Consequently, any product will probably be repositioned several times during the course of its product life cycle as customer tastes and preferences change. And this is precisely why a small company that is flexible and can move more quickly can take on a giant in a market niche that the giant has not yet tackled.

It is also important to note that not only will you position the product, but the company, distribution channel, and technology as well. Savvy customers today are concerned more and more about the reputation of the company they are dealing with, so if a company, for example, associates with distributors whose level of service is not up to its standards, it will ultimately reflect on the company. Realistically a product's position in the market will be a function of the customers' perception of where it should be. That is, you may have designed your product to replace another established product, whereas the customer sees it as a product they would like to have once they have already bought the existing product. Precious marketing dollars will be wasted if you don't respond to the customers' perceptions.

> *Not only will you position the product, but the company, distribution channel, and technology as well.*

In positioning the new product, refer to the customer profile developed when you did your market research. However, be aware that you must constantly receive feedback from customers to stay on top of changes in tastes and preferences that may call for a repositioning of the product later on. Most products will have primary market segments and then sub-sets of those segments. Sub-sets are other markets or uses for the product. Just as you studied the primary market, you must also understand the sub-sets to correctly position the product in those markets.

It is also important to carefully study your competitors to determine their strengths and weaknesses and how they might respond to your entry into the market. If a competitor is a publicly traded company, annual reports are available. In the event they are not, talking to distributors, customers, and advertisers can provide valuable information to help plan a strategy. If you find out a competitor holds the position you wish to occupy, you have three choices: 1) find another opportunity; 2) try to overtake the competitor in the position; or 3) attempt to reposition the competitor. Overtaking the competitor is very difficult to achieve and is rarely accomplished. If you have positioned the business in an emerging niche, there may be an opportunity to re-educate the customer about the competitor's product as well as introduce them to the different benefits of yours.

Studying the market carefully can produce niches that may not have been considered or vulnerabilities in competitors not previously apparent. It may also result in positioning the product a little differently than originally planned. Remember, however, to look not only for evidence to support a particular positioning but also to refute it.

Once you have determined the position you wish to occupy and have written the positioning statement, it needs to be tested in the marketplace. There are several methods that can be used, and they vary in the time and cost involved. In all cases, however, news of the product will be shared prior to market entry, so have anyone who participates in the testing sign a Statement of Nondisclosure.

- **Peer Review.** Ask anyone and everyone you know to give an opinion on the positioning statement. Ask for their impressions and perceptions of how the product will do in this position.
- **Distribution Channel Review.** Ask salespeople, distributors, and retailers what they think of the position statement. These are people who understand the industry and will have a pretty good sense of where you and your product might fit in.
- **Focus Groups.** Bring together a representative sample of the customer base and get their opinions.
- **Test Marketing.** This involves producing a limited amount of product and selling it in a defined geographic region to determine if the product positioning is correct. For most start-up companies, test marketing isn't economically feasible so the cost of this approach must be weighed against getting out in the market as quickly as possible.

As discussed in Chapter 6, entrepreneurs need to consider the costs versus benefits of expensive market research. With most markets far more volatile than ever before, it usually pays to shorten the development and test time to get into the market quickly, particularly where a company can gain a first-mover advantage. When you have a good positioning statement that will produce the desired results, communicate this statement to everyone involved in the production and distribution of the product so the company and everyone involved with it will share a common philosophy and communicate a consistent message to the customer.

Product Mix

Product mix refers to all the products the business will produce and/or sell. If the business will offer multiple products, you must consider how these products relate to each other and if they all serve to communicate your company's identity and product positioning message. The products that comprise the product mix will be determined by the markets to be served; for example, a more diversified product mix may be needed when several markets are being served.

Catherine White, founder of Financial Architects, a financial services firm in Lexington MA., offers social screening of potential investments as an additional service in her "product mix." Clients who wish to invest in companies that have certain social goals can use her services as well as clients who invest based on purely financial criteria. In this way, she is serving a larger market with a more diverse product mix.

Price

Price is one of the most important features of a product. As a marketing tool, price more than any other factor affects customer acceptance of the product, the business's cash flow, and in general the profitability. Price is determined by many factors:

- The demand for the product is strong relative to the supply. Where demand is greater than supply, a higher price may be commanded.
- The demand for the product is inelastic; that is, people will buy no matter what the price because they need the product. This is typically true for commodities with no viable substitute, like milk.
- Intense competition may force the price of the product down.
- Additional features may warrant a higher price.
- New technology may call for a higher price.
- Product positioning may be associated with a certain price level. For example, positioning a product among luxury items commands a higher price.

Strategies for Pricing

Pricing becomes a feature of the product when it is the central selling point. The product that is considered a commodity or the product that faces intense competition will often be marketed on the basis of lower price for the same quality. How a product is priced is a function of a company's goals. Is the goal to

- *Increase sales?* This may entail lowering prices to raise the volume sold.
- *Increase market share?* Again, by lowering prices, volume may increase, thus increasing market share.

- *Maximize cash flow?* Increasing cash flow can be achieved several ways, including raising prices and reducing direct costs and overhead.
- *Maximize profit?* Similar to maximizing cash flow, this can be accomplished several ways, including raising prices, lowering prices and increasing volume, or decreasing overhead.
- *Set up entry barriers to competition?* Lowering prices based on using efficient production methods, achieving economies of scale, and keeping overhead low can often set up entry barriers to companies that can't compete on that scale.
- *Define an image?* Setting a higher price based on higher perceived and/or actual quality is one way of establishing a particular image in an industry.
- *Control demand?* Where a company does not have the resources to meet demand, prices can be set at a level that discourages sales to a particular degree.

Knowing what a pricing strategy is supposed to accomplish in advance of setting a price will ensure compatibility with the company's goals.

There are several components of a pricing strategy.

1. **Cost-based pricing.** This component adds the cost of producing the product, the related costs of running the business, and a profit margin to arrive at a market price.
2. **Demand-based pricing.** This component is based on finding out what customers are willing to pay for the product, then pricing it accordingly. For new products with no direct comparison, a combination of this approach and cost-based pricing is often used to arrive at a satisfactory price. In general, customers recognize several prices for any one product: the standard price, which is the price normally paid for the item; the sale price, the price paid for specials; and the relative price, which is the price of the item compared to a substitute product. For some products, customers may have to add to the normal cost of shipping, handling, or installation in their comparison with other like products.
3. **Competition-based pricing.** Where the product has direct competition, the entrepreneur can look at competitors' pricing strategy and price the product in line with theirs, higher if it is determined that the product has added value, or lower if competing on price.
4. **Psychological pricing.** Using an odd-even strategy can suggest a pricing position in the market, an odd number ($12.99) to suggest a bargain, an

even number ($40.00) to suggest quality, or higher than average pricing to suggest exclusivity.

5. **Distribution channel pricing.** The channel of distribution through which the entrepreneur chooses to move the product will affect the ultimate price to the customer as allowance for each intermediary in the channel must be made to make a certain percentage of profit.

6. **Extrapolating from other industries.** It is important to look at the pricing strategies of businesses in other industries. Just because your industry does not seem to employ that strategy does not mean it won't work. Staying competitive on price means always looking for new methods of pricing products.

Gross Margins

Gross margin percentage is a way to examine the productivity of the company as well as aid in determining the price of a product. Be aware, however, that it is not always an accurate measure of profitability because it is based on sales. Gross margin is affected by manufacturing costs, distribution costs, selling costs, and inventory costs. Even where two businesses have equal gross margins, their profitability levels may differ dramatically. That difference may be attributable to higher or lower costs for handling, stocking, and marketing costs, which are typically lumped into the category of administrative and selling expenses below the gross margin line. Consequently, most businesses are not able to achieve an accurate true unit cost for a product, especially for multi-product companies. According to Walter J. Salmon of the Harvard Graduate School of Business, the business is better served by tracking "Direct Product Profit" or DPP.[2] DPP allows a business to identify products that carry higher than normal variable costs such as handling, so the entrepreneur can figure out ways to improve that aspect of the operation. DPP tracks total cost per unit rather than just gross margin.

Place

The place strategy will dictate how products get to the customers. This is essentially the distribution strategy, which was discussed in detail in Chapter 7. In this section, however, the scope of distribution and some issues related to transportation are addressed. As in any aspect of marketing, consistency is important. Naturally, the location of the business is a relatively stable feature so customers

---

[2]Parrott, M.D. (1988). "Margin for Error." *Do It Yourself Retailing.* Vol. 154, No. 6, p. 11.

always know where to find it. It is equally important to establish stable distribution channels so customers don't have to think about how to find your products. Once a customer associates your product with a particular outlet, whether wholesale or retail, a major change—such as moving to a mail order channel—may cause frustration and lead the customer to seek a substitute product.

The distribution strategy dictates how broadly your products are distributed. Choosing to distribute to all possible outlets involves using an intensive distribution strategy. Limiting distribution to select outlets is a selective strategy. With an exclusive distribution strategy, distribution is limited to one outlet per geographic area.

Dealing with Multiple Channels of Distribution

More often than not, as a company grows and the diversity of its customer base increases it develops more than one channel of distribution. It may, for example, use direct sales to service the largest customers and intermediary channels of resellers and manufacturer's reps to bring in new customers. It is often not easy to determine which channel is the most effective. Indirect channels are generally associated with a lower level of marketing and sales expense because this task is taken on by the reseller. However, indirect channels are also associated with lower net margins because of the discounts given to resellers so they can make a profit as well, hence the source of the oft-stated "the cost is in the middleman."

What is rarely recognized, however, is that resellers often deal in competing products or several products from one manufacturer and can therefore usually achieve economies of scale, thus reducing their selling costs. Direct sellers, on the other hand, are less able to compete on price with a variety of accounts and typically incur the highest cost per sales call of the two methods. In addition, they are not generally equipped to economically provide products to multiple receiving points in the same way a distributor with regional warehouses can.

The advent of distribution computer software has encouraged the development of major distributors who can, more efficiently than a manufacturer, handle orders, shipping, invoicing, inventory management, and receivables. Today distributors are more than simply transfer agents or bulk breakers for smaller companies; they actually add value through services provided to both their suppliers and their customers.

Transportation is the Link in the Chain

Transportation is potentially the weakest link in the distribution chain because it usually receives the least amount of attention from manufacturers. However, when you consider that raw materials as well as finished goods spend a good part of their time in transit or in inventory, incurring costs at both stages, any savings in logistical functions brings more to the bottom line for everyone in the chain. Even where price differentiation is not feasible, value can be added through differentiation in logistical strategy. The goals of an effective logistics system include:

- Increasing information
- Reducing inventories
- Increasing cycle times
- Reducing variable costs
- Improving customer service

Information is the key. The company that has a communications system that lets it stay in touch with its distributors and sales force wherever they are will be a more efficient and effective company. Some trucking companies, for example, use two-way satellite communication and track shipments via computer, so they are never out of touch. Thus, logistics is a significant aspect of any marketing plan.

Promotion

A new business requires two promotional plans: one for opening the business and making customers aware of its existence, and the other for growing the business. The opening plan establishes the identity or philosophy of the business. Remember that identity and philosophy are quite different from **image.** An image is what you may aspire to be, while your business character and philosophy define who you are in reality. The marketing plan for growing the business is the one you will implement and use consistently for the long term. It is the plan you invest in to build a customer base. It will define the target market and market share you wish to achieve, what people and resources it will take to reach that share, and which services will be needed.

The promotion function of the marketing strategy is the creative one, for this is where advertising, publicity, sales promotion, and personal selling tactics—in short, your promotional mix—is decided. Not every business has the same promotional mix; it is a function of the type of business, the target market, and, of course, the budget. For entrepreneurs with new ventures, the last item—the budget—usually dictates a creative approach.

Creativity begins with a clear understanding of the customer, the economy, current trends, and even the daily news. You never know where a creative idea will come from or what current event will trigger an idea for an ad campaign. In the 1990s, for example, social responsibility is a big issue, hence the proliferation of ads like those of The Body Shop that depict a company that cares about people and natural resources. In fact, the ad may never mention the product they are trying to sell. Tying a marketing strategy to current trends like social responsibility means you must remain flexible and willing to change the strategy should the current trend change. Customers are fickle, and no matter how sound or beneficial a trend may be, they will eventually tire of it, and a new tactic must be employed.

Advertising

Advertising media generally fall into two categories: print and broadcast. The following sections examine the various types of media and their uses. It is not the purpose of this book to provide all the information needed to use each medium presented, only to create awareness of how and when each is used so a decision can be made about which media will best serve the business

Print Media—The Newspaper. The purpose of a *newspaper* is to distribute the news in a direct, to-the-point fashion. Today that doesn't just mean the town gazette. Most cities have one or more major newspapers in addition to business newspapers, shopper newspapers, ethnic newspapers, and national newspapers. How does an entrepreneur know which is most appropriate for the product or service being sold? With businesses spending nearly one-third of their advertising dollars on newspaper ads, this question becomes critical.

Newspaper advertising offers the advantages of:

- Broad coverage in a selected geographic area
- Flexibility and speed in bringing an ad to print and changing it along the way
- Generating sales quickly
- Costing relatively little

Newspapers have disadvantages as well. Broad coverage means you are paying to reach people who may not be part of the target market. Furthermore, since newspapers carry hundreds of ads every day, it is not easy (short of taking out a full page) to attract the attention of the reader. Then too, a newspaper has a very short life. A person may read it with breakfast and throw it out before leaving for work. Even an ad that was noticed may be forgotten by the end of the day. Therefore, you may want to consider a specialized newspaper that will better reach the customer you want. Here are some tips for using newspaper advertising.

- Determine which newspaper is best for your business by placing ads in all of the ones in your target region the first time. Include in the ad a coupon or 800 number so the potential customer will either bring the coupon into your place of business or call on a special line. In either case, ask them where they heard about the business. The papers with the highest response rates should be continued and all others dropped. Once this has been done in one or two geographic regions, you can safely assume that a similar type newspaper in another part of the country will give similar results.
- Be sure you or someone you have paid designs the ad so it doesn't look like every other one on the page. Often a distinctive border will make the ad stand out.
- Create a basic design for advertising that reflects the philosophy of the business and use that design consistently in all advertising. Customers will eventually recognize that the ad is for your company before they even read it.
- The best location for the ad is the right-hand page, above the fold of the newspaper, but it is probably also the most costly.
- Keep track of the results of your ads, particularly if you are experimenting with size and design.
- A national newspaper like *USA Today* offers a good opportunity to do national advertising for less money and a broader reach than a magazine.

Magazines. A number of national magazines offer businesses the opportunity to advertise to certain broad-based target markets. Magazines like *People, Newsweek, Business Week,* and *Time* reach hundreds of thousands of people every week. In addition, there are specialty magazines like *Sports Illustrated, AARP, Rolling Stone,* and *Road & Track* that focus on specific interests. These magazines are useful for businesses that are targeting a particular interest like cars and car accessories or senior citizen issues. There are also a great number of trade magazines that reflect the needs of specific trade organizations like *Advertising Age* and *Variety.* Magazine advertising, however, is more costly and the time lag for printing is generally 6-8 weeks, so it lacks the flexibility of newspapers. These things must be weighed against the fact that you may be doing a better job of reaching the target market.

Magazines also offer the entrepreneur one thing newspapers can't: credibility. According to Jay Levinson, "A properly produced magazine ad, preferably of the full-page variety, gives a small business more credibility than any other mass marketing medium."[3] Obviously, you would want to run the ad more than once; but it is possible to run the ad one time and order reprints at a fraction of the original cost to use in direct mail campaigns and in brochures.

Here are some tips for magazine advertising.

- If the magazine has a regional edition, run the ad in the region you are targeting.
- Use a media buying service to gain real cost advantages.
- Ask the magazine if you can run a split-run ad, that is, run one headline in half the magazines and another in the other half. Be sure to code them so you can keep track of responses.
- Code all ads to reflect publication, date, run, and ad size.
- Use color effectively and take advantage of the fact that you can provide more information in a magazine ad than in a newspaper ad because the reader generally spends more time with it.
- Always give a phone number or mail-in coupon in the ad to encourage people to contact you for a full brochure or a video.
- Check on "remnant space," leftover space that must be filled before the magazine goes to print. It will be a fraction of the original cost of an ad.

Database Marketing. Database Marketing (DBM) is a system to gather and use information on customers and prospects with the goal of increasing profitability. A well constructed database will contain names, addresses, and attributes of people who are likely to purchase what the company has to offer. It will help the entrepreneur define a trading area, reach new customers in the marketplace, select specific target audiences, and survey current customers. DBM is not merely a way to more easily contact customers by mail. Today retaining and maintaining current customers is more important than spending money to find new customers. It has been reported that 65 percent of a company's business comes from current customers. In fact, it costs five to 10 times more to go after a new customer than it does to serve an existing one.[4] With good customer

---

[3]Levinson, J.C. (1993). *Guerrilla Marketing.* Boston: Houghton-Mifflin.
[4]"Firms Now Spend More on Old, Not New, Customers," *Los Angeles Times,* November 1, 1994.

profiles, an entrepreneur can match demographic information on current customers with demographic data in the geographic area of interest to find prospects more effectively. Information contained in the database can be used in advertising, sales promotion, public relations, direct mail, and personal selling.

The competitive advantages to DBM are many. It helps entrepreneurs increase their response rates, aids in the development of new products, helps in the forecasting of sales, and improves mass marketing decisions. Database marketing also allows the company to personalize advertising, cross-sell related products, and increase customer loyalty.

> *Direct mail has the highest response rate of any type of advertising.*

Database marketing is really an overall approach to doing business that requires the total commitment of everyone in the organization. The payoff to this approach takes time—many frustrated entrepreneurs will give up before seeing the results of the efforts. To successfully implement DBM, there must be measurement standards in place to ensure that the efforts are producing the desired results.

Direct Marketing. Direct marketing includes direct mail, mail order, coupons, telemarketing, door-to-door, and TV shopping networks. The essence of direct marketing is that the entrepreneur attempts to close a sale at the moment the advertising takes place. Direct marketing also permits coverage of a wide geographic area while, at the same time, targeting specific customers; therefore, more sales can be generated with fewer dollars. Much more information can be provided in a direct-response brochure; in other words, it can answer all the *customer's* potential questions so *they* can make an immediate decision. Consequently, direct mail has the highest response rate of any type of advertising, and the responses received from a purchased mailing list become the business's personal direct mailing list. Another way to create a personalized mailing list is to have people who "walk in" to the place of business fill out a database card and suggest other people who may be interested in the product or service.

The average response rate for direct mail is two percent. That rate can be increased 50 to 100 percent if you include an 800 number in the advertising, which is easier than filling out an order form. That response rate can be increased from 100 to 700 percent by following up the mailing with a phone call—telemarketing—within 72 hours. As a small, growing company, it is important to consider the staff resources you have and to control mailings to the number you can reasonably follow up on within the 72 hours.

Telemarketing Law

Be sure you understand the Telephone Consumer Protection Act, which says you must maintain a "do-not-call" list and bans unsolicited advertising via fax machines.

You can find out more about this law by writing for "Marketing by Telephone," to the Direct Marketing Association's Ethics and Consumer Affairs Department, 1101 17th St. NW, Suite 705, Washington, DC 20036-4704.

To get the highest response rate possible, you have to do several repeat mailings. For catalogs, four times a year is typical. Also, since most customers have a tendency to throw out direct, unsolicited mail before reading it, it is important to put the central selling point on the envelope as well. Customers must be enticed to open the envelope. A tag line that suggests that what is contained in the envelope will bring the customer money, health, love, or success will certainly encourage people to see what you have to offer. Be sure to continuously update the mailing list and refine it so the number of non-responses declines.

> *More than half of any success with direct mail is attributable to using a good mailing list.*

More than half of any success with direct mail is attributable to using a good mailing list, followed by offering something the customer wants, and being creative in the marketing of the product or service. If you use a targeted mailing list, offer a real benefit to the customer, and send that offer in a business envelope with no return address, the chances of getting a response climb significantly. Not all products are suitable for direct mail, however. Those that are not consumable (requiring repeat orders), short-lived as in a fad, too seasonal, not easily shipped, or too easily available in stores are not good bets for direct mail advertising.

If you are dealing in a consumer item, you may also want to consider interactive TV shopping shows or infomercials to sell the product. The interactive version where the viewer can see the product and order it immediately is in place in several test markets and will eventually be accessible by anyone who wishes it. Interactive TV allows you access to the consumer you seek by sex, age, special interests, occupation and so forth. It is estimated that 70 million people watch Home Shopping Network; 28 million watch Cable Value Network; and 18 million watch QVC. This is definitely a growing market for direct market sales and as soon as interactive TV becomes a reality for anyone who wants it, those numbers will increase. Computer online services like

Prodigy and *Compuserve* also provide an outlet for consumer products and will be something to look at carefully in the future.

The Yellow Pages. Many businesses can benefit from placing ads in the Yellow Pages of their telephone directory. If you are in the retail business or offer a service not considered a professional service (consultant, lawyer, accountant), there is a good chance people will look for what you offer in the Yellow Pages. However, remember that the Yellow Pages is fairly expensive advertising space and only targets the local market for your product or service, so it should not be considered a major source of advertising, particularly if you market nationally or globally.

Signs. Signs are a relatively inexpensive way to expose a lot of people to the business. They also encourage impulse buying of consumer products. Naturally, signs play the most important role in retail businesses where they become part of the total advertising campaign. In other types of businesses, the sign is merely a feature to help someone locate the business. Signs do, however, outlive their usefulness fairly quickly. If a sale sign is left in a window too long, people will tune it out; they will no longer see it, and it will have lost its value.

Broadcast Media—Radio. Radio is an excellent medium for local or regional advertising as the audience can be targeted geographically and generally by age group. Radio stations keep extensive records on the demographics of their listening audience to help determine if this audience will be interested in any product or service. It is useful to advertise on more than one station to saturate your market. Recently many companies have been able to gain a national presence by sponsoring a national radio program. This was the case with Snapple Beverage Company, who bought time on the Rush Limbaugh radio talk show and immediately gained access to 20 million listeners a week. Sales for the company soared as a result.

When dealing in radio advertising it is important to understand that the ad can't be a one-shot ad. As radio listeners are fickle and tend to change channels often, the ad needs to be played several times a day, several days a week to achieve an impact. Keeping track of the responses received from the ad indicates where the greatest impact has been made. A general rule of thumb is that prime radio time is during commuting hours in the morning and late afternoon. The cost will be higher at those times, but you will also reach the most people. Be sure to provide finished recorded commercials to the station so you can maintain quality and consistency in your advertising. Don't rely on the radio station personnel to give your ad the energy and professionalism it needs. Here are a few more tips for radio advertising.

- Stick to shorter spots. You can usually achieve just as much in a well-designed 30-second ad as you can in a one-minute ad.
- Use music and sound effects to set the tone for the commercial. Both can be rented from most radio stations for a modest amount.
- Be sure to design the commercial to catch the listener's attention in the first few seconds.
- Run your ads three weeks out of every four for good coverage at less cost.

Television. Many businesses spend one quarter of their advertising dollars on television; consequently, it is the second-most-popular form of advertising after newspapers for consumer products. With television, people can see as well as hear about the product or service, and the audience can be targeted at the national, regional, or even local level as well as by interest group by using cable channels. However, television advertising is expensive, not only for the actual on-air time but for the preparation and filming of the commercial.

Television time is based on the GRP (Gross Rating Point), which very simply put means that you will pay per GRP, a rate that differs based on whether you are in a small town or a large city. The range is about $5 to $500 per GRP. A rule of thumb for deciding whether or not to use television as an advertising medium is to calculate if you can purchase 150 GRPs per month for three months. If this level of advertising is not within the budget, forget TV; you will probably be wasting your money. When using television seek the help of a media buying service. They are the equivalent of buying health insurance through group pools, and they can get your media time much more cheaply than you can because they buy millions of dollars' worth every month.

While learning how to produce a television spot is a book by itself, here are two pieces of advice: 1) Write the script yourself and let the television studio provide the product equipment and expertise; and 2) do not appear in the commercial yourself unless you are a professional actor.

Miscellaneous Advertising. Many simple advertising tactics have been very successful for new and growing consumer products or service businesses. Offering for sale (or as a give-away) T-shirts and baseball caps with the company's name emblazoned on them has been a very successful tactic. Using searchlights to attract people to your business site is an attention getter. Couponing has certainly been an advertising staple, and there are many coupon magazines in which you can buy space. These magazines are distributed to households across the country and have been an excellent source of new customers for businesses. Look for any and all opportunities to demonstrate the product free to potential customers. One young entrepreneur who developed a successful, easy-to-use cleaner for silk plants reports his sales always increase when he does demonstrations in stores. Creating a video tape of the product in action is another useful technique, especially where the product is not easily transported. Many firms like PictureTel Corp. of Massachusetts incorporated videos into free seminars. An outstanding 80 percent of people who attend these seminars end up purchasing one of their products.

This section has provided just a few of the hundreds of tips and techniques available to entrepreneurs who wish to advertise products or services in the most efficient and effective ways while the new venture is growing. The series of books on guerrilla marketing by Jay Conrad Levinson is highly recommended for its marketing suggestions geared specifically to young, growing companies.

Publicity and Public Relations

Publicity is essentially free advertising for a product or business, through newspaper articles, radio and television stories, and talk shows. Public relations, on the other hand, is the way a marketing campaign is structured so as to present the desired perception to the public.

The key to publicity is having a unique or newsworthy product or business. For example, your product may be environmentally friendly, where your competitor's is not. Or the way your business was founded may be an interesting story. If the business or product is newsworthy, there are several ways to get some publicity. Write to a reporter or editor to tease them with an idea, and follow up with a phone call. Issue a press release answering the who, what, where, when, and why of the business and include a press kit containing the press release, bios, and photos of the key people in the story, any necessary background information, and copies of any other articles written about the company. The key is to make it as easy as possible for the reporter to write or tell the story. When an article is written about the business, use reprints in future advertising and brochures to get even more value for the effort.

Whenever possible, get to know people in the media on a first-name basis, even take them to lunch. This gives you instant clout when you need free publicity. The media are always looking for news and appreciate the effort to give them something newsworthy. An effective news release should contain the following:

- The date, your name and phone number
- The release date (for immediate release, or after a certain date)
- An appropriate headline
- The release information typed double spaced with wide margins
- The who, what, where, when, and why
- A photo if appropriate
- A note explaining briefly why you sent the release

There are also several publishing services that can be used to distribute information on the business. The *Contact Sheet*, a monthly publication, prints news releases written and paid for by companies. It is sent to over 1,800 editors and reporters nationally who have free use of the material. Another publication is the *PR Newsletter,* which is a membership electronic service that also assists the company in writing a message targeted to a specific media audience.

Personal Selling

Traditional selling techniques just don't meet the needs of today's customers. Today, people *expect* a quality product at a fair price with good service. That's a given. If you start with this in mind, you will find that the way you sell your products and your business is quite different from the traditional approach. Today, a business distinguishes itself in the marketplace by identifying and meeting specific customer needs. So even if you are "selling" a commodity, you need to figure out some way to add value to the product.

A good example of this is a small manufacturer of molded plastic parts in Massachusetts. Its largest account is a major acoustic speaker manufacturer, also in Massachusetts. The speaker company asked the plastics company to assign a full-time salesperson to their plant, which would help them eliminate some of the costs of buyers and planners and, at the same time, let the plastics plant concentrate on service rather than trying to acquire new accounts. As a result, the plastic company's sales have increased nearly 40 percent per year.

Becoming a value-added company, tailoring products to meet customers' needs, requires that everyone in the company become service oriented, a time-consuming task that necessitates training and educating employees. It also demands an opportunity mindset, rather than a selling mindset. And as this type of selling is usually accomplished at higher levels in an organization, it is a more lengthy process; however, the returns are potentially greater. Working more closely with customers can translate into reduced selling and marketing costs.

One of the most difficult issues an entrepreneur faces with regard to selling is that of compensation—what and how to pay sales representatives. The possibilities are endless: Incentives can be tied to profit or gross margins, contract size, the number of new accounts acquired, company goals, and so on. One of the latest techniques is to pay sales people a salary plus a percentage of the profits. Yet another issue is how to compensate those who provide service to customers. Service is the key to customer retention, and the people who provide that service are becoming increasingly more important to a firm's success. Studying the compensation practices in your industry as well as those of other industries will help you decide which method is best for your business.

Trade Shows and Exhibits

For some entrepreneurs trade shows, fairs, and exhibits are a primary way to expose their products.

Trade shows are a good way to find out who the competitors are and what marketing techniques they are using. It is also the place to meet and negotiate with sales reps and to get names for a mailing list. But the primary reason to display your products at a trade show is to eventually sell more product. To accomplish this, you should do the following:

1. Rent booth space. Hire a display designer to design and produce a quality display booth that will attract attention. Visiting several trade shows prior to doing your own will give you some ideas as to what works and what doesn't. You may also be able to work out a deal with a company that has compatible products to share a booth and combine resources.
2. Hire a model to distribute an information sheet to as many people as possible at the trade show that invites people to stop by the booth. Save the expensive brochures to hand out at the booth to potential customers. Also be sure to ask for business cards so you can follow up with people who took the brochure.

Trade Show Savvy

To learn about trade shows and conventions where you can display your products, check your library for *Tradeshow and Convention Guide,* which can also be ordered from Budd Publications, P.O. Box 7, New York, NY 10004.

3. Have enough knowledgeable, personable people in the booth so that potential customers are not waiting to talk to someone. Stagger breaks to keep the booth manned at all times.
4. Consider renting a hospitality suite in the hotel where the trade show is located to entertain key people in your industry.
5. Offer something free at your booth: a sample or a contest.
6. Follow up with letters to anyone whose business card was collected and phone calls to all serious prospects.

Marketing to Industrial Customers

When the target market you are trying to reach is other businesses, the marketing strategy is somewhat different in terms of advertising and promotion. Consumer products and services require a lot of high-profile advertising and promotion to entice customers away from the myriad of other choices they have. With industrial products and services, the focus is on letting the targeted businesses know the product or service is available and what it can do for the business.

In general, industrial products and services do not use broadcast media or most popular print media. Instead, they rely heavily on direct mail, personal selling, trade shows, and articles and advertisements in trade journals. As most industrial product manufacturers distribute their products through wholesalers, it becomes the wholesalers' job to market to and locate retail outlets. If you are dealing with industrial customers, investigate how products and services are marketed in your particular industry.

Online Market Research

With the addition of so many new electronic databases to the "information superhighway," it is now possible to do at least some of the needed market research online. Electronic bulletin boards catering to special interests, U.S. Census data, real-time stock quotes, financial and product information on foreign companies, Dun & Bradstreet's *Financial Profiles and Company Reports,* demographics, active trademark listings, and analysts' reports are but a few of the information sources now available.

If there was ever too much of a good thing, it might be the information superhighway. There are so many options and so much information that it boggles the mind. Plus, the convenience of online information must be weighed against the cost of retrieving it. Most database services charge either a monthly

Figure 12.1: Online Sources for Market Research

COMPUSERVE: **Business Demographics, Iquest** (gateway to more than 850 databases)
Magazine Database Plus: Full text articles
Marketing/Management Research Center: Full texts of major business magazines
Neighborhood Report: Demographics by zip code

DIALOG: **ABI/INFORM:** Business publications
Arthur D. Little/Online: Industry forecasts
Business Software Database
D&B Donnelley Demographics
D&B-Dun's Electronic Business Directory
Employee Benefits Inforsource
Moody's Corporate Files
PTS Newsletter Database

DOW JONES NEWS RETRIEVAL: Comprehensive Company Reports
Business Newswires
Text Library: Full text articles from over 500 publications
Dun & Bradstreet Financial Profiles & Company Reports
Japanese Business News: Same-day coverage
Statistical Comparisons of Companies & Industries:
Standard & Poor's Profiles & Earnings Estimates: Company reports
Top Business, Financial & Economic News

NEXIS: **Analyst Research:** Brokerage Houses
Computers and Communications: full text sources
Company: Company & industry research reports
Consumer Goods: Trade publications
LEXPAT®: Full text of U.S. patents
Marketing: Trade publications and general sources on marketing information
PROMT/PLUS: Trends in markets and technology

service fee, a per-search fee, an hourly rate, a print charge, or all of the above. This can run into a considerable amount of money in a short time. Figure 12.1 presents a summary of some of the services available from the most common database sources. Before signing up for any of these, arrange for a demonstration of several at once so you can compare them for speed, ease of use, and information provided.

Writing the Marketing Plan

While this chapter has covered a lot of material that will help you write your marketing plan, it has barely scratched the surface of information available to you in creating a unique plan that will work for you. Therefore, check some of

Figure 12.2: Marketing Plan Outline

- The purpose of the marketing plan. What are you trying to accomplish?
- The plan for achieving that purpose and the benefits that will accrue to the customer.
- The target market that the marketing plan will reach.
- The unique market niche that the business will occupy.
- The business's identity and how customers will perceive it.
- The distribution channels used to reach the customer.
- The marketing tools used to reach the target market (advertising, direct mail, trade shows, etc.).
- The media plan with the schedule of use and costs of each of the marketing tools.
- The total marketing plan budget as a percentage of sales.

the sources at the end of the chapter for more details on a specific topic that may interest you. Including a marketing plan in your business plan is essential as it helps ensure the business stay on track with its sales goals. It also lets others who may read the plan (bankers, investors, potential employees) know something about the company's philosophy, identity, and goals. See Figure 12.2 for an outline of a marketing plan.

This plan, like the rest of the business plan, is a living document subject to change based on new information. However, a marketing plan should not be changed often. It takes time to implement an effective plan, and it takes time to see the results. The plan you create should be the best one achievable, given the resources available.

✓ New Venture Checklist

Have you

☐ Analyzed the marketing options and rank ordered them?

☐ Written a clear, concise, one-paragraph statement of the marketing plan?

☐ Written a position statement for the product/service?

☐ Determined the distribution channels for the product/service?

☐ Developed an advertising, publicity, and promotion strategy?

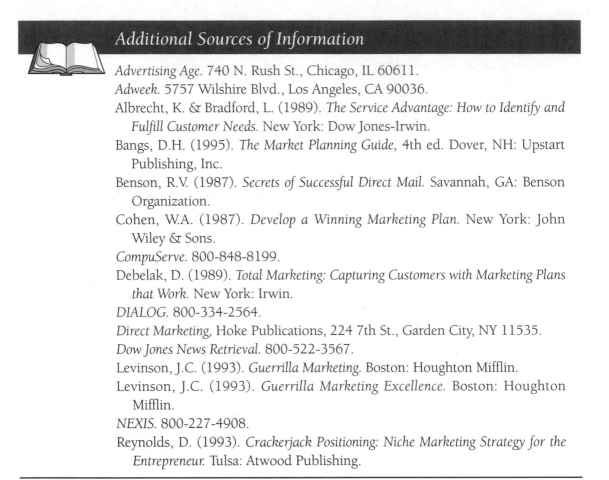

Additional Sources of Information

Advertising Age. 740 N. Rush St., Chicago, IL 60611.

Adweek. 5757 Wilshire Blvd., Los Angeles, CA 90036.

Albrecht, K. & Bradford, L. (1989). *The Service Advantage: How to Identify and Fulfill Customer Needs.* New York: Dow Jones-Irwin.

Bangs, D.H. (1995). *The Market Planning Guide,* 4th ed. Dover, NH: Upstart Publishing, Inc.

Benson, R.V. (1987). *Secrets of Successful Direct Mail.* Savannah, GA: Benson Organization.

Cohen, W.A. (1987). *Develop a Winning Marketing Plan.* New York: John Wiley & Sons.

CompuServe. 800-848-8199.

Debelak, D. (1989). *Total Marketing: Capturing Customers with Marketing Plans that Work.* New York: Irwin.

DIALOG. 800-334-2564.

Direct Marketing, Hoke Publications, 224 7th St., Garden City, NY 11535.

Dow Jones News Retrieval. 800-522-3567.

Levinson, J.C. (1993). *Guerrilla Marketing.* Boston: Houghton Mifflin.

Levinson, J.C. (1993). *Guerrilla Marketing Excellence.* Boston: Houghton Mifflin.

NEXIS. 800-227-4908.

Reynolds, D. (1993). *Crackerjack Positioning: Niche Marketing Strategy for the Entrepreneur.* Tulsa: Atwood Publishing.

Issues to Consider

1. What is the difference between an entrepreneurial marketing strategy and a large corporation's market strategy?
2. Why is it important to stick with your marketing plan even if it isn't returning immediate results?
3. What does the marketing plan do for the business?
4. Why should an entrepreneurial venture not engage in image positioning like large corporations?
5. How can a position statement be tested?
6. How is price for a product or service determined?
7. How does the promotion strategy for consumer-oriented businesses differ from that of industrial businesses?

The Management and Organization Plan

Overview

- *The entrepreneurial approach to organizational structure*
- *Ownership and compensation issues*
- *Hiring decisions*
- *The employee handbook*

The Organizational Chart—Fact or Fiction

How to manage and organize the business is a fundamental decision every entrepreneur must make, one that impacts all aspects of the business, from product design to customer service. The way a business is organized and staffed can also affect communications, morale, and performance in ways the entrepreneur never expected. Entrepreneurs traditionally have resorted to the ubiquitous line and staff organizational charts as seen in Figure 13.1 to formulate a structure for their businesses.

This chart depicts a company that is established, so it is more hierarchical than a typical entrepreneurial venture. While the entrepreneur and the founding team probably perform all these functions when the business is just starting, they also have to think ahead to their requirements as they grow. The organizational chart on p. 256 appears to spell out very clearly the relationships among the staff, indicating lines of authority and responsibility. Because this type of organizational structure focuses on functions, however, it often tends to result in dependent relationships; therefore when a problem occurs, it is sent up to the next management level for decision making.

Figure 13.1: Traditional Line and Staff Organizational Chart for a Simple Manufacturing Plant

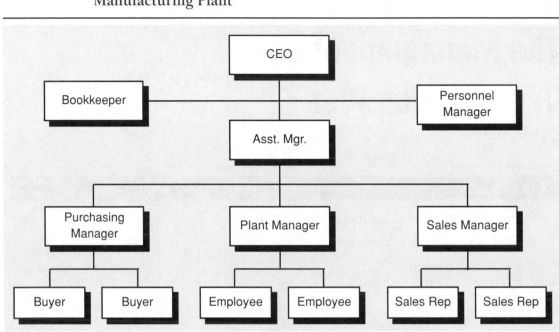

What is not depicted by this traditional, hierarchical chart is the informal organization or network of relationships that account for a significant portion of the daily work. Informal networks of people consist of those who tend to gravitate toward each other in an effort to accomplish tasks in a more efficient and effective manner than may be dictated by the chart. These networks form the shadow organizational structure that brings the business through an unexpected crisis, an impossible deadline, or a formidable impasse. They are social links that form the real power base in the organization. Metaphorically speaking, the organizational chart may be thought of as the skeleton of the body, while the informal network constitutes the arteries and veins that push information and activity throughout the organization—in other words, the lifeblood of the organization.

Research has found three types of informal networks: the advice network, which includes those people who are the problem solvers in the organization; the trust network where political information is shared; and the communication network, which consists of employees who discuss work-related issues on a frequent basis.[1] Often the people in these networks come from various functional areas in the organization that don't typically deal with each other on a

[1]Krackhardt, D. & Hanson, J.R. (1993). "Informal networks: The company behind the chart." *Harvard Business Review,* Vol. 71 (4), p. 105.

daily basis. For example, the political/trust network might include the book-keeper, a sales rep, and a plant employee.

Entrepreneurs seem to have intuitively recognized the value of informal networks in the organizational structure and often the most successful new ventures adopt a team-based approach with a more flat structure. Figure 13.2 depicts the nature of this structure. The lead entrepreneur is the driving force for the entrepreneurial team, which normally consists of people with expertise in at least one of the three functional areas of a new venture: marketing, operations, and finance. The organization consists of interactive, integrative teams. In the new venture, these are rarely "departments" in the traditional sense, but rather functions, tasks, or activities. The statistics reflect this pattern. Fifty-one percent of the growing companies that have made it to the *Inc. 500* list do not have a marketing director, while 61 percent have neither a COO nor a personnel director. Thirty-two percent do not have a CFO, and an astounding 67 percent have no one to manage information systems in their companies.[2]

What is the explanation for this? For one thing, entrepreneurs are usually too creative and flexible to be bound by the strictures of a formal organizational structure. They are more comfortable bringing together resources and people as a team and making decisions on the spot without having to go through layers of management. Another reason is that growing new ventures must be able to adapt quickly as they muscle their way into the market. Uncertainty and instability are a way of life for young ventures, and a rigid, formalized, bureaucratic structure would unduly burden a new venture both financially and operationally.

Three components make up the entrepreneurial organizational structure: formal processes, people, and culture. Formal processes include the planning system, control mechanisms, compensation and reward policies, and other processes that make the organization run more efficiently and effectively. These processes are not independent units, but rather are linked to all functions of the organization that require them. For example, quality control mechanisms are

Figure 13.2: Informal Networks in the Organizational Structure

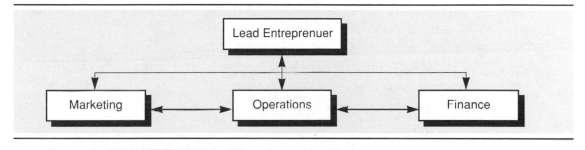

---

[2]*Inc.* magazine, October 1993, p. 86.

not solely the purview of a single department, but flow from product development through manufacturing, to distribution, and throughout all of the support functions needed to facilitate the process of getting the product to the customer.

People who work in market-oriented, entrepreneurial companies must not only think of their individual tasks but of the product and company as a whole. People required to make the business work need to have team building skills as well as the ability to make decisions and implement them with very little input from top management or the CEO. In new ventures those teams may consist of independent contractors whose skills are being "rented" on an as-needed basis.

Informal networks create flexibility and speed up operations. They also have the advantage of managing the personal issues not easily handled through policies and structure.

The Entrepreneurial Approach to Organizational Structure

If entrepreneurs have always recognized the value of an integrative, team-based approach (ITB) to management and organization, huge corporations—like Xerox—are also attempting to mimic this entrepreneurial style. They have learned that one of the greatest benefits of the entrepreneurial or market-oriented style of management is that relationships with customers improve. Xerox, for example, finds itself working with its customers to redesign the customers' business processes instead of merely selling them copiers. They are focusing on what the customer needs and then structuring their business accordingly.

What does this new market orientation look like? It begins with a *purpose* or *mission statement* for the business that reflects the reason the business exists. The mission then becomes the catalyst and driving force for everything the business does. All strategies planned and decisions made derive from the core mission of the business. The following is an example of a mission statement from a market-oriented company:

> DV Industries, Inc. will be recognized as a world-class provider of finishing processes and services to the aerospace and other industries requiring performance to demanding specifications.
>
> We will maximize the economic well-being and quality of life of our customers, employees, owners, suppliers, and neighbors by creating an environment of continuous improvement and by our commitment to excellence.

The purpose defines the *opportunities, innovations,* and *parameters* the business will pursue. DV Industries, for example, seeks to meet the specialized materials finishing requirements of customers in the aerospace and related industries. They do this by developing innovative processes customized to the customer's specifications.

The combination of purpose with innovation results in positioning the business in a *unique market niche*. DV Industries services customers whose needs require the highest level of quality and service in very specialized tasks. Because innovation and the development of new processes is time consuming, DV must sense changes and trends in the market they serve *before* they occur so they can stay ahead of their competitors. To succeed in the market niche, the business has to use or develop **collateral technologies** that keep it on the leading edge in the industry. DV Industries is continually developing innovative and environmentally sound finishing processes that set it apart from other businesses in its market, based on discussions with its customers.

> *Organizing a business in a way that it is flexible, and competitive in terms of operational costs requires an integrative, team-based approach.*

Entrepreneurs find that organizing a business in a way that it is flexible, quick to respond to market changes, and competitive in terms of operational costs requires an integrative, team-based approach. Teams come in many varieties: self-directed work teams, problem-solving teams, quality teams, cross-functional teams. Essentially they serve the same underlying purpose: "A team is a small number of people with complementary skills who are committed to a common purpose, set of performance goals, and approach for which they hold themselves mutually accountable.[3]

What makes the entrepreneur's situation unique is that, at least when the venture is in the start-up or initial growing phases and capital resources are limited, the team the entrepreneur develops will most likely consist of several people outside the organization, namely, independent contractors. For example, the entrepreneur may decide to sub-contract the manufacturing of a product to an established company. This means he or she needs to understand how that sub-contractor works and will, of necessity, become a part of that company's team in the production of the product. The entrepreneur's marketing, sales, operations, and finance people must also be able to work with the manufacturing sub-contractor to ensure that the goals of the new venture are met with the timeliness and level of quality desired. This requires skills on the part of the team that are not normally learned in school, skills such as diplomacy in the management of intra- and inter team relationships, problem-solving skills, and the ability to take responsibility for innovative changes on the spot, often without the direct approval of the entrepreneur.

---

[3]Katzenbach, J.R. & Smith, D.K. (1993). *The Wisdom of Teams*. Boston: Harvard Business School Press.

A Market Orientation for Thermos

You are no doubt familiar with Thermos, the manufacturer of Thermos bottles and lunch boxes. You may not have known, however, that they are also a major producer of gas and electric cookout grills. These "barbecue" grills have become a commodity in the marketplace—virtually everyone has one—and as a consequence, Thermos was experiencing flagging growth in this segment of its market. Thermos had always had a traditional, hierarchical structure organized by function, but this structure was no longer working in a dynamic marketplace.

Thermos decided to take a big chance and pulled together a development team consisting of managers from engineering, marketing, manufacturing, and finance. The focus was to be on the market; the goal was to learn about the cookout needs of their customers and then invent a brand new product to meet those needs. Leadership of the team would vary depending on what stage of the process was dominant at any point in time. Initially, marketing took the lead and everyone on the team went out to find out everything they could about how people cook out-of-doors. They used focus groups, visited people in their homes while they were barbecuing, and ultimately learned that the product they were to develop should be attractive to women (who were doing more of the barbecuing), not use charcoal (which is banned in some cities), avoid gas (which is banned in some condos), and cook good food. The solution was an electric grill that looked like a piece of furniture.

In the first phase of prototyping, the team took two rough models out to consumers and retailers to gauge their reactions; while this was going on, engineering was developing an innovative way to raise the cooking temperature of the electric heating rod using their core technology—the vacuum technology that keeps liquids cold or hot. At the same time, the designers were looking at ways to differentiate the product in the stores with features that added value; and the manufacturing segment, who had been involved from the beginning, was preparing for production.

Their first 100 grills went to employees to test and from that came some minimal design changes. Then they were on the road to the trade shows to debut the new product. The team approach was a success and increased revenues 13 percent in the first year.

Building a team that works well together is a long process that involves training the team in both interpersonal and job-related skills. In the beginning of a new venture, that learning may come through trial and error, but later as the budget allows, it may come through hiring a team facilitator or consultant who can help fine-tune the team's efforts. Integrative team building demands bringing in people who have a vested interest in the success of the business and are not content to simply do their job but want increasing responsibility, authority, and accountability. Entrepreneurs must be careful to make that requirement very clear when bringing someone new into the team.

TQM—Panacea or Solution

Total Quality Management, or TQM, became the buzzword of the early 1980s. As a management plan it requires businesses to become flexible and more responsive to their internal and external environments. TQM is an integrated, systematic, organization-wide management philosophy that helps to build customer-driven businesses. It strives to improve product and service quality in all aspects of the business by empowering employees to change processes. It demands systematic changes in management practice, the redesign of tasks, and the redefinition of managerial roles.[4]

Recently TQM has come under attack because despite its popularity, only 20 percent of those companies that institute TQM can identify significant improvement in their performance.[5] Furthermore, it is a difficult concept to measure without benchmarks as the traditional appraisal and reward systems do not work with TQM. Some people suggest that TQM will be replaced by the current buzzword, **business process reengineering**, which means constantly questioning and re-evaluating whether or not current processes in the organization are working and make sense. In any case, the basic concept of total quality throughout the organization is here to stay.

Ownership and Compensation in a Corporation

Two of the most perplexing management issues facing an entrepreneur with a new corporation are how much of the company to sell to potential stockholders and how much to pay key management. There is a tendency on the part of small, privately held companies to use minority shares as an incentive to entice investors and to pay key management, primarily because new companies do not have the cash flow to provide attractive compensation packages. The

[4]Grant, RM., Shani, R; Krishnan, R. (1994). TQM's challenge to management theory and practice. *Sloan Management Review*, Vol. 35, Iss. 2, pp. 25–35.

[5]Fisher, Liz (1994). Total quality: Hit or myth? *Accountancy*, Vol. 113, Iss. 1208, p. 50.

prevailing wisdom is that providing stock in the new company will increase commitment, cause management to be more cost conscious, reduce cash outlay for salaries, and induce loyalty to the company in the long term. But recent studies have found this is not always the case.[6] More often than not the person to whom you have given stock in good faith will ultimately leave the company, taking the stock with him with the potential for future harm to the business.

In the initial growth stage of a new venture, it is difficult to determine with any degree of accuracy what long-term role a particular person may play in the organization. Often the entrepreneur, due to limited resources, is not able to attract the best person to take the company beyond the start-up phase, so a person with fewer qualifications will be hired for little salary plus a minority ownership in the company. The entrepreneur is literally betting on the potential contribution of this person, an eventuality that usually doesn't pay off. Later when the company can afford to hire the person it needs, the entrepreneur has to deal with a minority shareholder who has developed territorial "rights." When minority ownership is an important issue to a potential employee, it is important to make clear to that person what it means. There are few legal and managerial rights associated with a minority position; thus, for all practical purposes, minority ownership is simply the unmarketable right to appreciated stock value that has no defined payoff period and certainly no guarantee of value.

Founder's Stock

Founder's stock (144 stock) is stock issued to the first shareholders of the corporation or assigned to key management as part of a compensation package. The payoff on this stock comes when the company goes public or is sold. Assuming the company is successful, founder's stock at issuance is probably valued at the lowest level it will ever be relative to an investor's stock value. Consequently, one tax problem that arises as a result occurs when private investors provide seed or working capital to the new venture. Often the value of the stock the investors hold makes it very obvious that the founder's stock was a bargain and not the true value of the stock. According to IRC 83, the amount of the difference between the founder's price and the investor's price would be taxable as compensation income.

One way to avoid this problem is to issue common stock to founders and key management, and convertible preferred stock to investors. The preference

<hr>

[6]Osborne, R.L. (1992). "Minority ownership for key employees: Dividend or disaster?" *Business Horizons,* Vol. 35 (1), p. 76.

upon liquidation should be high enough to cover the book value of the corporation so the common stockholders would receive nothing. This action would effectively decrease the value of the common stock so it would no longer appear to be a bargain for IRS purposes.

Founder's stock is restricted, and the SEC rules (Rule 144) state that the restriction refers to stock that has not been registered with the SEC (private placement) and stock owned by the controlling officers and shareholders of the company (those with at least 10% ownership). If a stockholder has owned the stock for at least three years, and public information about the company exists, Rule 144 can be avoided in the sale of the stock. If the stockholder has held the stock for less than three years, the rules must be strictly complied with. It is not the intent of this chapter to discuss the details of Rule 144. Suffice it to say that the rule is complex and the appropriate attorney or tax specialist should be consulted.

Compensating with Stock

Giving someone ownership rights in the company is a serious decision that should be given very careful consideration. There are several things to contemplate before taking on an equity partner, whether an investor or key management.

1. Anyone brought in as an investor/shareholder or partner with the entrepreneur does not have to be an equal partner. An investor can hold whatever share of stock you have determined is warranted based on what that partner will contribute to the business.
2. Never bring someone in as a partner/investor if you can hire that person to provide the same service, no matter what you may feel the urgency of the situation is. The most advantageous way to hire someone for a new venture is to hire the person as an independent contractor.
3. Do not lock yourself into future compensation promises like stock options. Use cash as bonuses whenever possible.
4. Establish the company as yours before taking on partners unless, of course, you have founded the company as a team.
5. Consider having employees work for the company at least two years before they are vested and given stock or stock options.

Issuing Stock When the Company is Capitalized. The number of shares you authorize when you form the corporation is purely arbitrary. Suppose you decide to authorize one million shares in the new venture. This means you have one million shares available to be issued to potential stockholders. If you value each share of stock at $1 and capitalize $100,000, you will have issued 100,000 shares; if each share is valued at $10, you will have issued 10,000 shares. The value you place on each share is arbitrary; for psychological reasons you may wish to value a share at $1, so a shareholder who contributes $10,000 to the business can say that he or she owns 10,000 shares of stock as opposed to 1,000 shares at $10/share. In short, the number of shares issued depends on the initial capitalization and the price per share.

Now suppose that you, the entrepreneur, will be initially contributing $250,000 in cash and $300,000 in assets (equipment, furniture, etc.) to the company. At $1 a share, you issue yourself 550,000 shares of stock and own a 100% interest in the company because you have only issued 550,000 shares total. At a later date you issue 29,000 additional shares at $5 a share to an investor. Your minority shareholder has therefore contributed $145,000 to the company and owns a five percent interest in the company (29,000/579,000 issued stock). The investor will require that the current value or future additional income of the company be sufficient to justify the increase in price per share. You can see that as additional shares are issued, the original stockholder's percentage ownership in the company declines. However, the founder's shares will not go below 55 percent (550,000/1 million) unless the company authorizes additional shares and issues a portion or all of those additional shares.

> *Holders of common stock share in both the successes and failures of the business and benefit through dividends and the appreciating value of the company.*

The type of stock you will be issuing is common stock, which is a basic ownership interest in the company. This means that holders of common stock share in both the successes and failures of the business and benefit through dividends and the appreciating value of the company. Once common stock is issued, a company can issue preferred stock, whose holders are paid first if the company is liquidated. Preferred stockholders, however, must accept a fixed dividend amount, no matter how much profit the company makes. If you form a sub-chapter S corporation, you may only issue one type of stock.

One form of stock you may want to offer investors as an inducement is called IRC Sec. 1244 stock, which permits a shareholder of a corporation with capital and paid-in surplus of $1 million or less to treat a portion of any loss on the disposition of the stock as an ordinary loss, rather than a capital loss. The amount the shareholder can take as a loss is limited to the shareholder's original investment.

Buy-Sell Agreements. One of the real concerns entrepreneurs with privately held corporations face is what to do when a stockholder wants to sell stock or an employee with stock decides to leave the company to work for a competitor. A buy-sell agreement spells out the terms and conditions for the sale of stock to people outside the organization. It is a way to maintain control of the company. Usually a buy-sell agreement provides for a right of first refusal to the company to buy the stock before it is sold to someone else. To determine the value of the stock at that point in time, it's a good idea to call for an appraisal of the company. Then the stock can be purchased using savings, insurance, or asset sales. All investors, stockholder, and employment contracts involving stock should contain buy-sell clauses.

Prenuptial Agreements. Entrepreneurs with family businesses face the additional threat from divorce from their spouses or the divorces of their children from spouses. One way entrepreneurs protect themselves from losing a significant ownership interest in the company to a divorcing spouse, whether theirs or their children's, is to have a prenuptial agreement. If the "prenup" is properly structured, the couple would not be allowed to hold company stock jointly. This is particularly important where a son or daughter who is a minority shareholder marries and subsequently divorces. The entrepreneur does not want to have to deal with an ex-in-law. A prenuptial agreement, while not fool-proof, will probably be upheld in a court of law if it is not vague and is reasonable in its terms.

Trusts. An irrevocable trust offers the greatest protection for the ownership of stock. For example, you may set up a trust for your child that contains his or her stock in the family corporation. The trust will stipulate that creditors have no rights to the trust. This also includes a potential spouse that your child might divorce. The important thing to remember is that you, the entrepreneur, must set up the trust using an attorney specializing in that area of the law.

Alternatives to Equity Incentives

There are other ways to compensate key management that will not require the entrepreneur to give up equity in the company.

Deferred Compensation Plans. In a deferred compensation plan, the entrepreneur can specify that awards and bonuses be linked to profits and performance of both the individual and the company, with the lion's share being on the individual's performance. The employee does not pay taxes on this award until it is actually paid out at some specified date.

Bonus Plans. With a bonus plan, a series of goals are set by the company with input from the employee, and as the employee reaches each goal, the bonus is given. This method is often used with sales people and others who have a direct impact on the profitability of the company. The key to success with bonus plans is to specify measurable objectives.

Capital Appreciation Rights. This type of program gives employees the right to participate in the profits of the company at a specified percentage, while not being full shareholders with voting rights. Capital Appreciation Rights, or "phantom stock," provide for long-term compensation incentives whose value is based on the increase in the value of the business. The phantom stock will look, act, and reward like real stock, but will have no voting rights and will limit the employee's obligation should the business fail. Typically the employee has to be with the company for a period of three to five years to be considered vested, but otherwise they do not have to pay for these rights.

Profit-Sharing Plans. Profit-sharing plans are distinct from the previously discussed plans in that they are subject to the ERISA rules for employee retirement programs. These plans must include all employees without regard to individual contribution to profit or performance. They are different from pensions in that owners are not required to contribute in any year and employees are not "entitled" to them.

Whatever plan you choose to compensate and reward key management, understand that these rewards may not produce the desired performance. You should carefully consider alternative plans before granting minority ownership status, as you may be able to achieve the results you are looking for without having to give up a portion of ownership.

Hiring—Job Descriptions and Specifications

One of the most important decisions made by any business is a hiring decision; yet, more often than not, those who are doing the hiring don't know what they're doing. They hire quickly, based on instinct, and then have to worry about how to get rid of the person. Today, with more employees suing their bosses for wrongful discharge, sexual harassment, and racial/gender/age discrimination, it is increasingly important that the entrepreneur understand how to hire. Hiring, however, is not a simple matter of placing a help wanted ad in the newspaper, receiving résumés, and then holding interviews to select the best candidate. The bulk of the work of hiring comes before the person is actually needed.

Job Profiles

Part of organizing the business is determining what positions are needed to do the required tasks of the business. Naturally, in the start-up phase most entrepreneurs do the biggest share of the work themselves, but they know that at some point they will have to hire employees, even if it's only a receptionist or administrative assistant. Preparing profiles and job descriptions for all the functions of the business ensures that you have them when you need them. Typically when entrepreneurs (and managers) develop job descriptions, they focus entirely on the duties and responsibilities of a particular job. While this is important, it is equally important to develop behavioral profiles of these jobs; in other words, what behavioral traits are typical of and vital to a particular position. An effective bookkeeper, for example, may require the following attributes: detail orientation, focused, can work alone, is responsible and organized.

In addition to looking at the best behavioral traits for each position, the entrepreneur must have a good sense of the business culture. While a job candidate may have the education and experience required by the job description and display some of the behavioral traits necessary for success in the position, the candidate's chemistry may not fit in well with the culture of the organization. This is an important distinction because education and experience can be achieved, behaviors can in most cases be taught, but chemistry—fitting in with the company culture—must already be present in the job candidate.

The Employee Search

The first and best place to look for an employee is your current employees, subcontractors, or professional advisors. Referrals from people you know and trust and who know the business have a greater likelihood of producing a successful hire. That is why if you can induce a key management person to leave an organization and join your business, that person will probably induce someone else you need later on to come as well. Even during start-up, be constantly on the lookout for good people who might come on board as the business grows.

The help-wanted ads is another source. An estimated 75 percent of those who read the ads are actually employed with no intention of seeking another job—unless they see an opportunity that interests them. Consequently, you must make certain your ad stands out and presents an opportunity to a qualified person that they can't pass up. You may also consider executive search firms for key management positions.

Résumés

The most important thing to know about a résumé is that it is a selling document. The person is attempting to convince you to give him or her an interview. Therefore, expect most résumés to exaggerate a person's importance somewhat. If a résumé indicates a person has had a number of jobs in a relatively short period of time or a number of "very important" positions—vice president of this company and president of that company—it may either mean this person truly is in demand and has been wooed away from several companies, or it may mean that this person can't hold a job. Consequently, you need to think of the résumé as a screening tool to see if the candidate has the requisite skills and experience. The more important information will be gained in the interview.

Interviews

Most entrepreneurs dread interviewing job candidates, primarily because they don't know what to say and they don't understand that they should ask questions that get at the person's personality, how they might react in certain situations. This can be accomplished in part by asking open-ended questions, questions that call for more than a yes or no answer. For example,

- What is your greatest strength? Weakness?
- How would you handle the following hypothetical situation?

While the person is answering the questions, be careful to note the nonverbal communication being sent through body language. Does the person appear confident, at ease with what is being discussed? Does the person look at you directly? Does the person sit with a very closed posture (arms crossed as if to protect) or in a more open, relaxed manner. It is said that 90 percent of communication is nonverbal, so if you don't trust what a person is saying verbally, check to see if the nonverbal signals match the verbal ones.

Entrepreneurs should know that certain questions may never be asked in an interview situation because they are illegal and leave you open to potential lawsuits. Under the laws administered by the EEOC (Equal Employment

Opportunity Commission) before the point of hire, you may not ask about a person's:

- Religion or religious background
- Nation of origin
- Living arrangements or lifestyle choice
- Plans for pregnancy
- Age (to avoid discrimination against people over 40 and under 21. You may ask a young person who must be 21 to hold the job if proof of the required age can be shown after hiring.)
- Criminal arrest record (You may only ask "Have you ever been *convicted* of a crime?")
- Military record

Screening Potential Employees

In an effort to screen potential employees for drugs, criminal records, false information, and workers' compensation history, some entrepreneurs are resorting to hiring firms that do background checks. Whether or not you need to run a background check is a function of the type of job for which you are hiring. A receptionist position probably does not require more than contacting previous employers to verify information on the résumé. But hiring a bookkeeper or Chief Financial Officer may call for checking for a criminal record. Likewise, a truck driver position may require verifying a clean driving record.

Some companies are requiring drug tests as well, and those jobs with physical requirements may call for medical exams. In addition, many companies are using integrity tests, which are psychological tests that measure whether a candidate is more or less likely to steal, take drugs, or be violent. Still others use personality assessment tests to see how a person matches a job profile or fits in with the company culture. Since psychological tests can be wrong, however, it is important to give them as only one part of a comprehensive interview and hiring process. To avoid the possibility of a discrimination suit, all these tests should be given *only after a job offer has been made.*

The recent surge in sexual harassment, wrongful termination, and discrimination suits against employers has prompted a new form of business insurance called employment-practices liability insurance. It came about after many businesses found to their dismay that their standard business liability insurance did not include, or specifically excluded, employment practices suits. These new policies generally have limits from $50,000 to $10 million and are not inexpensive, averaging about $150 per employee annually.

Employee Contracts

Once you have decided to hire someone, it is crucial to put the terms of the agreement in writing to avoid misunderstandings about salary, benefits, duties, and responsibilities. What is *not* included in the agreement should be spelled out clearly as well. Include in the contract a clause that calls for mandatory arbitration in the event of a dispute and a non-compete clause to prevent someone from leaving your business to start their own competing business with your confidential information and customer/supplier lists.

The Employee Handbook

Every new business should have an employee handbook that spells out the company policies and procedures, the mission, the expectations for employees, and the company philosophy. It is at once a legal document that protects both owners and employees and an enthusiastic rendition of the company culture. The handbook serves as documentation of everything from compensation and promotion to vacations and health care. It also lets employees know under what circumstances their employment can be terminated and what that process is. If a dispute arises, you may find your state court will bind you to the handbook as written, not intended; therefore state all policies and procedures clearly without leaving room for ambiguity. Any vague provisions will likely go in favor of the employee since the handbook was written by you, the employer.

The Company History

Relating the story of how the company was founded should definitely be the first entry in the handbook, because it sets the tone and gives the employees a sense of history, of belonging to something potentially great. Tell the story like a story, in other words, make it personal, entertaining, and readable (you never know when this portion of your handbook will end up in some magazine!). Remember that honesty about some of the troubles you faced starting the business will make your employees feel that they are part of a *human* effort rather than a serendipitous occurrence in a moment of extraordinary luck.

The Company Philosophy

Recall in the chapter on the Marketing Plan the discussion of identity versus image. The company philosophy is essentially a statement of the identity of your company—who you are and what you stand for. If the history section describes the birth of the company's culture, the philosophy section ingrains that culture in the minds of the employees. After reading this section, the employees should have a good sense of what you believe in, where the company is going, and how they fit into the picture. If your philosophy is that employees should be creative, assertive, productive, self-motivated problem-solvers who aren't afraid to be wrong, then let them know that up front. Remember that the experiences of most employees with company cultures has been quite the opposite. Shake them up a bit and help them to clearly see that their experience with your company will be very different.

What Goes into the Handbook?

The best way to determine what to put into the handbook is to first consider what *your* employees want to know about the business; then take a look at the handbooks of other companies for comparison purposes to see what you like and don't like. In general, include the following information in the handbook:

- A section stating that the handbook is not a contract and is subject to changes. This is important as business conditions may force work hours or vacation times to change, and employees should be forewarned of this possibility. State also that the employment relationship may be terminated at any time, for any reason, with or without cause or notice. Have the employee sign a copy of this statement, acknowledging receipt of the handbook and agreement with its terms.
- Employment policies on such things as opportunity, work hours, pay, performance reviews, vacations, sick leave, jury duty, and so forth.
- Benefits such as health, dental, insurance, disability, workers' compensation, and retirement. Include something on the Family and Medical Leave Act as required by law.
- Guidelines for employee conduct, including a written sexual harassment policy and dispute resolution procedures. State clearly that included are merely examples of unacceptable conduct and not a comprehensive list.
- An organizational chart so the employees know who is who and where they fit in the big picture.
- Phone numbers of key people.

- Table of contents, question/answer sections, and an index. The handbook should not be too cumbersome, 20-30 pages is plenty for a young company. It should be designed so information is easily accessed.

Other Policies

Besides policies relating to employees, create policies and procedures for the routine tasks that are accomplished each day in the business. For example, procedures for order taking, shipping, handling invoices, billing, and all of the other administrative functions the business undertakes will be needed. One way to figure out what procedures may be required is to take the business through a hypothetical, typical day or week and list all the activities that occur from the point an order is received to the point at which it is shipped, or from the point a sale is solicited to the point at which the sale is closed. Activities that take place over and over again require established procedures to promote efficiency and effectiveness. Naturally, many of the procedures you develop when you start the company will be modified as you bring on employees and receive their input. But it's still a good idea to start with something.

The Management/Organizational Plan Section of the Business Plan

Most of what has been discussed in this chapter will become part of the employee handbook, which is a supplement to the business plan and is not normally given to potential investors and the like unless asked for. Basically, in the management plan section of the business plan describe:

- The entrepreneur's general management philosophy (i.e. team-based, flat structure, etc.) and company culture
- The legal structure and form of ownership of the company
- The formal organizational chart of the business to depict who the key players are and their duties and responsibilities
- The compensation programs and incentives for key management
- The key policies on orders, billing customers, and paying suppliers
- Any major benefits offered to employees

The management plan is where the philosophy of business gets implemented. It should reflect the entrepreneur's beliefs about customers, suppliers, and employees, and should give the reader a clear sense of the company culture.

✓ New Venture Checklist

Have you

☐ Determined the personnel required to run the business at start-up and over the next three to five years?

☐ Written a mission statement for the new venture?

☐ Determined the ownership and compensation requirements of the business?

☐ Created job profiles for positions in the business?

☐ Formulated a plan to find the best candidates for positions in the company?

☐ Established policies and procedures for the business?

☐ Drafted an employee handbook?

Additional Sources of Information

Small Business Reports. (February, 1990). "Right employee, right job."

Directory of Executive Compensation Consultants. Kennedy Publications, 17 Templeton Rd., Fitzwilliam, NH 03447, 603-585-6544.

Alexander Hamilton Institute. *The Employee Handbook Audit.* 201-587-7050.

Balkin, D.B. (1988). "Compensation strategy for firms in emerging and rapidly growing industries." *Human Resource Planning,* Vol. 11 (3), pp. 207-213.

Bruce, S.D. (1993). *How to Write Your Employee Handbook.* Madison, CT: Business & Legal Reports, 800-727-5257, extension 169.

Nobile, R.J. (1995). *Guide to Employee Handbooks.* Boston: Warren Gorham Lamont, 800-950-1216.

Sack, S.M. (1990). *The Hiring and Firing Book: A Complete Legal Guide for Employers.* New York: Facts on File, 800-255-2665.

Tibbetts, J.S. Jr. & Donovan, E.T. (1989). "Compensation and Benefits for Start-Up Companies." *Harvard Business Review,* January-February, pp. 140-147.

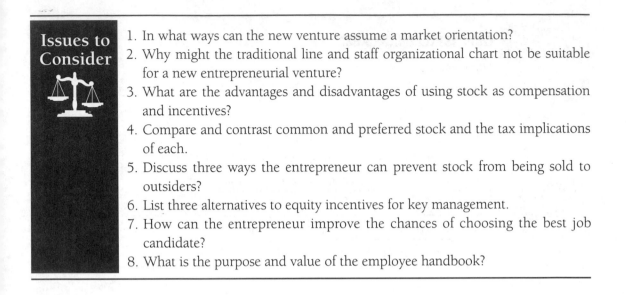

Issues to Consider

1. In what ways can the new venture assume a market orientation?
2. Why might the traditional line and staff organizational chart not be suitable for a new entrepreneurial venture?
3. What are the advantages and disadvantages of using stock as compensation and incentives?
4. Compare and contrast common and preferred stock and the tax implications of each.
5. Discuss three ways the entrepreneur can prevent stock from being sold to outsiders?
6. List three alternatives to equity incentives for key management.
7. How can the entrepreneur improve the chances of choosing the best job candidate?
8. What is the purpose and value of the employee handbook?

Case Study

4

OXO GOODGRIPS

OXO (A)[1]

I n the summer of 1989, Sam Farber had persuaded Davin Stowell, owner of Smart Design, to develop a line of kitchen gadgets (e.g. peeler, can opener, pizza cutter, garlic press) that would be functional, comfortable, ergonomically sound, attractive, and affordable. Stowell decided to accept the challenge for a three percent royalty agreement and a small advance. Farber was expecting Smart Design to have the kitchen gadgets prototyped and ready for manufacture so they could introduce the new line at the San Francisco Gourmet Show in April 1990. Before Davin Stowell would begin the process of generating prototypes, the Smart Design team needed to meet to reinforce or expand on Sam Farber's initial product criteria and help set the design goals for these new products.

The Seed of an Idea is Planted

Sam Farber had considerable experience in the housewares industry. He had founded COPCO, a company that produced well-designed cookware and related housewares items in 1960. COPCO's first products were enameled cast iron cookware made in Denmark. The cookware was designed by an American, Michael Lax. Up to that time, all enamel on cast iron cookware had been traditional designs. COPCO's products were the first modern designs. The company continued to expand its sales of well-designed products in enamel and plastics and was especially known for its tea kettles. At COPCO the concentration was on the shape and color of the products. The products were useful, but there was little thought given to how products could be made more "user friendly."

In 1983 Sam Farber sold COPCO, but he continued to head the company under a management contract for the next five years, until he retired at age 65. Sam and his wife, Betsey, had very strong interests in the field of outsider art,

---

[1]©1994, Corporate Design Foundation. This case was written by Professor William B. Gartner, San Francisco State University School of Business, with the support of the Corporate Design Foundation as a basic for class discussion rather than to illustrate either effective or ineffective handling of a business situation.

and they were looking forward to spending more time writing articles and curating art shows. They had done both in the past, but only in a limited way because of the demands of their work. They also loved to entertain and cook, and they decided they would spend at least a few months each year in the south of France, writing and cooking.

While they had never been happy with many of the tools they used in the kitchen, they didn't realize just how bad these tools actually were until they began "marathon cooking" for all of their friends that just happened to be traveling through Provençe. It became apparent that most of the kitchen tools didn't seem to meet the basics of good design: aesthetics, function, and form. Attractive products, when they found them, were a functional disaster. The bit of arthritis affecting Betsey's hands made it difficult for her to use the kitchen tools. She is one of over 20 million Americans who currently suffer from arthritis, so Sam and Betsey were particularly aware of how virtually none of the products considered user comfort.

They kept asking, "Why was the kitchen environment at best indifferent and at worst hostile to human use? Isn't it possible to combine form with utility in design, and combine them in such a way that it becomes accessible to the entire population? And doesn't it reason that such a design would have great consumer appeal? Why can't a kitchen tool be comfortable, easy to use, of good quality, aesthetically pleasing, and easy to clean?" The seed was planted and Sam Farber began to think about bringing this idea to market.

Market Research

Sam Farber devised a strategy to generate information on the market for kitchen gadgets with as few interviews as possible. He decided to interview buyers in different areas of distribution.

- Department stores—Bloomingdales, Macy's
- Specialty store chains—Crate and Barrel, Williams and Sonoma
- Mass merchants—Target Stores
- Mail order catalogs—Chefs Catalog

These discussions centered primarily on best-selling items, price, design, packaging, display, and service. Sam was surprised (and a little disturbed) to find that buyers did not comment on the function of the product. When Sam mentioned some of his preliminary product goals, the only criteria the buyers seemed to respond to were dishwasher safe, good quality, and design. Most buyers didn't mention the latter two. Function and user comfort did not enter into the discussion at all.

All the buyers suggested the same best-selling items: peeler, can opener, garlic press, grater, pizza cutter, measuring spoons, and measuring cups. The mail order catalog buyers preferred higher unit retails, and therefore wanted sets that combined two or three items. All distribution areas were selling kitchen gadgets in lower price ranges than the prices Sam Farber had contemplated (e.g. peelers ranged from $.99 to $4.99). Sam was considering a peeler at a price much higher than $4.99.

Sam Farber decided to confine his interviews with consumers to five or six people he knew were good cooks. Some of these individuals were professional chefs, but the majority were very good amateur cooks. Sam reasoned that they, like he and his wife, would have thought a lot about the tools they use in the kitchen. Their answers concentrated on quality, comfort, and function.

Design Partners

Concurrently with Sam Farber's exploration of the market, he engaged the design firm, Smart Design, to undertake the design process from concept to product. Smart Design had done work for Sam previously at COPCO. Sam felt Smart Design was forward-thinking, they had good technical expertise, and they were willing to take chances. The firm also had a wide variety of experience. Their client list included Corning Glass, Johnson & Johnson, Citibank, Clairol, the University of Southern California, and JC Penney.

Sam knew Smart Design would make a good partner, and he wanted them to be partners, not just hired hands. He worked out a three percent royalty agreement with Smart Design, plus a small advance. This way their success was dependent on the success of the products. In addition, Sam wanted to keep overhead costs (i.e. product design and development) minimal, as much as possible, rather than start the company with little working capital.

The Design Process

The designers discussed the product goals Sam Farber had already outlined, and most importantly, they attempted to identify the final customer. Was it a product for people with arthritis? Yes. Was it a product for older infirm people with weak hands? Yes. But it was really a product for everyone to use in the kitchen. Shouldn't everyone who cooks have comfortable tools? From a marketing point of view, Sam wanted to appeal to the broadest possible market, not just a very specific market for arthritics and the infirm. Sam wanted the design of these products to be of transgenerational, or universal, design.

Universal design stresses the need to make the design of any product or service fit the needs of as broad a spectrum of the populace as possible. Products that make life more comfortable for everyone. Products that are easy for everyone to use. Universal design acknowledges that people change over time, that their needs vary with ordinary events like pregnancy, an armful of groceries, carpel tunnel syndrome, skiing injuries, or the unavoidable changes of aging. Universal design attempts to extend the useful life of both the object and the user. Sam was hoping to push the boundaries dividing the able from the encumbered. Transgenerational design considers all these variations in strength and dexterity. It is a form of ecological thinking because it extends the life of the product and its materials by anticipating the whole life experience of the user. One of the designers put it this way: "We'd better design the stuff now because we'll need it when our abilities sag." Sam's comment was, "I think that's why I'm here."

Sam and Davin Stowell of Smart Design decided to bring in Patricia Moore as a project consultant. Moore was trained as a designer and had devoted herself to design problems addressing the older generation. For example, Procter and Gamble had asked her to help them redesign the Tide soap box to make it easier to open. So she helped them develop the snap-top box. Smart Design had collaborated with Moore on a number of universal design projects. There were eager to demonstrate that designing for a general population that included the elderly or those suffering from hand infirmities was not an excuse to make "frumpy prosthetic devices," but the opportunity to make products that are better for everybody.

Design Research

The next step was to have the design team do their own research. Information transmitted from the marketing managers to the designers can lose a lot in translation. The design team went out into the market. They talked to consumers. They examined all the competitive products. They interviewed chefs and spent many hours with volunteers from the New York arthritis group to learn the problems in hand movement. They used the products that were on the market for weeks to pinpoint areas that needed improvement. This involvement as the final user brought the designers close to the project and helped them share Sam Farber's passion and belief.

It was now time to sit down and determine the product goals.

1. What are the primary product goals for these kitchen tools in terms of customer needs?
2. Once these product goals are determined, what should happen next in terms of product development?
3. What problems in the areas of product development, quality control, and pricing is this business likely to face before the introduction of these products at the San Francisco Gourmet Products Show?
4. What does Sam Farber need to do before creating a marketing plan?

PART 5

The Financial Plan

*Money is the seed of money, and the
first guinea is sometimes more difficult
to acquire than the second million.*

—JEAN JACQUES ROUSSEAU

CHAPTER 14

Financing the New Venture

Overview

- *Bootstrapping savvy*
- *Equity versus debt financing*
- *Venture capitalists and angels*

Sources of Financing in the 1990s

Financing the start-up of a new venture in the 1990s is truly an exercise in creativity and optimism. The period of tremendous growth and availability of venture capital in the 1980s has been replaced by ultra conservative lending practices on the part of banks and retrenchment on the part of investors. Fueled by the savings and loan association crisis and the subsequent draconian regulations imposed on banks, bankers are less likely to invest in a new venture with no track record as their portfolios are continuously scrutinized by regulators. Similarly, the recession of the early 1990s, which sent the real estate market into collapse and many businesses into bankruptcy, has made private and professional investors alike nervous. As a result, they are cautiously awaiting some indication of the long-term direction the economy will take in light of new economic policy at the federal level. Therefore, it is very important that the entrepreneur become aware of creative sources of start-up capital.

Bootstrapping

Creativity is one of the key watchwords for financing start-ups in the 1990s. Techniques for creative financing are collectively known as "bootstrapping," which means getting by on as few resources as possible and using other peoples' resources whenever possible. Bootstrapping means begging, borrowing, or leasing everything needed to start the venture. It is the antithesis of the "big money model" espoused by many when they talk about entrepreneurial ventures.[1] More often than not, bootstrapping is a model for starting a business without money—or at least without any money beyond that provided by the entrepreneur's personal resources.

Entrepreneur Resources

Most entrepreneurs start their ventures with their own resources, at least initially. These resources include savings, credit cards, and friends and family. The Department of Commerce reports that 67 percent of all businesses were started without borrowed money. Enita Nordick liquidated her stocks and sold her home to contribute the required capital to start Unity Forest Products, which re-manufactures lumber blanks into such things as siding and paneling and sells them to retailers. Bill Gates and Paul Allen started the software giant Microsoft in a cheap apartment in Albuquerque with virtually no overhead, a borrowed computer, and very little capital. Ross Perot, one of the great bootstrapping success stories, started EDS with $1,000. These entrepreneurs comprise the rule, not the exception; most new ventures are initially funded through the resources of the entrepreneur. Gates, Perot, and Nordick realized early on that no one except friends and family would consider investing in the new venture until they had gotten it off the ground and had a viable business.

Hire as Few Employees as Possible

Normally the greatest single expense a business has is its payroll (including taxes and benefits). Subcontracting work to other firms, using temporary help, or hiring independent contractors can help keep the number of employees and their consequent costs down. This is the tactic taken by

---

[1]Bhide, A. (1992). "Bootstrapping Finance: The Art of Start-Ups." *Harvard Business Review,* Vol. 70, No. 6, pp. 109-117.

Maritime Services, an internal outfitter of cruise ships founded in 1986 with $1,000. As of 1991 it was doing $3.9 million in sales with only three employees. Similarly, Marianne Szymanski founded Toy Tips Inc., a nationally recognized, independent product testing and research firm in Milwaukee, using student interns from Marquette University and bartering for office space. The interns received university credit for working with her, and she didn't have to deal with payroll.

Lease, Share, or Barter Everything

Virtually all new ventures at some point need to acquire equipment, furnishings, and facilities. By leasing rather than purchasing major equipment and facilities, precious capital is not tied up at a time when it is badly needed to keep the new venture afloat. With a lease there is usually no down payment and the payments are spread over time. A word of caution, however. Be careful about leasing new and rapidly changing technology for long periods of time or you may soon find yourself with obsolete equipment and a continuing obligation.

Some entrepreneurs have shared space with established companies not only to save money on overhead but to give their fledgling ventures the aura of a successful, established company. This was the strategy used by Michael Kempner of Strategic Communications, Inc., a public relations firm. Kempner moved in rent free to space in a friend's elegant advertising offices with the agreement that he would refer clients to his friend's business in exchange for the space. When Marianne Szymanski of Toy Tips, Inc. found she needed a professional wardrobe for her media tour, she went to JH Collectibles and explained her situation. As a young businesswoman with a start-up company, she didn't have much money to spend, but she wanted their clothes to wear on the tour. JH Collectibles liked her idea and gave her a wardrobe of clothes she could promote on the tour while also promoting her business.

Bartering is a well-established tradition among entrepreneurs with new ventures. In fact, it is even used by large corporations going into global markets. In Russia, for example, Pepsi Cola traded its surplus cola for vodka which could be sold in the United States. Similarly, New Zealand had traded dairy products for Russian coal. These barter arrangements are known as "one-to-one trades." There are also barter exchange groups where a member can earn credits by providing products or services and then use those credits to "buy" products or services from another company when needed.

Other People's Money

Another key to bootstrapping success is getting customers to pay quickly and suppliers to allow more time for payment. Entrepreneurs must be willing to stay on top of receivables. Sometimes that means walking an invoice through the channels of a major corporation in person (a favorite tactic of Talli Counsel of Interfleet) or locating the person who can adjust the computer code that determines when a government agency pays its bills.

Suppliers are an important asset of the business and should be taken care of. If you establish a good relationship with your major suppliers, you may be able to arrange favorable payment terms. After all, the supplier also has an interest in seeing the new venture succeed. Use several suppliers to establish credit. Often a young company can't get sufficient credit from one supplier, so it helps to seek smaller amounts of credit from several reputable suppliers. In this way when you can qualify for a larger credit line, you will know which supplier is the best source.

If possible, sell wholesale rather than retail. By dealing with wholesale distributors, you make your life easier because they are the experts at working with the customers. They have already set up the consumer and industrial channels you may need to expand your market.

PROFILE 14.1

The Importance of Ethics

Scott Cook, founder of Intuit, the software developer known for its product *Quicken*, reported in *Inc.* magazine that "being truthful is good business."[2] A common practice in the software industry is to use promotional schemes to "load" the dealers with excess product in the belief that the dealer will then push that product to get rid of it before taking on a competitor's product. The practice also involves overstating demand.

Intuit refused to participate in this scheme and preferred to communicate their expectations for sales honestly to the dealers. In this way the dealers were not burdened with excess inventory, and Intuit kept its manufacturing facilities operating at an even keel rather than in costly boom and bust cycles.

---

[2]*Inc.* magazine, September 1992, p. 87.

Bootstrapping Ethics. Whenever bootstrapping tactics are employed to allow a new venture to survive long enough to use other sources of financing, the issue of ethics arises. This is because when an entrepreneur bootstraps, by definition he or she is making the new venture appear much more successful than it is to gain some credibility in the market. But the entrepreneur must be careful, because credibility, if it is ill-gotten, comes at a tremendous price to the business. Lying to survive will return to haunt the business at some future time. Intuit, a very successful software manufacturer, spent several start-up years bootstrapping, during which they quickly learned that trust is an essential element to long-term success.

Financing with Equity

One way to raise capital for the new venture is by having people invest their money for an ownership share in the business. This ownership share is termed **equity.** It is distinguished from debt in that the equity investor puts his or her capital at risk; there is usually no guaranteed return, and no protection against loss. For this reason, most entrepreneurs with start-up ventures seek investment capital from people they know who believe in them. There are a variety of sources of equity financing.

Personal Resources

As stated earlier, the number one source of start-up money is the entrepreneur's personal resources: savings, credit cards, parents, and friends and family. The reasons are many:

1. New ventures by definition have no track record, so all the estimates of sales and profits are pure speculation.
2. An enormous number of new ventures fail, so the risk for an outside investor is usually too high.
3. Many new ventures have no proprietary rights that would give them a competitive advantage.
4. The founders often do not have a significant track record of success.
5. Too many new ventures are "me too" versions of something that already exists, so they have no competitive advantages.

In addition to the personal resources already mentioned, entrepreneurs can also tap the equity in their brokerage accounts. Margin is, in effect, another

Some Money Terms

Angel: Business jargon for a private investor who holds an equity interest in the venture.

Asset-Based Loan: A loan collateralized by accounts receivable, inventory, or other assets. If the entrepreneur defaults on the loan, the lender can seize the assets.

Equity: An ownership interest in a company based on an investment of capital.

Factor: A lender who purchases a company's accounts receivable and then advances cash at a certain percentage of the value of the receivables.

Securities: The interest of a creditor or investor in the property or business of a debtor or owner, pledged to secure repayment of the debt or investment.

Seed Money: Money needed to complete research and development prior to starting the business.

Senior Debt: Usually a bank loan that has seniority over all other financial interest should the business fail.

Subordinated Debt: Non-bank debt that is repaid after senior debt in the event of business failure. Can often contain rights to convert to equity.

Venture Capital: Professional groups of individual investors whose purpose is to invest money in new and growing businesses. They typically supply second-stage or buyout financing.

source of credit, and when interest rates fall below those of the typical credit card, this source of funds becomes very attractive. With a margin loan, the security in your brokerage account is pledged as collateral for the money borrowed, just like pledging the equity in your home against a second mortgage. You can still trade the collateralized security (buy or sell), but cannot take possession of it until the loan is repaid.

Private Investors—Angels

The next source usually investigated for funding is private investors, typically people the entrepreneur knows or has met through business acquaintances. These investors who are part of the informal risk capital market—the largest pool of risk capital in the United States, over $50 billion—are called **angels.** They can't be found in a phone book, and they don't advertise. In fact, their intentions as investors are often well-hidden until they decide to make themselves known. They do, however, have several definable characteristics:

- They normally invest between $10,000 and $500,000 and usually focus on first-stage financing, that is, start-up funding or funding of firms younger than five years.

- They are well-educated, often entrepreneurs themselves, and tend to invest within a relatively short distance from home, as they like to be involved in their investment.
- They tend to prefer manufacturing, energy and resources, and service businesses. Retail ventures are less desirable because of their inordinately high rate of failure.
- They typically look to reap the rewards of their investment within three to seven years. The risk/reward ratio is a function of the age of the firm at the time of investment. They may want to earn as much as ten times their original investment, if the venture is a start-up, to five times their investment, if the venture has been up and running for a couple years.
- They find their deals principally through referrals from business associates.
- They tend to make an investment decision more quickly than other capital sources, and their requirements as to documentation, business plan, and due diligence may be lower.

In general, angels are an excellent source of seed or start-up capital. The secret to finding these elusive investors is networking—getting involved in the business community—so you come into contact with sources of private capital or people who know these sources—lawyers, bankers, accountants, and other

Stages of Financing for the New Venture

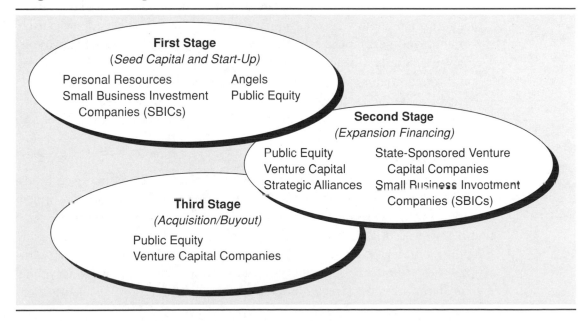

First Stage
(*Seed Capital and Start-Up*)
Personal Resources   Angels
Small Business Investment   Public Equity
    Companies (SBICs)

Second Stage
(*Expansion Financing*)
Public Equity   State-Sponsored Venture
Venture Capital   Capital Companies
Strategic Alliances   Small Business Investment
                                      Companies (SBICs)

Third Stage
(*Acquisition/Buyout*)
Public Equity
Venture Capital Companies

business people. Developing these contacts takes time; you can't wait until you need the capital to look for it. Of course, taking on an investor means giving up some of the ownership of the company. It is, therefore, probably wise to plan at the outset for a way for the investor to exit. Including a buyout provision in the investment contract with a no-fault separation agreement will ensure that the entrepreneur doesn't have to wait for a criminal act like fraud to end the relationship. Structuring the buyout to be paid out of earnings over time will avoid jeopardizing the financial health of the business. Above all, avoid using personal assets as collateral to protect an angel's investment.

Private Placement

Private placement is a formal vehicle for seeking funding from private investors who are "sophisticated" in terms of the rules of private placement, which are stated in Regulation D. Regulation D was designed to simplify the private offering process and allow the entrepreneur to seek funding from private investors as long as they met the requirements. Doing a private placement memorandum involves the completion of a business plan and a prospectus detailing the risks of the investment. The rules for private placement must be carefully followed; they are discussed in detail in Chapter 17 on financing growth.

As with any complex legal document, it is crucial to consult an attorney well versed in the preparation of the private placement memorandum and disclosure of information about the company and its principals. Problems don't usually arise if the business is successful; however, if the venture fails and the investors uncover a security violation, you and other principal equity holders may lose your protection under the corporate shield and become personally liable in the event of a lawsuit. Security violations have been dealt with severely by the courts, and there is no statute of limitations on the filing of such a suit.

Venture Capital

In general, venture capital companies are professional pools of managed funds that often operate in the form of a limited partnership. Equity venture capital funds are the most common type. While some venture capitalists invest in start-up companies, it is probably prudent not to attempt to seek venture capital funding at this stage for several reasons. Venture capitalists recognize that start-up is the riskiest time for a business, and as there are many growing young companies with a track record of performance (however short) available, their funds are probably better placed with these companies. Venture capitalists require substantial returns on their investments, generally in the 60 to 70 percent annual return range, and a significant ownership interest, which may force the entrepreneur to give up controlling interest in the new venture before the company gets off the ground.

In general funds are not as prolific as they were in the 1980s, and almost 60 percent of available venture capital funds are held by megafunds, usually institutional investors who prefer to invest in increments of $2 million and up. Consequently, most start-up ventures do not waste the time and money seeking venture capital funding. Instead, they see it as a source of second stage or growth funding. For this reason, venture capital funding is discussed in detail in Chapter 17.

Strategic Alliances

A partnership—whether formal or informal—with another business is a strategic alliance. Through strategic alliances, entrepreneurs can structure deals with suppliers or customers that will help reduce expenditures for marketing, raw materials, or R&D. By reducing expenditures, cash flow is increased, providing capital that wouldn't have otherwise been available.

Another type of strategic alliance is the R&D limited partnership. This vehicle is useful for entrepreneurs starting hi-tech ventures that carry significant risk due to the expense of research and development. The limited partnership contracts with the new venture to provide the funding for the R&D to develop a market technology that will ultimately be profitable for the partnership. This is advantageous for both the limited partner and the new venture. Limited partners are able to deduct their investment in the R&D contract and enjoy the tax advantages of losses in the early years on their personal tax returns; they also share in any future profits. In the R&D limited partnership, the new venture acts as a general partner to develop the technology and then structures a license agreement with the R&D partner whereby the venture can use the technology to develop other products. Often the limited partnership's interest becomes stock in a new corporation formed to commercialize the new technology.

An alternative to this arrangement is an agreement to pay royalties to the partnership. Yet another vehicle is the formation of a joint venture, which allows the entrepreneur to purchase the joint venture interest after a specific period of time or when the company reaches a certain volume in sales. As with the private placement, strategic alliances should involve an attorney. The new venture may incur significant costs in creating the partnership, a process that could drag on for up to a year. In addition, giving up the ownership of the technology may be too high a price if the partnership does not survive.

Small Business Investment Company (SBIC)

Small Business Investment Companies are actually venture capital firms licensed by the Small Business Administration. They get financing through the government to invest in small and growing businesses. Since their repayment terms with the government are generous, they are able to invest over longer periods of time. They can be found by contacting the SBA.

Venture Capital Institutes and Networks

Many areas of the country offer access to venture capital networks through institutes established on the campuses of major universities. The university acts as a conduit through which the entrepreneurs and investors are matched and assumes no liability for or has no ownership interest in either the new venture or the investor's company. The entrepreneur typically pays a fee, in the $200 to $500 range, and submits a business plan to the institute. The plan is then matched to the needs of private investors in the database who subscribe to the service. If an investor is interested in the business concept, he or she contacts the entrepreneur. In general, venture capital networks are a way for entrepreneurs to gain access to investors they may not be able to find through other channels. Furthermore, the investors in the database are there voluntarily, so they are actually looking for potential investments.

Financing with Debt

When an entrepreneur chooses a debt instrument to finance a portion of the start-up expenses, he or she provides a business or personal asset as collateral in exchange for a loan bearing a market rate of interest. The asset could be equipment, inventory, real estate, or the entrepreneur's house or car. There are several sources of debt financing.

Commercial Banks

In depressed economic climates, banks are not a readily available source of either working capital or seed capital to fund a start-up venture. Today banks are highly regulated; their loan portfolios are scrutinized carefully, and they are told in no uncertain terms not to make loans that have any significant degree of risk. Consequently, if established firms with good credit risks are being denied loans and credit lines, it stands to reason that a new venture with no track record would not be likely to get an unsecured loan from a commercial bank.

Generally, banks make loans based on what is termed "the five Cs": character, capacity, capital, collateral, and condition. In the case of the entrepreneur, the first two—character and capacity—become the leading consideration because the new business's performance is based purely on forecasts. Therefore, the bank will probably consider the entrepreneur's personal history carefully. It is important, however difficult, for the new venture to establish a lending relationship with a bank. This may mean starting with a very small amount of money and demonstrating the ability to repay in a timely fashion. Bankers also look more favorably on ventures with hard assets that are readily convertible to cash.

Commercial Finance Companies

As banks have tightened their lending requirements, commercial finance companies have stepped in to fill the gap. They are able to do this because they are not as heavily regulated and they base their decisions on the quality of the assets of the business. Thus, they are often termed **asset-based lenders.** They do, however, charge more than banks by as much as five percent over prime. Therefore, the entrepreneur must weigh the cost-benefit of taking on such an expensive loan. Of course, if it means the difference between starting the business or not, or surviving in the short term, the cost may not seem so great.

Small Business Administration

When a commercial bank loan does not appear to be a viable option, the entrepreneur may want to consider an SBA guaranteed loan. Between 1980 and 1991, the SBA guaranteed $31 billion in loans, principally for start-up and expansion. In 1993 alone, the SBA backed $6.4 billion in loans, which was a 40 percent increase since 1991. The SBA guarantees to repay up to 90 percent of the loan to the commercial lender should the business default. A further incentive to banks is that SBA-funded ventures tend to be growth-oriented and have a higher survival rate than other start-ups. In a study conducted by Price-Waterhouse, SBA-funded businesses versus non-SBA businesses were compared during the period between 1984 and 1989.[3] The results were astounding.

---

[3]"SBA Loans Spur Start-Up Growth," *Inc.* magazine, November 1992, p. 66.

	SBA Funded	Non-SBA Funded
Employee Growth	167%	0%
Revenue Growth	300%	37%
Survival after 4 years	75%	<65%

Of course, since these loans are backed by the government, the documentation and paperwork are extensive, and interest rates are usually no different than with a conventional loan.

The Small Business Administration also has a new program, the micro loan, that makes it easier for entrepreneurs with limited access to capital to borrow small amounts (up to $25,000). Instead of using banks as in their guarantee program, they use nonprofit community development corporations. The Answer Desk at the SBA, 800-827-5722, can provide information on micro lenders in a particular area of the country.

State-Funded Venture Capital

Many states now provide a range of services to help new and growing ventures. From venture capital funds to tax incentives, states like Massachusetts, New York, and Oregon are seeing the value of establishing business development programs. They usually receive their funding from the state government, which enables them to seek larger investment amounts from private sources. In states where equity funding is not available, there is typically a loan program aimed at new ventures. For example, in Massachusetts, favorable debt financing is often exchanged for warrants to purchase stock in the new company. Pennsylvania was the first to create a funding program aimed at minority-owned businesses.

Grants

The Small Business Innovation Development Act of 1982 requires that all federal agencies with research and development budgets in excess of $100 million give a portion of their budgets to technology-based small businesses in the form of grants. Small businesses find out about these grants by checking the published solicitations by the agencies (see Figure 14.1) to see if they can provide what the agency needs.

The grants have three levels:

1. Phase I is the concept stage, providing up to $50,000 for initial feasibility.
2. Phase II provides up to an additional $500,000 for projects that have the most potential after completing Phase I.
3. Phase III brings in private sector funds to commercialize the new technology.

Figure 14.1: Small Business IR Agencies

- Department of Defense
- Department of Energy
- Department of Transportation
- Department of Interior
- Department of Education
- National Aeronautics & Space Administration (NASA)

- Nuclear Regulatory Commission
- Environmental Protection Agency
- Health and Human Services
- National Science Foundation
- U.S. Department of Agriculture

To qualify for an SBIR grant, the company must employ fewer than 500 people, be independently owned, and be technology-based.

The entrepreneur with a new venture has many options. Crafting a capital structure for the new venture that works, however, depends in large part on the creativity and persistence of the entrepreneur in securing the capital needed at the right price to successfully launch the venture.

☑ New Venture Checklist

Have you

☐ Considered how many personal resources you have to help fund the new venture?

☐ Determined ways to bootstrap the start-up of the new venture?

☐ Networked to come in contact with potential "angels"?

☐ Identified an attorney who can help structure a private placement agreement if needed?

☐ Investigated the sources of debt financing in the community?

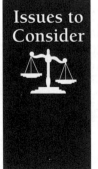

Additional Sources of Information

The Best of Inc. Guide to Finding Capital. (1988). The Editors of *Inc.* Magazine, New York: Prentice Hall Press.

Blechman, B. & J.C. Levinson (1991). *Guerrilla Financing.* Boston: Houghton Mifflin.

Canadian Reciprocal Trade Association, Box 82008, Burnaby, BC V5C 5P2, 604-521-7911, FAX 604-521-7944.

Garner, D. (1991). *The Ernst & Young Guide to Raising Capital.* New York: John Wiley & Sons.

Hicks, T.G. (1990). *Business Capital Sources.* Rockville Centre, NY: International Wealth Success, Inc.

International Reciprocal Trade Association, 9513 Beach Mill Road, Great Falls, VA 22066.

Latus, J. (1992). *Cashing in on Free State Government Money.* San Diego, CA: Lion Publishing Col.

National Association of Trade Exchanges, 9790 Southwest Pembrook St., Portland, OR 97224.

O'Hara, P.D. (1989). *SBA Loans: A Step-by-Step Guide.* New York: John Wiley & Sons.

Wilmeth, J.R. (Ed.) *Directory of Operating Small Business Investment Companies.* Washington, DC: Small Business Administration, Semiannual: June and December.

Issues to Consider

1. What are some ways a new venture can bootstrap to conserve capital?
2. What are some of the pitfalls of bootstrap financing?
3. What is the role of angels as a source of new venture funding?
4. At what stage of venture development do venture capitalists typically become involved and why?
5. What is the purpose of a private offering?
6. Why are commercial banks not usually a reliable source of new venture financing?
7. What are three additional sources of debt financing?

CHAPTER 15

Preparing the Financial Plan

Overview

- *Projecting sales and capital expenditures*
- *Calculating how much start-up capital is needed*
- *Preparing the pro forma financial statements*
- *Preparing the financial plan*

What Every Entrepreneur Should Know

No matter how many financial tools entrepreneurs use or how many complex analyses are constructed, the bottom line for any new venture is *cash*. Income statements and balance sheets can make a company look good—these are accounting measures—but cash pays the bills and allows the company to grow. Cash is the lifeblood of the business. The financial statements considered in this chapter describe various aspects of the new venture and need to be included in the business plan. However, significantly more attention is paid to the cash flow statement because this is a working statement that tells the entrepreneur how much start-up capital is needed and becomes a budget that guides the start-up and growth of the business.

While this book has promoted creativity in all aspects of developing the business concept, this creativity should not be reflected in the financial statements. Financial statements must follow "generally accepted accounting principles (GAAP)" so the reader of the business plan recognizes standard terms and sees items in their normal order of presentation. This familiarity instills confidence that the numbers are genuine. Furthermore, every assumption made in constructing the statements must be justified with supporting evidence, because with a new venture you are forecasting not based on historical performance but on your belief as to how the new venture will perform. Industry expertise, test marketing, and/or experience with a similar business goes a long way toward imbuing the reader with a sense of trust. In addition, having your accountant prepare and/or review the financials also adds credibility.

Projecting Sales and Capital Expenditures

Certainly, one of the more critical issues for the entrepreneur is forecasting sales and capital expenditures for the new business, but it is not an easy feat to accomplish. The problem stems from the volatile nature of new ventures in general—any effort to derive an accurate estimate is fraught with difficulty.

An example will make this dilemma clear. Gentech Corporation was a new company manufacturing a technology-based industrial machine. It had to purchase motors and other parts from its suppliers. In the start-up phase, the company did not have enough sales to buy parts in sufficient volume to warrant the maximum discount from the supplier, so initially material costs were high. To compensate, the founders subcontracted some of the work, performed the assembly themselves, and sold products with little or no gross margin. The question then became: When would the business generate enough sales to buy in adequate volume, thereby reducing costs and increasing profit? However, once the volume was attained, the business would likely need to purchase additional equipment, perhaps expand facilities, and add employees. At what point should they do this, and how much should they spend?

This is the dilemma of the new venture. To answer these difficult questions, the entrepreneur must gain a great deal of knowledge about the industry and how similar businesses operate within it, and then extrapolate from that until the business has been in operation for a while and has developed some patterns of its own that better define it.

The information needed to complete the pro forma financial statements includes demand, cost, and operating figures. The goal is to forecast the financial condition of the new venture for the next three to five years based on the information collected. These pro forma statements reflect the entrepreneur's best estimate of how the company will perform and what the associated expenses will be. The entrepreneur will also probably assume the ability to acquire credit and take on debt at some time. It is important, then, to understand that as these pro forma statements are estimates, they are subject to change based on the more accurate information gained when the business actually begins operating. This is why entrepreneurs typically re-evaluate the financial statements on a monthly basis for the first year.

The sales forecast should be calculated first because sales affects the other expenditures of the business. The method for forecasting sales varies depending on the general product or service category. For example, with a new product that is a line extension or the next generation of an established product, the entrepreneur can rely on historical data that will help ensure a more accurate estimate. With a brand new or breakthrough product, however, the entrepreneur is left to rely on market data, comparison of similar products, and the opinions of market experts. Therefore, to improve the estimate, it is useful to calculate best case, worst case, and most likely case scenarios that will cover about 90 percent of all the possible sales results.

Forecasting Sales with Consumer Products and Services

If the product or service being offered does not currently exist in the market, you must find a competing product or service that is similar or is a substitute product to study. The information needed includes the volume of "sell-in" to the retailer and the volume of "sell-through" to the customer—that is, the amount of product that is sold by the manufacturer or distributor to the retailer and the amount of that product that is ultimately sold to the customer. Naturally, since a service business generally operates with direct channels of distribution, it concerns itself only with the sell-through volume. In addition, you want to determine if there is any seasonality in the market that would affect the volume of sales during any particular period of time.

The mistake made by many companies who sell to retailers is focusing on how much product they are selling to the retailer and structuring their production and/or inventory accordingly. They do not carefully monitor retail sales to the customer. Consequently, when consumer buying slows and the retailer cannot move sufficient product, the manufacturer or producer is left with excess inventory. The entrepreneur with a new product or service, therefore, should monitor retail sales of competing products to consumers in the same category to arrive at an estimate of sales demand. Best case and worst case scenarios should also be calculated.

One word of caution: when choosing competing companies for comparison purposes, be aware that if the company is a publicly held company or a well-established company, you as a new venture will probably not achieve the same level of sales for some time. Therefore, the sales figures you gather serve merely as an upper limit benchmark as you determine how much below that figure your sales level will be. The percentage increase in your sales over a three- to five-year period will depend on:

- Growth rates in the market segment of the product or service
- The innovations offered that will make your product/service more attractive to the consumer, even at a higher price
- The technological innovations employed that permit you to produce the product or service at a lower cost than your competitors, thus making it more accessible and enticing to the consumer.

Forecasting Sales with Industrial Products

With industrial products, which are generally sold business to business, it is important to understand the needs of the customer and the buying cycles of the industry. Again, talking to experts (i.e. distributors) in the field, getting sales figures from noncompeting product manufacturers in the same industry, and generally determining the size of the market niches you intend to enter all help in arriving at an estimate of sales demand. Like the consumer market, in the industrial market it is vital to bracket the estimate with best case/worst case benchmark figures so you are prepared for the most likely contingencies. The rate at which sales increase is a function of the same three factors listed under consumer products.

Forecasting Expenditures

In wholesale businesses, once the sales forecast has been determined, you can apply the figures for inventory purchases as a percentage of sales and forecast from that. So if inventory cost is 25 percent of sales, you can apply that percentage to sales as they increase to forecast changes in the volume of inventory. In manufacturing businesses, it is a bit more complex because you must first derive the Cost of Goods Sold (COGS), which usually consists of direct labor, cost of materials, and factory overhead. Looking at the sales forecast in terms of units produced to arrive at a dollar figure for COGS and then applying costs of goods sold as a percentage of sales will probably suffice for purposes of pro forma statements when the business is starting. Month-by-month analysis of outcomes and use of a cost accounting model that considers raw materials inventory, work-in-process inventory, finished-goods inventory, total inventory, factory overhead, work-in-process flow in units, and weighted-average cost per unit will give a more accurate estimate as the business grows.

In service businesses, the COGS is equivalent to the time expended for the service. The rate at which you bill the service, say $100 an hour, is comprised of the actual expenses incurred in providing the service, a contribution to overhead, and a reasonable profit. The actual expenses incurred is the cost of goods sold equivalent.

General and administrative expenses—the expenses of running the business—are considered fixed but must be forecast separately in a detailed breakout statement. This is because some of these items may vary over a 12-month period, while others remain stable. Therefore, do not use a percentage of sales figure for G&A expenses. Only the totals of G&A expenses for each month will be used in the financial statements, with a footnote directing the reader to the G&A breakout statement. Selling expenses, which include advertising, travel, sales salaries, commissions, and promotional supplies, should be handled in the same manner, with a breakout statement, and totals only in the financial statements. Sample lists of manufacturing or construction expenses, distribution and warehouse expenses, and selling expenses are shown in Figure 15.1 on p. 302.

The last item to forecast is taxes. While many businesses may be able to take advantage of a tax-loss carry-forward for losses during R&D, ultimately the business will have to account for state, federal, and possibly local taxes that are paid at varying times of the year.

Preparing the Pro Forma Income Statement

The income statement, also known as a profit and loss statement, gives information regarding the profit or loss status of the business for a specified period of time. It is normally calculated first so income tax liability can be determined. The taxes owed based on the profit made by the company appear on the cash flow statement when they are paid. As income taxes vary from state to state, the financial statements presented here are not indicative of tax rates in every state. Figure 15.2 on p. 303 displays an example of an income statement for a corporation. Note that should the business be structured as a sole proprietorship or partnership, the reference to taxes will be deleted as taxes are at the personal tax rates of the owners.

The income statement should also contain footnotes for each item to refer the reader to supporting material in the "Notes to Financial Statements." Any unusual major expenses like the cost of participating in a trade show, should be footnoted separately and explained.

It is not uncommon for a new business to not show a profit in the first year and it really is a function of the type of business and the cost of start-up. In particular, high technology and manufacturing start-ups are capital intensive and generally take longer to realize a profit than service businesses. In the hypothetical example of NEW VENTURE INC., (see Figure 15.2) the company ended the year with a net profit before taxes of $15,250 on which it must pay taxes. For purposes of illustration, a 40 percent tax rate was used to include federal and state income taxes.

Figure 15.1: Sample Lists

Sample Manufacturing or Construction Expenses List

Manager's Salary Paid	Employees Salaries
Payroll Taxes	Vehicle Lease and Maintenance
Related Travel	Packaging Costs
Supplies	Depreciation on Owned Equipment

Sample Distribution and Warehouse Expenses List

Manager's Salary	Employees' Salaries
Drivers' Salaries	Payroll Taxes
Vehicle Lease and Maintenance	Warehouse Loading Vehicles
Lease/Maintenance	Depreciation on Owned Equipment
Freight Expenses Supplies	

Sample List of Selling Expenses

Sales Manager's Salary	Inside Sales Salaries
Inside Sales Commissions	Telephone Sales Salaries
Telephone Sales Commissions	Field Sales Salaries
Field Sales Commissions	Payroll Taxes for Sales Employees
Sales Vehicles Lease and Maintenance	Sales-Related Travel
Advertising and Promotion	Depreciation on Owned Equipment

Sample List of General & Administrative Expenses

Advertising	Rent
Salaries & Wages	Utilities
Office Supplies	Insurance
Office Equipment	Business Taxes
Payroll Taxes	

Figure 15.2: Pro Forma Income Statement for NEW VENTURE INC. (in thousands)

Month	1	2	3	4	5	6	7	8	9	10	11	12	Totals
Sales	$15.00	$19.50	$25.35	$32.96	$42.84	$55.69	$72.40	$94.12	$122.36	$159.07	$206.79	$268.82	$1,114.90
Less COGS	$9.00	$11.70	$15.21	$19.77	$25.70	$33.42	$43.44	$56.47	$73.42	$95.44	$124.07	$161.29	$668.93
Gross Profit	$6.00	$7.80	$10.14	$13.19	$17.14	$22.27	$28.96	$37.65	$48.94	$63.63	$82.72	$107.53	$445.97
Operating Expenses General &													
Administrative *	$3.75	$4.88	$6.34	$8.24	$10.71	$13.92	$18.10	$23.53	$30.59	$39.77	$51.70	$67.21	$278.74
Selling Expenses *	$5.00	$2.34	$3.04	$3.95	$5.14	$6.68	$8.69	$11.29	$14.68	$19.09	$24.81	$32.26	$136.97
Depreciation	$1.25	$1.25	$1.25	$1.25	$1.25	$1.25	$1.25	$1.25	$1.25	$1.25	$1.25	$1.25	$15.00
Total Operating Expenses	$10.00	$8.47	$10.63	$13.44	$17.10	$21.85	$23.04	$36.07	$46.52	$60.11	$77.76	$100.72	$430.71
Profit (Loss) Before Taxes	($4.00)	($0.67)	($0.49)	($0.25)	$0.04	$0.42	$0.92	$1.58	$2.42	$3.52	$4.96	$6.81	$15.26
Taxes	$0.00	$0.00	$0.00	$0.00	$0.00	$0.00	$0.00	$0.00	$0.00	$0.00	$0.00	$4.41	$4.41
Net Profit (Loss) After Taxes	($4.00)	($0.67)	($0.49)	($0.25)	$0.04	$0.42	$0.92	$1.58	$2.42	$3.52	$4.96	$2.40	$10.85

*See Figure 15.1 on p. 302 for examples of categories of items to include in a detailed statement.

How Much Start-Up Money is Needed?

Probably the key question to be answered when developing the financial plan for the new business is how much money will be needed to start the business and keep it operating until a positive cash flow is achieved. The first thing to understand is that the best estimates of the start-up total are just that—estimates. There is no way to guarantee that you have figured correctly. You can, however, achieve figures that prevent the business from dying before it has a chance to succeed through the careful collection of information on both potential revenues and expenses.

This section starts with a summary of pre-start-up costs, then moves to the pro forma cash flow statement. At that point there will be enough information to calculate the total start-up funds needed to keep the business running for a year. From there the pro forma balance sheet and the sources and application of funds statement for the new venture will be constructed.

Summary of Start-Up Costs

The bulk of expenses in the first year of a new business probably occur prior to the business opening its doors for the first time. Purchasing furniture, equipment, start-up inventory, and supplies can quickly add up to a substantial amount. Add to that deposits for leases and utilities, and you may have used up the first year's profits, assuming there would have been profits. See Figure 15.3 for typical expenses to start up the business.

Figure 15.3: Summary of Typical Pre-Start-Up and Start-Up Cost Categories

NEW VENTURE INC.	
Office lease—deposit	$ 2,000
Furniture and fixtures	25,000
Equipment (computer, plant equipment, etc.)	50,000
Business cards and brochures	2,500
Office supplies	1,000
Fees and licenses	500
Legal & accounting	2,000
Initial inventory	15,000
Employee training & wages	8,000
Pre-start-up marketing/promotion	10,000
Signage	1,000
Utility deposits and installation	3,000
	$120,000

A manufacturing start-up might also include product development costs, a plant lease deposit, and raw materials costs. Manufacturing start-ups with new products typically accrue heavy pre-start-up development costs that include engineering, prototyping, and patent work. These are one-time expenses to get the business started. For accounting purposes, some of these initial costs like equipment must be depreciated over a period of time on the income statement; others, such as organizational and formation expenses, must be amortized as start-up costs. For determining start-up funding requirements, however, these costs are treated as a lump sum. Your accountant can advise as to the correct disposition of all start-up costs.

Forecasting Cash Flow

The cash flow statement is the most important financial statement to the entrepreneur because it depicts the cash position of the company at specified points of time and lets the entrepreneur know when the company is expected to generate a positive cash flow based on sales—in other words, the company's liquidity position. It is important to others (bankers and investors) because it reflects the company's ability to generate future positive cash flow, meet its obligations, and pay dividends (assuming a corporate structure).

To begin to forecast cash flow in an effort to determine how much start-up capital is needed, you must have a good estimate of potential sales. This is no easy task. Certainly, the market research you conducted has given you a sense of the demand for your product or service. That research probably included discussions with suppliers, competitors, and customers as well as studying industry trends. As discussed previously, projecting sales is an educated guessing game at best; therefore, entrepreneurs will normally forecast sales based on three scenarios: best case, worst case, and a conservative, most likely case. For each case the justification should be stated so the reader (investor, banker, and others) can make his or her own judgments. Typically the entrepreneur forecasts five years into the future (investors usually want a return of capital in five years), monthly for years one and two, quarterly or yearly for years three to five.

Figure 15.4 on p. 307 gives an example of a cash flow statement for a business that has inventory to sell and is structured as a corporation. As with all financial statements, each item on the statement should be footnoted in the "Notes to Financial Statements" to explain what the assumptions were and how the figures were derived.

The first section of the statement, cash inflows or receipts, records all the sources of cash that come into the business when they are received. This is an important point to remember about a cash flow statement: it records cash inflows and outflows when they occur. Therefore, if a sale is made in March, for example, but payment is not received until April, the sale is counted in April on the statement. This explains the differences in figures on the income statement and the cash flow statement.

The next section records operating cash outflows or disbursements. These include such things as COGS, general and administrative expenses, selling expenses, and other expenses of running the business. Recall that only the totals of G&A and selling expenses should be reported with a separate, detailed breakout statement prepared to present the individual expenditures.

The next section reports priority outflows. Priority outflows are those obligations that must be paid first, generally interest expense and debt repayment. When the business has sufficient positive cash flow, it may also incur some discretionary expenses, which might include capital expenditures, R&D, and dividends. If the business is a partnership or sole proprietorship, the lines referring to dividends as well as the line for taxes are deleted, since sole proprietors and partnerships do not distribute dividends and pay taxes based on their personal income level. In the case of NEW VENTURE, no debt was projected for the first year.

The final section gives the crucial information to the entrepreneur: the net change in cash flow—in other words, whether the business had a positive or negative cash flow in that month. Note that in each month the net cash flow reflects only the cash inflows and outflows for that month assuming no start-up capital. With the net change computed for each month of Year One, it is now possible to calculate how much total cash is needed to start the business. The ending balance line provides the total of positive and negative cash flows for the year plus the start-up expenses for a total capital requirement of $273,340 as follows:

One-Time Start-Up Costs	$120,000
Add Negative CF/Subtract Positive CF	153,340
Total Cash Required	$273,340 (round up to $275,000)

By doing this analysis you learned that the business will probably not generate a positive cash flow from sales until the 12th month, so, at a minimum, there is a need to raise sufficient capital to not only cover the start-up costs but the first 12 months of operation as well. Once the start-up capital is obtained, a new cash flow statement can be generated to reflect the effect of the infusion of

Figure 15.4: Pro Forma Cash Flow for NEW VENTURE INC. (in thousands)

	Start-up	Month 1	2	3	4	5	6	7	8	9	10	11	12	Totals
Cash Inflows														
Sales		0	9.25	12.95	18.13	25.38	35.53	49.75	69.65	97.51	136.51	191.11	267.56	913.33
Capitalization	$0.00	$0.00	$0.00	$0.00	$0.00	$0.00	$0.00	$0.00	$0.00	$0.00	$0.00	$0.00	$0.00	$0.00
Total Cash Inflows	$0.00	$0.00	$9.25	$12.95	$18.13	$25.38	$35.53	$49.75	$69.65	$97.51	$136.51	$191.11	$267.56	$913.33
Cash Outflows														
Cost of Goods Sold	$15.00	$9.00	$11.70	$15.21	$19.77	$25.70	$33.42	$43.44	$56.47	$73.42	$95.44	$124.07	$161.29	$668.93
General & Administrative	$94.00	$3.75	$4.88	$6.34	$8.24	$10.71	$13.92	$18.10	$23.53	$30.59	$39.77	$51.70	$67.21	$278.74
Selling Expenses *	$11.00	$5.00	$1.11	$1.55	$2.18	$3.05	$4.26	$5.97	$8.36	$11.70	$16.38	$22.93	$32.11	$114.60
Total Cash Outflows	$120.00	$17.75	$17.69	$23.10	$30.19	$39.46	$51.60	$67.51	$88.36	$115.71	$151.59	$198.70	$260.61	$1,062.27
Net Cash Flow Before Taxes	($17.75)	($17.75)	($8.44)	($10.15)	($12.06)	($14.08)	($16.07)	($17.76)	($18.71)	($18.20)	($15.08)	($7.59)	$6.95	($148.94)
Taxes	$0.00	$0.00	$0.00	$0.00	$0.00	$0.00	$0.00	$0.00	$0.00	$0.00	$0.00	$0.00	$4.41	$4.41
Net Cash Flow	($17.75)	($17.75)	($8.44)	($10.15)	($12.06)	($14.08)	($16.07)	($17.76)	($18.71)	($18.20)	($15.08)	($7.59)	$2.54	($153.35)
Beginning Balance	$0.00	($120.00)	($137.75)	($146.19)	($156.34)	($168.40)	($182.48)	($198.55)	($216.31)	($235.02)	($253.22)	($268.30)	($275.89)	
Ending Balance	($120.00)	($137.75)	($146.19)	($156.34)	($168.40)	($182.48)	($198.55)	($216.31)	($235.02)	($253.22)	($268.30)	($275.89)	($273.35)	

*See Figure 15.1 on p. 302 for examples of categories of items to include in a detailed statement.

capital as can be seen in Figure 15.5. With an infusion of $275,000 in investment capital, the company maintains a positive cash flow and finishes the first year with an ending cash balance of $1,650, which will be recorded on the end-of-year pro forma balance sheet as cash available. This is not sufficient cash with which to begin the second year; the $275,000 must therefore be considered the absolute minimum amount of capital to start given the current situation.

Use a spreadsheet program to set up the cash flow statement as well as the other financial statements. When you make a change in one item, the computer recalculates all the relevant figures to give you a new net cash flow figure. Because it is relatively easy to produce very detailed analyses, however, there is a tendency to overwhelm the potential reader with page after page of financial statements. This will hurt more than help. Instead, be concise and to the point, and be sure to understand and document how figures were calculated so you can explain them if asked.

Spreadsheets make it easier to forecast best and worst case scenarios for your financial statements. Doing these optimistic and pessimistic analyses is extremely valuable because they provide a range of capital needs based on three different economic scenarios. To attempt to reconcile the three cash amounts, it is often suggested that you calculate a contingency factor.[1] Take the annual cash flow figures for the most optimistic and most pessimistic scenarios and calculate the difference between them and the conservative cash flow figure (most likely). You will now have a range of values. The greatest negative difference becomes the contingency factor. The calculations using hypothetical best and worst case figures would be as follows:

Best case or most optimistic cash flow	$ 50,000
Worst case or most pessimistic cash flow	($300,000)
Most likely or conservative cash flow	($153,000)

Pessimistic	*Optimistic*
$(300,000)	$ 50,000
- (153,000)	-(153,000)
$(147,000)	$ 203,000

In this example, the most optimistic case produces a positive cash flow of $50,000, which means that $203,000 less capital would be needed to fund the

---

[1]Stancill, J.M. (1991). "How Much Money Does Your New Venture Need?" In Sahlman, W.A. & Stevenson, H.H. (1992).*The Entrepreneurial Venture*. Boston: Harvard Business School Publications.

Figure 15.5: Pro Forma Cash Flow for NEW VENTURE INC. (in thousands)

	Start-up	Month 1	2	3	4	5	6	7	8	9	10	11	12	Totals
Cash Inflows														
Sales		0	9.25	12.95	18.13	25.38	35.53	49.75	69.65	97.51	136.51	191.11	267.56	913.33
Capitalization	$275.00	$0.00	$0.00	$0.00	$0.00	$0.00	$0.00	$0.00	$0.00	$0.00	$0.00	$0.00	$0.00	$0.00
Total Cash Inflows	$275.00	$0.00	$9.25	$12.95	$18.13	$25.38	$35.53	$49.75	$69.65	$97.51	$136.51	$191.11	$267.56	$913.33
Cash Outflows														
Cost of Goods Sold	$15.00	$9.00	$11.70	$15.21	$19.77	$25.70	$33.42	$43.44	$56.47	$73.42	$95.44	$124.07	$161.29	$668.93
General & Administrative	$94.00	$3.75	$4.88	$6.34	$8.24	$10.71	$13.92	$18.10	$23.53	$30.59	$39.77	$51.70	$67.21	$278.74
Selling Expenses *	$11.00	$5.00	$1.11	$1.55	$2.18	$3.05	$4.26	$5.97	$8.36	$11.70	$16.38	$22.93	$32.11	$114.60
Total Cash Outflows	$120.00	$17.75	$17.69	$23.10	$30.19	$39.46	$51.60	$67.51	$88.36	$115.71	$151.59	$198.70	$260.61	$1,062.27
Net Cash Flow Before Taxes	$155.00	($17.75)	($8.44)	($10.15)	($12.06)	($14.08)	($16.07)	($17.76)	($18.71)	($18.20)	($15.08)	($7.59)	$6.95	($148.94)
Taxes		$0.00	$0.00	$0.00	$0.00	$0.00	$0.00	$0.00	$0.00	$0.00	$0.00	$0.00	$4.41	$4.41
Net Cash Flow	$155.00	($17.75)	($8.44)	($10.15)	($12.06)	($14.08)	($16.07)	($17.76)	($18.71)	($18.20)	($15.08)	($7.59)	$2.54	($153.35)
Beginning Balance	$275.00	$155.00	$137.25	$128.81	$118.66	$106.60	$92.52	$76.45	$58.69	$39.98	$21.78	$6.70	($0.89)	
Ending Balance	$155.00	$137.25	$128.81	$118.66	$106.60	$92.52	$76.45	$58.69	$39.98	$21.78	$6.70	($0.89)	**$1.65**	

*See Figure 15.1 on p. 302 for examples of categories of items to include in a detailed statement.

start-up. In the most pessimistic case, however, $147,000 more capital is required for start-up. This is the amount that should become the contingency factor, bringing the total investment to $420,000 ($153,000 plus the contingency factor of $147,000—the greatest difference—plus the start-up capital requirement of $120,000). Rather than investing the $275,000 as calculated using simply the conservative cash flow statement, it is probably more prudent to seek an investment of at least $420,000 so the probability of covering all possible contingent situations is higher. Besides, the company ends the first year with a positive cash balance of only $1,650, which is a very weak position, leaving little room for error heading into the second year.

Using the Cash Flow Statement to determine the amount of capital needed to start and run the business is certainly not its only use. Particularly during the first year of operation, compare the monthly cash flow statement against *actual* inflows and outflows of cash to the business to determine where estimates deviated. Making adjustments to the remaining projections avoids any surprises later on. Essentially the cash flow statement becomes a budget for the business. As the business grows, it is also a good idea to put someone in charge of monitoring cash flow throughout all functions of the organization. That person should be familiar with all the operations of the business; consequently, the accountant is often not the best choice for someone to manage cash flow at the operational level.

Preparing the Pro Forma Balance Sheet

The balance sheet shows the condition of the business in terms of its assets and liabilities and the net worth of its owners at a specific point in time. Unlike the cash flow and income statements, the balance sheet is usually prepared to reflect the condition of the business at the end of each of the first five years of a new business. Figure 15.6 on p. 311 displays a sample balance sheet for a new business.

Forecasting Assets

The first section of the balance sheet is the **assets,** everything of value the business owns. Assets are valued in terms of actual cost for the item. Current assets are those consumed in the operation of the business during the year, while fixed assets are tangible assets used over the long term. Accounts receivable must be forecasted based on the seasonality experienced by the business. If the business experiences no pronounced seasonality, you may be able to assume a certain percentage of sales that will not be paid in cash each month based on industry averages or an accounts receivable turnover rate. Once the business is established, however, it develops its own pattern of receivables and a more accurate turnover rate can be calculated. To account for the fact that some accounts receivable will not be collected, some entrepreneurs choose to subtract from receivables an allowance for bad debt, a small percentage (two to five percent) based on typical bad debt figures for the industry. Again, your business will develop its own unique pattern over time and it will be easier to predict more accurately what the bad debt rate will be. See Figure 15.6 for an example of an end of first year pro forma balance sheet.

Figure 15.6: Pro Forma Balance Sheet: End of First Year

NEW VENTURE INC.
ASSETS

Current Assets	
Cash	$ 1,650
Accounts receivable	201,560
Inventory	23,000
Supplies	1,000
Total Current Assets	227,220
Fixed Assets	
Equipment	75,000
Less depreciation	15,000
Total Fixed Assets	60,000
Total Assets	287,210

LIABILITIES AND OWNER'S EQUITY

Current Liabilities	
Accounts payable	$ 2,000
Current portion of long-term debt	0
Total Current Liabilities	2,000
Long-term Liabilities	
Notes payable	0
Total Long-Term Liabilities	$ 0
Owners' Equity	
G. Brown, capital	$137,500
P. Smith, capital	137,500
Retained Earnings	10,210
Total Owner's Equity	$285,210
TOTAL LIABILITIES AND OWNERS' EQUITY	$287,210

Inventory turnover must also be forecasted. Again, if the business experiences seasonality, it is not feasible to employ a constant turnover rate based on cost of goods sold. Inventory is a more complex issue for a manufacturing firm than accounts receivable, because at any time a business may have raw materials, work in process, and finished goods. In the beginning stages of the business, you will probably estimate the amount for each of these stages and then use the total of the three for each month as the estimate for the year-end balance sheet. As the business grows, however, using a cost accounting model in which the three totals are shown separately on the balance sheet is a preferred method.

Liabilities

Liabilities are everything the business owes to its creditors. Those that are due within one period are called **current liabilities.** New ventures generally have to pay for materials and inventory with cash until they have established a line of credit with suppliers, so you need to show a separate schedule that depicts when you expect to begin to use credit. Indicate only the total of materials and inventory for the year on the balance sheet, however. If the business paid cash for the entire year, which is not uncommon for a start-up, there will be no accounts payable. The current portion of long-term debt is that portion owed in the coming year.

Owner's or Stockholder's Equity

Owner's equity, also known as stockholder's equity in the corporate form, represents the excess after liabilities have been subtracted from assets and is the net worth of the business. Note that the individual investment contributions of the owners are also stated in this section. Retained earnings is the profit (loss) from the business that was not distributed as dividends.

When the balance sheet is completed, the total of the assets must equal the sum of the liabilities plus owner's equity. In other words, the balance sheet must balance! Understand that should you decide to use venture capital, private investors, or bank financing, the party involved may want a say in your debt-to-equity ratio; therefore, as capital is raised, the balance sheet is subject to adjustment.

Preparing the Pro Forma Sources and Applications of Funds Statement

To understand how net operating income and other sources of funds to the business were used to increase assets or pay off debt and what effect this had on working capital, the Sources and Applications of Funds Statement is created. Figure 15.7 displays such a statement.

New Venture Inc. earned an after-tax profit of $10,850 during the year, which becomes a source of funds for the business. Depreciation, which is not a cash expense, is added back into the equation. Typical uses of funds include paying dividends, increasing assets like equipment, paying off long-term debt, and decreasing owner's equity. The net increase in working capital is the difference between total funds received (sources) and total funds applied. Notice that the statement must balance, with the balance item being working capital.

Break-Even Analysis

The break-even analysis is a useful tool the entrepreneur can use to calculate when the business will make a profit in terms of either units sold or total sales dollars. In order for a business to break even and begin to make a profit, it must be able to generate a volume of sales that will cover both fixed and variable costs of running the business.

Figure 15.7: Pro Forma Sources and Applications of Funds: End of First Year

ABC Company—New Venture Inc.	
Sources of Funds	
Personal funds (capitalization)	$275,000
Net income from operations after taxes	10,850
Add depreciation	15,000
Total of Funding Sources	$300,850
Applications of Funds	
Purchase of equipment/furnishings	$ 75,000
Inventory	23,000
Total Funds Applied	98,000
Net Increase in Working Capital	202,850
	$300,850

Mathematically speaking, the break-even point is reached when total revenue (TR) equals total costs (TC). Total revenue is comprised of the quantity of units (Q) produced times the price (SP) per unit. Total costs are comprised of fixed costs (FC) plus variable costs (VC) per unit times the quantity of units (Q). Variable costs are associated with the production of the product such as materials, selling expenses, and direct labor. The break-even formula is as follows:

$TR = TC$ $SP(Q) = FC + VC(Q)$
Selling price = $50/unit   Variable Cost = $30/unit
Fixed Costs = $278,740

$$BE\ (Q) = \frac{FC}{SP/unit\text{---}VC/unit\ (marginal\ contribution)} = \frac{\$278,740}{\$50\text{-}\$30} = 13,937\ units$$

Whenever the unit selling price exceeds the unit variable cost, there will be some contribution to cover fixed costs. When the excess is enough to cover all fixed costs, break-even has been achieved. Using the continuing example of New Venture Inc., it can be seen that the business has fixed costs of $278,740, variable costs per unit of $30, and a selling price of $50 per unit. Therefore, the break-even quantity is 13,937 units. This means that before New Venture can begin to make a profit, it must sell 13,937 units.

Reporting the Financial Plan in the Business Plan

Preparing financial statements and a financial plan for the new venture is a tedious and time-consuming process, but it is absolutely essential for two reasons. Up to this point you have determined that your business concept has a market and is operationally feasible. First, the financial plan lets you know if you can turn this concept into a viable business that will be self-sustaining over the long term. Second, it proves to others (investors, bankers, key management) that you have a credible concept with potential for growth.

As the financial plan can be a fairly complicated and intimidating section of the business plan, include a brief summary of the highlights of the forecasted performance of the business—namely, sales, earnings, and cash flow. The reader can then selectively read the financials while still maintaining a sense of the whole picture.

The financial plan should include all the elements in Figure 15.8.

Figure 15.8: The Financial Plan

Summary of Financial Plan Highlights
Sales
Earnings
Cash Flow

Pro Forma Cash Flow Statements
Years 1-5, monthly years 1-2
Notes to cash flow statements

Pro Forma Income Statements
Years 1-5, monthly years 1-2
Notes to cash flow statements

Pro Forma Balance Sheets
Years 1-5
Notes to balance sheets

Pro Forma Sources and Applications of Funds Statements
Years 1-5
Notes to sources and applications statements

☑ New Venture Checklist

Have you

☐ Collected all the operating cost data needed to construct the financial statements?

☐ Studied competitor products to learn about seasonality, sales volume, and market share?

☐ Calculated the amount of start-up capital required to start and operate the business until a positive cash flow is achieved?

☐ Forecasted best and worst case scenarios for the pro forma financial statements, as well as the most likely case scenario?

☐ Calculated a break-even analysis for the first year?

☐ Completed a summary of the highlights of the financial plan?

Additional Sources of Information

Financial record keeping for small stores, *SBA Small Business Management Series*, Stock No. 045-000-00142-3.

Andrews, E.L. (January 1986). "Running Out of Money." *Venture*, pp. 32-25.

Frankston, F.M. (January 1981). "A Simplified Approach to Financial Planning." *Journal of Small Business Management*, pp. 7-15.

Stickney, C.P. (1990). *Financial Statement Analysis: Theory. A Strategic Perspective.* New York: Harcourt Brace Jovanovich, pp. 275-90.

Issues to Consider

1. Why is the cash flow statement the most important statement for the entrepreneur?
2. What kinds of information must be collected to complete the financial statements?
3. How is forecasting sales for consumer products different from forecasting sales for industrial products?
4. What three factors affect the percentage increase in sales over a three-to-five year period?
5. What are the distinct purposes of the income statement, the sources and applications of funds statement, and the balance sheet?

Case Study

5

✈ *FLIGHT TIME*
I N T E R N A T I O N A L

Flight Time
Air Charter Worldwide:
Start-Up of an Air Charter Broker

Case #93-32 Flight Time. Start-Up of an Air Charter Broker (A) This case was written by Alberto Bonacini, Candida Brush and Clifton Smith. Used with permission.

"Unfortunately, our request for the $300,000 loan has been rejected," stated Patricia Zinkowski to her two partners, Dara Zapata and Jane McBride, co-founders of Flight Time Corporation, a six-month-old air charter broker company based in Chestnut Hill, Massachusetts. It was June 1985 and the three partners were seated in the restaurant of the Suffolk Downs race track in East Boston to discuss Flight Time's first period of operations and future financial needs. The business had not taken off the way they expected. Clients, and consequently cash inflows, had not been enough to support the company beyond six months and the relevant net loss had eroded the initial investment of the three entrepreneurs. They had estimated that $300,000 was needed to continue Flight Time's operations, but their request for these funds to Shawmut Bank had been turned down and their personal finances were not sufficient to keep the company in business.

They all agreed their new company had potential and the possibility of dissolving the corporation was not even considered. However, as Patti observed, what had started as a desire for independence and challenge, "was now becoming a much more serious game."

Founder's Background

Dara A. Hoy Zapata

Dara Zapata had gained extensive experience in the airline business after graduating from Cardinal Cushing College, an affiliate of Notre Dame, with a degree in Business Administration in 1971. She began her career as a tour coordinator with one of the first wholesale tour operators in Massachusetts. The firm specialized in arranging vacations to Europe, particularly to Spain, for large groups of retirees. Dara's job was to organize the air charter flight and the hotel sojourn for these tour groups.

In 1976 she left this company and worked for a short period of time as a sales person, first for a Boston-based yacht brokerage company and then for a local travel agency, selling air tickets and all-included vacation packages. In 1977, while working for this agency, Dara co-founded A.H. Zapata, Inc. with her Chilean husband. The company offered bilingual translation and interpreting services in Spanish and English, English as a Second Language programs for foreign employees, and Spanish classes for U.S. personnel of Boston metropolitan service-oriented companies, such as Beth Israel Hospital, Mass General Hospital, Brigham and Women's Hospital, Mass Defenders, Boston Housing. Dara worked alternately part-time and full-time setting up programs, marketing services, hiring and training language teachers. In 1983 Dara's husband decided to accept a full time position at the Brigham and Women's Hospital and consequently the company ceased its operations in the same year.

> It was the end of 1984 when Dara began to vaguely conceive the idea of an air charter clearinghouse.

In 1979, while working part-time for A.H. Zapata, she joined Braniff International, a Texas-based airline, where she was employed as a manager of Boeing 747 flight operations, responsible for organizing time schedules of international pilots and crew. Dara subsequently became a manager of in-flight services in charge of catering contracts for provisions and other supplies, until she was dismissed by Braniff in 1982 due to a corporate-wide layoff.

Prior to starting Flight Time, Dara became an independent aviation consultant providing assistance to start-up airlines in meeting government regulatory requirements. She was particularly involved with the short-term leasing of aircraft and worked closely with Lusoair, a U.S. carrier that operated between Boston and Ponta Delgada in the Azores. She helped them managing "wet aircraft leasing," where, along with the plane and crew, maintenance agreements were included. It was the end of 1984 when Dara, observing the business operations between this carrier and its clients—large international tour operators—began to vaguely conceive the idea of an air charter clearinghouse.

Jane F. McBride

Jane McBride, Dara's cousin, was 25 years old at the time of Flight Time's incorporation. Jane graduated from Wesleyan University in 1981 with a degree in Cultural Anthropology and her first job was teaching English at A.H. Zapata,

Inc., Dara's enterprise. Jane also had a passion for aviation and had obtained her license as a private pilot, flying more than 200 hours on a Piper Dakota, her father's private plane.

The summer of 1982 she left Zapata, Inc. and went to work for International Weekends, an American tour wholesaler operator which at the time moved the largest number of passengers per year.[1] Jane was a tour escort guiding tourists to London, Amsterdam and Paris. Because her job at International Weekends was seasonal, in 1983 she joined American Adventures, a U.S.-based travel operator, as a tour leader. In this job, Jane led ten tours of foreign tourists throughout the States, doing everything from driving the 20-seat van to coordinating the trip, arranging sightseeing and planning overnight accommodations. A year later, Jane left American Adventures and went to work for Trans National Travel (TNT), the travel-related wholesaler division of Trans National, a financial services company based in Boston. As a tour director, her responsibilities involved organizing trips and traveling to Asia, Europe, and the Caribbean.

Jane found her job "challenging and satisfying" and stayed with TNT until the end of 1984. It was then that she had a conversation over dinner at Jane's sister's wedding with her cousin Dara, who convinced her that joining their business knowledge and skills to start a new company was a good idea.

Patricia A. Zinkowski

Patti Zinkowski, 27 years old, grew up in the Boston area and went to University of Massachusetts at Amherst, planning to become a veterinarian. Before graduation Patti switched her major to the Physics/Astronomy Department and was especially interested in climatology and aviation weather. However, due to the small number of climatology and meteorology courses, she graduated with a degree in Physics and, according to her, "with no intention of using it."

After graduation in January 1980, she went to Europe backpacking with a friend. She spent time in Switzerland, skiing and working as a ski instructor at summer camps for kids. In November 1980, the head of a Philadelphia-based company that sent American tourists overseas offered her a temporary six-month position as tour guide at a hotel in Switzerland. "I had a lot of fun organizing the stay of our clients and socializing with them. I had the best time, made a few bucks and decided that I liked to travel." After this assignment, she came back to Boston for a visit, but ended up being hired in January 1982 by the same company Jane was working for, International Weekends, at their U.K. accounting office. Patti was appointed Accounts Supervisor and sent to

London, where she oversaw the bookkeeping activities of related tour agencies. It was here she met Jane in 1982, who was working for International Weekends as a tour escort.

In 1983, Patti left International Weekends to join Trans National Travel (TNT), where she worked as Director of European Accounting, managing all the financial aspects of tour operations in Switzerland, Italy, and Germany. In the autumn of 1984, after discussing with Jane the possibility of starting their own company, Patti decided to leave TNT in December of that year.

The Business Opportunity

The Idea

The idea for Flight Time was conceived by Dara during her consulting experience, which involved the short-term leasing of aircraft for new airlines. The leasing agreements typically required that the lessee guarantee a certain number of flight hours[2] to the owner of the airplane. Dara found that the more flight hours the operator guaranteed, the more favorable the lease rate. As a consultant, she tried to increase the number of guaranteed hours by making some phone calls to tour operators whom she felt might need aircraft space for tour groups. One of these contacts was a tour operator whose 80 clients had been stranded in San Juan because of a last-minute flight cancellation. Scheduled flights were fully booked and the tour operator had no ideas for providing alternative air travel, so the angry tour group was unable to leave the island. After a few more phone calls, Dara "discovered that there was quite a demand for some type of a central clearinghouse, serving airlines operators, who could let us know about aircraft availability, and the customer, who needed airplanes."

In September 1984, Dara, who desired to be "independent and to do things in the [air travel] industry better than they were done", approached her cousin Jane at a wedding and over a glass of wine at the dinner party told her about the business idea, already having selected the company's name: "Flight Time." Dara wanted Jane to be involved because she "knew her cousin had the necessary background for the tour operator component needed by the envisioned enterprise." Dara believed Jane's experience was a necessary complement to her own expertise in aircraft operations and flight contract agreements. Jane was extremely interested in the opportunity because of its "excitement, sense of adventure. I [also] could not imagine working for anybody else."

Dara was aware that "the third piece needed would have to be someone with a solid background in computers, accounting and finance." Jane remembered Patti, who was now head of European accounting for TNT, and called her about the Flight Time idea. Patti, who in her experiences had seen travel groups getting stranded at various airports around the world, thought that the possibility of offering air charters to travel groups was very feasible and decided to join Dara and Jane in the new venture.

Getting Started

The initial business concept was to operate in the air charter industry as a pure charter broker.[3] As Dara explained: "We thought of setting up an intermediary company that would help aircraft owners to increase their utilization and assist tour operators in finding an aircraft, whatever their needs might be." From September to November of 1984, Dara and Jane met several times to explore the feasibility of the potential start-up company. Patti, who was abroad at the time, joined them in December when she returned to Boston. During that period, they called contacts in the travel business they had made over the years, to see "if the idea was really off the wall or not." Patti recalled the outcome of those phone calls and meetings:

> We asked them if we opened a business like this, 'Would you use our service?' And it was an overwhelming response: 'Are you in business now? Do you know of any place [that provides this type of service]?'
>
> We just couldn't see that anything was so wrong with the idea. We just thought it was a great idea since we also had personal experiences with people needing planes.

In addition to talking to potential clients, they met with advisors from the Service Corps of Retired Executives (SCORE)[4], experienced in providing free business and technical consulting to businesses and corporate start-ups. Even though these counselors did not know very much about the industry or specific business, they concluded if Dara, Jane, and Patti wanted to start this business, it was feasible. The three entrepreneurs felt quite reassured with this advice. Jane recollected later that excitement was growing because "at the time we did not think there was any other company doing this."

Enthusiastically they discussed the business idea with their families, but all their parents expressed reservations and thought it was risky to start a new company considering the young age of the three partners: "Why don't you get a real job?" was a recurrent suggestion. On the contrary, Jane felt "we did not have anything to lose [because] we were between seasons with our tours" and Patti thought that "if it was not going [to work], we could have gone back to what we were doing before."

In December, Dara, Jane, and Patti met several more times and decided their bread and butter would be Part 135[5] aircraft. Larger aircraft also were considered but they decided to concentrate on the smaller aircraft first. They agreed to target customers who traveled where scheduled service was lacking or when times weren't convenient. The following description characterizes Flight Time's target customer:

> In the beginning, their main objective was to get the word out, to let people know about the new service their business would provide.

"If you went Boston to Atlanta no problem: you got eight flights a day. But if you had to go from Biloxi, Mississippi, to Daphne, Alabama, there was not good service. You had to go back to Atlanta, change planes, go to Daphne, go back to Atlanta, change planes, go back to Biloxi. It was this hub-and-spoke. You just couldn't get around the wheel. You always had to come to the center where the airlines were."

Tour operators' small track programs, which involved prearranged periodical flights to and from the same destination, were also targeted as a major source of revenues. Other segments the three principals identified, in no specific order, were the leisure market (defined as "vacationers"), corporate business travel, and sports team travel. Dara stated their "target was to have a wider client base. If one end did not pan out, the other part of the client base could pick up the slack."

In the beginning, their main objective was to get the word out, to let people know about the new service their business would provide. Jane and Dara would concentrate on contacting potential clients and operators to find out what type of aircraft they were operating and what type of utilization they would have liked to have.

By chance, Dara met an administrator of the U.S. Military Travel Management Command (MTMC), a federal military representation division. This official explained to her how the Military Command arranged air charter flights for its troops, how the contracts were filled out, and what kind of information was needed when dealing with air carriers. After this conversation, Dara decided to adopt this framework for Flight Time's operations.

A hired designer created a windrose high-tech logo, that represented the three founders and an aircraft style design (see p. 317). Even though a formal business plan had not been written, time had come to meet with the lawyer for the official incorporation of the company.

Business Environment

Between 1976 and 1982, the commercial airline industry was characterized worldwide by high fragmentation and intense competition. The top 15 airlines flying between the United States and Europe, the most traveled international route, had an overall passenger market share on that route of less than 70 percent in 1984. Pan Am, TWA, and British Airways, the top three international carriers, were separated only by one percentage point.[6] U.S. carriers had the largest share of world traffic in 1984 with 40 percent of the total Revenue Passenger Miles (RPMs)[7] flown, only a three percent increase from 1976.[8]

Commercial air carriers provide regularly scheduled and/or charter flights for both passenger and cargo operations. Scheduled flights serve a specific route on a regularly scheduled timetable (for instance, biweekly) and are sold to the public. For charter flights, either public charters (i.e. typically a wholesale tour operator resells the seats of the leased aircraft to the general public) or single entities (i.e. a corporation charters a flight for its employees, without reselling single seats), are purchasers of the services and negotiate their own routing and timetables. A scheduled airline may provide both scheduled and charter air service, while charter operators generally offer only the latter. Revenues from charter flights varied greatly among single airlines, ranging from less than $100,000 a year for the airline operating a single Part 135 aircraft, to nine-digit figures for non-scheduled flights of major national scheduled carriers. In 1984, scheduled air operations accounted for 89 percent of the total airline traffic measured in Revenue Ton Miles (RTMs)[9] and 90 percent of world RPMs (see Exhibit 1). The Department of Transportation (DOT) estimated that in the United States 5.5 million people—business travelers and vacationers—took air charter flights in 1984.

Before the introduction of the Airline Deregulation Act (ADA) in 1978, the competition among U.S. domestic airlines was regulated similar to public utilities by the Civil Aeronautics Board's (CAB's) control of new entries, entries into existing markets, routes, and pricing policies. Since 1978, when President Jimmy Carter introduced the competitive aviation policy and the CAB was dissolved, airlines were allowed to voluntarily modify their route networks and marketing strategies. One of the most visible effects of the deregulation was the accelerated growth of "hubbing." Five years from the adoption of the ADA, some airlines more than doubled their hub-and-spoke operations, with up to 10 percent increase of the load factor and a 15–20 percent increase of air travelers who flew a complete journey on a single airline.[10] Major commercial airlines began to cut regular services to and from locations considered not profitable enough, while small commuter, corporate jets, and charter operators blossomed. According to the *Financial Times*, in the early 1980s "businessmen are increasingly taking to the air in small, light transport aircraft either owned by, or chartered on behalf of, their companies. This concept of 'business aviation'—as opposed to 'business travel' on scheduled airlines—has been winning favor . . . [because of] . . . the greater convenience and time savings involved, by comparison with the scheduled airlines, together with a significant saving in cost."[11]

In 1984 there were more than 12,000 airports in the U.S. but only 400 were serviced by scheduled flights.[12] Worldwide, there were 300 scheduled airlines, of which fewer than 30 were the U.S. scheduled carriers, accounting for more than $100 billion in revenues.[13] Approximately 4,000 carriers operated air charter flights in the U.S. accounting for $2.4 billion in sales, flying more than 14,000 aircraft. Revenues from vacationers (the so-called "leisure travel") comprised more than 60 percent of the $2.4 billion dollar sales, while 20 percent of the revenues came from incentive houses[14] and corporations. The remainder was split among the U.S. government (i.e. troops movements), sports teams, and entertainment.

> In 1984 there were more than 12,000 airports in the U.S. but only 400 were serviced by scheduled flights.

The largest share of the air charter market was represented by public charter flights, sold directly to the public or, more often, to tour operators. Most scheduled and non-scheduled airlines marketed their charter flights through in-house brokerage operations or through their own sales people. The rest was managed by wholesale and retail tour operators and by a handful of regionally dispersed and privately held independent brokers, whose revenues rarely surpassed the one million dollars. Tour operators, corporate incentive planners, government departments (such as the Defense Department), and sports teams were, in order, the four main purchasers of the these brokerage services.

Few charter airplanes were large jet aircraft (such as DC-9, B737 and B757) produced by major aircraft manufacturers, like Boeing and McDonnel-Douglas.[15] Instead, single-engine and two-engine piston planes, produced by specialized smaller manufacturers, such as Fokker, and having fewer than 20 seats were most frequently chartered. The Part 135 aircraft made up 60 percent of the 80 seats or less segment.[16] Total shipments of general aviation aircraft to scheduled and charter carriers were declining since 1979 (see Exhibit 2 on p. 332) and in 1984 experts were forecasting a steady negative trend.

This downturn in the shipment of aircraft was mainly the result of the airlines' attempt to contain fixed costs and to strive for better use of the available equipment, to be obtained partially by increasing the number of flight hours. For airline operators, the average utilization of large equipment was 6 to 7 flight hours a day including scheduled flights, while for smaller airplanes utilization barely reached 2 flight hours a day. Even though fixed costs such as aircraft, maintenance, and personnel were steadily increasing, other variable costs, such as jet fuel and oil prices, after a steady increase and a sharp rise in 1979, were declining beginning in 1981 (see Exhibit 2.)

The Start-Up

On January 2, 1985, Patti, Jane, and Dara went downtown to meet with their lawyer for the first step of the legal incorporation of the business.

Initial Resources

Each of the three partners was able to withdraw ten thousand dollars from their personal savings without involving family funds. Flight Time, Inc. was organized so that the Dara, Patti and Jane had equal partnership in the business, each owning one third of the three hundred shares issued at no par value. Dara described the initial financing: "We figured that $30,000 would let us go on forever. We would have enough income from our business to perpetuate the business." Then, they gave each other titles, a legal condition when an incorporation occurred. Dara was named President because she had the original idea, Patti was appointed Treasurer because she was doing the bookkeeping, and, considering that the State of Massachusetts required someone to be clerk, Jane was made Secretary by default.

They leased a one room office with no windows at a travel agency in Chestnut Hill. To provide the new location with the necessary office supplies, they went to friends' basements and dug out old file cabinets, then to yard sales, other companies, and offices to obtain second hand desks and appliances. On the first day of business, their office furnishings consisted of a few telephones, a couple of typewriters, an answering machine, a photocopier, a $4,700 Hewlett Packard computer with dot matrix printer, and a coffee machine. They distributed various Rolodex cards with the names and the addresses of all the contacts that Dara, Jane, and Patti had made in the airline industry and the tour operator business. Besides these contacts, they subscribed to *Aviation Daily, Travel Weekly,* and other periodicals and newspapers, useful to keep updated aviation-related news and to be used as possible sources for their first clients. Flight Time did not have a firm commitment from anyone who prior to start-up had demonstrated interest in using the services of an air charter broker.

At Work

The first day of Flight Time's operations, Jane, Dara and Patti went to work in business attire promptly at 8:30. According to their new business cards, Jane was Director of Operations, Dara was President and Director of Sales and Marketing, and Patti was Director of Finance. After a few weeks at the office, however, while it was clear that finance and accounting were Patti's main responsibilities, most of the other functions were managed together. Decisions other than those involving ordinary operations, had to be made unanimously.

Most of their time was spent jointly, searching for clients and available airplanes. Jane recalled that "how to get the word out was our marketing plan." Sitting in the same room facing each other, they looked in the *Boston Globe* for companies that were growing and called people they knew, from professional contacts they had in the tour operator business, to friends and family, as well as friends of friends and referrals. Through letters and follow-up calls, their efforts in convincing potential Part 135 clients to consider chartering a small aircraft were based on comparing charter planes to scheduled carriers: "Why change planes and why stay overnight in a hotel, when you can fly with your own plane?"

> Travel people began to identify them as "The Three Women in Boston."

With the goal of getting the word out and reaching potential clients, Flight Time joined the National Business Aircraft Association (NBAA). Patti was able to generate few descriptive articles about the company for the trade magazines and local newspapers. Looking for new ideas, Patti went to a Public Relations seminar, where she conceived the first press release of Flight Time. As she mentioned, "it was necessary to have a lot of common sense. We did not have a lot of money to spend in advertising, but we needed to get our name out there." Thus, the initial press coverage resulted in many phone inquiries that were used to build up a list of possible clients. To expand this press coverage, in April Flight Time also started a two-page newsletter that was sent to prospective customers and air charter operators (see Exhibit 3 on p. 333). Travel people began to identify them as "The Three Women in Boston." In an attempt to enhance Flight Time's image and business network, Patti joined the New England Women Business Owners (NEWBO) and Jane the National Association of Female Executives (NAFE.) They were sure that being three women in a "male" dominated industry would create a stronger awareness of their service.

Operationally, when a potential customer called for a price estimate, a standard client request sheet was completed and input into the computer. Information included the desired time of departure, date, place of departure and arrival, number of people traveling, and special equipment carried along. Flight Time then searched for the possible carriers in a computerized database they created, in the *World Aviation Directory*, and in any other publications that could provide a profile of different airlines and included information such as contact names, types of the aircraft, and number of seats. In order to match the customer's request to an aircraft, Dara, Patti and Jane would call various carriers and ask for a quote. Considering that the quoted price already included a 5 percent to 10 percent commission, they did not add any extra charge to the client. When a client accepted the price and aircraft type, Flight Time linked the customer and the charter airline, with only those two parties signing the final air transportation contract. A database of available Part 135 and Part 121 aircraft organized by state was set up on the computer, even though it was mostly used for the newsletter and business correspondence to clients and airlines. Another database, containing information about possible clients also was developed.

On March 31, after 3 months of operations, they had their first official board meeting at the Emerson Place of Charles River Park. The three partners decided to form an international executive committee to assist them in searching for contacts and business advice, with no obligation or compensation for its members. About at the same time, the three founders discovered that they were not the only pioneers of the air charter brokerage industry; in fact another company, Charter Services, had been operating in Albuquerque since 1979. This discovery reinforced Flight Time's moral: "if there is someone doing what we are doing since '79, there must be a lot of business out there."

First Clients

Dara recalled how many of Flight Time's early contacts originated from the consulting service she used to provide. "They were not a lot of contacts, but certainly enough to get going. I knew the business well enough so that I could call any airline, introduce ourselves and explain about our company." In February, the American Soy Bean Association travel planner called Flight Time because some of the members had to inspect properties located in Massachusetts and needed a Part 135 airplane for the tour. This was the first deal for the newly born clearinghouse.

The second month of operation the phone rang again. A casino operator wanted to fly 15-20 people daily from Boston and from Providence, Rhode Island, to the casinos of Atlantic City, New Jersey.[17] The three businesswomen were speechless: it was a $1,000,000 yearly contract, one hundred thousand dollars in brokerage fees. They located a start-up airline in New Hampshire operating just the right size plane, a Dornier 228-201. The casino operator signed the original contract. Because this track program was a long-term commitment, he asked for a credit extension. As per Flight Time's policy he would pay for the first flight before the departure and then settle the other trips a few days later. The plane flew smoothly for two weeks, then suddenly the aircraft was not being filled, the casino operator stopped paying and the contract failed. "But it was an eye-opener," Patti recollected later, "we had this one contract, but it got screwed up so fast. If there was one of these trips there were more of these trips."

A few weeks later, a former client of Dara, a hardware distributor from Southeastern Massachusetts, was contacted by Flight Time. The owner of the company was a pilot himself who easily understood the air charter concept. He decided that instead of picking up his clients at Boston's Logan Airport, it would be better to fly them directly to his factory. This $700 deal, paid a few days prior to departure, generated a profit of $70 to Flight Time.

By June 1985, the five month old clearinghouse had generated $150,000 in revenues, primarily from trips arranged at least 3-4 weeks in advance although some flights were arranged on one-day notice. For every 10-12 price quote requests, Flight Time was able close one deal, usually settled before the departure and subject to a cancellation policy of 2 to 3 weeks in advance. Most of the booked planes could carry between 10 and 50 passengers, with the 8 seater Learjet being the most chartered aircraft. However, the time spent to shape a deal on a Learjet with 8 people was the same as for a Boeing 727, a 100 seat jet. At the end of the fifth month the names of several potential clients had been entered into the database and it was clear to Jane that "the only limitation to our success was creating awareness of our services."

Second Financing?

During the first week of June, Patti inspected Flight Time's financial position. The business had less than $4,000 in cash. Most of the start-up money had been used for office supplies, rent, utilities, promotional activities and salaries to the principals. But Dara, Jane and Patti were not ready to give up.

"The track program we had set up was not going to sustain itself, which was what the original plan was. We knew that the business we anticipated was on the books. We were waiting for the big one to come along and get us over, [but] the numbers decided for us that we needed a secondary financing."

After a quick analysis of the situation, they determined that $300,000 was needed not only to keep the business running, but also to expand it. They approached a local bank for the $300,000 loan. The bank requested that Flight Time present a business plan and disclose relevant financial information. Suggestions from SCORE helped them to construct the business plan (see Exhibit 4 on p. 334) and a certified public accountant was hired to produce the financial statements (see Exhibit 5 on p. 338). However, because of Flight Time's lack of track record and brief business history, the bank refused to lend Flight Time the $300,000.

Watching the horses race, Dara, Patti, and Jane were wondering what kind of future Flight Time could expect.

Footnotes

[1] International Weekends was later bought by TWV, another U.S. wholesaler tour operator.

[2] Flight hours are measured block to block, only when the aircraft in moving.

[3] An air charter broker is a fee-based business intermediary that links an airline having aircraft space to rent, with another entity, usually a corporation or a tour operator, needing to fly people or goods. A pure broker does not own or personally lease aircraft, but acts only as an agent for the two parties.

[4] SCORE, is an affiliate of the Small Business Administration (SBA).

[5] In 1985, Part 135 referred to section of the U.S. Federal Aviation Regulation (FAR) governing safety and operating procedures for aircraft having, among other requirements and limitations, fewer than 20 seats and not more than a 12,500 pounds gross takeoff weight. Over these two limits, FAR Part 121 regulations applied. Aircraft operating under Part 135 and those operating under Part 121 can be generically defined as "small airplanes" and "large airplanes" respectively.

[6] Source: *International Air Transport Association* (IATA), 1985.

[7] *Revenue Passenger Mile* (RPM): As defined by the Federal Aviation Administration (FAA,) "one revenue passenger transported one mile in revenue

service. Revenue passenger miles are computed by summation of the products of the revenue aircraft miles flown during a flight stage, multiplied by the number of revenue passengers carried on that flight stage."

[8] Source: *U.S. Department of Transportation,* 1985.

[9] *Revenue Ton Mile (RTM):* As defined by the FAA, "one ton of revenue traffic transported one mile."

[10] Source: *U.S. Department of Transportation,* 1984.

[11] Source: *Financial Times,* April 2, 1984.

[12] Source: *TravelAge East,* May 12, 1986.

[13] Source: *International Civil Aviation Organization (ICAO),* 1985.

[14] Incentive Houses are service companies organizing the work incentive plans (such as travel bonuses) for the employees of their corporate clients.

[15] For a more detailed description of aircraft manufacturers in the 1970s and in the 1980s, see Professor Sushil Vachani, "The Commercial Aircraft Industry In 1987," (1990), *Management Policy Department,* Boston University.

[16] Source: Federal Aviation Administration 1984 Forecast, *Federal Aviation Administration,* 1985.

[17] See Exhibit 3 on p. 333.

EXHIBIT 1

Flight Time

DISTRIBUTION OF WORLD AIRLINE TRAFFIC IN 1985

	International	U.S.	Total
Freight Services - Note A			
Scheduled	84%	96%	90%
Charter	16	4	10
Passenger Services - Note B			
Scheduled	81	97	89
Charter	19	3	11

Source: International Air Transport Association, Historical Data Report, 1985.
Note A: Measured in Revenue Ton Mile (RTM).
Note B: Measured in Revenue Passenger Mile (RPM).

SELECTED DATA FOR WORLD AIR TRANSPORT

	1981	1982	1983	1984
Scheduled Airlines				
Scheduled Services				
Passengers Carried (millions)	752	767	798	845
Freight Tons Carried (millions)	11	12	12	13
Passenger-Miles Flown (billions)	703	717	745	798
Available Seat-Miles (billions)	1,109	1,132	1,166	1,236
Ton-Miles Performed (billions)	84	86	91	99
Available Ton-Miles (billions)	145	148	152	164
Charter Services				
Passenger-Miles Flown (billions)	30	30	28	30
Ton-Miles Performed (billions)	3.9	3.6	3.5	3.7
Available Ton-Miles (billions)	6.1	5.7	5.5	5.8
Charter Airlines				
All Services				
Passenger-Miles Flown (billions)	32	37	40	43
Ton-Miles Performed (billions)	4.2	4.8	5.0	5.4
Available Ton-Miles (billions)	5.7	6.6	6.6	7.0

Source: International Air Transport Association, Historical Data Report, 1985.

EXHIBIT 2

Flight Time

U.S. General Aviation Aircraft Shipments

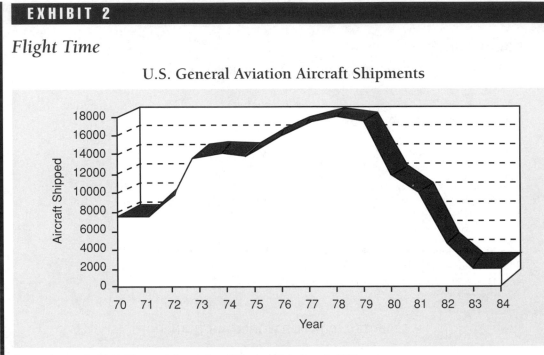

Source: International Air Transport Association, Historical Data Report, 1985.

Jet Fuel Prices
Real (FY—1982) Dollars

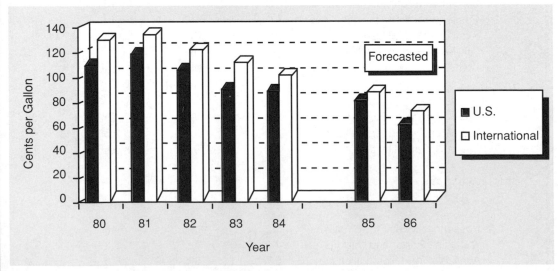

Source: International Air Transport Association, Historical Data Report, 1985.

EXHIBIT 3

Flight Time

Flight Time's Newsletter
April/May 1985 Issue

FLIGHT LINE BY FLIGHT TIME   April/May 1985

Congratulations, consider yourself an innovator in your company!

Every business needs individuals who think ahead, who are open to new ideas, and are not afraid to try new products. By showing your interest in FLIGHT TIME you are supporting a pioneer concept in the aviation industry.

This month FLIGHT TIME launches its first newsletter and introduces you to new opportunities in air travel.

OPPORTUNITY No. 1—FLIGHT TIME

FLIGHT TIME is not a travel agency. We are not an airline nor a tour operator. What we are is a resource, and information station, dedicated to securing cost-efficient and reliable private charter air transportation for individuals, corporations, groups, and associations. FLIGHT TIME fills requests for charter aircraft for groups of all sizes, whether it be for you or your entire company.

Since you may have received some information on FLIGHT TIME prior to this newsletter, here is a brief synopsis of the services offered by FLIGHT TIME.

FLIGHT TIME: 1. HELPS you decide if private charters are your best alternative in air travel.
2. LOCATES certified aircraft which best suit your needs.
3. PROVIDES quotes and options which include aircraft descriptions, per hour costs, and technical data.
4. CONFIRMS and coordinates charter arrangements and itineraries.

Best of all, FLIGHT TIME offers these services FREE of charge.

OPPORTUNITY No. 2—PRECISION AIRLINES/ATLANTIC CITY HOLIDAYS

FLIGHT TIME is pleased to announce that Atlantic City is now accessible from Boston and Providence via Precision Airlines.

Atlantic City Holidays, a New England based tour operator, is now offering daily departures from Boston and Providence to Atlantic City, New Jersey. Round-trip air, complete overnight packages including casino transfers shall be available starting April 5, 1985.

Precision Airlines puts into service its new DORNIER 228-201 for this program. The Dornier is a new-generation commuter aircraft known for its speed, high passenger comfort, and STOL capabilities.

Further information on price and schedule may be obtained by calling: (800) 442-1162 (Mass. only) or (800) 447-2250 (outside Mass.).

OPPORTUNITY No. 3

According to the National Business Aircraft Association, the average business trip involves 4.1 people traveling 338 miles with a four-hour turnaround.

Suppose you and your team of key salesmen want to blitz a customer in Syracuse. Instead of dealing with complex schedules, two-hour layovers, and missed connections, you jump into your private plane, make a three-hour presentation and fly back again. You get the job done fast. Your plane waits for you rather than you waiting for the plane.

Many businesses do not even consider the possibility of chartering aircraft for their business travel due to the myth that the cost is prohibitive. (Not all itineraries merit a chartered airplane.) You could be pleasantly surprised to find that on many occasions a business trip would be more cost-efficient if key employees traveled by private charter rather than scheduled carrier.

For more information call FLIGHT TIME at (617) 965-7060.

OPPORTUNITY No. 4—EASTERN CHARTER/NANTUCKET

Eastern Air Charter is planning to offer first class service to Nantucket Island from Norwood, MA airport this upcoming summer season. Service is tentatively scheduled to begin May 15th.

The price of a ticket will include: First class comfort aboard executive aircraft (planes are fully air conditioned), champagne, full liquor, and soft drinks, inflight snacks, free airport parking, onboard telephone and entertainment systems.

The schedule is designed to accommodate weekend passengers with departures Friday evenings and early Saturday mornings returning on Sunday evenings. The fare for this trip will be $175.00–$180.00 per person round trip.

EXHIBIT 4

Flight Time

FLIGHT TIME'S BUSINESS PLAN
As Provided by Flight Time to Shawmut, for the Loan Request Application

STATEMENT OF PURPOSE

FLIGHT TIME is a service business dedicated solely to security charter air transportation for individuals, groups, associations, and corporations. FLIGHT TIME specializes in screening and locating Part 135 and Part 121 aircraft for this client base. FLIGHT TIME neither owns nor operates any aircraft.

FLIGHT TIME acts as a charter clearinghouse. The company is in the business of distributing information on aircraft prices and availability, negotiating terms of charter contracts and coordinating details of charter flight operations. Upon authority by client, FLIGHT TIME acts as agent for the client in security aircraft and arranging charter flight.

FLIGHT TIME charters aircraft (on behalf of clients) from carriers certified for charter. This means that both commercially scheduled airliners and nonscheduled airliners may be used in the selection process.

Note: FLIGHT TIME does not engage in activities such as the following, which are traditionally associated with retail travel agencies, i.e.:

- reserve and ticket airline seats on commercial or charter flights.
- arrange tours of any kind for individuals or groups.
- arrange "package deals" associated with tourism.
- reserve and confirm hotel accommodations or any other land arrangements.
- reserve or promote rental cars or ground transportation.

BUSINESS PLAN—MARKET SECTION

The market for FLIGHT TIME Corporation's charter air service may be subdivided into the following segments, each with its own particular requirements.

CORPORATE

According to Travel Weekly, a trade journal, over 500 million business trips of one night or more are made each year. The report concludes that because few corporation have any organized business travel policy, millions of dollars are wasted annually.

FLIGHT TIME works, with corporations of all sizes, many of which are listed in the Fortune 1000. We recommend the following checklist to our clients as a yardstick to determine air charter feasibility:

- When 3 or more people are charter feasibility.
- When key personnel travel business or first class.
- When the limitations of scheduled airline service mean unnecessary hotel overnights with other added expenses.
- When the destination or point of origin is more than 45 minutes from a major airport.
- When a destination does not have non-stop or direct air service.

Responses to FLIGHT TIME's service have been extremely positive. Due to the wide array of available aircraft, FLIGHT TIME has been able to accommodate requests for 15 passenger turboprops, 5 passenger jets, and 80 passenger jets, just to name a few.

TOUR OPERATORS

There is a very high concentration of tour operators and wholesalers in the Northeast and for many, the key to the success of a track program is contingent upon reliable and economical chartered air space. In an industry where last minute changes and failed contracts are commonplace, FLIGHT TIME assists tour operators in negotiating contracts with FAA certified air carriers.

FLIGHT TIME recently negotiated a contract between a Boston based tour wholesaler and regional air carrier for daily flights from Boston and Providence to Atlantic City.

TRAVEL AGENTS

Travel agents are prime targets for FLIGHT TIME's services with their corporate, leisure, and affinity markets already established. Since most travel agents, as well as the traveling public, are unfamiliar with general aviation, FLIGHT TIME's services complement those of retail and corporate agents.

FLIGHT TIME has targeted reputable agents with upscale clientele who have expressed an interest in private charter. Agents receive a percentage of FLIGHT TIME's commission.

In addition to F.I.T.s, many agencies organize their own group tour programs and frequently need larger aircraft. FLIGHT TIME has received requests from agents for groups of 15–100 passengers.

CASINOS

FLIGHT TIME, sponsored by Claridge's Casino of Atlantic City, is awaiting confirmation of its vendor registration number, a license to contract directly with New Jersey casinos. FLIGHT TIME applied for the license in response to several queries from casino operators looking for charter aircraft to transport VIP clients in from the greater Northeast region.

Casinos are constantly seeking ways in which to entice "high rollers" to their establishments: flying them directly into Bader Field, located in downtown Atlantic City, is one such way. Bader Field, however, has a very short runway—only 2950 feet, and few aircraft can land there. FLIGHT TIME has located a number of high performance STOL aircraft capable of flying directly into Bader, and is actively marketing these aircraft. Several casinos have expressed interest in working with FLIGHT TIME once the vendor registration number has been assigned.

REFERRALS

Referrals from airlines constitute a major market segment, and these clients are usually already qualified buyers. To date, we have received referrals for trips to Cincinnati, Minneapolis, Bowling Green, Cleveland, and Atlanta.

Personal contacts and referrals have also generated considerable business.

HOTELS

Deluxe hotels are constantly seeking extra amenities to offer their clients. FLIGHT TIME has contacted general managers of upscale hotels in MA to introduce our services. Executive charter, like limousine service, is considered by many as a necessity rather than a luxury. Over-sized folded business cards, which include a brief description of FLIGHT TIME's services and are displayed in selected areas of a hotel, are an inexpensive yet effective way to reach the discerning business or leisure traveler.

Travel and Meeting Planners, as well as Incentive Houses, are also good sources of potential business.

LOCATION ANALYSIS FOR BUSINESS

FLIGHT TIME operates primarily via telephone, telex and written correspondence, therefore, location is not a major factor. FLIGHT TIME is located in close proximity to the 128 belt, and is convenient to Norwood airport.

COMPETITION ANALYSIS

As of this writing, there exists no other company operating exactly like FLIGHT TIME. The existing competition consists of:

A. Direct Airway - New Jersey - Primary focus is corporations utilizing fleet based in Teterboro, NJ.

Charter Clearinghouse - Pennsylvania - Primary focus is on bringing clients from Pennsylvania to Atlantic City.

Charter Services - New Mexico - Concentrates on Midwest sports teams.

Netair Int'l - Colorado - Organized 12 air taxi operators in the western U.S. under the Netair name and uniform.

F. Miscellaneous Charter Operators - Charter operators who do not own or operate a particular aircraft requested, but broker it out and charge hefty commissions.

PRICING PHILOSOPHY

The difference between FLIGHT TIME and its competition lies in our pricing philosophy. FLIGHT TIME strives to offer its services free of charge to its clients. Because of the soft general aviation market, aircraft owners and operators are extremely eager to maximize aircraft utilization, and pay a sales commission to FLIGHT TIME. FLIGHT TIME receives a commission based on the overall contract value:

- 10% on Part 135 operators—i.e. aircraft with fewer than 20 seats
- 5% on Part 121 operators—i.e. aircraft with more than 20 seats.

Unlike the competition, which levies 5–10% commission on both the operator and the client, FLIGHT TIME's prices are among the lowest in the industry. We believe that by keeping prices low, we will be able to better demonstrate to our clients that private air charter can be cost-effective and competitively priced.

CREDIT POLICY

FLIGHT TIME operates on a cash or credit card basis with the majority of sales prepaid. A 3% bank charge will be assessed on credit card sales. (Once a client has established a favorable credit history, FLIGHT TIME will extend credit on a net-10 basis, but only in situations where FLIGHT TIME has at least the same terms with the carrier.)

EXHIBIT 5

Flight Time

BALANCE SHEET
as of May 31, 1985
(Note A)

ASSETS

Current assets

Cash	$3,797
Supplies	866
Prepaid Expenses	229
Deferred Expenses - Note B	5,779
Total Current Assets	10,671

Property and Equipment

Computer	4,700
Equipment	1,853
Total Property and Equipment	6,553
Accumulated Depreciation - Note C	(175)
Total Net Property and Equipment	6,378

Other Assets

Deposits	575
Organization Expenses, Net of Amortization	596
Total Other Assets	1,171

Total Assets	$18,220

LIABILITIES AND STOCKHOLDERS' EQUITY

Current Liabilities

Accounts Payable	$978

Long-Term Debt

Loans Payable, Stockholders'	26,000

Commitments - Note D

Stockholders' Equity

Common Stock - Note E	3,000
Retained Earnings	(11,758)
Total Stockholders' Equity	(8,758)

Total Liabilities and Stockholders' Equity	$18,220

Note A: Balance Sheet as Prepared by Robert M. Hurst & Company, Certified Public Accountants.

Note B: This Amount Represent Expenses Incurred Prior to the Date Operations Commenced and, Accordingly, Are Being Amortized Over the First Twelve Years.

Note C: Property and Equipment Are Being Depreciated Using the Straight-Line Method of Depreciation Over Their Estimated Useful Lives of the Assets for Book Purposes and the Accelerated Cost Recovery System for Tax Purposes.

Note D: As of May 31, 1985, the Company Was Obligated Under a One-Year Lease Agreement Expires December 31, 1985 Covering the Premises in Chestnut Hill, Massachusetts. The Terms of the Lease Stipulate a Monthly Rental Payment of $300.

Note E: No Par Value; 15,000 Shares Authorized; 300 Shares Issued and Outstanding.

STATEMENT OF INCOME AND RETAINED EARNINGS
for the Period from January 2, 1985 (Date of Inception) to May 31, 1985
(Note A)

		% to Sales
SALES - Note B	$123,919	100 %
COST OF SALES - Note C	117,356	94.7
Gross Profit	6,563	5.3
SELLING, GENERAL AND ADMINISTRATIVE		
EXPENSES - Note D	18,864	15.2
Net Profit (Loss) Before Other Income and (Expenses)	(12,301)	(9.9)
OTHER INCOME AND (EXPENSES)		
Gain on Sale of Stock	687	0.6
Interest Income	85	0.1
Depreciation and Amortization	(229)	(0.2)
Net Profit (Loss)	(11,758)	(9.5)

Note A: Income Statement as Prepared by Robert M. Hurst & Company, Certified Public Accountants.
Note B: Dollar Amount as from Billing to Customers.
Note C: Dollar Amount as from Billing from Aircraft Carriers.
Note D: See SCHEDULE OF SELLING, GENERAL AND ADMINISTRATIVE EXPENSES.

SCHEDULE OF SELLING, GENERAL AND ADMINISTRATIVE EXPENSES
for the Period From January 2, 1985 (Date of Inception) to May 31, 1985
(Note A)

		% to Sales
Office Supplies and Expenses	$4,011	3.2 %
Promotion and Entertainment	3,801	3.1
Auto and Travel	3,405	2.7
Rent	1,567	1.3
Dues and Subscriptions	839	0.7
Equipment Rental	833	0.7
Telephone	715	0.6
Training	698	0.6
Postage	423	0.3
Maintenance and Repairs	418	0.3
Professional Fees	410	0.3
Insurance	383	0.3
Taxes, Other	228	0.2
Advertising	187	0.2
Organization Expense	131	0.1
Miscellaneous	815	0.7
	$18,864	15.2

Note A: Schedule of Expenses as Prepared by Robert M. Hurst & Company, Certified Public Accountants.

STATEMENT OF CHANGES IN FINANCIAL POSITION
for the Period From January 2, 1985 (Date of Inception) to May 31, 1985
(Note A)

SOURCE OF FUNDS

To Operations

Net Income (Loss)	($11,758)
Add Back Non-Cash Expenses:	
Depreciation and Amortization	229
Net to Operations	(11,529)
Proceeds from Loans Payable, Stockholders'	26,000
Proceeds from Issuance of Capital Stock	3,000
Total Source of Funds	17,471

APPLICATIONS OF FUNDS

Acquisition of Computer	4,700
Acquisition of Equipment	1,853
Increase in Deposits	575
Acquisition of Other Assets	650
Total Applications of Funds	7,778

INCREASE (DECREASE) IN WORKING CAPITAL	$9,693

COMPONENTS OF WORKING CAPITAL

Increase (Decrease) in Current Assets

Cash	$3,797
Deferred Expenses	5,779
Supplies 866	
Prepaid Expenses	229
Total Increase (Decrease) in Current Assets	10,671

Decrease (Increase) in Current Liabilities

Accounts Payable	(978)

INCREASE (DECREASE) IN WORKING CAPITAL	$9,693

Note A: Cash Flow Statement as Prepared by Robert M. Hurst & Company, Certified Public Accountants.

1. What was the window of opportunity, and what allowed these three entre-preneurs to take advantage of it?
2. How much did the three really know about the market and the economic feasibility before start-up?
3. Was there any advantage (or disadvantage) to the three entrepreneurs being female?
4. Should they continue operations?

PART 6

A Plan for Growth

My candle burns at both ends,
It will not last the night.
But ah my foes, and oh, my friends,
It sheds a lovely light.

—EDNA ST. VINCENT MILLAY

CHAPTER 16

Growing the Business

Overview

- *Positioning the new venture for growth*
- *Growth strategies within and outside the industry*
- *Preparing for globalization*
- *Issues to consider when exporting*

Beyond Start-Up

Although some entrepreneurs, for a variety of personal reasons, may ultimately choose not to grow their businesses, most founders of entrepreneurial ventures are growth-oriented. Expansion is a natural by-product of a successful start-up. It helps a new business secure or maintain its competitive advantage and establish a firm foothold in the market. Contrary to popular opinion, the fastest growing small companies come from a variety of industries; albeit, the ubiquitous computer software industry does dominate the high-growth companies. When *Business Week* (May 23, 1994) listed the hottest growth companies in America, included among the top 20 were:

- A fast-food pizza business
- A sports sandal company
- Five software companies
- A product marketing firm
- Three telecommunications companies
- A rehabilitation services business

- Three casual clothing companies
- A saloon
- A slot machine manufacturer
- A magnetic ink character reader manufacturer
- A leather goods manufacturer
- A computer hardware manufacturer

What made these companies high-growth companies and set them apart from others was that they displayed several of the following characteristics. They were:

- First into the market
- Better at what they did
- Leaner in their operations
- Unique in what they offered

Being first in the market with a new product or service is one of the strongest competitive advantages there is, as it presents the opportunity to establish brand recognition so that customers immediately think of your company when they think about a particular product or service. This was certainly the strategy of Xerox in the copier industry and Microsoft in the operations and applications software industry.

Many high-growth businesses have developed *innovative processes* that allow them to do what they do better and to *run leaner operations*. For example, Papa John's Pizza, which topped the *Business Week* list, restricted its menu to pizza, breadsticks, cheesesticks, and soft drinks, while offering a small tub of garlic butter and two hot peppers with each pizza as a value-added item. They also have three centralized commissaries that make all the sauce and dough for their 485 stores, which brings costs down substantially while also producing revenue.

A fourth way these companies have achieved high growth is by offering a *unique, innovative product or service*. This is the strategy of Davidson & Associates, the highly successful educational and entertainment software company that has looked at software development from a child's point of view and has succeeded in bringing technology to education.

Factors that Affect Growth

The degree and rate at which a new venture grows are dependent on both the market and the management strategy. Market factors that affect a firm's ability to grow include:

The size, characteristics, and buying power of the target market. If the niche market into which the company is entering is by nature small and relatively stable as to growth, it will be more difficult to achieve the spectacular growth and size of the fastest growing companies. On the other hand, if the product or service can expand to a global market, growth and size are more likely to be attained.

The nature of the competition. Entering a market dominated by large companies is not in and of itself an automatic deterrent to growth. A small, well-organized company is often able to produce its product or service at a very competitive price while maintaining high quality standards because it doesn't have the enormous overhead and management salaries of the larger companies. Moreover, if an industry is an old, established one, entering with an innovative product in a niche market can produce rapid rates of growth.

The degree of product innovation in the market. In some industries like the computer industry, innovation is a given, so merely offering an innovative product is not in itself enough. In highly innovative industries, the key to rapid growth is the ability to design and produce a product more quickly than competitors. By contrast, in an industry that is stable and offers products and services that could be considered commodities, entering with an innovative product or process will provide a significant competitive advantage.

The status of intellectual property rights like patents, copyrights, trademarks, and trade secrets. Intellectual property rights are also a competitive advantage to a new venture as they permit a grace period in which to introduce the product or service before anyone else can copy it. However, relying on proprietary rights alone is not wise. It is important to have a comprehensive marketing plan that allows the new business to secure a strong foothold in the market before someone attempts to reproduce the product and compete with it. True, you have the right to take someone who infringes on your proprietary rights to court, but it is a time consuming and costly process, one which the small company can ill afford to undertake at a time when it needs all its excess capital for growth.

The volatility of the industry. Some industries are by their very nature volatile; that is, it is difficult to predict what will happen for any length of time and with any degree of accuracy. The computer industry in the 1980s was such an industry; it has lately become somewhat more predictable as the leading players in the industry have emerged. The young and dynamic telecommunications industry, however, is very volatile at this time. Consequently there are opportunities for extraordinary growth in new ventures and, at the same time, a higher risk of failure. A new entry into such an industry needs to maintain a constant awareness of potential government regulations, directions the industry is taking, and emerging competitors.

The barriers to entry. Some industries, simply by their size and maturity, make it difficult for a new venture to enter and achieve sufficient market share to make a profit. Others by the cost of participating (plant and equipment or fees and regulations) in the industry prohibit entry by new ventures. Yet, in the right industry a new venture can erect barriers of its own to slow down the entry of competing companies. Proprietary rights on products, designs, or processes, for example, can effectively erect a temporary barrier to allow the new venture a window of opportunity to gain market share.

Management factors that affect a firm's ability to grow include:

The entrepreneur's ability to move from controlling all aspects of the company to delegating authority and responsibility for major functions. Rapid growth requires different skills from start-up skills. In the beginning of a new venture, the entrepreneur has more time to take part in and even control all aspects of the business. But when rapid growth begins to occur, systems must be in place to handle the increased demand without sacrificing quality and service. Unless the entrepreneur is able to bring in key management who have experience in high-growth companies, chances are the growth will falter, the window of opportunity will be lost, and the business may even fail needlessly. Many entrepreneurs have found that at some point in the business's growth, they must step down and allow experienced management to take over.

The ability to encourage entrepreneurship in the entire venture team. Growing the business does not have to mean that the entrepreneurial spirit is lost, but the entrepreneur has to be very creative about how to maintain that sense of small-ness and flexibility while growing. Subcontracting some aspects of the business is one way to keep the number of employees down and retain that team spirit. Developing self-managing teams is another way.

Stages of Growth in a New Venture

Rates and stages of growth in a new venture vary by industry and business type; however, there appear to be some common issues that arise at shared points in time. The importance of knowing when these issues will surface cannot be overstated, for they should become part of a well-orchestrated plan on the part of the entrepreneur to anticipate events and requirements before they occur. The stages of growth (see Figure 16.1) can be defined as four phases through which the business must pass to move to the next level of activity.

Figure 16.1: Phases of Growth

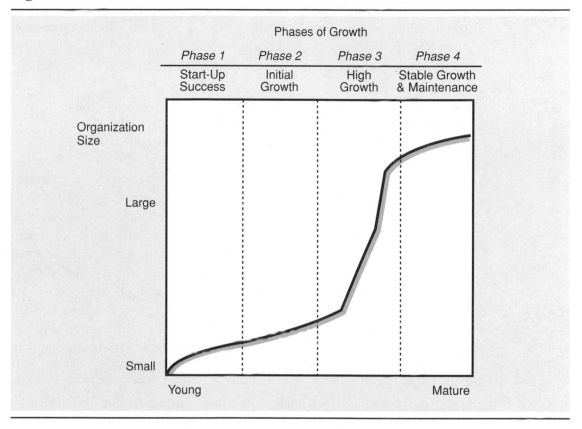

Start-Up Success. At the first level, the main concerns for the entrepreneur are to ensure sufficient start-up capital, seek customers, and design a way to deliver the product or service. At this point, the entrepreneur is a jack of all trades, doing everything that needs to be done to get the business up and running. This includes securing suppliers, distributors, facilities, equipment, and labor.

Initial Growth. If the new venture makes it through the first and most difficult phase, it enters the second level of activity with a viable business that has enough customers to keep it running. Now the concerns become more focused on the issue of cash flow. Can the business generate sufficient cash flow to pay all the expenses and support the growth of the company? At this point, the business is usually relatively small with few employees and the entrepreneur still playing an integral role. This is a crucial stage for the business, for it is here that the business will either remain small or move to the next level, high growth, which entails some significant changes in the organization and strategy of the business. The owners need to decide if they are going to grow the business to a much larger revenue level or remain stable yet profitable.

High Growth.   If the decision is to grow, all the resources of the business have to be gathered together to finance the growth of the company. This is a very risky stage as growth is expensive, and there are no guarantees the entrepreneur will be successful at attempting to reach the next level. Planning and control systems must be in place and professional management hired. The problems faced in this stage center on maintaining control of rapid growth. This is accomplished successfully by delegating control and accountability at various levels and usually fails due to uncontrolled growth, running out of cash, and not having the necessary management expertise to deal with the situation. If growth is accomplished, it is in this stage that entrepreneurs often sell the company at a substantial profit, assuming it will remain successful in its growth. It is also at this stage that some entrepreneurs are displaced by their boards of directors, investors, or creditors, so many entrepreneurial ventures reach their pinnacle of growth with an entirely different management team than the one that founded the company.

Stable Growth and Maintenance.   Assuming the business has successfully passed through the rapid growth phase and is able to effectively manage the financial gains of growth, it will have reached Phase 4, stable growth and maintenance of market share. Here the business, which is usually now large, can remain in a fairly stable condition as long as it continues to be innovative, competitive, and flexible. If it does not, sooner or later, it will begin to lose market share and could ultimately fail or revert back to a much smaller business. Allowing decision making at the lowest levels in small operating units is one way to permit the company to continue to grow without losing that entrepreneurial spirit and flexibility.

High-tech companies seem to be an exception to the traditional growth patterns. Because they typically start with solid venture capital funding and a strong management team (dictated by the venture capitalists), they move out of Phases 1 and 2 very rapidly. During Phases 3 and 4, if the structure is effective, they become hugely successful. If, on the other hand, the structure is weak, they can fail rapidly.

Problems with Growth

New business growth, for the most part, is a very positive thing; however, it does bring with it some issues for which the entrepreneur must be prepared. For example, if the new venture is a retail business, and you expand by opening additional stores, you need to decide whether or not to retain control of all functions in one main store, or delegate the day-to-day management and solely control marketing, accounting, finance, and purchasing. It may be necessary to establish a computer network to keep track of sales at all locations. For a manufacturing firm, expansion may entail significant capital investment in additional plant and equipment, or developing new strategic alliances to keep production in line with demand. It may also mean locating additional distributors and even new channels of distribution. For a service business, growth may mean taking on additional associates or employees and investing in computer systems to manage information.

This chapter looks at several strategies for growing the business:

- **Intensive growth strategies,** those that exploit opportunity in the current market
- **Integrative growth strategies,** those that involve growth within the industry as a whole
- **Diversification strategies,** those that exploit opportunities outside the current market or industry
- **Global strategies,** those that take the business into the international arena

Intensive Growth Strategies: Growing within the Current Market

Intensive growth strategies focus on exploiting the current market fully, that is, expanding the market share to the greatest extent possible. This is accomplished by increasing the volume of sales to current customers and the number of customers in the target market. There are generally three methods for implementing an intensive growth strategy: market penetration, market development, and product development.

Market Penetration

With market penetration, the entrepreneur attempts to increase sales using more effective marketing strategies within the current target market. The classic example of this strategy is the repositioning of Arm & Hammer Baking Soda. The manufacturer began advertising and educating its customers about additional uses for the product beyond cooking, such as a refrigerator deodorizer, a toothpaste, and a cleaning agent. Having additional uses for the product causes customers to buy more. Another way to employ market penetration is to attract customers from your competitors by advertising product qualities, service, or price that distinguishes your product from others. A third way is to educate nonusers of product or service as to its benefits in an effort to increase the customer base.

Market Development

Market development consists of taking the product or service to a broader geographic area. For example, if you have been marketing on the East Coast, you may decide to expand across the rest of the United States. One of the most popular ways to expand a market geographically is to **franchise** because it is generally less costly than setting up a national distribution system. Franchising allows the business to grow quickly in several geographic markets at once. The franchiser sells to the franchisee the right to do business under a particular name; the right to a product, process, or service; training and assistance in setting up the business as well as ongoing marketing and quality control support once the business is established. The franchisee pays a fee and a royalty on sales, typically three to eight percent. What the franchisee may get for the fee, depending on the business, is:

- A product or service that has a proven market
- Trade names and/or trademarks
- A patented design, process, or formula
- An accounting and financial control system
- A marketing plan
- The benefit of volume purchasing and advertising

Franchises generally come in three types. Dealerships allow manufacturers to distribute products without having to do the day-to-day work of retailing. Dealers benefit from combined marketing strength, but are often required to meet quotas. Service franchises provide customers with services such as tax preparation, temporary employees, payroll preparation, and real estate services. Often the business is already in operation before it applies to become a franchise member. The most popular type of franchise is one that offers a product, a brand name, and an operating model. Some examples are Kentucky Fried Chicken and Golf USA.

Franchising is not without its risks, however. It is virtually like creating a whole new business, because the entrepreneur must carefully document all processes and procedures in a manual that will be used to train the franchisees. Potential franchisees need to be scrutinized to ensure they are qualified to assume the responsibilities of a franchise. Moreover, the cost of preparing a business to franchise is considerable and includes legal, accounting, consulting, and training expenses. Then, too, it may take quite a long time to show a profit, as many as three to five years.

Not all businesses are suitable for franchising as a growth strategy. A successful franchise system will need to have the following characteristics:

- A successful prototype store (or preferably stores) with proven profitability and a good reputation so the potential franchisee will begin with instant recognition
- Registered trademarks and a consistent image and appearance for all outlets
- A business that can be systematized and easily replicated many times
- A product that can be sold in a variety of geographic regions
- Adequate funding, as establishing a successful franchise program can cost upwards of $150,000
- A well-documented prospectus that spells out the rights, responsibilities, and risks to the franchisee
- An operations manual that details every aspect of running the business
- A training and support system for franchisees both before they start the business and on-going after start-up
- Site selection criteria and architectural standards

Developing a franchise program requires the assistance of an attorney and an accountant whose advice should be carefully considered before undertaking the effort.

Product Development

The third way to exploit the current market is to develop new products and services for existing customers or offer new versions of existing products. That is the tactic of software companies, who are constantly updating software with new versions their customers must buy if they want to enjoy all the latest features. Savvy businesses get their best ideas for new products from their customers. These new ideas usually come in two forms: incremental changes in existing products or totally new products. Incremental products often come about serendipitously when engineers, sales personnel, and management spend time out in the marketplace with the customers learning more about their needs. Bringing all these team members together on a weekly basis to discuss ideas helps the business to quickly zero in on those incremental products that are possible within the current operating structure and budget. The advantage of incremental products is that since they are based on existing products, they can usually be designed and manufactured fairly quickly.

New or breakthrough products, on the other hand, have a much longer product development cycle and are therefore more costly to undertake. Breakthrough products cannot be planned for; instead, they usually come about through brainstorming, exercises in creativity, and problem-solving sessions. In other words, if the entrepreneur creates a business environment that encourages creative, "off-the-wall" thinking, the chances are greater that it will eventually come up with breakthrough products. The breakthrough environment of necessity has no budget or time constraints and does not run on a schedule. A combination of incremental and breakthrough products is probably the most effective way to go. The speed and cost efficiency of the incremental products keeps cash flowing into the business that helps fund the more costly breakthrough products.

Branding

The most successful entrepreneurs recognize the power of a brand name; therefore, they strive to gain brand-name recognition for their products and services as quickly as possible so they can use the recognition to create a family of related products and services under that name. A company that is able to establish brand recognition will find its marketing effort that much easier and its costs reduced. A brand name that reflects quality, service, and value is an asset that can ultimately generate huge profits for the business. One example of the value of brand name recognition is the T-shirt industry. Companies like Mossimo and Nike buy basic T-shirts from an apparel manufacturer and then print their design and logo on the shirt. Customers will pay more for a T-shirt with the Mossimo name on it than they will for the same T-shirt with an unknown company name on it—that's brand recognition.

To establish brand recognition:

• Know what you're good at. In other words, list the strengths your company and its products possess. For example, do you offer a higher quality product, a wider range of accessories or models, or exciting new colors?

- Educate customers about your strengths. Once you have identified your core strengths, communicate them over and over again in all your marketing efforts, from brochures to signs to advertising. They should literally become a mantra for the customer. The minute customers think of your product, they should associate it with its strengths.

- Develop a set of rules for using the brand name. If you want your brand name to only be associated with wholesome things, you probably would not want to advertise during a television show that contained violence, for example. How the brand name will be used also needs to be decided. Gentech Corporation, for instance, wanted the trade name for their product, *PowerSource*, always to be associated with the company name, so in all its advertising and promotion, the product is referred to as the Gentech *PowerSource*. In this way, when additional products are developed in the future, the common thread will be the company name, Gentech.

- Get feedback on brand-name recognition. To make sure the brand name is achieving the recognition level you are seeking, check periodically with the target customer.

Once brand name recognition has been established, take advantage of it by developing related products under the same brand name. This only works, however, when you are offering new benefits to your target market or taking the same benefits to a new market. If you take a new product to a new market, the brand recognition will not necessarily follow.

Integrative Growth Strategies—Growing within the Industry

Traditionally when entrepreneurs have wanted to grow their businesses within their industry, they have looked to vertical and horizontal integration strategies, but with the mantra of the 1990s being "lean and mean," entrepreneurs with growing businesses are more often than not looking to a modular or network strategy. This section examines all three strategies.

Vertical Integration Strategies

An entrepreneurial venture can grow by moving backward or forward within the distribution channel. With a backward strategy the company either gains control of some or all of its suppliers, or it becomes its own supplier by starting another business from scratch or acquiring an existing supplier that has a successful operation. This has been a common strategy for businesses that have instituted a just-in-time inventory control system. By acquiring the core supplier(s), the entrepreneur can streamline the production process and cut costs. With a forward strategy, the company attempts to control the distribution of its products by either selling directly to the customer (i.e. acquiring a retail outlet) or acquiring the distributors of its products. This strategy gives the business more control over how its products are marketed.

Horizontal Integration Strategies

Another way to grow the business within the current industry is to buy up competitors or start a competing business (i.e. sell the same product under another label). For example, suppose you own a chain of sporting goods outlets. You could purchase a business that has complementary products such as a batting cage business so your customers can buy their bats, balls, helmets, and so forth from the retail store and use them at the batting cage.

Another example of growing horizontally is to agree to manufacture your product under a different label. New York designer Mark Eisen manufactures a line of clothes for Spiegel Catalog under a different name in addition to his designer label line. This strategy has been used frequently in the major appliance and grocery industries. Whirlpool, for example, produced Sears' Kenmore washers and dryers for years. Likewise, major food producers put their brand name food items into packaging labeled with the name of a major grocery store.

Modular or Network Strategies

The latest way to grow within your own industry is to focus on what you do best and let others do the rest. If the core activities of the business include designing and developing new products for the consumer market, other companies can make the parts, assemble the products, and market and deliver them. In essence, your company with its core activities becomes the hub of the wheel with the best suppliers and distributors as the spokes. By doing this, the business can grow more rapidly, keep unit costs down, and turn out new products more quickly. In addition, the capital saved by not having to invest in fixed assets can be directed to those activities that provide a competitive advantage. The electronics and apparel industries used this growth strategy long before it became trendy. Today many other industries are beginning to see the advantages to a modular approach. Even service businesses can benefit from outsourcing functions like accounting, payroll, and data processing, which require costly labor. The key to success with a network strategy such as this is to have a good relationship with suppliers and distributors so that as the business begins to grow rapidly, they are willing to ramp up to meet demand.

Diversification Growth Strategies—Growing Outside the Industry

When entrepreneurs expand their businesses by investing in or acquiring products or businesses outside their core competencies and industry, they are employing a diversification growth strategy. Usually, but not always, this strategy is used when the entrepreneur has exhausted all growth strategies within the current market and industry and now wants to make use of excess capacity or spare resources, adapt to the needs of customers, or change the direction of the company because of impending changes in the market or economy. The latter is exemplified by the collapse of the Houston oil economy in 1984. Many entrepreneurs who saw their oil ventures drying up found they had to diversify into new product lines or services to survive and grow.

One way to diversify is to use a **synergistic strategy** where you attempt to locate new products or businesses technologically complementary to your business. For example, a food processor may acquire a restaurant chain that can serve as a showcase for the food. Another way to diversify is to employ a strategy where you acquire products or services that are *unrelated* to your core products or services. For example, a manufacturer of bicycle helmets may acquire an apparel manufacturer to make clothing with the company logo on it to sell to helmet customers. A final strategy for diversifying is called **conglomerate diversification** and involves acquiring businesses that are not at all related in any way to what you are currently doing. An entrepreneur might use this strategy to gain control of a related function of doing business—for example, purchasing the building in which the business is housed and then leasing out excess space to other businesses to produce additional income and gain a depreciable asset. Many entrepreneurs whose work causes them to travel extensively find it advantageous to acquire a travel agency to reduce costs and provide greater convenience.

A diversification strategy for growth is not something to undertake without careful consideration of all the factors and potential outcomes, particularly when it involves an acquisition. While it is true that the entrepreneur can find consultants who are experts in mergers and acquisitions to help smooth the path financially and operationally, what is difficult to predict with any degree of certainty is how the cultures of the two businesses will merge. Acquisitions and mergers cannot be successful based on financial and operational synergy alone. Organizational styles and individual personalities of key management all come into play when an acquisition or merger takes place. As a result, the human side of the two businesses must be analyzed and a plan developed for merging two potentially distinct cultures into one that can work effectively.

PROFILE 16.1

The Case of a Commercial Printer[1]

Quick Press is a commercial printer located in Connecticut. Its owner/entrepreneur, Sam Quick, saw significant changes beginning to take place in the printing industry toward the end of the 1980s. It was obvious that traditional printing methods were being overtaken by desktop publishing via computers. Not wishing to become an obsolete business, he hired a computer consultant to determine the best way to computerize the company so it could continue to grow. The consultant informed Quick that the cost would be high and the learning curve steep. It was then that Quick decided it might be more cost efficient to acquire a company that already had the capability he needed.

In 1991, Quick was able to buy such a company, Graphical Arts. On the surface the deal appeared to have synergy. With the capabilities of the two companies, Quick could offer their customers a wider variety of services and could also do some of the work in-house that he had previously had to outsource, tasks like color-scanning. However, many of Quick's customers are large companies who have also gone to doing much of their printing in-house. The marketplace is extremely competitive with very tight margins.

The first thing Quick found out after the acquisition had taken place was that much of the technological expertise for which he paid, although excellent, was still in the R&D stage; this started things off on the wrong foot. The next problem was the clash of cultures. There were significant differences in management style and workplace attitude, with the Quick Press employees being a more laid-back group and the Graphical Arts employees much more disciplined, professional, and serious. With no preparation for the merger, it was no surprise that the two groups found it difficult to adjust. The bottom line is that the acquisition definitely positioned the company for future growth, but until the people issues were resolved, that growth remained stalled.

---

[1]The actual names of the parties in this case are not being used.

Many researchers have attempted to determine the most effective growth strategy for a new venture. In general, it has been found that horizontal integration, vertical integration, and synergistic diversification have been more successful than unrelated diversification. This is true whether the entrepreneur acquires an existing company or starts another company to achieve the goal. This is not to say that unrelated diversification should never be chosen as a growth strategy. If the potential gains are by comparison extraordinarily high, the risk may be worth the taking. It is also generally true that an acquired business has a better chance of success than a start-up for the obvious reason that it has usually already passed the crucial two stages of start-up and survival and is more likely to be poised to grow.

Growing by Going Global

Today the question for a growth-oriented company is not *should we go global*, but *when should we go global?* There are many reasons why entrepreneurial ventures must consider the global market even as early as the development of their original business plan. Today technology is not the sole province of the United States. Gone are the days when the United States could ship its obsolete technology to other countries to extend its market life. Other countries now expect to receive the latest technology in the goods they purchase, and it may not always come with a United States label on it. In fact, the United States, while a huge market, represents less than half of the total global market.

Furthermore, due to rapidly changing technology, product lives are increasingly shorter and with R&D being so expensive, companies are forced to enter several major markets at once to gain the maximum advantage from the window of opportunity. Entrepreneurs who attend world trade shows know their strongest competition may as easily come from a country in the Pacific Rim as from the company next door. Entrepreneurs also know they may have to rely on other countries for supplies, parts, and even fabrication to keep costs down and remain competitive.

With increasing competition and saturated markets in some industries, looking to global markets can add a new dimension to the entrepreneur's business. Many entrepreneurs have found new applications for their products in other countries or complementary products that help increase the sales of their product domestically. Several events have made exporting United States products to other countries more attractive than ever before.

- Relatively low United States interest rates have made it easier for businesses to finance the exporting of their products.
- The North American Free Trade Agreement (NAFTA) eliminates trade barriers among the United States, Mexico, and Canada, which makes exporting to those countries more attractive.
- The decline of the U.S. dollar, while not good for U.S. travelers in other countries, certainly makes U.S. goods more affordable for other countries.
- The opening up and growth of untapped markets like China and Vietnam means more potential customers for U.S. products.
- The establishment of the first four Federal Export Assistance Centers give businesses considering exporting a new source of help. The four centers are located in Baltimore, Long Beach, Miami, and Chicago.
- The Uruguay Round of GATT (the General Agreement on Tariffs and Trade) potentially will reduce or eliminate tariffs among 117 countries starting in 1995. It will also provide for improved patent and copyright protection, which has been a problem for businesses exporting protected products to other countries where proprietary rights may not be recognized or protected.

While you should include a global strategy in any business planning, you will probably not be able to export until the business is somewhat established and offering a high-quality product or service at a competitive price. Exporting is a long-term commitment that may not pay off for some time. During that period you may have to adapt the product or service somewhat to meet the requirements of the importing country and develop good relationships with agents in the country. If you are dealing in consumer products, target countries that have disposable income and like American products. If, on the other hand, you are dealing in basic or industrial products, look to developing countries that need equipment and services for building infrastructures and systems. One example is Mexico, which is taking on the enormous task of building bridges and roads as it positions itself as a major player in the world market.

Finding the Best Global Market

Finding the best market for a product or service can be a daunting task, but there are some sources and tactics that help make the job easier. Start with the *International Trade Statistics Yearbook of the United States,* which is available in any major library. Using the SITC (United Nation's Standard Industrial Trade Classification) codes found in this reference book, you can find information on international demand for your product or service in specific countries. The

SITC system is a way of classifying commodities used in international trade. You should also be familiar with the Harmonized System of classification, which is a ten-digit system that puts the U.S. "in harmony" with most of the world in terms of commodity tracking systems. If your international shipment exceeds $2,500, you must know your HS number for documentation.

Demand for American products is usually reflected in three areas:

1. The dollar value of worldwide imports of a specific type of product to a country
2. The level of growth of these imports as seen by import demand records over time. Look for a country whose level of import demand exceeds worldwide averages for a product or service.
3. The share of total import demand to a country that is enjoyed by U.S. products. This figure should exceed five percent. A lower figure could indicate that tariffs might be affecting growth.

Consult additional sources of information like the District Office or the Washington DC office of the International Trade Administration, and the Department of Commerce (DOC). The Commerce Department's database links all the DOC International Trade Administration offices and provides a wealth of valuable research information.

The successful launch of a program of global growth should include a marketing plan and budget directed toward that goal in the business plan. You also need to bring someone onto the team who has international management experience or export experience. Depending on your budget, you may choose to hire a consultant who specializes in this area. It is also important to attend foreign trade shows to learn how businesses in the countries in which you are interested conduct business, who the major players are, and who the competition is. Finally, this chapter cannot present all the detailed information needed before beginning to export. Consulting a source dedicated to exporting, such as Jack Wolf's *Export Profits* (Upstart Publishing), is a must.

Export Financing

To make a sale in the global market, the entrepreneur must have the funds to purchase the raw materials or inventory to fill the order. Unfortunately, many entrepreneurs assume that if they have a large enough order, getting financing will be no problem. Nothing could be further from the truth. Export lenders, like traditional lending sources, want to know that the entrepreneur has a sound business plan and has the resources to fill the orders. Entrepreneurs desiring to export can look for capital from several sources:

- Bank financing
- Internal cash flow from the business
- Venture capital or private investor capital
- Prepayment, down payment, or progress payments from the foreign company making the order

A commercial bank is more interested in lending money to a small exporter if the entrepreneur has secured a guarantee of payment from a governmental agency such as the Import-Export Bank, which limits the risk undertaken by the bank. Asking buyers to pay a deposit up front, enough to cover the purchase of raw materials, can also be a real asset to a young company with limited cash flow.

Foreign Agents, Distributors, and Trading Companies

Every country has a number of sales representatives, agents, and distributors who specialize in importing American goods. It is possible to find one agent who can handle an entire country or region, but if a country has several economic centers, it may be more effective to have a different agent for each center. **Sales representatives** work on commission; they do not buy and hold products. Consequently, the entrepreneur is still left with the job of collecting receivables which, particularly when you're dealing with a foreign country, can be costly and time consuming.

Agents are a way to circumvent this problem. Agents purchase your product at a discount (generally very large) off list and then sell it and handle collections themselves. They solve the issue of cultural differences and the ensuing problems inherent in these transactions. Of course, with an agent you lose control over what happens to the product once it leaves your hands. You have no say over what the agent actually charges customers in his or her own country. If the agent charges too much in an effort to make more money for himself, you may lose a customer. If you are just starting to export or if you are exporting to areas not large enough to warrant an agent, consider putting an ad in American trade journals that showcase American products internationally. If you are producing a technical product, you may be able to find a manufacturer in the international region you are targeting who will let you sell your products through their company, thus giving you instant recognition in the foreign country. Ultimately, they could also become a source of financing for your company.

Another option is to use an Export Trading Company (ETC) that specializes in certain countries or regions where they have established a network of sales representatives. ETCs may also specialize in certain types of products. What often happens is that a sales rep may report to the ETC that a particular country is interested in a certain product. The ETC then locates a manufacturer, buys the product, and sells it in the foreign country. Trading companies are a particularly popular vehicle when dealing with Japan.

Choosing an Intermediary

Before deciding on an intermediary to handle the exporting of your products:

1. Check their current listing of products to see if your company seems to fit in with their expertise.
2. Understand with whom will you be competing; that is, does the intermediary also handle your competitors?
3. Find out if the intermediary has enough representatives in the foreign country to adequately handle the market.
4. Look at the sales volume of the intermediary. It should show a rather consistent level of growth.
5. Make sure the intermediary has sufficient warehouse space and up-to-date communication systems.
6. Examine the marketing plan.
7. If needed, make sure the intermediary can handle servicing your product.

Once you have decided on the intermediary, draft an agreement detailing the terms and conditions of the relationship. As it is very much like a partnership agreement, consult an attorney specializing in overseas contracts. The most important thing to remember about the contract is that it must be based on performance so you do not tie yourself up for many years with someone who is not moving enough product for you. Negotiate a one- or two-year contract with an option to renew should performance goals be met. This will probably not please the intermediary as most want a five- to ten-year contract. Be firm; it is not in your best interests to do a longer contract until you know that the person is loyal and can perform. Other issues that should be addressed in the agreement include:

- Your ability to use another distributor; in other words, negotiate for a nonexclusive contract so you have some flexibility and control over the situation.

- The specific products the agent or distributor will represent. This is important because as your company grows, you may add or develop additional products and not want this agent to sell those products.
- The specific geographic territories for which the agent or distributor will be responsible.
- The specific duties and responsibilities of the agent or distributor.
- A statement of agreed-upon sales quotas.
- A statement of the jurisdiction in which any dispute would be litigated. This will protect you from having to go to a foreign country to handle a dispute.

Choosing a Freight Forwarder

The freight forwarder's job is to handle all aspects of delivering the product to the customer. The method by which you ship a product has a significant impact on the product's cost or the price to the customer, depending on how the deal is structured, so consider the choice of a freight forwarder carefully. The ability to fill a shipping container to capacity is crucial to reducing costs. Freight forwarders prepare the shipping documents, which include a bill of lading (the contract between the shipper and the carrier) and an exporter declaration form detailing the contents of the shipment, and they can present shipping documents to your bank for collection. The entrepreneur, however, is responsible for knowing if any items being shipped require special licenses or certificates, as in the case of hazardous materials or certain food substances.

Additional Sources for Exporting

Directory of American Firms Operating in Foreign Countries	*Major Companies of the Far East*
	Moody's International Manual
Europa World Year Book	*Predicast's F&S International Index*
European Directory of Marketing Information Sources	*Predicast's F&S Index Europe*
Exporters Encyclopedia	*U.S. Importers and Exporters Directory*
Guide to Canadian Manufacturers	*United Nations Statistical Yearbook*
International Marketing Handbook	*Worldcasts*
Japan Trade Directory	

Global Franchising

The first franchisors on the global scene were primarily the large food franchises such as MacDonalds, Kentucky Fried Chicken, and Burger King. Today even smaller franchisors are going global. Franchisors are generally welcomed by foreign governments because they bring not only a product to the country but a way of doing business, which provides jobs for the citizens of the country. Those who have chosen to try their luck in developing countries or the old Eastern Block countries have consistently found the cost of doing business there much higher. In addition, they are likely to have to deal with unstable governments, volatile currencies, and a general lack of understanding of competitive market systems. Many international franchisors have discovered that having a local partner is one of the keys to a successful global effort because it allows them to acquire an understanding of the business and consumer culture in the country. They also tend to look to establish master franchise agreements, which gives the franchisee the rights to the entire country or region.

One of the challenges facing international franchisors is achieving the same level of productivity and service they experience in the United States. In some countries low productivity is simply a way of life, and changing old habits can require hours of training. One source of help for potential international franchisors is the International Franchise Association (IFA) located in Washington, DC. This organization has established a Code of Ethics and, through its Franchisee Advisory Council, provides dispute resolution for both franchisees and franchisors.

PROFILE 16.2

Domino's Goes Global

Domino's went into Japan literally against all odds. Other pizza companies had failed, suggesting that the Japanese simply didn't like pizza. Moreover, free delivery, which was the way Domino's had differentiated itself in the domestic market, was an expected service in the Japanese market. Still, after extensive research, Domino's decided to move ahead and successfully captured the Japanese market by reducing the size of their pizzas to accommodate the smaller appetites of the Japanese customer, using scooters to maneuver the crowded streets, and creating exciting packaging and brochures, which the Japanese appreciate. Today Domino's stores in Japan do twice the volume of those in the United States.

To Grow or Not to Grow ...

Some entrepreneurs make a conscious choice to control growth even in the face of extraordinary market demand. This is not to say growth is slowed to single digits. Instead the entrepreneur may choose to maintain a stable growth rate of 35 to 45 percent per year rather than subject the young venture to a roller coaster ride in the triple digits. In general, entrepreneurs who restrain growth do so because they are in the business for the long term, so they don't advertise heavily or aggressively seek new customers beyond their capabilities. Instead, they diversify their product or service line from the beginning to make themselves independent of problems that may face their customers or their industries.

It is intoxicating for a new venture to realize potential demand is great and that the company could virtually fly off the scales in terms of industry averages. But "speed of light" growth has destroyed many companies that did not have the capacity, skills, or systems in place to meet demand. The growth phase of a new business can be one of the most exciting times for an entrepreneur. But if the entrepreneur has not prepared for growth with a coherent plan and budget to match, it can be instead a disastrous time for an otherwise successful start-up. The keys to successful growth are to be the best at what you do, be the first in the market where possible, operate lean and mean, offer something unique, and *have a plan.*

☑ New Venture Checklist

Have you

- ☐ Identified market factors that may affect the growth of the business?
- ☐ Determined which growth strategy is most appropriate?
- ☐ Identified potential international markets for the product or service?
- ☐ Developed a plan for globalization of the company at some point in the future?

Additional Sources of Information

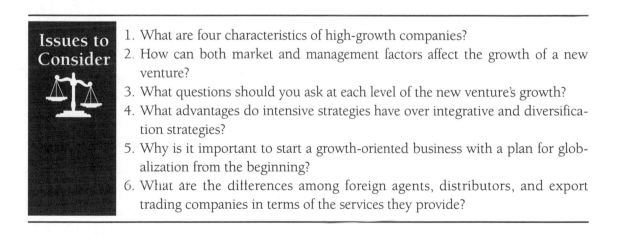

Commerce Department, "Flash Facts," a 24-hour free fax line for information on specific international regions. Eastern Europe, 202-482-5745; Mexico, 202-482-4464; Pacific Basin, 202-482-3875; Africa, Near East, and South Asia, 202-482-1064.

Commerce Department—District Offices. *The Export Yellow Pages,* includes U.S. export companies, intermediaries, and freight forwarders.

Export-Import Bank, Washington, D.C. 202-566-4490, for a list of lenders who handle international transactions.

Export-Import Bank's City/State Program, 800-424-5201.

Rager, L. (June 1989). "How to Expand by Franchising." *Nation's Business.*

Roberts, M.L. & Berger, P.D. (1989). *Direct Marketing Management.* Englewood Cliffs, NJ: Prentice-Hall, Inc.

Trade Information Center, 800-USA-TRADE (800-872-8723). Ask for an industry desk officer who specializes in your industry.

U.S. Small Business Administration, *Bankable Deals,* a book on export finance, 202-205-6720. Also has lists of trade events.

Wolf, J.S. (1992). *Export Profits.* Dover, NH: Upstart Publishing Company, Inc.

Issues to Consider

1. What are four characteristics of high-growth companies?
2. How can both market and management factors affect the growth of a new venture?
3. What questions should you ask at each level of the new venture's growth?
4. What advantages do intensive strategies have over integrative and diversification strategies?
5. Why is it important to start a growth-oriented business with a plan for globalization from the beginning?
6. What are the differences among foreign agents, distributors, and export trading companies in terms of the services they provide?

CHAPTER 17

Financing Growth

Overview

- *The nature of the venture capital industry*
- *How to obtain venture capital*
- *Using the Private Placement Memorandum to raise growth capital*
- *Going public*
- *Using strategic alliances as a growth vehicle*
- *Valuing the growing venture*

Finding Growth Capital

Seed capital is the money the entrepreneur raised or used to develop and start the business. Growth capital, or second round financing, refers to those funds needed to take the venture out of the start-up phase and move it toward becoming a contender in the global marketplace. To the extent that the entrepreneur has met the sales and earnings targets estimated in the start-up business plan, the choices available increase substantially when growth financing is sought. The fact that more choices are available is important because the amount of money needed to grow the business is normally significantly larger than that required to start the business. One exception is high-tech companies that incur considerable R&D costs prior to start-up. These types of companies may spend millions of dollars and accrue several years of negative income before their first sale.

Most venture capital today is still going to the biotechnology, software, and computer ventures, but, in general, the best companies in any industry have the easiest time finding capital. To become one of the "best" companies requires an excellent track record (however short), a sound management team, and potential for high growth. Often the bottom line criterion for securing a bank loan is to be a company that doesn't really need the money. The same can be said for suppliers of growth capital. They typically will not go into a situation where their "new money" is paying off "old debt," or where a company has poor cash flow. They want to know that the infrastructure is in place, sales are increasing, and the growing venture needs capital only to take that next leap up the sales ladder.

Make no mistake about it, raising growth capital is a time-consuming and costly process. Many entrepreneurs opt instead for growing slowly, depending exclusively on internal cash flow to fund growth. They have a basic fear of debt and giving up any control of the company to investors. This attitude is fine if it works, but new ventures that begin with obvious high-growth potential will find themselves hamstrung and frustrated by a level of growth that prohibits them from meeting demand. Plan for growth from the very beginning so you will be prepared for the expense and the demands on your time when they come.

> *The first thing to understand about raising growth capital is that it will invariably take at least twice as long as you thought.*

The first thing to understand about raising growth capital (or any capital for that matter) is that it will invariably take at least twice as long as you thought to actually have the money in the company's bank account. If you are attempting to raise a substantial amount of money, several million dollars for instance, you can expect it to take possibly several months to find the financing, several more months for the potential investor or lender to do due diligence and say yes, and then up to six months more to receive the money. In other words, don't wait to look for funding until you need it; it will be too late, which—if you're not prepared with a backup source—could spell disaster for the business. Moreover, as this search for capital can take the entrepreneur away from the business when he or she is needed most, it is helpful to use financial advisors who have experience raising money, and to have a good management team in place so you don't have to worry about the business while you're out seeking money.

The second thing to understand about raising growth capital is to never rely on the person you have identified as the financial source to actually come through for you. Keep looking for additional investors, if only as backups, because you may ultimately determine that the terms of the first investor are not compatible with your goals. Often second round financiers request a buy-out of the first round funding sources, who could be friends or family, because they feel the first round has nothing more to contribute to the business and they no longer want to deal with them. This can be a very awkward situation, as the second round funder has nothing to lose by demanding the buy-out. They can certainly walk away from the deal; there are thousands more out there.

In figuring out how much capital the venture needs to grow, many entrepreneurs concentrate on the cost of the capital in terms of interest rate or return on investment and fail to include the cost of seeking the capital, which can be substantial. The costs incurred before the money is received must be paid up front by the entrepreneur, while the costs of maintaining the capital can often be paid from the proceeds of the loan, or in the case of investment capital, from the proceeds of a sale or internally generated cash flow.

If the business plan and financials have been kept up-to-date after the start of the business, you have taken the first step in preparing the company for presentation to a funding source and saved some money in the process. If you are seeking capital in the millions, however, growth capital funding sources prefer that your financials have the imprimatur of a financial consultant or investment banker, someone who regularly works with investors. This person is expert in preparing loan and investment packages that are attractive to potential funding sources. Your CPA will prepare the business's financial statements and work closely with the financial consultant. All of these activities result in costs to the entrepreneur. In addition, if you are seeking equity capital, you need a prospectus or offering document, which requires legal expertise and often has significant printing costs. Then there are the costs to market the offering; such things as advertising, travel, and brochures can become quite costly.

In addition to the up-front costs of seeking growth capital, there are "back-end" costs when the entrepreneur seeks capital by selling securities (shares of stock in the corporation). These can include investment banking fees, legal fees, marketing costs, brokerage fees, and various other fees charged by state and federal authorities. The total cost of raising equity capital can go as high as 25 percent of the total amount of money sought. Add that to the interest or return on investment paid to the funding source(s) and you can see why it definitely costs money to raise money.

The Venture Capital Market

Private venture capital companies have been the bedrock of many high-growth ventures, particularly in the computer, software, biotechnology, and telecommunications industries. As venture capitalists rarely invest in start-up ventures outside the high-tech arena, the growth stage of a new venture is where most entrepreneurs consider approaching them. Waiting until this stage is advantageous to the entrepreneur because using venture capital in the start-up phase can mean giving up significant control. Private venture capital is, quite simply, a pool of money managed by professionals. These professionals usually assume the role of general partner and are paid a management fee plus a percentage of the gain from the investment by their investors. The venture capital firm takes an equity position through ownership of stock in the company. It also normally requires a seat on the board of directors and brings its professional management skills to the new venture in an advisory capacity.

In the 1980s the number of private venture capital firms grew by 199 percent, while the average amount of money under professional management grew from $2.9 billion in 1979 to over $49.5 billion in 1989. It was an easy time for entrepreneurs seeking this type of capital. However the growth in venture capital firm formation peaked in 1987 and has been on the decline ever since. One reason is the relative demise of the junk bond market, and with it the leveraged buy-out and mergers and acquisitions market. Another reason is that most of the new opportunities lie with smaller, innovative companies that have not held the interest of the venture capitalists. A third reason is the poor performance of many venture capital funds, due in large part to a weak economy. Two experts on venture capital markets, Bill Bygrave and Jeff Timmons, believe the venture capital system is at a "crossroads" with the need for a new vision.[1] Others agree, calling venture capital the "incredibly shrinking venture capital industry."[2] On the other hand, the possibility of global venture capital is now very attractive. Europe, for example, has 342 million inhabitants, making it arguably the richest market in the world.

The Venture Capital Sequence of Events

To determine if venture capital is the right type of funding for the growing venture, the entrepreneur must understand the goals and motivations of venture capitalists, for they dictate the potential success or failure of the attempt. The venture capital company invests in a growing business through the use of debt and equity instruments to gain long-term appreciation on the investment within a specified period of time, typically five years. By definition, this goal is often different from that of the entrepreneur, who usually looks at the business from a much longer frame of reference. The venture capitalist (VC)

---

[1]Bygrave, W.D. & Timmons, J.A. (1992) *Venture Capital at the Crossroads.* Boston: Harvard Business School Press.

[2]*Venture Capital Journal*, Special Report, April 1990, p. 1.

also seeks varying rates of return depending on the risk involved. An early-stage investment, for example, characteristically demands a higher rate of return, as much as 50 percent or more, while a later-stage investment demands a lower rate of return, perhaps 30 percent. Very simply, as the level of risk increases, so does the demand for a higher rate of return as depicted in Figure 17.1. This relationship is certainly not surprising. Older, more established companies have a longer track record on which to make predictions about the future, so normal business cycles and sales patterns have been identified, and the company is usually in a better position to respond through experience to a dynamic environment. Consequently investing in a mature firm does not command the high rate of return that investing in a high-growth start-up does.

Usually the first thing venture capitalists look at when scrutinizing a potential investment candidate is the management team to see if experienced people with a good track record are in place and able to take the company to the next level of growth. In addition to experience, they are looking for commitment to the company and to growth because they recognize that growing a company requires an enormous amount of time and effort on the part of the management team. Once they have determined that the management team is solid, they look at the product and the market to see if the opportunity is substantial and if the product holds a unique or innovative position in the marketplace. Product uniqueness, especially if protected through intellectual property rights, helps create entry barriers in the market, commands higher prices, and adds value to the business.

Figure 17.1: Risk vs. Rate of Return

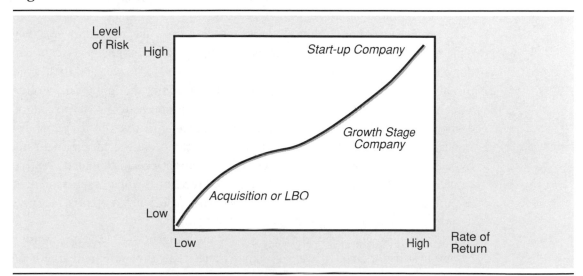

The other major factor is the potential for significant growth and the amount of growth possible, because it is from the consequent appreciation in the value of the business that the venture capitalist will derive the required return on investment. The venture capitalist weighs that potential for growth against the risk of failure and the cost to achieve the growth projected. Therefore, when negotiating with venture capitalists, the entrepreneur should have a good sense of the value of the business, a topic discussed at the end of this chapter.

Armed with an understanding of what venture capitalists are looking for, the entrepreneur is prepared to begin the search for the company that meets his or her needs. As the venture capital community is fairly close knit, at least within regions of the country, it is wise not to "shop" the business around looking for the best deal. Do some research on the venture capital firms in your state first to see if any specialize in your particular industry or type of business. Get recommendations from attorneys and accountants who regularly deal with business investments. In fact, the best way to approach a venture capitalist is through a referral from someone who knows them. Once a venture capital company has been chosen, it is preferable to stay with that company until you are certain the deal will not work. Under no circumstances should you be talking to two companies at once.

> *The best way to approach a venture capitalist is through a referral from someone who knows them.*

The venture capital company will no doubt ask for a copy of the business plan with an executive summary. The executive summary is a screening device—if it can't be immediately determined that the entrepreneurial team's qualifications are outstanding, the product concept innovative, and the projections of growth and return on investment realistic, they will not bother to read the entire business plan.

If, on the other hand, after studying the plan they like what they see, they will probably call for a meeting to determine if the entrepreneurial team can deliver what they project. This may or may not call for a formal presentation of the business by the entrepreneur. During this meeting, the initial terms of an agreement may also be discussed; however, the entrepreneur should not be too eager to discuss issues like owner compensation until the venture capitalist indicates a deal is imminent. It is also very important that the entrepreneur not hype the business concept or make claims that cannot be substantiated. Venture capitalists have literally seen it all and readily recognize when an entrepreneur is puffing. The entrepreneur should, however, disclose any potential negative aspects to the business and ways to deal with them.

If the meeting goes well, the next step is due diligence—that is, the venture capital firm has their own team of experts check out the entrepreneurial team and the business thoroughly. If they are still sold on the business, they draw up legal documents to detail the nature and terms of the investment and declare that "the check's in the mail." Don't spend the money, however, as it may take some time to receive it. Some venture capitalists wait until they know they have a satisfactory investment before putting together a partnership to actually fund the investment. Others just have a lengthy process for releasing money from the firm.

You should not be surprised if the money is released in stages based on meeting agreed-upon goals. Also realize that the venture capital firm will continue to monitor the progress of the new venture and probably want a seat on the board of directors to have a say in the direction the new venture takes.

Capital Structure

It may seem that the entrepreneur is totally at the mercy of the venture capitalist. That, unfortunately, is true if the entrepreneur enters the negotiation from a weak position, desperately needing the money to keep the business alive. A better approach is to go into the negotiation from a position of strength. True, venture capitalists have hundreds of deals presented to them on a regular basis, but most of those deals are not big hits; in other words, the return on the investment is not worth their effort. They are always looking for that one business that will achieve high growth and return them enough gain on their investment to make up for all the average or mediocre-performing investments in their portfolio. If the entrepreneur enters the negotiation with a business that has a solid record of growth and performance, he or she is in a good position to call many of the shots.

Any investment deal has four components:

- The amount of money to be invested
- The timing and use of the investment moneys
- The return on investment to investors
- The level of risk involved

How these components are defined will affect the venture for a long time, not only in constructing its growth strategy but in formulating an exit strategy.

Venture capitalists often want both equity and debt—equity because it gives them an ownership interest in the business, and debt because they will be paid back more quickly. Consequently, they tend to want redeemable preferred stock or debentures so that if the company does well, they can convert to common stock, and if the company does poorly or fails, they will be the first to be repaid their investment because they have preferred stock. If you have entered the negotiation from a position of strength, you will more likely be able to convince them to take common stock, which makes things much easier for you. In another scenario, the venture capitalists may want a combination of debentures (debt) and warrants, which allows them to purchase common stock at a nominal rate later on. If this strategy is carried out correctly, they can conceivably receive their entire investment back when the debt portion is repaid and still enjoy the appreciation in the value of the business as a stockholder.

There are several other provisions venture capitalists often ask for to protect their investment. One is an antidilution provision, which ensures that the selling of stock at a later date will not decrease the economic value of the venture capitalist's investment. In other words, the price of stock sold at a later date should be equal to or greater than the price at which the venture capitalist could buy the common stock on a conversion. One way to ensure that dilution does not occur is to have a full ratchet clause that allows the venture capitalist to buy common stock at the lowest rate at which it has been sold. For example if the lowest price at which the stock has been sold to this point is $1, then that is the conversion rate for the VC. However, if subsequently the stock is sold at $.50, then all the VC's convertible shares can be purchased at the new lowest rate. Where their $1 million investment would have bought 1 million shares at $1/share, they now can buy 2 million shares at $.50 a share, effectively reducing the equity holding of the founders.

> Venture capital is only one source, and with the advice of experts, the entrepreneur should consider all other possible avenues.

A better method from the entrepreneur's point of view is to use a weighted ratchet approach, which uses the weighted price per share of all the stock issued after the founder's stock and before the lowest stock price that will cause dilution. This is certainly fairer to the founders and prevents them from losing control of the company should the value of the stock decrease substantially.

In addition, the VC may often request a forfeiture provision, which means that if the company does not achieve its projected performance goals, the founders may be required to give up some of their stock as a penalty to the VC to guard against their having paid too much for their interest in the company. This forfeited stock increases the VC's equity in the company and may even be given to new management that the VC brings on board to steer the company in a new direction. One way to mitigate this situation is for the entrepreneur to request stock bonuses as a reward for meeting or exceeding performance projections.

Using venture capital is certainly an important source for the entrepreneur with a high-growth venture. It is, however, only one source, and with the advice of experts, the entrepreneur should consider all other possible avenues.

The best choice is one that gives the new venture the chance to reach its potential and the investors or financial backers an excellent return on investment.

Private Placement

Private placement is a way of raising capital from private investors by selling securities in a private corporation or partnership. Securities are common and preferred stock, notes, bonds, debentures, voting-trust certificates, certificates of deposit, warrants, options, subscription rights, limited partnership shares, and undivided oil or gas interests. It is a less costly, less time-consuming process than a public offering, and many states now offer standardized, easy-to-fill-out disclosure statements and offering documents.

The advantages of a private offering are many. The growing venture does not have to have a lot of assets or credit references, which they would need for bank financing, or a lengthy track record. They also don't have to file with the Securities and Exchange Commission (SEC). They do, however, have to qualify under the rules of Federal Regulation D. Not all states recognize the exemptions under Regulation D in their "Blue Sky" laws, so the issuer of a private placement memorandum may have to register with the state. Essentially, Regulation D says:

- The entrepreneur must file five copies of Form D with the SEC within 15 days after the first sale of securities, then every six months thereafter, and 30 days after the final sale.
- The entrepreneur must follow the rules for notices of sale and payment of commissions.
- Rule 504 permits the entrepreneur to sell up to $1 million worth of securities to any number of investors, whether they are sophisticated or not during a 12-month period. *Sophisticated* in this context refers to people who invest on a regular basis and have a net worth of at least $1 million.
- Rule 505 allows the founders to sell $5 million of unregistered securities in a 12-month period to up to 35 investors of any type in addition to an unlimited number of accredited investors. **Accredited investors** include institutional investors such as banks and insurance companies, investors who purchase at least $150,000 of securities in the entrepreneur's venture, investors with a net worth over $1 million or annual income of over $200,000 in the previous two years, and directors and officers of the company.
- Rule 506 allows the founders to sell an unlimited number of securities to 35 investors and unlimited accredited investors and relatives of the founders but

without general solicitation through advertising. An issuer under this rule can sell securities to accredited investors without any disclosures whatsoever. An example might be selling securities to someone with whom you have an ongoing business relationship and who qualifies as an accredited investor.

The burden is on the issuer to document that the exemption from registration requirements have been met. Therefore, the "sophistication" of all offerees should be examined closely and the reasons why they qualify carefully documented. The issuer should also number each private placement memorandum and keep a record of who has looked at the memorandum or discussed the offering with the issuer. The memorandum should have a qualifying statement on it that the contents must not be copied or disclosed to anyone other than the offeree. If an offeree becomes an investor, the issuer should document when and where the offeree examined the books and records of the company. When the offering is complete, the issuer should place a memo in the offering log stating that only those persons listed in the log have been approached regarding the offering.

> *Within the structure of the corporate private placement, the entrepreneur can sell preferred and common stock, convertible debentures, and debt securities with warrants.*

Even if the offering qualifies as exempt from registration, it is still subject to the antifraud and civil liability provisions of federal securities laws and state Blue Sky securities laws. Many states have adopted the Small Corporate Offering Registration Form, also called SCOR U-7, which makes the registration process much simpler by providing 50 fill-in-the-blank questions that ask for the basic financial, management, and marketing information for the company. Your lawyer should be consulted as some of the adopting states restrict who can use Form U-7.

Within the structure of the corporate private placement, the entrepreneur can sell preferred and common stock, convertible debentures, and debt securities with warrants. Recall that preferred stock has dividend and liquidation preference over common stock in addition to antidilution protection and other rights as may be specified in a stockholder agreement. Common stock, on the other hand, carries with it voting rights and preserves the right of the corporation to elect S-Corporation status. Convertible debentures are secured or unsecured debt instruments that can be converted to equity at a later date as specified in the agreement. In its debenture form, however, it provides for a fixed rate of return (interest), which can be deducted by the corporation. Debt securities with warrants give the holder the right to purchase stock at a fixed price for a specified term. Purchasing common stock under this instrument does not invalidate the preferred position of the debt holder as creditor.

PROFILE 17.1

The Private Placement Process

As an example of what the private placement process is like, consider the following situation of a company that wanted to raise $1 million to grow. These are the steps it took.

1. Using a SCOR software program provided by the state securities agency, the entrepreneur, Tom Lauder, wrote a prospectus detailing the terms, conditions, risks, and rewards of the offering.

2. Lauder refined the document with the aid of his attorney. The 60-page document took about three weeks to complete at a total cost of about $50,000.

3. He hired a nationally known accounting firm to audit the corporation's most recent financial statements. This cost was approximately $15,000.

4. Comparing his company with others in the industry, he was able to arrive at a value for the company of three times present earnings or $15 million.

5. He registered the corporation in ten states where the SCOR filing was permitted, with filing fees ranging from $50 to over $2,000.

6. He then had to decide to whom he should present the offering. A logical choice was his major customers and suppliers. To those people he sent an announcement of the offering. From the announcement he received requests from 3,000 people for a prospectus and from that group he received enough commitments to be fully subscribed within the year.

The Initial Public Offering (IPO)

The initial public offering, or "going public," has an aura of prestige and represents an exciting time in the life of a high-growth business. However, the decision whether or not to do a public offering is difficult at best because once the decision has been made to go ahead with the offering, a series of events is set in motion that will change the business and the relationship of the entrepreneur to the business forever. Moreover, returning to private status once the company has been a public company is an almost insurmountable task.

An initial public offering is simply a more complex version of a private offering, in which the founders and equity shareholders of the company agree to sell a portion of the company (via previously unissued stocks and bonds) to the public by filing with the Securities and Exchange Commission and listing their stock on one of the stock exchanges. All the proceeds of the IPO go to the company in a primary offering. If the owners of the company subsequently sell their shares of stock, the proceeds go to the owners in what is termed a secondary distribution. Often there is a combination of the two events; however, an offering is far less attractive when a large percentage of the proceeds are destined for the owners, as it clearly signals a lack of commitment on the part of the owners to the future success of the business.

More and more smaller corporations are using the IPO vehicle to raise growth capital; in fact, well over half of all IPOs are companies with an asset value under $500,000. This trend has been helped by SEC Form S-18, which applies to offerings of less than $7.5 million and simplifies and reduces the disclosure and reporting requirements. There is no "rule of thumb" for when to go public; but, in general, many companies consider it as an option when their need for growth capital has exceeded their debt capacity. On average, the company should have an attractive rate of annual growth, at least $10 million in annual sales and $1 million in earnings, and a history of audited returns.

Advantages and Disadvantages of Going Public

The principal advantage of a public offering is that it provides the offering company with a tremendous source of interest-free capital for growth and expansion, paying off debt, or product development. With the IPO comes the future option of additional offerings once the company is well-known and has a positive track record.

A public company has more prestige and clout in the marketplace so it becomes easier to form alliances and negotiate deals with suppliers, customers, and creditors. It is also easier for the founders to harvest the rewards of their efforts by selling off a portion of their stock as needed or borrowing against it. In addition, public stock and stock options can be used to attract new employees and reward existing employees.

There are, however, some serious disadvantages to the public offering. Of the 3,186 firms that went public in the 1980s, only 58 percent are still listed on one of the three major exchanges. Moreover, the stock of only one third of these firms was selling above its issue price.[3] It is a very expensive process. Where a private offering can cost about $100,000, a public offering can run well over $300,000, a figure that does not include a seven to ten percent commission to

---

[3]Zeune, Gary D. (February 1993). "Ducks in a Row: Orchestrating the Flawless Stock Offering." *Corporate Cashflow.*

the underwriter, which compensates the investment bank that sells the securities. One way to prevent a financial disaster should the offering fail is to ask for stop-loss statements from lawyers, accountants, consultants, and investment bankers. The stop-loss statement is essentially a promise not to charge the full fee if the offering fails.

Going public is an enormously time-consuming process. Entrepreneurs report that they spend the better part of every week on issues related to the offering over a four- to six-month period. Part of this time is devoted to educating the entrepreneur about the process, which is much more complex than this chapter can express. One way many entrepreneurs deal with the knowledge gap is to spend the year prior to the offering preparing for it by talking to others who have gone through the process, reading, and putting together the team that will see the company through it. Another way to speed up the process is to start running the private corporation like a public corporation from the beginning, that is, doing audited financial statements and keeping good records.

A public offering means that everything that the company does or has becomes public information subject to the scrutiny of anyone interested in the company. The CEO of a public company is now, above all, responsible to the shareholders and only secondarily to anyone else. The entrepreneur, who before the offering probably owned the lion's share of the stock, may no longer have the controlling stock (if the entrepreneur agreed to an offering that resulted in the loss of control), and the stock that he or she does own can lose value if the company's value on the stock exchange drops, an event that can occur through no fault of the company's performance. World events and domestic economic policy can adversely (or positively) affect a company's stock regardless of what the company does.

A public company faces intense pressure to perform in the short term. Where an entrepreneur in a wholly owned corporation can afford the luxury of long-term goals and controlled growth, the CEO of a public company is pressured by stockholders to show almost immediate gains in revenues and earnings which will translate into higher stock prices and dividends to the stockholders. Last, but not least of the disadvantages, the SEC reporting requirements for public companies are very strict, time-consuming, and, therefore, costly.

The Public Offering Process

The first step in the public offering process is to choose an underwriter, or investment banker. This is the firm that sells the securities and guides the corporation through the IPO process. Some of the most prestigious investment banking firms only handle well-established companies because they feel smaller companies will not attract sufficient attention among major institutional investors. Consequently, the entrepreneur should contact anyone he or she knows who has either gone public or has a connection with an investment bank to gain entry.

The importance of investigating the reputation and track record of any underwriter cannot be stressed enough, as investment banking has become a very competitive industry with the lure of large fees from IPOs attracting some firms of questionable character. The entrepreneur should also examine the investment mix of the bank. Some underwriters focus solely on institutional investors, others on retail customers or private investors. It is often useful to have a mix of shareholders, as private investors tend to be less fickle and more stable than institutional investors. The investment bank should also be able to provide the IPO support after the offering by way of financial advice, buying and selling stock, and helping to create and maintain interest in the stock over the long term.

> The importance of investigating the reputation and track record of any underwriter cannot be stressed enough.

Once chosen, the underwriter draws up a letter of intent, which outlines the terms and conditions of the agreement between the underwriter and the entrepreneur/selling stockholder. It normally specifies a price range for the stock, which is a tricky issue at best. Typically, underwriters estimate the price at which the stock will be sold by using a price/earnings multiple that is common for companies within the same industry as the IPO. That multiple is then applied to the IPO's earnings per share. It should be emphasized that this is only a rough estimate. The actual going out price will not be determined until the night before the offering. If the entrepreneur is unhappy with the final price, the only choice is to cancel the offering, something that is highly unpalatable after months of work and expense.

A registration statement must be filed with the SEC. This document is known as a "red herring," or prospectus, because it discusses all the potential risks of investing in the IPO. This prospectus is given to anyone interested in investing in the IPO. Following the registration statement, an advertisement, called a "tombstone," in the financial press announces the offering. The prospectus is valid for nine months; after that the information becomes outdated and cannot be used except by officially amending the registration statement.

Another major decision to make is which exchange to list the offering on. In the past, smaller IPOs automatically listed on the American Stock Exchange (AMEX) or National Association of Securities Dealers Automated Quotation (NASDAQ) only because they couldn't meet the qualifications of the New York

Stock Exchange (NYSE). Today, however, the NASDAQ, with companies like Microsoft and Apple, is the fastest growing exchange in the nation.

There is a difference between the way NASDAQ and the other exchanges operate. The NYSE and AMEX are auction markets with securities traded on the floor of the exchange, enabling investors to trade directly with one another. The NASDAQ, on the other hand, is a floorless exchange that trades on the National Market System through a system of broker-dealers from respected securities firms who compete for orders. In addition to these three, there are also regional exchanges like the Pacific and Boston stock exchanges that are less costly alternatives for a small, growing company.

The high point of the IPO process is the road show, a two-week, whirlwind tour of all the major institutional investors by the entrepreneur and the IPO team to market the offering. This is done so that once the registration statement has met all of the SEC requirements and the stock is priced, the offering can virtually be sold in a day. The coming out price determines the amount of proceeds to the IPO company, but those holding stock prior to the IPO often see the value of their stock increase substantially immediately after the IPO.

Strategic Alliances

Chapter 16 talked about how to use strategic alliances to create the virtual company or grow the business. Strategic alliances with larger companies are also an excellent source of growth capital for young companies. Sometimes the partnership results in major financial and equity investments in the growing venture. Such was the case of United Parcel Service of America, which acquired a 9.5 percent ownership interest in Mail Boxes Etc. for $11.3 million. This gave Mail Boxes Etc. capital to grow and UPS additional pickup and drop-off outlets. Growing companies that link with established companies can usually get a better deal than they would have gotten from a venture capitalist. In addition, they derive some associated benefits that give them more credibility in the marketplace. The large, investing partner is, at a minimum, looking for a return of the cost of capital, but in general a return of at least ten percent on the investment.

Strategic alliances are every bit as tricky as partnerships, so the entrepreneur must evaluate the potential partner carefully as well as do "due diligence" on the company. It is also crucial not to focus on one partner but consider several before making a final decision. For the partnership to really work, the benefits should flow in both directions; that is, both partners should derive cost savings and/or revenue enhancement from the relationship. It is probably best not to form a partnership that requires one of the partners (usually the smaller company) to be too heavily dependent on the other for a substantial portion of their revenue-generating capability. It is a dangerous position to be in should the partnership dissolve for any reason.

Valuing the Business

A key component of any growth strategy is determining the value of the company, as a realistic value figure is needed no matter which financial strategy is undertaken to raise growth capital. However, understand at the outset that value is a subjective term with a myriad of meanings. In fact, at least six different definitions of value are in common usage. Summarized, they are as follows:

- **Fair Market Value.** This is the price at which a willing seller would sell and a willing buyer would buy in an arm's length transaction. By this definition, every sale would ultimately constitute a fair market value sale.
- **Intrinsic Value.** This is perceived value arrived at by interpreting balance sheet and income statements through the use of ratios, discounting cash flow projections, and calculating liquidated asset value.
- **Investment Value.** This is the worth of the business to an investor and is based on the individual requirements of the investor as to risk, return, tax benefits, and so forth.
- **Going Concern Value.** This is the current status of the business as measured by financial statements, debt load, and economic environmental factors such as government regulation that may affect the long-term continuation of the business.
- **Liquidation Value.** This value assumes the selling off of all assets and calculating the amount that could be recovered from doing so.
- **Book Value.** This is an accounting measure of value and refers to the difference between total assets and total liability. It is essentially equivalent to shareholder's or owner's equity.

Accountants tend to value a business by using earnings and multiplying a year's worth of earnings by some multiple. However, the variation in ways that a company can calculate earnings makes this a dubious measure at best for purposes of valuation. Similarly, financial analysts use a price/earnings ratio from which to figure a multiple; however, this approach only makes sense for valuing publicly traded companies. The point is that neither of these approaches considers what the investor will receive for his or her investment. If valuing the business as a whole is the goal, the most common measure and the one that gives more accurate results is future cash flows, because only cash or cash equivalents are used in the calculations. The method is called **discounted cash flow analysis** or **capitalization of future cash flows to the present value.** What this means is simply calculating how much an investor would pay today to have a cash flow stream of X dollars for Y number of years into the future.

For this analysis, the entrepreneur uses pro forma cash flow statements for the business and determines a forecast period. To do this, the length and nature of business cycles in the industry must be understood so a forecast period that goes either from trough to trough or peak to peak in a cycle is chosen. In other words, you need to have at least one complete business cycle within the forecast period to give a fair representation of the effect on cash flow. (See Figure 17.2)

The forecast period is also affected by macroeconomic cycles, particularly if the business is in the consumer products area. A study of leading, lagging, and coincidental indicators can provide information on macroeconomic cycles that may affect the future cash flow of the business in some industries. For example, leading indicators such as Manufacturers' New Orders for Consumer Goods or Orders for Plant and Equipment have typically declined for nine months prior to the beginning of a recession. One way to mitigate the problems associated with business and macroeconomic cycles is to calculate a weighted average of three cash flow projections: worst case, best case, and most likely case. The entrepre-

Figure 17.2: Business Cycles and the Forecast Period

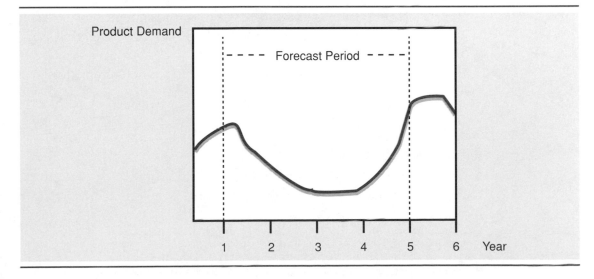

neur should assign a subjective probability to each case based on best estimates of the chances for that case occurring, given certain economic conditions.

Once the forecast period has been defined and the cash flow projections prepared (See Chapter 15 for a discussion of pro forma cash flow statements), a discount rate must be chosen. This is not a purely arbitrary exercise. The decision should be based on two factors:

1. The rate achievable in a risk-free investment such as U.S. Treasury notes over a comparable time period. For example, for a five-year forecast, the current rate on a five-year note is appropriate.
2. A risk factor based on the type of business and industry should be added to the interest rate in #1. Several precedents for determining what these factors are have been established over years of study. The most recent, widely accepted standards are offered by Schilt[4] and Pratt.[5] in the form of five categories of business. Note that even within each category there is room for degrees of risk.
   a. Category 1: Established businesses with good market share, excellent management, and a stable history of earnings: *6-10%*
   b. Category 2: Established businesses in more competitive industries, still with good market share, excellent management, and a stable earnings history: *11-15%*
   c. Category 3: Growing businesses in very competitive industries, little capital investment, average management team, and a stable earnings history: *16-20%*
   d. Category 4: Small businesses dependent on the entrepreneur or larger businesses in very volatile industries, and the lack of a predictable earnings picture: *21-25%*
   e. Category 5: Small service businesses operating as sole proprietorships: *26-30%*

The following example illustrates this valuation method:

Assume: 6% risk-free rate
<u>14%</u> risk factor (Category 2 business)
20% discount rate

---

[4]Schilt, James H. (1982). "A Rational Approach to Capitalization Rates for Discounting the Future Income Stream of Closely Held Companies." *The Financial Planner.*

[5]Pratt, Shannon P. (1989).*Valuing a Business,* 2nd Edition, Homewood, IL: Business One Irwin.

End of Year	Cash Flow ($000)	Factor (20%)	Present Value
1	200	.8333	166.7
2	250	.6944	173.6
3	300	.5787	173.6
4	375	.4823	180.9
5	450	.4019	180.9
Totals	1,575		874.7

Assuming the current rate on a ten-year treasury note is 6 percent and you are dealing with a Category 2 business at a 14 percent risk factor, the adjusted discount rate becomes 20 percent. Using a calculator or a present value table, the present value of the five-year cash flow stream can be calculated. What this example shows is that this hypothetical business will throw off $1,575,000 of positive cash flow over five years. Hence, a buyer would be willing to pay $875,000 today for that business, given the discount rate.

In addition to the discount rate and risk factor, a business may have an ability to generate cash virtually into perpetuity, assuming a strong position in the marketplace and an excellent management team. Tuller and others have advanced similar proposals to deal with what they call "continuing value" of the business.[6] It involves choosing a period of time subsequent to the forecast period of at least 30 years so the final years will have little or no impact on the cash flow stream being discounted and applying the last year's cash flow figure from the forecast period as if it would go on unchanged for the next 50 or more years. In other words, multiply the last year's cash flow figure by 50 (or 75 or 100 depending on the period chosen). Discount that product using a discount factor of double the original factor (or triple depending on subjective assessment of risk) to account for the unknown probability that the business will continue for that period of time and produce that amount of cash flow. The total for the discounted continuing period can then be added to the discounted cash flow from the forecast period to arrive at an estimate of value. If you have prepared three scenarios—best, worst, and most likely cases—you will end up with three values for the business. At this point the "real" value for the business is determined through negotiation with investors, lenders, or the underwriters who are helping to take the company public. However, doing the calculations just discussed provides an excellent jumping off point for the negotiations.

As careful as this procedure is, it still has a significant "crystal ball" aspect to it because at several crucial points in the process subjective decisions are made by

---

[6] Tuller, Lawrence W. (1994). *Small Business Valuation Book.* Holbrook, MA: Bob Adams, Inc.

the entrepreneur. There is really no way to avoid this dilemma; it is the nature of the beast. The entrepreneur, nevertheless, must recognize that everyone interprets value differently and must be prepared to discuss and defend the assumptions used to estimate value. Another point needs to be made. While the entrepreneur is attempting to place a value on the business as a whole, the potential investor/owner is looking at the business in terms of what the business will *return to the investor/owner*. This is a very specific type of return and includes three categories of items: cash flow returns, appreciation, and tax benefits.

- *Cash Flow Returns.* The investor/owner can receive the benefits of cash flow through "perks" such as expense accounts and company cars, the repayment of debt which is a tax-free transaction, interest, salary, and dividends. Each of these has personal advantages and disadvantages to the investor/owner.
- *Appreciation.* The investor/owner can sell off a portion of his or her interest in the company and enjoy a tax-free event up to the amount of his or her cost basis.
- *Tax Benefits.* The investor/owner may be able to receive pass-through losses that generally occur in the early years of a venture, if the business has elected an S-corporation status.

This chapter has focused on one accepted method for valuing a young, growing business. Valuation is by its very nature an incremental process that involves bringing together key pieces of information that will, hopefully, give some insight into the health and future of the business. In all discussions of value, the entrepreneur should be clear on whose definition of value is being used.

Final Thoughts on Growth Capital

Recall from Chapter 1 that entrepreneurs work with a vision of where they see their company going and what it will look like when they get there. That vision sustains them through the ups and downs of start-up and the breathless speed of growth when the company finally takes off. It also supports them in the difficult search for capital to feed that growth and ensure that the business remains successful. The growth period of a world-class venture can be an extraordinarily exciting time for everyone if the entrepreneurial team has prepared for growth by:

- Networking, researching, and lining up potential capital sources well in advance of need
- Determining at least three years in advance if the company will go public at the most appropriate window of opportunity. This is so the company can

begin, if it hasn't already, to regularly prepare audited financial statements using a nationally recognized accounting firm and put in place the financial and control systems required of a public company.

- Updating the comprehensive business plan

New Venture Checklist

Have you

- ☐ Determined how much growth capital will be needed?
- ☐ Developed a strategy for seeking growth capital?
- ☐ Established a value for the business?

Additional Sources of Information

Bygrave, W.D. & Timmons, J.A. (1992). *Venture Capital at the Crossroads.* Cambridge: Harvard Business School Press.

Gladstone, D. (1988). *Venture Capital Handbook.* Englewood Cliffs, NJ: Prentice Hall.

Tuller, L.W. (1994). *Small Business Valuation Book.* Holbrook, MA: Bob Adams, Inc.

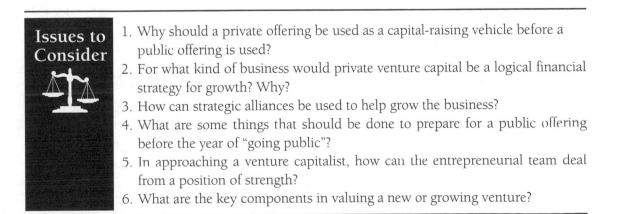

Issues to Consider

1. Why should a private offering be used as a capital-raising vehicle before a public offering is used?
2. For what kind of business would private venture capital be a logical financial strategy for growth? Why?
3. How can strategic alliances be used to help grow the business?
4. What are some things that should be done to prepare for a public offering before the year of "going public"?
5. In approaching a venture capitalist, how can the entrepreneurial team deal from a position of strength?
6. What are the key components in valuing a new or growing venture?

6

OXO
GOOD GRIP**S**

OXO (B)[1]

In the summer of 1989, Sam Farber and a design team lead by Davin Stowell from Smart Design, were involved in the development of a line of kitchen gadgets (e.g., peeler, can opener, pizza cutter, garlic press) that would be functional, comfortable, ergonomically sound, attractive, and affordable. Farber expected the Smart Design team to have the kitchen gadgets prototyped and ready for manufacture so they could introduce the new line at the San Francisco Gourmet Show in April 1990. A number of design, marketing, and manufacturing challenges would need to be solved in the next nine months.

Determining the Product Goals

When OXO and Smart Design conducted a consumer survey about kitchen gadgets, they found users complained about: rusting metal, cracking plastic, dull peeler blades, and can openers that didn't cut. Users wanted nonslip handles, easy-to-read measurements on all devices, simple directions, easy-to-clean tools, dishwasher-safe tools, a self-cleaning garlic press, and comfortable handles, especially for scissors.

The design team decided to spend most of the investigative time looking at the range of manual limitations, from serious permanent disabilities to the limited mobility and declining strength associated with aging. The team believed that by making tools that most of this group could use comfortably, they could satisfy the needs of all users.

The designers divided motions into twist (used to scoop, stir, and peel), push/pull (graters and knives), and squeeze (used to work scissors, garlic press, and can opener). The design team made hundreds of models and tried them all. They discovered that it was necessary to use a combination of motions to work most tools. The project would narrow down to three

---

[1]©1994, Corporate Design Foundation. This case was written by Professor William B. Gartner, San Francisco State University School of Business, with the support of the Corporate Design Foundation as a basic for class discussion rather than to illustrate either effective or ineffective handling of a business situation.

functional groups: gadgets and utensils with a general multipurpose handle, squeeze tools, and measuring devices.

A general handle was to be used for the twist and push/pull motions. The handle would be large to increase leverage and oval to keep it from rotating in the hand. The short round end would fit comfortably into the palm and evenly distribute the pressure in motion.

When the group sat down to determine the product goals, they generated the following criteria:

Comfort: This was the key goal. A new product has to be able to differentiate itself from all the ones on the market. Almost every tool they held was the wrong shape or so hard that it hurt the hands. They also experienced hand and wrist fatigue after using many of them. All the scissors on the market were a disaster. Sore fingers were a common complaint. It was actually in the conversation with one of their consumer cooks that the word "soft" appeared. They all agreed that a soft handle would be a comfortable handle and that it should be a key goal.

Easy to Use: They decided to stick to simple hand tools—ones that served one purpose and did it well.

Good Quality: This was a key recommendation from most of the consumer cooks. They complained about the inferior quality of the kitchen tools on the market. They rusted. Peeler blades became dull (or started out dull). Plastic cracked. Consumer cooks were willing to pay more for a longer-lasting tool.

Aesthetically Pleasing: There was a consensus that all the tools on the market were ugly or old-fashioned. Many people left their kitchen tools out in jugs on the counter and wanted them to be attractive.

Dishwasher Safe: A lot of people were afraid to put their kitchen tools in the dishwasher. Their previous experiences were disastrous: rusting, cracked handles. All agreed they would like tools they could just throw into the dishwasher. This was important in their search for the right soft materials for handles and led to their choice of Santoprene.

From Prototype of Product

In order to develop the general handle to be used for the different gadgets, hundreds of prototypes were constructed. Besides determining the shape of the handle, the design team also needed to specify a material to make the handle from. The design team wanted the material for the handle to be soft and flexible. However, the material had to be easy to mold and dishwasher safe. The team chose "Santoprene," a material from Monsanto. Santoprene is composed of polypropylene plastic and rubber. This material has a warm non-slip feel to it. Since Santoprene is used for dishwasher gaskets, there was no doubt that it was dishwasher safe. By using Santoprene it was also possible for the designers to incorporate another feature of the handle, "fingerprints softspots," which are flexible fin sections. These resilient fins help the handle to bend to an individual finger grip, thereby giving the user more cushion and control, even when hands are wet or soapy. The flexible fin feature was subsequently patented. The "fingerprints softspots" were added to the handle because Sam Farber saw a need to make an innovative feature of the general handle (soft spots) visible.

> Sam Farber felt that "the handle should invite involvement."

In conducting their research on the usability of different handle prototypes, the Smart Design team had identified the need for "soft spots," a portion of the handle that was softer than the rest of the handle in order to make the handle easier to grip and maneuver. The Smart Design team had originally designed in many of the prototypes for the soft spots to be "invisible," that is, the handle looked the same from tip to end, but when grasped, a portion of the handle where the finger gripped the tool, gave more, and therefore provided a better grip. Sam Farber felt that this feature needed to be visible to the customer: "the handle should invite involvement." By creating flexible fin sections for the soft spots on the handle, the handle had a distinctive and visually descriptive design. Much like an elegant sneaker built for the hands, the flexible fins on the handle were a sign to prospective customers that this was not another "me too" product.

In order to achieve the necessary rigid inner structure in the handle to support the tool end of a particular gadget as well as provide a base for the soft flexible outer handle, the metal part of the tool was molded to an inner core of inexpensive ABS plastic. The injection-molded Santoprene handle was then slipped over the ABS core.

The squeeze tools were designed with wide flat handles, so that in the clenching motion of the whole fist, the pressure on the hand was evenly distributed to alleviate sore spots and finger cramps. In designing the scissors they added a hidden spring in the hinge that opens the blades automatically. The user does not have to use the tender backside of the thumb to pull the blades apart. The scissors were designed to use the strength of the whole hand for cutting. They were designed so that the bottom of the handle was flat, so that a user could press the scissors down on a table or countertop and, therefore, put the weight of one's shoulder into cutting through tough items like poultry joints or tree branches. The scissors were also designed to be used in either the right or left hands. A pair also latches shut for safe storage in a drawer or on a hook.

The measuring cups and measuring spoons were designed with wide handles for extra control and big easy-to-read size markings that were color coded. This feature helps the eye perform better, as well as the hand. Finally, big holes on the gadgets, and big rings for the measuring items enhance their ease in hanging.

Manufacturing

The key group of items that would be Sam Farber's focus of attention when selecting a factory for production involved the peeler group of gadgets. Peelers are the biggest selling item in a line of kitchen gadgets. A factory was required that could manufacture a high quality peeler and OXO peelers would require a factory that had expertise in both metal parts production and plastic production. Because of Sam Farber's prior experience at COPCO in manufacturing kitchen products abroad and in selling kitchen wares in the United States market, he knew that OXO's products would have to be made in the Far East to be price competitive. Sam knew that the cost of tooling in the Far East would be lower and that he could get factories to share in the costs of making the tooling. Yet, Sam did attempt to coax American manufacturers to bid. When Sam approached a factory in the United States that was making bicycle grips with a material similar to Santoprene, the factory manager looked at the Santoprene/ABS composite prototype handle and said, "It can't be done." When Sam visited a Japanese factory, the factory manager looked at the prototype handle and said. "Very interesting—why not?" Sam selected a Japanese factory to make the peelers. He had used this factory before to make knives for COPCO.

Sam turned to other factories in the Far East to manufacture the scissors. garlic press, measuring cups and spoons. He researched many factories in Taiwan and found three quality producers offering competitive prices. For manufacturing the large stainless steel tools, such as spoons and turners, Sam sought out factories in China. These large tools require a great deal of hand labor for a polished finish, and labor for this type of work is cheaper in China. Sam worked with a Hong Kong company that would ensure quality control in China. Sam sought companies that had experience selling to the German market. German consumers demanded higher quality than American consumers. The Hong Kong company was producing products for a number of quality German importers.

In summary, all of the factories that Sam Farber choose met the following criteria:

1. They were producing similar products, so that they were familiar with the production problems that could arise and could consult effectively with the designers during the final stages of design.
2. They were quality conscious.
3. They understood the process of exporting to the U.S. market.
4. They were willing to help pay for the cost of tooling as well as accept low minimum quantities on the original order.

Developing a Time Table

After selecting the factories to produce the products, Sam Farber established a time schedule with each factory, laying out a time frame from the day final drawings would be received to the shipping date of the gadgets. When he returned to the U.S. from this trip, Sam Farber met with the design team to map out a design and production schedule. Sam planned to show the line at the Gourmet Products Show in San Francisco in April 1990. Working back from this date, the following activities would have to be accomplished:

1. The preliminary conceptual designs would be ready on October 15. A design direction would be chosen. If none of the designs were accepted, the design team would try again.
2. The final designs would be presented for approval on November 15.
3. Prototypes would be made by Smart Design or their model maker on December 15.
4. Final drawings and prototypes would be sent to the factories on January 1, 1990.
5. The lead designer and Sam Farber would visit the factories and finalize all designs and give approval to start the tooling.
6. In order to show something at the Gourmet Show by April, temporary molds of the gadgets made at the Japanese factory would be made, and prototypes of the items made at the Taiwanese and Chinese factories would be shown.
7. Stock would be in the warehouse by July 1 for shipment.

While this schedule was ambitious, Sam felt it could be achieved. In bringing the kitchen gadgets into production. Sam never went to the Far East without someone from the design team. He believed that the designer needed to be familiar with the factories and their production capabilities, what a factory can and cannot do. Sam felt that "factory guys" are notorious for saying "it can't be done." Sam found that the design team couldn't just work in the studio, but had to be actively involved in the early marketing studies and in the production techniques and manufacturing. "You can't accomplish design innovation in a vacuum. All the players have to participate and feel they are partners all along the way."

Other Considerations

All of the distribution areas (e.g., department stores, specialty kitchen shops, mail order catalogs, discount retailers) suggested the same best selling items: peeler, can opener, garlic press, grater, pizza cutter, measuring spoons, and measuring cups. The mail order catalogs preferred higher unit retails and were therefore interested in selling sets that combined two or three items.

All distribution areas were used to selling kitchen gadgets in lower price ranges than OXO had contemplated, e.g., most peelers were selling from $.99 to $4.99 while the OXO peeler would be sold from $5.99 to $7.99. The mass market companies were interested in the lower end of the price range. This was an important factor in the decision to produce a second line for this distribution area that would be lower priced. This line, labeled "Prima," would sell peelers for $3.99, which is at the higher end for mass merchants. In order to manufacture gadgets at this lower price, tradeoffs in the quality of the product would have to be made. While the handle would be "user friendly," it would be made of hard plastic and in one piece, rather than made from Santoprene, and in two pieces. Farber also decided he was willing to take a lower gross margin on the Prima line in order to sell the product for a lower price.

Department stores and mass merchants wanted items packaged on cards in a traditional manner. Farber and the design team realized that their "story" was in the handle, so they designed cards so that the handle swung free. Customers could actually grab the handle and feel it. OXO also realized that many specialty stores didn't like cards, so gadgets were also sold uncarded, or with small counter top displays. The demands from the mail order catalogues were mixed. Some wanted cards for customer information and some didn't.

The accepted display technique in all stores was to hang the items on the "gadget wall." The team's marketing observations were that these walls were unsightly—it was difficult to find a product and none of the lines were presented together as one package. Since OXO had a story to tell, they wanted to keep their line separate from the others. The department stores and specialty stores were receptive to the idea of a free-standing display. The mass merchants only used the wall. The design team created a large display at first and subsequently created a smaller revolving display, and finally, a display that holds six items that could be placed near the cash register.

Most department stores wanted service, either complete service such as inventory counting and display maintenance, or display maintenance. Some mass merchants were not interested in service because they had sophisticated scanning devices for quick reordering through EDI setups as well as trained stocking people in the stores. Other retailers wanted merchandise sold to a distributor who would handle the stocking and service. For example, they found that Target stores wanted merchandise sold directly to them, while Caldor wanted merchandise to be sold to Federal Wholesale, who maintains their inventories and displays.

Because the handle was the key to the whole line, they realized that they needed to have a name for the gadgets that told the customer what was special about the product. "Good Grips" proved to be a perfect name. This name communicated the major advantage of the line to the customer quickly: these products were comfortable kitchen tools.

Expanding the Team

While Sam Farber had invested his own money in the venture during these initial stages of development, he realized that as the company began manufacturing the product, he would likely need more capital for inventory expansion and working capital. He approached a few of his friends, explained his idea, and received assurances from them that they would like to participate as investors. When Sam talked to his son John, a vice president at Prudential Bache in mergers and acquisitions, about OXO, John agreed to become Sam's business partner, but not actually work full-time for the company However, a few months later, John changed his mind and decided to become an active participant. Sam and John decided to form OXO as a limited partnership with four of Sam's friends as the other partners. Through the assistance of Sam's accountant, the partners arranged for a line of credit with Chemical Bank. Surprisingly, because of strong initial sales and inventory purchases on a just-in-time basis, OXO had a healthy positive cash flow and never did borrow any money from the bank.

Sam's wife Betsey had shared the same passionate beliefs about the products from the very beginning. Her experience in the kitchen and her arthritis were key factors in the original concept. She decided to join the company rather than return to the practice of architecture. She came to be in charge of all publicity, trade shows, brochures, copywriting, and in-house graphic design.

Though Sam had many contacts with buyers, he knew he needed to focus his own efforts on developing new products. OXO would need a sales force and someone to manage this sales force. One of his former sales vice-presidents from COPCO, Ed Beren, was presently working as a sales consultant to two or three companies in the housewares field. When Sam explained the idea of "Good Grips" to Ed and showed him some of the initial models, Sam had another passionate believer. Ed agreed to work as OXO's sales manager and as a consultant to the company for a percentage of the sales and a small advance. Though OXO would not get all of Ed's time, they would only have to share in paying for his expenses, thereby turning what is often a fixed overhead expense into a variable cost.

The meeting with Ed took place in February. They agreed that Ed would find a sales force of manufacturers' representatives and bring them together for the first time at a sales meeting during the San Francisco Gourmet Show in April. The manufacturers' representatives would all work on commission.

A three-year marketing plan was developed. The initial line of kitchen gadgets would be sold to upscale distribution outlets to establish the concept and the name. They targeted January 1992 as the time to introduce a second line of kitchen gadgets geared to mass merchants, like Wal-mart, K-Mart and Target. By the end of 1993 they would produce a third line aimed at the supermarkets and lower-priced kitchen stores. Although the lines would be different from each other, they would adhere to the same basic principles of universal design: all of the tools would be easier to hold and use.

Last Minute Details

Right before the San Francisco Gourmet Show, Sam and Betsey contacted many of the trade magazines about the story of OXO and Good Grips. Trade magazines are looking for news of new products. The editors of these magazines jumped at the opportunity to write feature stories on the company and the concept. Magazine editors and writers were introduced to the Smart Design office. The entire design process was explained. Sam wanted them to become believers too. They did. A number of articles were written that celebrated the revolutionary qualities of the new designs for these kitchen gadgets.

In building a display booth for the Gourmet Show, the team realized they didn't have much product to display, and the products, themselves, were small.

In order to catch the buyer's eye quickly and communicate the features of these unique products, the booth was constructed of photo murals of the products.

A week before the Gourmet Show the Japanese factory sent the initial samples for the show. But the grade of material chosen for the handles was noticeably harder than what the design team had wanted. The Japanese worked around the clock and through the weekend to produce another set of samples in time for the show. Sam's view of this burst of cooperation was:

> They too had become believers. They felt involved as partners. Making the supplier a part of the team in the early stages is one of the keys to success of a project. In any innovative design project, you're probably pushing way beyond the boundaries of present products and present techniques—and in many cases present technology too. Those land mines hide all over the road. It is hard to imagine this statement in relation to a fairly prosaic item like the potato peeler. But we were using a material unfamiliar to our factories, and one never before used in kitchen tools. We were asking them to mold very thin uniform sections in the material. We were *convinced* it could be done and Monsanto felt it could be done.

> Naysayers are a serious impediment in the process of design innovation. They can be outside suppliers, technical people, or people within your own company who always follow the safe path. Safety and self-doubt don't flourish along the pathway of the entrepreneur. It's not the way of someone trying to push through a revolutionary design project. That's why it is so important to have the suppliers involved. When they believe, they will continually try to help you prove that it can be done.

The Good Grips line was an instant success when it was presented at the San Francisco Gourmet Show in April 1990. Everyone wanted the merchandise. While the product had been promised for delivery in July, shipments did not begin until September. OXO was able to place the products in all the major department stores and specialty stores. Sales did meet initial projections.

Expansion and Growth

In Spring 1991 OXO introduced a line of knives using the Santoprene handle. The handle has a slightly different shape, since knives are held differently than other kitchen gadgets. In July 1991 OXO introduced the "Prima" line for mass merchants in the 500-store western chain, Target. The Prima line has the same finger grip, but uses less of the Santoprene, which is an expensive material.

Other products that were introduced include a hand-held jar opener which easily twists off stubborn jar lids and bottle caps. A "flying nun" corkscrew, that has a large easy-to-turn knob, and wide wings contoured to the curve of the hand to facilitate the downward push which lifts out the cork. The screw is coated with zylon, a non-stick material that enables it to glide easily into the cork without tearing it.

OXO has also introduced a line of tools designed for the garden. The handle uses a soft material similar to the Santoprene. It has the patented fingerprint fins, but the shape of the handle has been altered slightly to conform to the different ways the hand moves when using a garden tool. OXO signed a licensing agreement with the Sierra Club to market the tools as "Good Grips Sierra Club Garden Tools." Part of the proceeds from the sale of these tools goes to the Sierra Club to help preserve and protect the environment.

The company is developing nonskid mixing bowls. They are also conducting extensive studies on arm and wrist movements when lifting a pot filled with food in order to design a line of cookware using a version of the patented handle. In terms of the future, Sam commented:

> We think there is still much more we can do in designing innovative items for the kitchen and related home areas. We also realize that our patented handle and our work in promoting universal design has potential even beyond that. At the present time we are licensing our knife handle to a major medical supply company. They are using it to produce a set of tableware—rocker knife, fork, and various spoons—for use by people who have physical difficulty holding ordinary silverware. Our factories manufacture the implements exclusively for them and we receive a royalty. We are also in the process of discussing licensing the patented handle to a paint tool company and to a hair brush company. Our scissors are about to be introduced in a number of poultry processing plants where relief of hand and wrist fatigue in repetitive motion is very important. We feel that we are just at the beginning, both in developing our own new products and in licensing our handles in other markets.

In the four years since the first showing, these products have won a number of design awards:

* *International Design Magazine* Annual Design Review, 1991. Selection for consumer products category out of 1,300 submissions.

- Industrial Design Excellence Awards. Gold Medal, 1992. A contest conducted by the Industrial Designers Society of American and sponsored by *Business Week.*
- Design Leadership Award for Growing Companies, 1993. Winner for product design. A context sponsored by *Inc.* magazine and the Corporate Design Foundation.

On October 20, 1992, General Housewares Corporation (GHW) announced the acquisition of OXO International L. P. In making the announcement, Paul A. Saxton, Chairman, President and CEO of General Housewares, said,

> The acquisition of OXO and its exceptional portfolio of distinctive products strengthens General Housewares' position as the leading domestic supplier to the highly involved, discriminating kitchen consumer. We are especially pleased to become associated with Sam Farber and John Farber, the principals of OXO. Sam and John will be joining the GHC executive team, continuing their direct management roles in OXO. They will also play a key contributory role in our sourcing and new product development programs. With the addition of kitchen tools, we provide to our customers a more comprehensive product assort-ment, as well as create for GHC new and exciting cross-merchandising opportunities building upon our existing products.
>
> OXO is an acquisition that fits very well with GHC's strategy. As with the Chicago Cutlery acquisition, OXO embodies a truly superior product line and an emerging brand franchise that we believe will add important value to GHC in the years to come.

Sam Farber commented,

> We are extremely excited about the combination with General Housewares. As our business continues to grow dramatically, we have become increasingly aware of the need to bring top-quality service as well as products to our customers. General Housewares is known in the industry for the superior quality of its marketing and customer service and I believe those capabilities, combined with our product development work, create a unique force in the housewares industry. Finally, we have been very impressed by the character and depth of the General Housewares management team and believe that our compatibility with them will ensure a very successful future.

Plans for the Future

With OXO now a part of a company with substantial resources for product development and marketing, Sam Farber felt that OXO needed to direct its energies to new opportunities. But, in order to do that Sam needed to determine the company's direction:

> What should we do next? Are we a kitchen company or are we a company developing comfortable universal design products for any place in the home or office or outside the home? I have posed this question to everyone at OXO and to our designers. We are in the middle of discussions.

1. How was OXO's philosophy and mission used to develop the product line?
2. Was it necessary for OXO to join forces with General Housewares Corporation to grow and why?
3. Is OXO a kitchen company or are they a company developing comfortable universal design products for any place in the home, office, or outside the home? Why is it important for Sam to answer this question?

PART 7

Contemplating the Future

We know not yet what we have done, still less what we are doing. Wait till evening and other parts of our day's work will shine than we had thought at noon, and we shall discover the real purport of our toil.

—HENRY D. THOREAU

CHAPTER 18

Planning for Change

Overview

- *The purpose and uses of a contingency plan*
- *The purpose and uses of an exit plan*
- *Issues related to the selling of a business as an exit strategy*
- *Mechanisms for cashing out of the business while still maintaining a degree of control*
- *Bankruptcy as an escape plan or an entrepreneurial tool*
- *Presenting the contingency plan in the business plan*

The Contingency Plan

There is no crystal ball that will tell an entrepreneur what the future holds for the new venture. Many entrepreneurs have started a business with a plan in mind for where that business would go, but along the way things changed. Forces beyond the control of the entrepreneur forced the venture into new directions and a new set of plans had to be constructed. This was the case with Talli Counsel of Interfleet, who found that the rewards for consulting and providing education to the major auto makers and others were much greater and provided less liability and fewer problems than the physical part of his business—servicing the fleet vehicles of the Fortune 500 companies worldwide. Consequently he is now changing the primary focus of the business to reflect changes in the environment as well as his personal goals.

It is a sad fact that most entrepreneurs with growing ventures do not have time for contingency planning; they are just too busy keeping the business alive. But planning is essential. In the absence of planning, the business puts itself in a reactionary mode, virtually at the whim of the environment in which it operates. Instead of dealing from a position of strength, entrepreneurs may find themselves reacting in panic and without information to situations for which they are not prepared. As a result, the quality of decision making is reduced and the business suffers.

By forcing entrepreneurs to consider multiple outcomes and possibilities, contingency plans help a growing business deal with the ubiquitous downturns and upturns in the economy, new regulations, changes in customer tastes and preferences, and many other events that regularly, and often without much warning, disrupt the equilibrium of the business. For example, the reason many businesses fail in a recession is that they haven't prepared for it by forecasting the potential impact on demand when signs of a recession appear and calculating how they can adjust and still maintain a positive cash position.

> *In the absence of planning, the business puts itself in a reactionary mode, virtually at the whim of the environment.*

Recessions do not happen overnight. There are signs, even within specific industries, that signal a slowdown. Since the government began compiling indices on the economy after World War II, some consistent trends have appeared. For example, the leading index, which consists of such items as the Producer Price Index, the Consumer Confidence Index, and the Manufacturers' Orders for Durable Goods, declines for nine months prior to the onset of a recession. The coincident/lagging index, which is a ratio of the coincident index (employment, personal income, industrial production) to the lagging index (Consumer Price Index, interest rates, unemployment), declines for 13 months prior to the onset of a recession.

Being able to recognize the signs of recession before they impact the business gives the entrepreneur the chance to prepare in many ways, including maintaining a higher degree of liquidity. In recessionary times it is more difficult to raise capital from either bankers or private sources, so being liquid allows the entrepreneur to take advantage of opportunities that become available only during recessions. For example, the entrepreneur may be able to purchase a building that in good economic times was beyond reach, or he or she may be able to negotiate more favorable terms from suppliers just to keep the business moving forward.

Growing entrepreneurial ventures need to engage in both short- and long-range planning. Short-range planning involves setting quantitative goals for the coming year and developing a plan for achieving them. If a business does any planning, it is usually short-range. Long-range plans, by contrast, are based on the business's mission and focus on the direction the business will take, accounting for potential changes in the environment in which the business operates. It is certainly not possible to account for all contingencies, but there are some key crisis issues that seem to occur for all high-growth ventures.

Taxes and Regulations

Government regulations and regulatory paperwork are severe problems for growing ventures, and the cost of compliance is rising to the point that entrepreneurs are looking for a way to avoid coming under the purview of some of the regulations. The Family Leave Act now has a threshold of 50 employees, so many small businesses fight to stay below that number, because the lengthy loss of an employee in a small, growing company can impact operations severely.

The cost of hiring an employee is becoming so prohibitive that many companies are solving the problem by subcontracting work and leasing employees. Take, for example, a growing manufacturing company with fewer than 50 employees. On an hourly basis, per employee base pay is $11; health coverage costs about $3 an hour; Social Security, Medicare, and unemployment insurance is about $1.50; and workers' compensation is $1, for a total hourly cost of $16.50. If you then factor in profit sharing, bonuses, and retirement plans, you can easily reach $20 an hour as the actual cost of hiring that employee. However, the government is cracking down on businesses that categorize people as independent contractors, so the IRS rules must be carefully followed. (See Chapter 4.)

Changes in the tax laws can place a significant burden on the business and the entrepreneur as well. The $135,000 ceiling on income subject to Medicare Tax has been eliminated, which could add several thousand dollars to the business's tax liability and to that of the entrepreneur in an S corporation. Growth in state and local taxes in some states makes it more important than ever to search for states that place a smaller burden on business. Changes in the tax law, however, can also provide a benefit to the entrepreneur; for example, the recent break for investors in businesses with less than $50 million in assets allows them to reduce their taxable gain by 50 percent if they have held the stock for more than five years.

Product Liability

The chances are fairly good that if you manufacture a product, your company will at some point face a product liability suit. The Administrative Office of the U.S. Courts in Washington, DC reports that in 1989 alone, 14,339 product liability claims were filed. The states with the most industry naturally had the highest claims, with Pennsylvania, Ohio, Texas, and New York leading the list. More and more the risk of product-related injuries has been shifted to manufacturers, creating a legal minefield that could prove disastrous to a growing company.

The problem stems from the fact that even if the company carefully designs and manufactures a product, and covers it with warnings and detailed instructions, it is still vulnerable to the misuse of and consequent injury from the product. For a company to be legally liable, the product must be defective and an injury must have occurred. But in a litigious society, those requirements don't stop people from suing. Most product liability insurance covers the costs of defense, personal injury, or property damage, but does not cover lost sales and the cost of product redesign. Moreover, if your insurance company must pay on a claim, your premiums will, no doubt, increase.

> A growing company must plan for potential litigation from the very inception of the business.

A growing company must plan for potential litigation from the very inception of the business. One proven method is to establish a formal safety panel that includes people from all the major functional areas of the business. During the start-up phase, that panel may only consist of the entrepreneur and one or two outside advisors with experience in the area. It is the job of the safety panel to review safety requirements on a regular basis, establish new ones when necessary, and document any injuries or claims made against the product. Prior to product introduction in the marketplace, the panel should see that careful records of all decisions regarding final product design, testing, and evaluation procedures are maintained. Any advertising regarding the product should not contain exaggerated claims or implied promises that may give customers the impression that you are claiming more safety features than the product actually has. Implied promises can be used against you in a court of law. Instruction manuals should be easy to follow and should point out potential hazards. They should also include guidelines for when and how to service the product, which components made by other manufacturers are not covered by your warranty (unless pass-through warranties have been negotiated), and statements that the warranty is invalidated by misuse, misassembly, or modification, and is only valid if the specified maintenance procedures are followed. Of course, the best insurance is to keep in contact with your customers so that if a problem occurs, you will be given the opportunity to fix it before legal action is taken.

Early on in the operation of the business, identify a qualified attorney familiar with your industry to handle any potential product liability claims. This attorney should handle the first case with which the business is faced. Thereafter, if other suits arise in various parts of the country, you can save money by hiring a "local attorney" in the jurisdiction of the claim. Then let the primary attorney brief the "local attorney" on the precedent-setting cases related to the claim and assist while the local attorney carries the case to court. In this way, you do not have to send your primary attorney on the road, incurring significant travel and time expenses.

Loss of Key Employees

Today more than ever before, no one can count on having the same management team over the life of the business—or even past the start-up phase. The demand for top-notch management personnel, particularly in some industries like high-tech, means that other companies will constantly be trying to woo away the best people from the best firms. Moreover, with more CEOs traveling, the chance for a fatal accident is greater. Then too, disease and heart attack often claim the lives of high-powered executives. This type of contingency planning is often called succession planning and involves identifying people who can take over key company positions in an emergency. Ideally that person will come from within the company, but in the case of a growing entrepreneurial company that has been operating in a "lean and mean" mode, that may not be possible, so outsiders must be found. To prepare for the eventuality that a key employee will be lost, the entrepreneur must have shared his or her vision for the company with others both inside and outside the company.

Bringing in a consultant to guide the management team in succession planning is a valuable exercise for any growing venture. Often consultants are even hired temporarily to take over a vacant position for a specified period of time during which they train a permanent successor. Another solution is to cross-train people in key positions so that someone can step in, at least for the short term, in the event of an emergency. Cross training is generally an integral part of a team-based approach to organizational management.

In the case of entrepreneurs who head family-owned companies there are special problems because they tend to look to a son or daughter to succeed them. Unfortunately, often that child will have no interest in doing so but will not have said anything to that effect to the parent/entrepreneur. One solution is to insist that the potential "successor" work for another company for several years to gain some business savvy and learn if they want to take over the family business.

Decline in Sales

When sales decline and positive cash flow starts looking like a memory, entrepreneurs often go into a period of denial. They start paying their suppliers more slowly to preserve cash; they lay off people; they stop answering the phone and insulate themselves against the demands of their creditors. Their panic often causes them to make poor decisions about how to spend the precious cash they have. They figure that if they can just hold on long enough, things will turn around. Unfortunately, this attitude only makes the problem worse, effectively propelling the business toward its ultimate demise. How can an entrepreneur lose touch with the business and the market so much that he or she puts the business at risk? What often happens is that entrepreneurs get so tied up with the day-to-day operations of the business that they don't have time to contemplate the "big picture" or stay in tune with their customers. Consequently, many times they don't see a potential crisis coming until it's too late.

When sales decline, the solution isn't necessarily to lower prices. If you have educated your customers about the value of your product or service, they will be confused by the sudden discounting. When there is a decline in sales it is especially important to look at all possible sources, not just the economy. You may have been lax about checking the credit status of customers and distributors, or the inventory turnover rate may have changed. You may have failed to notice an emerging competitor offering a product or service more in line with current tastes and preferences.

When a growing business first notices a dip in sales, it is time to find the cause and make the necessary changes. This will be easier if the business has a contingency plan in place. If, however, those changes cannot be made in time to forestall a cash flow problem, it is time to consult a debt negotiation company, a crisis management consultant, or a bankruptcy attorney who is willing to work through the problem outside of court. These experts can help the entrepreneur work with creditors until the problem is resolved. To make the best effort at avoiding a cash flow crisis, the entrepreneur must be continually committed to:

• Producing exceptional quality products
• Controlling the cost of overhead, particularly where that overhead does not contribute directly to revenue generation (i.e. expensive cars, travel, excessive commissions)
• Controlling production costs through subcontracting and being frugal about facilities

- Making liquidity and positive cash flow the prime directive, so that the company can ride out temporary periods of declining demand
- Having a contingency plan in place

The Exit Plan

Many entrepreneurs have questioned the need for an exit plan when they are more concerned with launching the business and making it a success. They find it difficult to think about how to get out of the business when they have barely gotten into it. While some entrepreneurs stay with their start-up for the rest of their lives or the business's, whichever comes first, the majority of entrepreneurs enjoy the challenge of start-up, the excitement of growth, and abhor with a passion the custodial role of manager of a stable, mature company. Exiting the business does not necessarily mean exiting the role of entrepreneur. It may in fact mean taking the financial rewards of having grown a successful business and investing them in a new venture.

There are entrepreneurs who do that very thing over and over again throughout their lives. Other entrepreneurs find that when the venture reaches a certain level, the business needs professional management skills that the entrepreneur often does not possess. In fact, the entrepreneur may actually be holding the company back without realizing it. At some point the board of directors will relegate the entrepreneur to R&D, public relations, or they may actually push the entrepreneur out of the company, as Apple Computer did with Steve Jobs. In any case, whether or not you intend to exit the business, you should have a plan for harvesting the rewards of having started the business in the first place.

Selling the Business

Selling the business outright to another company or an individual may be the goal if the entrepreneur is ready to move on to something else and wants to be free financially and mentally to do so. Unfortunately, however, selling a business is a life-changing event. For several years the entrepreneur has probably devoted the majority of his or her time and attention to growing the business, and it played an important role in structuring the entrepreneur's life. When the business is sold, the entrepreneur often experiences a sense of loss, much like the death of a loved one. If the entrepreneur has not prepared for this change in his or her life, serious emotional problems could be the consequence. There are several alternatives to selling the business outright that will be discussed in the next section. For now suffice it to say that before selling the business, the entrepreneur should plan for what will happen after the business is no longer part of his or her life.

The best way to sell a business is to know almost from the beginning that selling is what you want to do. This is so that you will make decisions for the business that will place it in the best position for a sale several years later. For one thing you will maintain audited financial statements that give the forecasts more credibility. The tax strategy will not be to minimize taxes by showing low profits but to show actual profits and pay the taxes on them because you will probably more than make up for the expense at the time of sale. Higher recorded profits will likely help the business be worth more. You will keep the business expenses and activity totally separate from the personal expenses and ensure that the business has value without you by preparing a successor. You will also plan for the time it will take to sell the business and wait to sell until the window of opportunity has opened.

Smaller businesses often use the services of business brokers to sell the business; however, a high-growth venture will more likely employ the services of an investment banking firm that has experience with the industry. Investment banks normally want a retainer to ensure the seriousness of your commitment, but that retainer will be applied against the final fee on the sale, which averages five percent of the purchase price. It is recommended, however, that a third party with no vested interest in the sale be employed to judge the fair market value of the business. This "appraiser" can also prepare financial projections based on the history of the company and their independent market research.

When a business is sold, the entrepreneur does not have to sell all the assets. For example, the building could be held out of the sale and leased back to the

Selling Your Name

If you have used your name as the name of the business, it becomes a negotiable asset in the sale. To sell the business you may have to give up the right to use your name in any future venture or in any advertising you do after the sale. Remember it has probably taken several years to establish your business's name in the marketplace. A purchaser will probably not want to change that name and confuse customers. You may, however, be able to pay for the right to use your name in a non-competing business, perhaps in a different industry. This is a serious issue that should be discussed with an attorney.

business purchaser, with the original owner staying on as landlord. While the potential purchaser is conducting due diligence on the entrepreneur and the business, the entrepreneur needs to do the same with the purchaser. The purchasing firm or individual should be thoroughly checked out against a list of criteria the entrepreneur has developed. The purchaser should have the resources necessary to continue the growth of the business, be familiar with the industry and the type of business being purchased, have a good reputation in the industry, and offer synergies that will ensure that the business continues in a positive direction. It is often helpful to make a complete list of criteria and then weight them by importance to fairly compare one potential buyer with another.

Cashing Out But Staying In

Sometimes entrepreneurs reach the point where they would like to take the bulk of their investment and gain out of the business but are not yet ready to cut the cord entirely. They may want to continue to run the business or at least retain a minority interest. There are several mechanisms by which this can occur.

Selling Stock.   If the company is still privately owned, the remaining share-holders may want to purchase your stock at current market rates so control doesn't end up in other hands. In fact, the shareholder's agreement that was drafted when you set up the corporation may have specified that you must first offer the stock to the company before offering it to anyone else. If the company is publicly traded, the task is much simpler; however, if you own a substantial portion of the issued stock, you must follow strict guidelines set out by the SEC in the liquidation of your interests. If the company had a successful IPO, the entrepreneur's founders stock will have increased substantially in value, which presents a tax liability the entrepreneur should not ignore. That is why many entrepreneurs in such situations cash out only what they need to support what-ever goals they have. This, of course, is based on the presumption that the company stock will continue its upward trend for the foreseeable future.

Restructuring.   Entrepreneurs who want to cash out a significant portion of their investment and turn over the reins of business to a son or daughter can do so by splitting the business into two firms, with the entrepreneur owning the firm that has all of the assets (plant, equipment, vehicles) and the child owning the operating aspect of the business while leasing the assets from the parent's company. See Figure 18.1 on p. 414.

Figure 18.1: Restructuring a Business

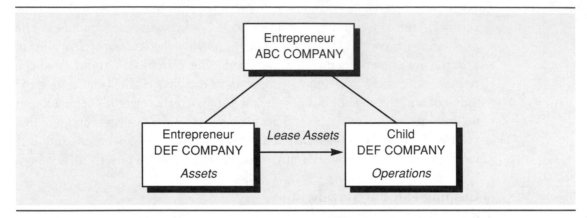

A Phased Sale.   Some entrepreneurs want to soften the emotional blow of selling the business, not to mention the tax consequences, by agreeing with the buyer—an individual or another firm—to sell the business in two phases. During the first phase the entrepreneur sells a percentage of the company but remains in control of operations and can continue to grow the company to the point at which the buyer has agreed to complete the purchase. This approach gives the entrepreneur the ability to cash out a portion of his or her invest-ment and still manage the business for an agreed-upon time, during which the new owner will likely be learning the business and phasing in. At the second phase, the business is sold at a price that is prearranged, usually as a multiple of earnings.

This approach is fairly complex and should always involve an attorney expe-rienced with acquisitions and buy-sell agreements. The buy-sell agreement, which spells out the terms of the purchase, specifies the amount of control the new owner can exert over the business before the sale is completed and the amount of proprietary information that will be shared with the buyer between Phases 1 and 2.

Using an ESOP.   If the business has more than 25 employees, one option for the entrepreneur is to cash out via an Employee Stock Ownership Plan (ESOP), but still maintain control for as long as desired. ESOPs, which are tax-qualified pension plans or defined-contribution plans governed by ERISA and IRS regu-lations, have long been considered viable devices for succession planning but work only where certain ingredients are present. The potential ESOP company should have revenues of at least $3 million and an annual payroll of at least $500,000, because the costs of setting up the plan can be substantial, around $100,000 for legal, bank, and accounting fees. The business also needs to have assets—inventory, accounts receivable, equipment—that can be used as collateral if a bank loan is required. Finally, the company should have excellent cash flow to repay the ESOP debt and buy back the stock of any employees who might leave the company over time.

The company sets up an ESOP trust fund into which it puts new or existing shares of stock. Another option is for the ESOP trust to take out a bank loan to buy stock and a minority interest in the company, at least 30 percent to trigger the capital gains exclusion. The shares in the trust are then allocated to individual employee accounts. The capital gains exclusion provides that the cash the owners receive from the ESOP is not taxed if it is reinvested in U.S. stocks or bonds. The banks too have an incentive to provide these ESOP loans because half of the interest the company pays to the bank is tax deductible to the bank if the ESOP owns 50 percent of the voting stock of the company. This can effectively raise the return on an eight percent loan to 12 percent.

The ESOP company makes tax-deductible contributions of up to 25 percent of the participant payroll to the ESOP to repay the bank debt. The cash-out price for the entrepreneur is based on the company's value at the time and results from a negotiation process with the trustee for the ESOP. The ESOP procedure is not something that can be completed quickly. Normally the entrepreneur prepares for the exit several years in advance, usually the length of time to repay the bank loan. See Figure 18.2.

There are several advantages to ESOPs:

- The entrepreneur can reinvest the proceeds of the sale in other securities within 12 months of the stock sale and thereby defer the gain until the new securities are sold. This assumes that the entrepreneur has owned the stock

Figure 18.2: ESOP Financing

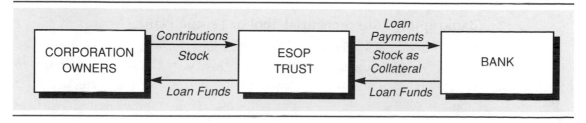

for more than three years. If the securities remain in the entrepreneur's estate at death, the heirs avoid having to pay a capital gains tax.

- The ESOP creates a ready market for any remaining owner shares in the entrepreneur's estate upon death. The heirs can sell those shares to the ESOP.
- ESOP loan interest rates are much lower than normal borrowing rates because banks can deduct 50 percent of the interest income when an ESOP owns 50 percent of the company's voting stock.
- Assuming the ESOP owns 50 percent of the stock, it can deduct interest *and principal* payments on the loan, which benefits cash flow enormously.
- ESOPs can also fund retirement plans and health care coverage.
- Employees participating in the ESOP can accumulate significant amounts of money over time, once they are vested.
- Employee shareholders have no voting rights but are represented by the trustee.

There are also several disadvantages the entrepreneur should be aware of:

- A company with an ESOP cannot elect a sub-chapter S corporation election, partnership, or professional corporation.
- ESOPs are expensive to set up and maintain, with annual expenses running about $10,000-$15,000.
- Private companies are required to repurchase the shares of employees who leave the company.
- New shares issued dilute the value of existing shares of stock.
- An ESOP creates a much more open environment in terms of information that must be shared with the ESOP participants than many entrepreneurs are accustomed to.

Entrepreneurs often find that with an ESOP in place, employees have a vested interest in the success of the business and tend to perform accordingly. In fact, the ESOP Association reports that about 71 percent of ESOP companies surveyed experienced higher performance after the ESOP. The employees will, however, also expect to be treated as partners in the venture and will want to be privy to full information on the operations of the company.

Bankruptcy: Entrepreneurial Tool or Escape Plan?

It is an unfortunate fact of life that some entrepreneurs must exit their businesses through liquidation. For whatever reasons, the business was unable to pay its obligations and unable to secure capital to float the business until it could. Certainly no entrepreneur starts a high-growth venture with liquidation in mind as the exit strategy; but sometimes the forces working against the business are so great that the entrepreneur must have an exit vehicle so he or she can move on to do something else. What forces a corporation into bankruptcy is difficult to pinpoint. The immediately precipitating cause is the failure to pay debt; however, a myriad of other events led up to that cause. They include economic and business cycles, excessive debt, surplus overhead, shifts in demand, excessive expenses, poor dividend policies, union problems, supplier problems, and poor financial management. Of course, the common denominator for all of these factors is poor management.

The title of this section referred to bankruptcy as a "tool," suggesting a vehicle by which the entrepreneur can accomplish something. The use of bankruptcy law as a tool stems from the fact that once any bankruptcy action is filed, all lawsuits and creditors' calls stop. This was certainly important to Manville Corporation, who filed for bankruptcy protection in 1982 based on an anticipated 32,000 lawsuits related to injury from asbestos products. Manville, which was a healthy corporation at the time, determined it could not stay in business and pay the lawsuits. Some firms have used Chapter 11 to nullify a union contract and force a change. At this point it should be noted that not all businesses can file for bankruptcy protection. Those that are exempt include savings and loans, banks, insurance companies, and foreign companies. Furthermore, a bankruptcy filing cannot occur where the intent is to defraud, and a company may file only once every six years.

Bankruptcy is normally a voluntary event; however, a company can be forced into bankruptcy by its creditors if they are:

• One or more creditors whose claims amount to $5,000 over the value of any assets if there are fewer than 12 claims, or
• Three or more creditors under the same above conditions where there are more than 12 claims, or
• Any number fewer than all the general partners in a limited partnership.

Involuntary bankruptcies are not common because the courts deal harshly with creditors that force a business into bankruptcy in bad faith.

The Bankruptcy Reform Act of 1978 and Public Law 95-958 provide for more than just liquidation of the business. Therefore, a clear understanding of the bankruptcy mechanisms available to the entrepreneur is essential in considering the options when a venture is faced with financial adversity.

• Chapter 7 discusses liquidation

- Chapter 9 deals with municipal debts
- Chapter 11 handles reorganization of businesses
- Chapter 13 deals with the debts of an individual with a regular income.

The two chapters that are pertinent to the entrepreneur are Chapter 11 and Chapter 7.

Chapter 11.   Chapter 11 under the bankruptcy code is really not a bankruptcy in the commonly used sense of the word. It is simply a reorganization of the finances of the business so it can continue to operate and begin to pay its debts. Only in the case where the creditors believe the management is unable to carry out the terms of the reorganization plan will a trustee be appointed to run the company until the debt has been repaid. Otherwise, the entrepreneur remains in control of the business while in a Chapter 11 position. After filing for reorganization, the entrepreneur and the creditors must meet within 30 days to discuss the status and organization of the business. The court then appoints a committee, which usually consists of the seven largest unsecured creditors, to develop a plan for the business with the entrepreneur. That plan must be submitted within 120 days and acceptance of the plan must come within 60 days of submittal. Of the total number of creditors affected by the plan, representing at least two-thirds of the total dollar amount, at least one half must accept the plan. Once the reorganization plan is approved by the court, the entrepreneur is discharged from any debts with the exception of those specified in the plan.

Chapter 7.   Chapter 7 of the Bankruptcy Code is essentially the liquidation of the assets of the business and the discharging of most types of debt. This vehicle is usually chosen when the business does not have sufficient resources to pay creditors while continuing to operate. The filing of a petition under Chapter 7 constitutes an Order for Relief. A trustee is then appointed to manage the disposition of the business, the goal of which is to reduce it to cash and distribute the cash to the creditors where authorized. After exemptions, the moneys derived from liquidation go first to secured creditors and then to priority claimants. Priority claimants include in order:

- Administrative expenses related to the bankruptcy
- Wages, salaries, or commissions
- Vacation, severance, and sick leave pay up to $2,000 per person if earned within 90 days of filing or the date of cessation of the business, whichever came first

- Contributions to employee benefit plans up to $2,000 per person earned within 180 days of filing or cessation
- Individual claims up to $900 each for services not rendered or products not received but paid for
- Taxes and customs duties
- General unsecured creditors
- Punitive penalties
- Accrued interest during the bankruptcy

Any surplus funds remaining after this distribution go to the entrepreneur. Prior to distribution, the entrepreneur has the right to certain exempt property. If the business is a corporation, those exemptions are minimal:

- Interest in any accrued dividends up to $4,000
- The right to Social Security benefits, unemployment compensation, public assistance, veterans' benefits, and disability benefits
- The right to stock bonuses, pensions, profit sharing or similar plan

If the legal form of the business is a partnership, the entrepreneur is entitled to exempt those properties specifically allowed for individuals filing bankruptcy petitions.

Lest it seem as though the entrepreneur is at the mercy of the creditors in a bankruptcy situation, it should be made clear that the entrepreneur in either type of bankruptcy petition, Chapter 7 or 11, has a great deal of power and control over the process. This power comes from the natural desire of the creditors for a quick and equitable resolution to the problem, and the protections inherent in the bankruptcy law. Often the creditors are better served by negotiating a restructuring of debt while the company is still operating and prior to a Chapter 7 liquidation where they are not likely to receive as great a portion of what is owed them. There are, however, certain things the entrepreneur will not be permitted to do within a certain period of time before the filing of a bankruptcy petition:

- Hide assets or liabilities
- Give preferential treatment to certain creditors 90 days prior to filing the petitions
- Make any potentially fraudulent conveyances up to one year prior to the filing of the petition

Any of the above conveyances may be recouped by the court during the bankruptcy proceedings.

Recently a new vehicle under Chapter 11 has emerged. Known as a "prepackaged bankruptcy," it can take from four to nine months to complete rather than the typical nine months to two years. The entrepreneur presents the creditors and equity owners with a reorganization plan *before* the bankruptcy filing actually goes to court. If the entrepreneur can achieve the required number of votes to agree to the plan (more than half the total creditors and two-thirds within each class of creditors), then the prepackaged plan can go forward expeditiously.

There is an obvious advantage to the entrepreneur using this approach. Under the traditional Chapter 11 approach, the creditors and everyone else

> *A new vehicle under Chapter 11 is the prepackaged bankruptcy.*

learn of the company's problems at the filing. With a prepackaged plan, by contrast, an approved plan is in place at the point at which the public becomes aware of the problem, and the creditors thus may experience a greater sense of confidence in the entrepreneur. Moreover, the prepackaged plan results in far less time in legal processes. For this approach to succeed, however, the statement of disclosure for the creditors about the positive and negative aspects of the business must be carefully constructed to give the creditors all the information they need to consider the plan and protect their interests.

Before considering bankruptcy as an option to either exit a troubled business or restructure the business in an effort to survive, you should seek advice from your attorney and/or a specialist in turnarounds in the industry. With the aid of an accountant, you need to audit your assets and liabilities to see if the business can qualify for and benefit from a Chapter 11 reorganization. Often seeking help before filing a bankruptcy petition can lead to alternative, less difficult solutions that are more beneficial to the entrepreneur and creditors alike.

Presenting the Contingency Plan in the Business Plan. The contingency plan is normally a small section of the business plan. It represents the entrepreneur's effort to demonstrate that the new venture has considered future contingencies that may affect the business's ability to perform as projected in the pro forma

Strategies for Avoiding Bankruptcy

- Avoid relying on one major customer or industry for revenue generation
- Keep overhead costs to essentials that directly contribute to support the generation of revenues
- Maintain a degree of liquidity equal to about several months of overhead expense
- Maintain current and honest relationships with bankers, creditors, and suppliers

financial statements. Those contingencies typically include such events as changes in the economic climate, changes in demand for the product, loss of key employees, and the potential for changes in laws and regulations affecting the business. Certainly no one expects the entrepreneur to account for all contingencies that may impact the business; only those that may significantly impact the business and have a real probability of occurring need be addressed.

✓ New Venture Checklist

Have you

☐ Identified the issues that could potentially affect the business at various points in the future?

☐ Developed a contingency plan for various scenarios that may impact the business at some future date?

☐ Determined your goals for the business relative to an exit strategy?

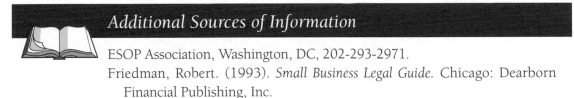

Additional Sources of Information

ESOP Association, Washington, DC, 202-293-2971.

Friedman, Robert. (1993). *Small Business Legal Guide.* Chicago: Dearborn Financial Publishing, Inc.

Freiermuth, Edmund P. (1988). *Life After Debt.* Homewood, IL: Dow Jones Irwin.

National Center for Employee Ownership, Oakland, CA, 510-272-9461.

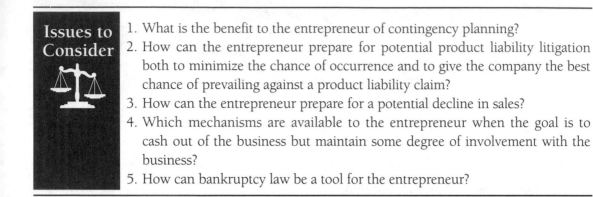

Issues to Consider

1. What is the benefit to the entrepreneur of contingency planning?
2. How can the entrepreneur prepare for potential product liability litigation both to minimize the chance of occurrence and to give the company the best chance of prevailing against a product liability claim?
3. How can the entrepreneur prepare for a potential decline in sales?
4. Which mechanisms are available to the entrepreneur when the goal is to cash out of the business but maintain some degree of involvement with the business?
5. How can bankruptcy law be a tool for the entrepreneur?

CHAPTER 19

Packaging and Presenting the Business Plan

Overview

- *The focus of the business plan*
- *The content of the business plan*
- *Oral presentation of the business plan*

Preparing the Business Plan

This book has focused primarily on launching a new venture and secondarily on growing the venture. In both instances, a business plan can be enormously helpful if not absolutely essential. The business plan is a living guide to the business that lets the reader understand the culture, mission, goals, and objectives of the new venture at various points in its life. Prior to start-up, the business plan helps the entrepreneur understand completely the nature of the venture being undertaken, and to that extent, it assists the entrepreneur in deciding if the business is viable or if new directions or new concepts should be developed. Too often entrepreneurs "fall in love" with their business concepts and charge ahead with no plan, only to discover after much time and money have been expended that there is no market for it. Doing a feasibility study can go a long way toward preventing these kinds of costly errors. Once the business concept has been judged feasible, the business plan establishes the direction the new venture will take in its effort to grow, and the means and methods by which it will get there. It is also a vital source of information for others as the entrepreneur seeks investment capital, a loan or credit line, or equity members for the management team.

You have no doubt noticed that this book was designed to carry you through the business planning process in a "logical" progression. Following this progression may be the ideal way to go about preparing a business plan, but, frankly, it doesn't often happen in such an orderly fashion. Typically, information for all parts of the business plan is gathered at various points in time, usually at the convenience of the entrepreneur. The entrepreneur may talk to a distributor in the industry seeking a sense of market demand for the proposed product and wind up getting, in addition, an understanding of typical gross margins in the industry, information that will not be needed until after it has been determined that there is a market for the product. From talking to suppliers during market research, the entrepreneur may become concerned that the cost to produce the product is too great, so he or she will quickly calculate the cost to produce and the probable selling price based on preliminary information to see if there will be enough money left over to pay overhead and eventually make a profit. If it looks as though there isn't enough profit in it to make the effort worthwhile, the entrepreneur may decide to abandon the concept even before finishing the market research.

> *Preparing a business plan doesn't often happen in an orderly fashion.*

As you can see, business planning is a fluid and dynamic process. One way to gain a measure of control of the information gathered over time is to set up files for each of the major sections of the business plan. As each piece of information is collected, it is filed in the appropriate folder. When it's time to analyze and prepare that section of the business plan, all the information needed to do it will be there.

You will find people who will proudly proclaim that they never had a business plan and yet were successful. That may be true—there are always exceptions to every rule—but more often than not, these entrepreneurs started small businesses rather than high-growth, world-class ventures, or perhaps never had to seek capital from outside sources. Also many of the more famous companies that were started without plans—Pizza Hut, Crate and Barrel, Microsoft, and Reebok—were started in the 1970s and early 1980s in a less global, less technologically complex business environment. Moreover, most of these companies eventually had to write business plans when expansion required taking on investors, going public, or being acquired by a major corporation. Then, too, you can't dismiss the luck aspect. Being in the right place at the right time has played a telling role in the early success of many ventures.

No one will deny that writing a business plan is a chore, but if you organize the information in advance and plan for the time it takes to actually do the writing, it can be accomplished with a minimum of pain and frustration. Be realistic. This is not a job that can be completed in a marathon weekend, but is a job that you as the lead entrepreneur and the key members of your founding team must tackle seriously if you are to ensure the best chance for achieving the goals of the business.

Writing with a Focus

Too often entrepreneurs approach the writing of the business plan with a "what do *I* need to know" approach without considering the reader's interests. It is important to know prior to writing the plan that different readers have different needs which must be addressed. How is it possible to write one business plan for several different audiences? It's not. You may need to have more than one version of the plan to appropriately address the specific needs and requirements of various audiences. For example, a business plan written with venture capitalists in mind would focus on growth and high return on investment, but might be considered too risky by a banker, who is more interested in how the bank's loan will be repaid. Likewise, a plan written to meet the needs of the banker will not capture the attention of a venture capitalist, because generally it is too conservative in its projections.

There are several audiences for the business plan. This section focuses on those typically encountered by entrepreneurs starting high-growth ventures: investors and venture capitalists, bankers or lenders, strategic alliances, customers and suppliers, and key management.

Focusing on Investors and Venture Capitalists

Anyone investing in the new venture has four principal concerns: rate of growth, return on investment, degree of risk, and protection. Investors are generally betting on the value of their ownership interest in the business increasing over time at a rate greater than that which could be gained in another type of investment or in a bank account. They want to know how fast the business is projected to grow, when that growth will take place, and what will ensure that the growth actually occurs as predicted. They expect that predictions will be based on solid evidence in the marketplace and a thorough knowledge of the target market. Investors are naturally concerned about when and how the principal portion of their investment will be repaid and how much gain on that investment will accrue over the time they are invested in the company. The answers to these concerns are largely a function of the structure of the investment deal, whether that be a limited or general partnership, or preferred or common stock, and so forth. Consequently, investors want to understand what the entrepreneur intends as far as deal structure, knowing full well that the investor will at some point have some input into how the deal is ultimately structured.

Investors want to thoroughly understand the risks they face in investing in the new venture, principally, how their original equity will be protected. They expect the entrepreneur to present the potential dangers facing the new venture and a plan for mitigating or dealing with them to protect the investors against loss. Finally, investors want to know how their equity will be protected if the business fails and how the business will protect its assets from seizure by creditors.

There are some typical errors that entrepreneurs frequently make when writing the business plan for investors or venture capitalists:

- *Projecting rapid growth beyond the capabilities of the founding team.* This is a common problem. The new venture shows potential for rapidly increasing demand, sales doubling or tripling on an annual basis in the first few years. The entrepreneur believes this will be very attractive to investors. What he or she doesn't realize is that there is no evidence in the business plan to prove that the founding team can manage and control this type of growth, and this is a cause for great concern on the part of the investors. Too often they have seen a business fail during rapid growth because management didn't have the systems in place to deal with it. The entrepreneur should be careful to project controlled growth and have a plan for bringing on the necessary personnel at the point at which the company is ready for more rapid growth. The other danger in projecting too high a level of success is that you increase the chances you will not be able to achieve it. It is better to project a little more conservatively and try to exceed those projections.

- *The three-ring circus with only one ringleader.* Many entrepreneurs pride themselves on being a "jack of all trades." They claim to have expertise in all the functional areas of the new venture. What they really have is general knowledge of all the functional areas and maybe a real expertise in only one. Investors are very nervous about relying on solo entrepreneurs to lead world-class ventures. They much prefer a team of founders with at least one person specializing in each of the functional areas.

- *Performance in some or all areas that exceeds industry averages.* While it is possible for a new venture to exceed industry averages in a particular area, it is not likely. Most averages, such as those for receivables turnover and bad debt losses, have come about as a result of economies of scale, which the new venture is not likely to achieve for some time. It is better for the business plan to initially indicate performance measures at or slightly below industry averages with a plan for how to exceed those averages at some point in the future.

- *Underestimating the need for capital.* Investors need to know that the business plan projects sufficient capital infusion to grow the company until internal cash flows can carry the load and then provide a plan for an additional infusion of capital when the company is ready for rapid expansion. If the entrepreneur underestimates the amount of capital needed, most savvy investors will recognize it and attribute the error to naiveté on the part of the entrepreneur, or, conversely, they will rely on the figures presented in the plan and ultimately suffer the potential loss of their investment as a result. Every estimate for capital should contain an additional amount for contingencies.

- *Confusing strategy with tactics.* It is much easier to develop tactics than strategies. Strategies define the overall focus of the business, while tactics are the methods by which those strategies will be achieved. When an investor asks what the entrepreneur's strategy is for achieving a projected market share by year three and the entrepreneur responds with "attending trade shows and advertising in trade journals," the entrepreneur has lost the confidence of the investor by responding with tactics. This mistake is often made, as many entrepreneurs focus too much attention on tactics, often to the exclusion of identifying the overall strategy those tactics will support. The strategy for achieving the market share may be to become the first mover in a market niche.

- *Focusing on price as a market strategy for a product or service.* This is similar to projecting performance above industry averages. It is rarely possible for a new venture with a product or service that currently exists in the marketplace to enter based on a lower price than competitors. Established companies have achieved economies of scale that the new venture is usually unable to do and will no doubt easily match the price set by a new entrant into the market. Furthermore, this strategy does not impress investors. They are more interested in how the new venture will differentiate itself in terms of product, process, distribution, or service.

- *The entrepreneur's investment in the business.* Investors are more comfortable investing in a new venture where the entrepreneur has contributed a substantial amount of the start-up capital. That signals to the investors a level of commitment necessary to achieve the goals of the company.

Focusing on Bankers or Lenders

Like investors, bankers or lenders want to know they are going to get their money back. When considering a business plan and an entrepreneur for a loan, lenders have several concerns:

- *The amount of money the entrepreneur needs.* Lenders are looking for a specific amount that can be justified with accurate calculations and data.
- *What positive impact the loan will have on the business.* Lenders would like to know that the money they are lending is not going to pay off old debt or pay salaries, but rather improve the business's financial position, particularly with regard to cash flow.
- *What kind of assets the business has for collateral.* Not all assets are created equal. Some assets have no value outside the business because they are custom-made or specific to that business and therefore cannot be sold on the open market. They prefer to see industry-standard equipment and facilities that can easily be converted to another use.
- *How the business will repay the loan.* Lenders are interested in the earnings potential of the business over the life of the loan, but more important, they want to know that the business generates sufficient cash flow to service the debt. While fixed expenses are fairly easy to predict, variable expenses—those related to the production of the product or service—present a more difficult problem. That is why lenders are also interested in the market research section of the business plan, which tells them what the demand for the product/service is, and the marketing plan, which tells them how the entrepreneur plans to reach the customer.
- *How the bank will be protected if the business doesn't meet its projections.* Lenders want to know that the entrepreneur has a contingency plan for situations where major assumptions prove to be wrong. They want to ensure they are paid out of cash flow, not by liquidating the assets of the business.
- *The entrepreneur's stake in the business.* Like investors, lenders feel more confident about lending to a business where the entrepreneur has a substantial monetary investment in the business. That way the entrepreneur is less likely to walk away, leaving the lender stranded.

Focusing on Strategic Alliances

Strategic alliances may involve formal partnership agreements with major corporations or simply an informal agreement through a large purchase contract. In either case, the larger company that is allying itself with the new venture is usually looking for new products, processes, or technology that complement its current line of products or services. Accordingly, it will search for a new venture management team that has some large corporate experience so the relationship will be smoother. They are also interested in strategic issues like the marketing and growth strategies of the new venture.

Focusing on Major Customers and Suppliers

Major customers and suppliers are concerned with the new venture's performance record since the company was founded. As it takes some time to establish a stable performance record, these third-party readers of the business plan will probably not be interested in seeing the plan until the business is up and running and beginning to demonstrate that its predictions for sales are fairly accurate.

Focusing on Key Management

Key management that the founding team wishes to attract during the growth phase of the new venture will also be concerned about how precisely and accurately the entrepreneur has forecasted demand for the product or service. Many of these targeted key management people will leave other jobs to join the new venture so they will want to feel confident that the business will not fail and has strong potential for growth. More than any other group mentioned, potential key management will be more interested in the details of the operations of the company.

At the beginning of this section, it was suggested that various versions of the plan be developed depending on the audience. The longest and most detailed version will probably be for internal use and for attracting key personnel. Investors, strategic alliances, and lenders in particular will probably prefer a more concise—perhaps 40-page—version of the plan, focusing on the specific areas of interest they have. It's a good idea to read other companies' business plans to get a sense of what works and what doesn't in terms of impressing the reader. If the style and organization of a particular plan makes the business concept seem more appealing, consider adapting the style to your business plan. But make sure the content is written in your own unique style—otherwise, it may sound like a "canned" or professionally prepared business plan and will win no points with a potential funder.

What to Include in the Business Plan

While there are no hard and fast rules about all the items to include in a business plan and where to put them, most business plans contain the sections discussed below. The major sections of the business that have already been discussed and outlined in detail in various chapters of the book will only be listed here.

The Cover Page for the Bound Document

Like any document designed to sell something, the business plan is attempting to convince various third parties—and the entrepreneur—of the viability of the new venture. Therefore, the cover page should convey in an attractive, professional manner the confidence and creativity of the entrepreneur. In the case of venture capitalists and lenders, most have dozens of business plans cross their desks every day, so it is important to make your plan stand out. Appearance may be only skin deep, but positive first impressions go a long way toward attracting the attention of a potential financial source. The typical information to have on the cover page is:

- The name of the company
- The words "Business Plan"
- The name of the contact person for the new venture and the address and phone number of the business

Some ways to make the business plan stand out are to use color on the cover, the business's logo with the name, or a design that reflects the personality of the business.

The Executive Summary

The executive summary is a two-page (maximum three-page) summary of the key points in the business plan. Often entrepreneurs use an executive summary to gauge interest in the business before handing out the complete business plan. It is also used to query venture capitalists as to their curiosity and desire to know more about the business. If first impressions count, the executive summary is one of the most crucial sections of the business plan, and probably the most difficult to write. It is not easy to condense the major sections of the business plan into a paragraph each, but it is an excellent exercise that forces the entrepreneur to truly understand the key elements of the business and state them in such a way that they entice the reader to want to know more.

Accordingly, the executive summary is first and foremost a selling document whose purpose is to get the reader to look at the complete business plan. Most venture capitalists and investors—as well as lenders—see so many plans that all they ever read in the first pass is the executive summary. If they aren't excited after reading that, they'll never look at the complete plan. So the first paragraph, even the first sentence, is critical. It must convey the excitement and personality of the business without using such time-worn, over puffed phrases as "There is nothing like this in the market today." Statements like that are sure to turn an investor off, because they know immediately that it isn't true; very few new ventures are based on concepts that are entirely new and nonexistent, and investors know this.

The first paragraph should also clearly show how the product or service being represented differentiates itself in the marketplace. One way to do this is to use the approach Gentech Corporation employed in its executive summary (See Figure 19.1, for a portion of that summary). They briefly described a problem in their industry and how they were going to solve it. This approach lets the investor know right away that the company is customer-oriented and has differentiated itself in the marketplace.

Another important thing to remember about the executive summary is that it should be a stand-alone document—that is, you should be able to hand it out independent of the business plan.

Figure 19.1: A Portion of an Executive Summary

GENTECH CORPORATION
EXECUTIVE SUMMARY
Businesses and individuals who use both power and pneumatic tools have always had to deal with using two distinct power units—a generator and a compressor—and leaving those units running continuously for extended periods of time. This inefficiency results in:
- Increased operating costs of using two units
- Increased fuel consumption
- Increased costly maintenance and repairs
- Increased nuisance level of noise associated with gasoline engine-powered generators and compressors running continuously
- Increased environmental pollution

GENTECH CORPORATION's *PowerSource*™ alleviates these problems by providing:
- A combination air compressor and generator unit driven by a single gasoline engine and providing both AC electric power and air power from one portable unit
- A patented start/stop system to control the engine remotely and automatically based on demand, which reduces fuel consumption, costly maintenance repairs and is less polluting to the environment as the engine only runs during tool usage or to replenish tank pressure
- Patented electronic switching between the generator and compressor to monitor AC and air power requirements to ensure maximum power output on demand
- A variable timer delay system which avoids numerous engine shutdowns if tools are being used frequently
- Portability through the use of one lightweight engine to power both functions

The executive summary goes on to describe how Gentech Corporation will compete in the marketplace and summarizes the other major sections of the business plan.

The Cover Page for the Business Plan

Between the executive summary and the table of contents for the business plan, it is useful to put another cover page containing the name of the business and the words "Business Plan."

The Table of Contents

The table of contents should display the major sections of the business plan and the key subheadings for each section.

The Body of the Business Plan

The body of the business plan contains all the major sections of information that were discussed throughout the book.

- The purpose and description of the business
- The management team
- The industry
- The target market
- Operations
- Marketing plan
- Financial plan
- Contingency plan
- Deal structure (if appropriate for the reader)
- List of references if footnotes were not used

Business plans contain a lot of private information, some of which you may not want to share with everyone who reads the plan. Again, that is the reason for several versions. A section like "Deal Structure," for example, should probably not be included when giving a plan to a lender or potential management employee, but is usually needed when dealing with investors or venture capitalists.

Be sure that the body of the business plan answers the basic questions:

1. Who are you?
2. What is the company?
3. What do you sell?
4. Who will buy?

5. Why will they buy?
6. How is your financial health?

Supporting Documents—The Appendices

Many items that might be important to the reader but would clog up the body of the business plan and make it more difficult to read quickly can be placed in appendices after the body of the plan. Some items that typically go in an appendix include:

- Résumés of the founding team
- Job descriptions
- Lease agreements
- License agreements
- Contracts
- Letters of intent
- Incorporation agreements or partnership agreements
- Evidence of patents
- Designs, architectural or product
- Personal financial statement (only where required, typically by a lender or investor)

Visual Presentation of the Business Plan

By now you know that the appearance of the business plan is the first step in getting the plan read. The trick, however, is to have the plan look professional without being too slick by making it a hard-bound, full-color, textbook-style business plan. Besides, a hard-bound plan suggests it's not subject to change any time soon, which is not an impression you want to convey. Here are some suggestions for ways to make the business plan stand out from the crowd.

- The plan should be bound in such a way that it lies flat when you read it. A spiral type binding or binder works well.
- Use index tabs to separate major sections and make it easier for the reader to find something.
- Use 12- or 13-point type fonts and an easily read font style like Times Roman for readability.
- Use bolded subheadings and bullets generously, again to facilitate finding information. (See Figure 19.2 on p. 434 for an example of one style of headings and sub-headings.)
- If you have a logo, use it at the top of every page.

Figure 19.2: Sample Formatting for a Business Plan

GENTECH CORPORATION

PRODUCT PLAN

Purpose   GENTECH CORPORATION, a privately held California corporation, was established to manufacture and distribute portable power equipment incorporating patented, state-of-the-art technology and satisfying a need for efficient, energy-saving and environmentally friendly power equipment. GENTECH CORPORATION has been actively involved since 1989 in the research and development of a portable dual-purpose power source for power and pneumatic tools.

Product   *PowerSource* ™, the first product to be offered by GENTECH CORPORATION, is a combination air compressor and generator unit mounted on a typical twin-tank, wheelbarrow-style frame. Driven by a single gasoline engine, the dual purpose *PowerSource* ™ provides both AC electric power and air power from one portable, lightweight unit. When operating as a generator, it supplies electrical power to 110 volt outlets. When an electrical tool is in use, an electronic switching device automatically sends a signal to open a valve to vent the compressor piston to the atmosphere, thus significantly reducing the demand on the engine. As long as there is air stored in the tanks, air tools and power tools can be used simultaneously. A powerful AC generator and a high-output air compressor, the *PowerSource* ™ eliminates the need to transport both a generator and compressor to the work site.

PowerSource ™ features a state-of-the-art, start/stop system which controls the engine remotely and automatically based on demand. This innovative system starts the engine immediately upon demand from a power tool or when the pressure in the air tank reaches the lower limit. The engine stops automatically when power tools are not in use and the pressure in the air tank reaches the upper limit. No special tools, electric cords, or air hoses are required. This system is considered to be fuel efficient and less polluting since the engine is only running while an electrical tool is being used or tank pressure is being replenished. To avoid numerous shutdowns if tools are used frequently, a variable timer delay mechanism can be activated to allow the gas engine to idle down for a set period prior to shutting down altogether. In addition, an override switch allows the option of operating the engine continuously when a constant power source is preferred.

- Make sure your writing is focused and concise. Prune excess words with a vengeance.
- Make sure all claims are supported by solid evidence.
- Ask several people to edit the plan.

- Do not use fill-in-the-blanks computer programs to write the plan. The result will not reflect the personality of your business.
- Revise and rewrite several times.
- Number each copy of the business plan and include with it a Statement of Confidentiality that the reader should sign. Keep track of who has which plan.
- Place a statement on the cover page prohibiting copying of the plan.

Oral Presentation of the Business Plan

It is not uncommon, particularly if the plan is being used to seek capital, for the entrepreneur to be asked to do a presentation of the business concept, high-lighting the key points of the business plan. Usually this occurs after the potential funders have read the executive summary and perhaps done a cursory reading of the complete business plan. In any case, they feel it is worth their time to hear from the entrepreneur and the founding team to see if they measure up to their expectations. While this presentation should not be confused with a formal speech, it does share with a speech many common elements.

- *Answer the fundamental questions* as discussed in the preceding section on the body of the business plan
- *Keep the presentation under a half hour.* That is plenty of time to present the key elements. Questions and discussion will probably follow the presentation.
- *Be sure to catch the audience's attention in the first 60 seconds.* Let them know you're happy to be there and immediately get them involved in the presentation by showing concern, for example, for whether or not they can easily see the presentation slides.
- *Stand without using a podium.* It will give you better command of the situation and make it easier to use gestures and visual aids.
- *Move around but don't pace.* It is deadly to stand constantly in one place, but it is equally annoying to pace back and forth with no purpose. Moving helps reduce stress and livens up the presentation.
- *Maintain eye contact with everyone.* Talk *to* the audience, not over their heads.
- *Use visual aids.* Color slides or overheads help keep the presentation on track and focused on key points. Be careful not to dazzle the audience with too many overheads, however, as the audience may find themselves more interested in the rhythm of the motions you subconsciously develop as you flip through the slides than in what you have to say. Keep the slides simple—no more than five lines per slide—and professional looking.
- *Make sure the key members of the founding team are involved* in the presentation.

- *Do a demonstration of the product or service where possible.* It helps generate excitement for the concept.
- *Practice the presentation in advance* for a small group of friends or colleagues who will critique it, or videotape the practice session so the founding team can critique themselves.
- *Anticipate questions* that may be asked by funders and determine how they should be answered.

If the founding team has successfully made it through the presentation, they have cleared the first hurdle. The second hurdle, however, is the hardest: answering questions from the funders. One thing to learn about funders is that they generally like to ask questions for which they already know the answers; this is a test to see if the founding team knows what they're talking about. Furthermore, they will ask questions that either require an impossibly precise answer or are so broad as to make the entrepreneur wonder what the questioner is looking for.

Another type of question typically asked is "What are the implications of...?" With this question they are looking for an answer that addresses their needs and concerns relative to the request for capital. Finally, the type of question that poses the most problems for the founding team is the inordinately complex question that contains several underlying assumptions. For example, "If I were to analyze your new venture in terms of its market share before and after this potential investment, how would the market strategy have changed and how much of the budget should be allotted to changing that strategy?"

The first thing the entrepreneur should do when faced with such a complicated question is to ask that it be repeated to ensure nothing has been missed that might cause the entrepreneur to make an incorrect assumption. Alternatively, you can restate the question and confirm that it has been understood correctly. Another suggestion is to ask for a few minutes to formulate your answer. With this type of question, you may only feel comfortable answering part of it, for example, you may have evidence to support a change in market share as a result of the capital infusion which you could present. On the other hand, you probably don't want to commit to any course of action or any budget amount without having had time to consider it further and gather more facts. Saying this in response to the question will no doubt gain you a measure of respect, for you will have demonstrated you don't make important decisions precipitously without considering all the facts.

If you are asked a factual question for which you do not know the answer (usually these are tangential to the business plan and asked to see how you will respond), admit that you don't have that answer off the top of your head but will be happy to find it after the meeting is completed and get back to them. If the presentation or anything the team has proposed is criticized (a likely possibility), be careful not to be defensive or turn the criticism in any way on the audience. If you do so, you will have lost your chance with them immediately and may never regain it. Remember, you are playing in their ballpark. They make the rules. If it appears they will be difficult people to deal with as investors or lenders, you don't have to use them. Chalk up the presentation to practice and go on to the next one.

Preparing and presenting the business plan is the culmination of months of work. The business plan represents the heart and soul of the new venture and, if it was researched and written well, it can enhance the chances of starting a successful, high-growth venture.

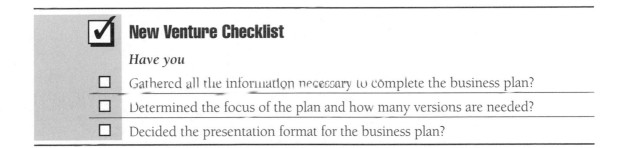

✓ New Venture Checklist

Have you

☐ Gathered all the information necessary to complete the business plan?

☐ Determined the focus of the plan and how many versions are needed?

☐ Decided the presentation format for the business plan?

Additional Sources of Information

Bangs, David H. Jr. (1992).*The Business Planning Guide*. Dover, NH: Upstart Publishing Company, Inc.

Detz, Joan. (1984). *How to Write and Give a Speech*. New York: St. Martin's Press.

Gumpert, D.E. (1990). *How to Really Create a Successful Business Plan*. Boston: Inc. Publishing.

Hoff, Ron (1992). *I Can See You Naked*. Kansas City: Andrew and McMeel.

Mancuso, Joseph (1985). *How to Write a Winning Business Plan*. New York: Simon & Schuster.

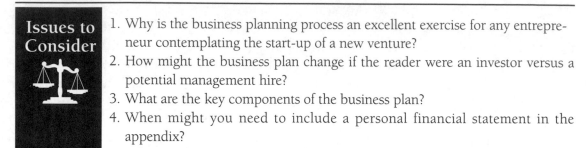

Issues to Consider

1. Why is the business planning process an excellent exercise for any entrepreneur contemplating the start-up of a new venture?
2. How might the business plan change if the reader were an investor versus a potential management hire?
3. What are the key components of the business plan?
4. When might you need to include a personal financial statement in the appendix?
5. What are three key elements of a successful business plan presentation?

Simtek, Inc.

I n July 1985, a California corporation called Simtek, Inc. was founded to produce and market patented consumer products. The company was initially capitalized in November 1986 by selling 60 percent of its stock to two private investors. Seed capital of $500,000 was raised to develop two products—the Tapemate electric Scotch tape dispenser, and the Tapemate box sealer. Simtek, Inc. initially chose to begin development and operations with the Scotch tape dispenser, a concept that the founder, Steven Johnson[1], had been developing since 1982.

The Product

Tapemate®, a registered trademark of Simtek, Inc,, is an AC electric tape dispenser that dispenses and cuts any desired length of tape by pressing a button. The TM-100 is designed to be quick and efficient and incorporates a patented disposable tape cartridge containing Scotch brand tape. The original Scotch brand tape did not sell well when it was introduced as there was no easy way to remove the tape from the roll. The first tape dispensers invented are those still in common usage today. They all contain a means for holding a roll of tape and a serrated blade for tearing a desired length of tape. 3M, the manufacturer of Scotch brand tape, produces an excellent adhesive product, but difficulties continue to arise when customers attempt to remove the desired length from a tape roll even with the use of a traditional dispenser. Invariably, the tape has unwanted finger prints, smudges, jagged edges, and so forth. The TM-100 solves this problem by pulling tape off the roll at a smooth three inches per second without finger prints or smudges and also cutting the dispensed length of tape cleanly without serrations or jagged edges.

To further ensure the quality of the Tapemate dispenser and its intended functions, Simtek also designed a disposable tape cartridge, much like a type-

---

[1]Steven Johnson is not the real name of the entrepreneur/inventor who founded Simtek.

writer ribbon cartridge. The cartridge helps keep the dispenser clean while ensuring that the correct type of tape is being used in the dispenser. The cartridge is easy to load into the dispenser and comes in several types of tape in a variety of widths, lengths, adhesives, thicknesses, and overall quality. Simtek felt it was important to control the type of tape used in the dispenser to guarantee the highest quality. It also planned to price the product at a price point similar to the electric pencil sharpener so it would sell well in major office supply outlets. A retail price point of $79.95 was determined.

Simtek applied for and was granted a United States Patent, #4,638,696, for the electric tape dispenser. Research found that previous similar inventions suffered from a number of difficulties, including the jamming of the operative mechanisms due to the adhesive surfaces contacting the operative mechanism of the dispensing device. Another chronic problem was the propensity for slack to form in the lead portion of the material within the device that would then become entangled in the operative mechanism, thereby jamming the dispenser. It was based on this research that Simtek believed that a need existed for its Tapemate product.

The Company Philosophy

Johnson planned to begin operations with a very small staff of multiskilled individuals, subcontract for manufacturing, and use independent sales reps for a sales team. The goal was to be a "highly service-oriented company with a firm belief in quality and customer satisfaction." It would strive to maintain a very low product defect ratio to promote customer loyalty. Furthermore, Simtek would not be a one-product company. It would continually search for new consumer products that were innovative and competitively priced.

The History of the TM-100

Johnson approached a prestigious design firm located in Palo Alto, California to engineer the product and complete the assembly drawings, and contracted with a well-known Southern California design firm to handle the packaging design. The cost of design and development was exceptionally high. It included about $60-70,000 for injection molding tools, $30-40,000 for engineering, and $25,000 for patents. Johnson then took the drawings to a model builder to develop a prototype. At this point a total of about $150,000 had been spent in

R&D. It was decided to produce the Tapemate in Korea to keep manufacturing costs down, and limited production was begun.

The initial feedback was positive; it appeared that the market for the electric tape dispenser was very large. However it was quickly learned that the product was more price sensitive than first anticipated and, in addition, manufacturing costs were coming in higher than estimated, due in large part to over-design of the product. In other words, the product had too many advanced features that resulted in excessive manufacturing costs.

Johnson decided to save money by acting as his own manufacturer's rep, initiating sales first in the United States and then in Europe through a contact he had made in Switzerland. He attended trade shows and demonstrated the product in major department stores like Bloomingdales and Macys. Demonstrating the product resulted in greater sales, in large part because of the design of the box in which the Tapemate was packaged. While very attractive (it won several design awards), it did not, however, show what was in the box beyond saying *Simtek* Tapemate®. There was no picture of the dispenser on the box, so potential customers didn't recognize the product for what it was when they saw it on the shelf. Still, Johnson's efforts produced sales of approximately 7,000 units domestically and 5,000 in Europe. In 1988 gross sales totaled $16,345 with a COGS of $10,945. In 1989, gross sales totaled $28,062 with a COGS of $21,092.

> The initial feedback was positive; it appeared that the market for the electric tape dispenser was very large.

At this point, the product had been in the market for three years. Simtek did additional market research and concluded that some key changes had to be made in the product—specifically, a DC battery-operated version so the product would not be geographically sensitive, and some minor design flaws had to be adjusted. For example, it was found that if a customer touched the start button too quickly and didn't hold it quite long enough, the dispensing mechanism would jam after several repetitions. Furthermore, there was the problem of the price point. Johnson's market research indicated that customers perceived the electric tape dispenser as an equivalent of an electric pencil sharpener rather than an electric stapler. This was a crucial distinction, as electric pencil sharpeners could be bought in the $15-$20 range, while the price on electric staplers was much closer to the price on the tape dispenser. At $79.95, the tape dispenser did well in gift stores because its design was very stylized and it worked well in demonstrations. However, it was not competitive in the office supply market where margins are very small.

Back to the Drawing Boards

Having determined that the original design was probably not the most market-able, Simtek approached two major California product design firms for estimates on the development costs for the battery-operated tape dispenser. The goal of re-design was to reduce the cost of manufacturing through component optimization, part reduction, and mechanism development. The design goals included:

- A battery-powered product with an optional AC adapter for extended operation
- An improved user interface via a switch separated from the tape dispensing area to eliminate accidental switch activation
- Easy access to internal components in the event of mechanism failure
- Control of the minimum length of tape dispensed to avoid mechanism failure
- Elimination of custom cartridges. Access to the internal feeding mechanism would be provided to facilitate the tape-loading process.
- Replacement of the solenoid-driven cutting mechanism with a mechanically equivalent solution to reduce the overall power consumption and compo-nent cost
- Cost of Goods Sold held to between $5 and $6
- Exploration of alternative motor and drive assemblies to optimize perfor-mance and minimize cost
- Reduction in the number of labor-intensive processes such as electrical assem-bly and soldering, and provide for unidirectional assembly of all components

It was estimated that to be competitive, the new unit must sell at a retail price of approximately $15. This translated to a manufacturing cost of $3-$4.50 per unit. The estimates from the product design firms came in at $74,000-$91,000 for concept design, breadboard design (the first stage of a design using models), documentation, prototyping, and pre-production. The entire process would take from 28 to 33 weeks to complete, with the deliverable being a production-quality prototype.

Estimate of Sales After Redesign

	Cost to Redesign	Unit Cost	Sales Price	Year 1 Sales	Year 2 Sales	Year 3 Sales	Year 4 Sales
Tapemate	$150,000	$6.00	$12.00	25,000 units $300,000	75,000 units $900,000	125,000 units $1,500,000	150,000 units $1,800,000

The Beginning of the End

With the design proposal and a revised financial project in hand, Johnson went in search of additional funds for redesigning and to buy out his original investors who, by 1990, were becoming frustrated. Tired of waiting any longer, though, the original stockholders finally forced a dissolution of the company and wrote off the investment on their taxes in 1991.

SIMTEK, INC.
Pro Forma Income Statement
(Year 1 after redesign)

	Monthly	Annual
Revenues		
Sales - Tapemate	25,000	300,000
Sales - Box Sealer*	100,000	1,200,000
Gross Revenues	125,000	1,500,000
Less: Cost of Goods Sold	62,500	750,000
Gross Profit	62,500	750,000
Expenses		
1. Promotion and Advertising	250	
2. Entertainment and Travel	500	
3. Meals	100	
4. Wages	12,083	
5. Payroll Tax	483	
6. Medical/Workers' Comp	725	
7. Telephone	400	
8. Supplies	250	
9. Rent	1,500	
10. Freight	300	
11. Model Making R&D	1,000	
12. Drafting R&D	2,500	
13. Materials R&D	1,000	
14. Tooling	11,000	
15. Legal	750	
Total Expenses	32,841	394,092
		355,908
Commissions		75,000
Net Profit Before Taxes		280,908

* Based on adding Box Sealer product to mix

1. Contract PR efforts	6. 6% of payroll	11. Appearance and check models
2. Trade show travel/buyer visits	7. Average including fax	12. ME drafting to work up Ideas
3. Employee travel/meals	8. Office supplies and equipment	13. Stuff
4. Staff salaries	9. Office/warehouse space	14. Tapemate - $50K; Box Sealer - $75K
5. 4% of payroll	10. UPS/Fed Ex/US Mail	15. Patent work

1. With regard to Simtek's product development process, what were the key problems with the process and how could they have made it more efficient and less costly?
2. What were the advantages and disadvantages of taking on venture partners during the product development phase?
3. With consideration to Johnson's pro forma statement for what he expects to happen after redesign, what should Steve Johnson do now that the partners have dissolved the company?

PART 8

A World-Class Venture

The quality of your work, in the long run,
is the deciding factor on how much your
services are valued by the world.

—OG MANDINO

CHAPTER 20

Achieving World-Class Status

On Becoming World Class

This chapter culminates a long process that started with an opportunity and an idea in the mind of the entrepreneur. Whether or not the reader is an entrepreneur, by this point it should be clear that the entrepreneurial mindset—the entrepreneurial vision, if you will—is the antithesis of the bureaucratic mindset found in so many large organizations today. It is also distinctly different from the mindset of the small-business owner. Unfortunately, in much of what is written about entrepreneurs (and the term is often used loosely) these distinctions are blurred, so the reader never comes away with a clear sense of why some ventures become the Microsofts of the world and others never go beyond providing a modest income for the owner.

This book has attempted to make that distinction clear by focusing on entrepreneurs as founders of high-growth, world-class ventures. It should also be apparent from the book that the birth of a Silicon Graphics or a Staples Office Supply begins in the mind of the entrepreneur with world-class intentions. The decisions made, even in the pre-start-up phase, reflect the global mindset of these entrepreneurs.

The defining factor for world-class ventures is no longer size; in fact, size may actually be a deterrent to world-class status in the 1990s. Certainly, there can be no doubt it is much easier to *start* a venture with world-class intentions than it is to change the habits of years in a large organization. A new venture with world-class intentions can set up the infrastructure and hire people who have the same mindset. It can measure all of its actions against the criteria for world-class companies. A monolithic, bureaucratic organization, by contrast, struggles constantly against resistance to change among its people and organizational structures that seem to be as firm as concrete. While the bureaucratic company may have the financial resources and clout to become world-class, they may be outdistanced by the scrappy entrepreneurial venture that understands how to *be* world class from the very beginning. In the 1990s, make no mistake about it, *being* world class is a distinct competitive advantage.

How do you know when you have achieved world-class status? While there certainly are exceptions, there seem to be eight characteristics common to world-class ventures:

- A global vision
- An established network of strategic alliances
- Innovative, proprietary technology
- A market-driven strategy
- A globally experienced management team
- An integrative, organizational team philosophy
- Absolute integrity
- A passion for excellence

A Global Vision

World-class ventures are born with a global view. From sourcing materials and parts, to distributing product, selling product, and setting goals for the future, these ventures know no geographic boundaries. It has often been said that new ventures should wait to go global until they are well established and have achieved a certain level of sales. If *Water Ventures, Inc.*, a resort watersports equipment and services company in California, had listened to that advice, it might not be in business today. *Water Ventures* found that the best markets for its products lay overseas, in particular the Middle East. Consequently, the domestic market is a relatively small portion of its total sales.

Having a global vision is not just a world-class attribute—it is a matter of survival. An entrepreneur has two choices: take the leap into the international arena or retreat within the boundaries of the U.S. and watch its market share being eaten up by international competitors. Of course, "taking the leap" does not necessarily mean establishing a physical presence in another country via a manufacturing or other facility. It may mean establishing a strategic alliance with a foreign company or simply exporting products internationally to gain a presence in a region before investing large amounts of capital in something more permanent. If you are an original equipment manufacturer (OEM), it may mean responding to a customer that has gone global by locating a distribution center in the region where the customer is selling product. In fact, in some countries, the only way to do business is through a joint venture or contract with a local company. The U.S. venture maintains control of its R&D, finance, manufacturing, and quality control, but uses locals for marketing and service functions.

Having a global vision is much more than merely recognizing an opportunity in another country, however. It entails understanding the way business is conducted in that country, learning the rules and regulations of trade, and having an awareness of global monetary markets.

An International Network of Strategic Alliances

Maintaining a global vision requires resources beyond any one company's ability to acquire or manage. The future of business lies in establishing successful relationships with other companies and sharing resources to the benefit of all. The so-called information superhighway is a global phenomenon still in its infancy, but it presents a wealth of opportunity not seen since the invention of the personal computer. It is touted to change completely how technology is used, to the extent that no one technological source (i.e. the PC) will dominate or be required. For the information superhighway to be a success, however, will take cooperation among the hundreds of new and established ventures seeking to grab a piece of the action.

Going into global markets also requires partnerships with experts in particular countries. Nowhere has this been more evident than in the former eastern block countries, including Russia. With capitalism and a market-driven economy still new concepts to the people of these countries, the local expertise that a U.S. venture intending to do business there will seek is expertise in government policy, monetary policy and exchange, and general "street smarts." Developing a relationship with a local business, no matter how small, will smooth the way into the business environment of the country.

Innovative and Proprietary Technology

For a company with a global vision, it is not enough to simply have a patent on a product and expect to maintain a competitive advantage on a global level. For one thing the global markets have not yet come to complete agreement on how to protect intellectual property rights outside the boundaries of the country in which they were executed. In some countries a patent application by a U.S. company is held in the "applied for stage" as long as eight years before a patent is issued. During that time it is not uncommon for a local company to "reverse engineer" the product and bring it into the market to compete with the proprietary company. Moreover, even if a company has secured patent rights in a country, it may be inordinately costly and time consuming to protect them against local infringers.

The problem that U.S. companies have long faced is the loss of technological preeminence and with it a competitive advantage in terms of proprietary technology. Relying heavily on foreign technology, by 1986 American companies had lost the lead to Japan in seven major areas that were key to future developments in electronics and optics.[1] The principal reason advanced for this decline in technological strength was a lack of sufficient investment in R&D and basic research. By 1985, almost 45 percent of all patents granted went to foreign applicants.[2] Moreover, American businesses were increasingly getting their high-tech components from foreign manufacturers.

But the solution to this problem is not to retreat within the political and economic boundaries of the United States, but to seek ways to regain technological preeminence while still dealing in the global marketplace. If innovation and proprietary technology are to be key components of a world-class venture, they must be interwoven so tightly in terms of product and process that "reverse engineering" becomes an exercise in futility. Businesses need to follow the lead of those industries that continue to pay attention to basic research: chemical, electrical equipment, and food products industries. Innovation in products in these industries has always necessitated innovation in process as, more often than not, companies have had to invent equipment and processes to produce their products. In doing so, they have gained a proprietary advantage both in their products and in the equipment used to produce them—a difficult barrier to overcome for those who would attempt to compete by infringement.

Innovation can often provide a competitive advantage even where legal protections are not available. An innovative marketing strategy or a unique distribution strategy, even using products or services not in and of themselves innovative, can give a new venture a niche advantage in the market. Innovation is not just about technology, or products, or processes. It is about looking at every aspect of the organization to see how things could be done better. Innovation... "is the specific tool of entrepreneurs, the means by which they exploit change as an opportunity..."[3] It's about what Drucker called, "creative

---

[1]*Advanced Processing of Electronic Materials in the United States and Japan; A State-of-the-Art Review Conducted by the Panel on Materials Science of the National Research Council.* (1986). Washington, DC: National Academy Press.

[2]Hayes, R.H., Wheelwright, S.C. & Clark, K.B. (1988). *Dynamic Manufacturing: Creating the Learning Organization.* New York: The Free Press.

[3]Drucker, Peter F. (1985). *Innovation and Entrepreneurship.* New York: Harper & Row.

imitation," waiting for something new to be developed and then jumping in and making it better. That is what IBM did after Apple introduced its successful personal computer. It designed a computer based on customer needs that became the standard in the industry, the PC. The idea was not IBM's; IBM simply exploited the success of Apple through creative imitation.

The world-class entrepreneurial venture of the 1990s must make innovation an ongoing process in every function of the business—not innovation for innovation's sake, but innovation that is market-driven, that will give customers what they want. New ventures have a distinct advantage over large businesses because they are used to thinking small, and it is many small experimental starts that ultimately lead to innovation. Paul Hawkin, in his book *The Next Economy,* observes that "...it is one thing to start a business that becomes large and entirely another to start things on a large scale. You should imitate nature, where meaningful beginnings are almost always unnoticeable."[4] The fact that most new ventures have little capital can also be an asset because the project stays small and simple and the pressure to succeed is much greater. Innovation in a world-class venture involves:

* Including customers at all stages from idea to design to prototype
* Using a team-based approach
* Testing the idea early and quickly
* Getting physical with a prototype quickly

Innovation is action-oriented; it happens quickly and usually without the formality of committees, boards of directors, and strategy sessions. Innovation welcomes failure, in fact, demands it, but quick failures that help the company change direction and move toward success. Innovation means breaking the old rules and creating new ones. In short, innovation is the new venture constantly renewing itself.

A Market-Driven Strategy

The world-class venture of the 1990s lives for its customers. Customers will decide what is produced, when and how it is produced, how much is produced, how much it will cost, and where it can be purchased and serviced. To paraphrase Ross Perot, the customers are the owners of the company. Keeping the customers happy is essential to the survival and success of the business. In a market-driven business, it is not just the sales personnel who

---

[4]Hawkin, Paul. (1983). *The Next Economy.* New York: Holt, Rinehart & Winston., pp. 172-3.

deal with the customer. Everyone from the engineers to the plant workers to the office staff knows the customers. This means that those responsible for product development spend time with customers assessing needs; those who handle billing and invoicing spend time with customers to assure that the service they provide is meeting its mark; and senior line management spends at least a third of the time with customers so they don't lose touch with the company's greatest asset. In short, all actions taken by the organization are first assessed based on their impact on the customer and secondarily on their impact on the business. Without the customers, there is no business.

In a world-class business, the customer is an integral part of the organization and is encouraged to participate in the company through letters, newsletters, visits to the company facilities, and attendance at special meetings. Customers are given numerous opportunities to express their feelings, give their suggestions, and are regularly sampled for their degree of satisfaction with the company and its products or services. When a world-class business makes promises to a customer, those promises are kept no matter what the cost to the business to do so. The customer is always right.

An Internationally Experienced Management Team

The new venture with a global vision must be led by people who understand the economy and the marketplace beyond their native country. That knowledge may have come from reading, vacations abroad, and television, but everyone in a world-class organization must have or acquire at least a basic understanding of other cultures and economies. Naturally, a start-up venture normally does not have the resources to hire international experts in management positions for some time, but the founding team can rely on international consultants and foreign agents to guide them through the process of internationalization until they can hire the expertise to become part of the team.

So much is now being written about how business is conducted in other parts of the world that it will not be difficult for any entrepreneur to start becoming internationally educated. Universities, corporations, and individuals regularly give seminars on global issues related to business. If the entrepreneur has targeted a certain region of the world for market introduction, it is always wise for key management to spend some time there in advance of introducing the product and the company. It can never be assumed that customers are the same everywhere or that suppliers or distributors operate by the same set of rules. Management should also acquire a working knowledge of international trade rules and agreements, such as the General Agreement on Tariffs and

Trade, the North American Free Trade Agreement, the European Community, and the Association of South East Asian Nations.

An Integrative, Organizational Team Philosophy

This book has stressed the team approach to entrepreneurship because it is believed that no one person has the expertise, experience, or energy to do everything or take control of every activity of a rapidly growing venture. The classical entrepreneurial leadership style is to do all of the crucial tasks yourself, hire others to do the secondary tasks, and direct and monitor everything yourself. This is, for the most part, how the majority of new ventures start out. The classical style works fine for a while, until the business outgrows the entrepreneur's

> Complex new ventures require an integrative, team-based approach to management.

ability to stay on top of everything. The classical entrepreneur, finding it difficult to delegate responsibility and authority, may hire management personnel to help, but will still stay directly involved in all major decisions. This approach does not work well when you're trying to build a world-class venture; in fact it more often than not inhibits the growth of the business and makes it difficult to achieve excellence.

Another approach is for the entrepreneur to act as the ringmaster in a three-ring circus. The entrepreneur outsources all the tasks he or she doesn't want to do and essentially coordinates all the efforts—the ultimate virtual corporation. It is possible to build a very large business this way; however, whether or not you can achieve world-class status is arguable. What many virtual corporations find is that it is often difficult to control the quality, service, and delivery timing of other companies' resources. That lack of control is no more apparent than when a member of the virtual channel suffers a loss such as fire that can cause a chain reaction throughout the entire channel of distribution with potentially devastating consequences for the entrepreneur's business. To build a world-class organization under this scenario requires the complete cooperation of all members of the virtual team, a difficult achievement at best.

Complex new ventures require an integrative, team-based approach to management. Some examples of complex organizations are manufacturing, service organizations that provide a variety of services, and retail operations with multiple locations. These types of ventures demand that the entrepreneur delegate authority in specific areas of the business to specific people and then let those people make their own decisions. Of course, the entrepreneur retains the right to terminate the employee if he or she feels those decisions are not appropriate to the goals or philosophy of the company. An integrative, team-based approach (ITB) means that key management in all the functional areas of the organization participate fully in the design, development, production, and distribution of the products or services that the business offers. This does not necessarily suggest that all members of the team are employees of the entrepreneur. They may, in fact, be virtual members of the organization, independent contractors who carry out specific functions of the entrepreneur's business within their own companies.

The advantage of the team-based approach is that it promotes skill, discipline, motivation, and learning—essential attributes of a world-class organization. It is not an approach that can be achieved overnight, however. That is where a new venture has an advantage over an established firm that is attempting to convert to a team-based approach to management. The new venture can begin with a team-based philosophy, infrastructure, and personnel prepared to take on the responsibilities inherent in this approach.

In a team-based approach, employees work in teams of perhaps six to seven people with a supervisor who really acts as a facilitator. The team in essence has

> *The advantage of the team-based approach is that it promotes skill, discipline, motivation, and learning— essential attributes of a world-class organization.*

a problem-solving mandate; consequently members of the team are paid based on their skill level rather than on the job they perform. This is a critical distinction, because in the ITB approach, problem-solving and people skills are rated as important, if not more important, than physical or task skills. All teams are charged with the responsibility of finding ways to improve all aspects of the product, process, and service. A particular job is measured by the number of physical operations involved in completing a task and the number of managerial or problem-solving skills involved. This means that no longer are there assembly-line jobs that can be done without thinking. Technical and managerial competence is required of all jobs; accordingly, the people who are hired to work in a world-class business must have both skills or at least be motivated to acquire them.

It is certainly much easier to form an organization with ITB in mind than it is to decide to convert later on after employees with a more traditional mindset have been hired. Nevertheless, even the entrepreneur with a new venture cannot simply announce to potential employees that they will have to think about their work and ways to improve it and expect it to happen automatically. Entrepreneurs dedicated to ITB must be willing to train employees in problem-solving skills and provide incentives for continual learning. They must also be willing to educate their employees on where they fit into the big picture of the organization.

Another advantage of ITB is that less information is required to coordinate the activities of all the functions of the business because control is much further down in the organization. In the case of a manufacturing firm, however, more information is typically needed on the plant floor because of the need to coordinate the efforts of the various teams to ensure the timely and efficient processing of the product. This information requirement can be met by the use of computer-integrated manufacturing technology (CIM), which allows those involved in the production process to manage quality control, production planning, machine setup, and problem diagnosis and resolution in real time and by interacting with staff via computer where necessary.

To balance the greater demand for information, teams are given the authority to respond to various situations as they occur. In this way valuable production time is not lost attempting to get approval from a higher level of authority. Of course, for teams to be able to make decisions on the spot, they must have a clear understanding of the entire production process and the impact any decision they make might have, hence, the importance of integration and continuing education. The best type of ITB is one in which all teams are cross-trained so no one aspect of production is dependent on a single team.

Furthermore, all production teams work directly with engineering teams, marketing teams, sales teams, and finance teams, with everyone rewarded based on the performance of the business. With an integrated, team-based approach, no one team and no one person is more important than any other. Management sends a clear message that the person who solders the wires is every bit as important to the company as the person who manages the finances, or the sales person who promotes the product. Accordingly, in an ITB organization, you will not see executive dining rooms, special parking places for certain people, or barriers of any kind to the free and open flow of communication and trust.

Of course, integrated, team-based management and process control must go hand in hand as well. It is only by streamlining materials flow and minimizing work-in-process inventory that problems and bottlenecks in the system readily surface so they can be detected and solved, not in a piecemeal fashion, but so the entire production process can continue unimpeded.

Absolute Integrity

To accomplish the successful networks of strategic alliances necessary to operate in a global economy requires integrity. The old adversarial mindset that business has traditionally held no longer works when you are striving to become a world-class venture. The environment for entrepreneurial ventures has always been volatile and uncertain. Add to that the global dimension and there aren't too many things that can be relied upon to remain constant. Hence, the one constant that must be present is the security that relationships are based on integrity, ethics, and trust. Often, in an effort to be competitive, companies promise what they can't deliver or change the terms of an agreement at the last minute when the other party is at its most vulnerable. These tactics may be successful in achieving certain ends in the short term, but the cost in loss of customers and reputation will be devastating in the long term.

Integrity is consistency in what the company says, does, and stands for. It is fair and uncompromising treatment of every supplier, every distributor, every customer, and every employee. If you are going to expect the best from these people and ask them to assume some of the risk with you, they must feel confident you will do what you promise. Integrity is confidence that the company is who they say they are. It means knowing that you will not be short-changed on a payment, or on a quantity order, that products will meet the level of quality advertised, and that service will be provided as promised.

In a global economy the issue of business ethics often displays its formidable presence. It is common knowledge that not all countries operate under the same rules of ethics as the United States. Is it OK for an American business to accept a bribe in another country or pay a government official under the table to speed up a process? For a world-class venture the question is moot. Absolute integrity means maintaining high ethical standards in all business dealings no matter where they take place. How can an entrepreneur expect employees to act fairly and honestly toward the business if the business is not doing the same? Honesty is still the best policy.

A Passion for Excellence

In their best-selling book, *A Passion for Excellence,* Peters and Austin said, "a passion for excellence means thinking big and starting small: excellence happens when high purpose and intense pragmatism meet." But they caution, "the adventure of excellence is not for the faint of heart."[5] Ten years later that message is probably even more relevant than it was when the authors wrote it. Like being a world-class venture, achieving excellence is not a stage in the life of business, but rather an ongoing process of improvement that never ends. Hayes, Wheelwright, and Clark call it "continual learning."[6] They assert that wherever U.S. manufacturers have lost competitive advantage, the source can be traced to problems with cost, quality, and innovation.

---

[5]Peters, Tom & Austin, Nancy. (1985). *A Passion for Excellence.* New York: Warner Books.
[6]Hayes, R.H., Wheelwright, S.C. & Clark, K.B. (1988). *Dynamic Manufacturing.* New York: The Free Press.

For companies dealing in a global market, cost is a function of productivity and the exchange rate. If U.S. companies do not keep pace with other countries in terms of their investment in plant and equipment, any productivity gains may be lost. Moreover, while American companies strive to dispel the perception of low quality, foreign companies are also moving ahead in that arena, making it difficult for American companies to catch up. Finally, with U.S. investment in R&D at low levels compared to other countries and with the majority of federal government money for research going to defense and aerospace rather than commercial development or basic research, it is difficult for American companies to regain technological preeminence with breakthrough products and technology. But it is not impossible. Waiting for the government to change its focus or for megacorporations to reinvent themselves is not the short-term solution. The short-term answer lies with new ventures and the entrepreneurs who start them. These entrepreneurs must:

- Hire the very best people and work hard to keep them
- Become experts in integrating product/process design
- Be flexible and fast
- Maintain a state-of-the-art philosophy in every area of the organization
- Manage on the leading edge
- Use an integrated, team-based approach
- Have a customer focus
- Take a return-on-quality approach to excellence
- Engage in lifelong learning
- Maintain a state of perpetual self discovery

One of the more recent buzzwords to hit the business world is "return on quality" (ROQ). ROQ is really a reaction to the frustration faced by those companies that took up the mantra of Total Quality Management in the 1980s and did not achieve the results they were seeking. TQM pushed for quality in all functional areas of the organization, a worthy goal, but it now appears that no one ever really considered the cost/benefit side of TQM; in other words, what was the return on the investment in TQM? Many companies leaped into TQM with total dedication, applying a good share of their resources to that end. Some, like Wallace Co., an oil equipment company, won the Malcolm Baldrige National Quality Award (1990). Unfortunately, Wallace filed for Chapter 11 two years later, due in large part to falling oil prices and mounting quality program costs.[7]

---

[7]*Business Week*, August 8, 1994, p.54.

Today, more and more companies are taking a bottom-line approach to quality control and measuring each quality improvement effort against its costs to judge the ultimate value. And the bottom line is whether or not a particular quality improvement makes good economic and business sense.

How does ROQ correlate with a customer focus? It is interesting that sometimes businesses think they really know their customers' needs when they don't because they haven't been asking the right questions. UPS, for example, always figured that on-time delivery was the number one concern of their customers, so that was their focus. They had delivery times down to a science. The reason they thought that on-time delivery was the most important thing to the customers was that all of their customer surveys had only asked about that particular issue. When they recently began asking more broad questions like how can UPS improve its service, they found to their surprise that what customers most wanted was greater interaction with the drivers. They actually wanted to get to know their drivers better. Accordingly, UPS, while it still emphasizes on-time delivery, encourages its drivers to spend more time with the customer. The ROQ for this new effort is increased sales—the bottom line.

Focusing on the return on quality forces everyone in the organization to think more about what they are doing. A common complaint about TQM in its later incarnations was that it had become mechanistic. True, costs were cut, defects were reduced, and cycle times were shortened, but along the way the customer was lost from the equation. Quality for quality's sake was the result. ROQ attempts to correct that situation by getting customers involved in the quality process from the beginning. It *is not* about short-changing the customer on quality just to make the bottom line look better. It *is* about finding out what is really important to the customer and getting the customer involved in bringing it about.

On Becoming Successful

A business's success is easily measured by total revenues, earnings, return on investment and so forth, but entrepreneurs don't typically measure success in these terms. Entrepreneurs seem to take a much more personal view of what constitutes success; consequently, the definition varies from entrepreneur to entrepreneur. Wally Amos of Uncle Noname Cookies believes that success is "turning lemons into lemonade." For Sue Szymczak of Safeway Sling in Milwaukee, success is "being happy with what you're doing and feeling as though you're accomplishing something." One group of entrepreneurs decided that measuring their success in terms of the financial performance of the business did not reflect their definition of success, even at the company level. These are the entrepreneurs who started many of the so-called "socially responsible" businesses, most of which came into being in the 1980s. Ben and Jerry's, The Body Shop, and Patagonia are just a few of these new-age businesses that set out to make a difference in the world by establishing very ambitious social goals that were virtually impossible to reach.

Consequently, success in their terms can never really be achieved. For example, one of The Body Shop's goals was to end Third World poverty. No one would dispute that this is a lofty and worthwhile goal. But realistically, can one corporation do what nations have been unable to accomplish? The Body Shop was setting itself up for failure. It should be noted that The Body Shop has since modified its goal to changing the lives of hundreds of poor people and has seen success in that effort.[8]

> *Entrepreneurs who aspire to socially responsible success must understand that unless the business of the business is conducted well, there will be no business from which to achieve the goal of social responsibility.*

The unfortunate thing for these companies is that they have used their social goals as the focus of all their advertising and promotion, so every day they are reminded by the ever-vigilant media of how they have not succeeded. They are also held to impossibly high standards by their employees, who expect working conditions to be substantially better than those at traditional, nonsocially responsible companies—and often they are not. Entrepreneurs who aspire to socially responsible success must understand that unless the business of the business is conducted well, there will be no business from which to achieve the goal of social responsibility.

No matter what your definition of success, there seem to be some constants that comprise the very essence of what is success. One of those constants is *purpose*. To feel successful, entrepreneurs need to know that what they are doing is taking them in the direction of a goal they wish to achieve. True success is a journey, not a destination—even the achievement of a goal will just be a step on the way to the achievement of yet another goal. Success attained serendipitously, without purpose, is usually fleeting. Entrepreneurs purposefully avoid the path of least resistance to success. An electric current will follow the line of least resistance; a light bulb will only glow

---

[8]As of this writing The Body Shop is embroiled in a controversy over assertions that it has been misleading customers in its claims. For example, one allegation is that the Body Shop uses non-renewable petrochemicals as ingredients in its products while it advertises them as all natural. In response, The Body Shop has hired an ethicist from Stanford University to look into the claims.

when there *is* resistance. Entrepreneurs striving to build world-class ventures will leave the path of least resistance to those who are seeking the quick successes that usually don't endure.

The second constant is that life has its ups and downs. *Failure is the other half of success,* and most entrepreneurs have experienced several failures of one sort or another along the way. But entrepreneurs do not fear failure, because they know intuitively that those who obsessively avoid failure are doomed to mediocrity. To avoid failing one has to virtually retreat from life, to never try anything that has any risk attached to it. Most entrepreneurs strive for a high batting average, in other words, more successes than failures. To ensure this high batting average they make sure that every time they come to bat they give it their best, and then win or lose, they strive to learn from the experience and go on. Entrepreneurs are generally optimists with great expectations.

The third constant is a *sense of satisfaction* with what they're doing. The most successful entrepreneurs are doing what they love, so the satisfaction level is usually very high. Does satisfaction with the work result in success or does success bring satisfaction? Probably both are true in many instances; however, being content with how things are progressing will not always bring a successful outcome, nor will success always bring with it lasting satisfaction.

> Failure is the other half of success.

For the most part, though, entrepreneurs do achieve a certain level of satisfaction when they consider themselves successful because they usually have predetermined what success means to them, so the ultimate achievement of that success is even sweeter.

The fourth constant of success is that *there is no free lunch*. Success rarely comes without work. Entrepreneurs do not have the luxury of a nine-to-five work day where at five o'clock the entrepreneur goes home, leaving thoughts of the business behind. Entrepreneurs are married to their businesses 24 hours a day. Recently Bill Gates of Microsoft got married and proudly proclaimed that he now leaves work at midnight instead of in the middle of the night as he has done since he founded the company. It is not just the number of hours of work that distinguishes entrepreneurs but how they use their time. Entrepreneurs make productive use of odd moments in their day—while they're driving, on hold on the telephone, in the shower, walking to a meeting. They make the best use of the time they have.

Success has another kind of price, however. Napoleon said that "the most dangerous moment comes with victory." Paraphrasing that statement, it can be said that the most dangerous moment comes with success. This is because people who forget that success is transitory tend to relax in their success and stop moving forward. Many entrepreneurs have suffered physical and emotional problems, divorces, financial problems, and a whole host of other maladies simply because they didn't know how to handle success. Many have seen their hugely successful venture crumble into dust because, buoyed by their success, they didn't keep striving for continued excellence. Many have subconsciously set themselves up for failure because they weren't prepared for success. There is a tendency on the part of many to focus on how to deal with failure, but equally important is how to deal with success, for if entrepreneurs are truly striving to raise their success/failure ratio, they will potentially have more opportunities to encounter success than failure over the long term and must therefore be equipped for that eventuality.

The best way to illustrate how success can turn into failure is to recall a meeting that took place in 1929 at the Edgewater Beach Hotel in Chicago. Attending the meeting were eight of the world's most successful and important financiers: the presidents of the largest steel, utility, and gas companies; the president of the New York Stock Exchange; a presidential cabinet member; the most successful Wall Street investor; the chairman of the world's largest monopoly; and the president of the Bank for International Settlements. Twenty-five years later, all of them faced ruin. Charles Schwab died bankrupt; Samuel Insull was a fugitive from justice; Howard Hopson became insane; Richard Whitney served in prison, as did Albert Fall, who was eventually pardoned so he could die at home; and Jesse Livermore, Ivan Krueger, and Leon Fraser all committed suicide.[9]

It is not within the scope of this book to fully treat the issue of the entrepreneur's inability to cope with success—that will be left for a later study—but suffice it to say that those entrepreneurs who seem to have found the formula for coping with success maintain a constant state of self renewal, a constant striving to be better at what they do and better at who they are as human beings—a constant pursuit of excellence in every aspect of their lives. Only the best is good enough for world-class entrepreneurs, these intrepid people who not only say "I can," but "I will"—and who envision their success long before it is achieved.

---

[9]Mandino, O. (1982). *University of Success.* New York: Bantam Books.

Index